WITHDRAWAL

The Consultation and Intervention Series in School Psychology
Sylvia A. Rosenfield, Series Editor

Lambert/Hylander/Sandoval • Consultee-Centered Consultation: Improving the Quality of Professional Services in Schools and Community Organizations

Consultee-Centered Consultation

Improving the Quality of Professional S
in Schools and Community Organiza

Consultee-Centered Consultation

Improving the Quality of Professional Services
in Schools and Community Organizations

Edited by

Nadine M. Lambert
University of California at Berkeley

Ingrid Hylander
University of Linköping, Sweden

Jonathan H. Sandoval
University of California at Davis

LAWRENCE ERLBAUM ASSOCIATES, PUBLISHERS
2004   Mahwah, New Jersey   London

9796191-1

Lawrence Erlbaum Associates, Inc., Publishers
10 Industrial Avenue
Mahwah, New Jersey 07430

Cover design by Kathryn Houghtaling Lacey

Library of Congress Cataloging-in-Publication Data

Consultee-centered consultation : improving the quality of professional
services in schools and community organizations / edited by Nadine M.
Lambert, Ingrid Hylander, Jonathan H. Sandoval.
     p. cm.
Includes bibliographical references and index.
ISBN 0-8058-4463-5 (alk. Paper)
     1. Educational counseling. 2. Counselors—Professional relationships. I.
Lambert, Nadine M.   II. Hylander, Ingrid.   III. Sandoval, Jonathan.

LB1027.5.C62215 2003
371.4—dc22

                                                                    2003056106
                                                                         CIP

Books published by Lawrence Erlbaum Associates are printed on acid-free
paper, and their bindings are chosen for strength and durability.

Printed in the United States of America
10 9 8 7 6 5 4 3 2 1

Contents

nization; specific features and description of the consultation process n the particular system; evaluation of consultation in ongoing or short-term relationships;

B. ways that the interaction between consultant and consultee promote conceptual change as evidenced by: changes in the ways that the problem is presented by the consultee and consultant; and, changes in the ways that the problem is represented or understood by the consultant and the consultee.

Preschool and Child Care

School

Health and Welfare

Corporate Settings

Evaluation Practice

Part III   The Consultation Process - Dialogues Across Settings and Disciplines to Activate Conceptual Change

The chapters in this section describe techniques and processes involved in consultee-centered consultation that promote engagement in the process and new conceptualizations in both the presentation and representation of the professional problem.

Part IV   Evidence of the Impact of Consultee-Centered Consultation

Models for evaluating change in the consultation process focus on the interplay between the consultants' and consultees' presentations of the problems and representations of its underlying dynamics. Documenting the impact of consultation involves assessing the conceptual development that occurs for the two or more participants in the process and the effects of this change on the clients.

I

Theoretical Advances in Consultee-Centered Consultation

These papers provide a history of consultee-centered consultation as a method for promoting the well-being of the population, and show how the method has evolved over the years to become an approach with broad applications serving professionals and their clients in school and community settings.

1

Consultee-Centered Consultation: An International Perspective on Goals, Process, and Theory

Nadine M. Lambert
University of California at Berkeley

CONSULTEE-CENTERED CONSULTATION IN SCHOOLS AND COMMUNITY MENTAL HEALTH PROGRAMS: HISTORICAL FOUNDATIONS

Consultee-centered consultation in the 21st century has its origins in the consultation methods introduced in the late 1950s and early 1960s. Mental health specialists were grappling with ways to broaden the application of mental health principles in community settings to reduce the prevalence of mental health disorders, and to develop strategies to intervene with the mental health, learning, and behavioral problems of the general population.

These efforts to design federal, state, and local mental health services with a broader out-reach culminated in the Federal Community Mental Health Centers Act (U.S. Public Health Service, 1963) followed by similar state legislative mandates. These legislative initiatives outlined a wide range of interventions by mental health specialists from consultation to hospitalization. The new models for comprehensive community mental health services envisioned a cadre of mental health professionals who would be available to offer mental health education, consultation to care giving professionals, brief mental health interventions, psychotherapy, and intensive long term psychological services depending on the setting and the presenting problems. These federal and state programs gave an impetus to the development of consultee-centered mental health consultation. (Caplan, G., 1956, 1963, 1970, 1980; Caplan, R.B. 1993; Caplan & Caplan, 1993) as an essential mental health service to schools, professional organizations, and community agencies.

The term *mental health* in consultee-centered consultation reflected the fact that the foundations of consultee-centered consultation were focused on services that were:

1. related to mental health disorder or personality idiosyncrasies of the client
2. promotion of mental health in the client, or
3. interpersonal aspects of the clients work situation (Caplan, 1970, p. 28–30).

As the method outlined by Caplan evolved over the intervening years, the work problems of the clients consultees sought help with, broadened to include, for example, child development issues, motivation, learning and behavior problems in schools, family disruption and conflict, and organizational and system concerns, not all of which could be considered as "mental health" problems, even though they might involve mental health components.

This volume reflects the advances in the method by mental health professionals in many countries, offers a contemporary definition of consultee-centered consultation, provides examples of the ways it can be used in serving clients with varying presenting problems in diverse settings, and presents some techniques that have proved valuable in enhancing the problem-solving repertoires of consultant and consultee professionals. The underlying theme of these presentations is the focus on the *process* of consultee-centered consultation and its goal of promoting conceptual change in both the consultee and the consultant as they jointly develop strategies for solving the consultee's work problem.

CONSULTEE-CENTERED CONSULTATION

All professional consultation involves a consultant, consultee, and a client, clients, or an organization, and takes into account the ecological or organizational system in which the presenting problem is discussed. It is important at the outset to distinguish between consultee-centered consultation and client-centered consultation as both methods involve consultants, consultees, and clients. Traditional or client-centered consultation takes place when a consultee seeks information or confirmation or advice from a consultant about a work problem regarding a client. The consultation process could involve discussions about assessment results, case findings, diagnoses, or recommendations for interventions. This type of consultation can include consultee requests for more diagnostic information about the presenting problems, advice about whether the services provided are appropriate, recommendations for practice, and clarification of facets of the client's problem that the consultant professional is in a position to answer.

The consultant who accepts the request to provide client-centered consultation acknowledges that his or her expertise is appropriate to evaluate the client's problem and to offer an expert perspective and recommendations to the consultee-professional. Client-centered consultation is hierarchical and prescriptive. The consultant is the expert who offers his or her opinion and makes recommendations for follow-up action. Although the consultant may not necessarily see the client in client-centered consultation—such as in cases where the consultant reviews a case file or diagnostic findings with the consultee—the relationship remains hierarchical, and the recommendations or "prescriptions" follow from the consultant's background and expertise.

Caplan (1970) outlined several characteristics that differentiated consultee-centered mental health case, program, or administrative consultation from client-centered consultation. All of these remain characteristic of consultee-centered consultation. The consultant has no administrative responsibility for the consultee's work, and no professional responsibility for the outcome of the client's case. The consultant is under no obligation to modify the consultee's behavior toward the client. Similarly, the consultee has no compulsion to accept the consultant's ideas or suggestions. There is a coordinate relationship between the consultant and consultee and an understanding that together they will discuss the work problem sharing respective views of the problem from their own perspectives. The discussion about the client occurs among two professional equals. This coordinate relationship is fostered by the consultant being a member of another profession. The consultant has no predetermined body of information that is to be imparted to the consultee. Although there is no predetermined body of knowledge to be imparted, the consultant has a wide range of professional experience and knowledge, and an array of theories that could be useful in assisting consultee to resolve the work problem, if he or she decides that it is relevant and wants to use it. A consultee asks for consultation from someone that he or she trusts and from one who has professional experience and knowledge in another field.

The consultant acknowledges that the consultee has relevant expertise about the client's work problem and aims to elicit this knowledge in the consultation process. The consultant hopes to help the consultee improve the handling or understanding of the current work problem with the goal of assisting the consultee to manage similar problems in the future. The aim is to effect changes in the consultee's performance and not his or her sense of well-being. Consultee-centered consultation does not involve the discussion of personal or private material, and the consultation process is understood to be a privileged communication. The responsibility for the outcome remains with the consultee.

CALIFORNIA INITIATIVES SUPPORTING CONSULTEE-CENTERED CONSULTATION IN SCHOOLS

At the time of the development and implementation of comprehensive community mental health programs, the California State Legislature (Joint Interim Committee on Education and Rehabilitation of Handicapped Children, 1959) authorized a major research program in 1958 to study and recommend methods for identification and education of children who were described as "emotionally disturbed," (later changed to "emotionally handicapped.") These were children with serious learning and behavior problems whose teachers found it difficult to manage in the regular classroom situation. It was generally recognized that there was a range of severity of such problems among school children, supported by state estimates of their prevalence by State Department of Education research staff (Bower, 1958, 1959–1960). The research program undertook the establishment and evaluation of the merits of an array of services reflecting the seriousness of the child's problems, from help to the teacher when a child could remain in the classroom, to learning disability groups for children whose primary problems were basic skill acquisition, to all day special classes for those whose needs were more intense and involved, and to home and hospital instruction for children who could not attend school. As model programs were being established in many school districts in California, the Federal Government was receiving testimony on the mental health needs of children from a National perspective. Many mental health and education professionals proposed strategies for reducing the prevalence of these problems and were active in the discussions about the roles of the schools and teachers in meeting the needs of emotionally handicapped children.

It was inevitable that the research team directing the California research on programs for emotionally handicapped children would become involved in the community mental health movement and its leaders, among whom were Gerald Caplan, borrowing from their experience those programs that might be adopted in the school setting. So, as directors of community mental health centers contemplated training for and programming the new models of mental health services, one of the promising directions they promoted was the adoption of consultee-centered mental health consultation, principally as described by Caplan (1956, 1963). The California research team included "consultation to teachers" as one of the programs to be implemented and evaluated. For the research effort mental health professionals from the community were employed to provide consultee-centered mental health consultation to teachers in the school district research sites. Some of the consultants had studied with Caplan at Harvard. In order to be sure that those providing consultation were cognizant of the objectives of consultee-centered mental health consultation and were conforming to the principles that had been laid out, a training consultant graduate of the Harvard program in Community Psychiatry was brought on board to guide the efforts of the consultants who were assigned to the teacher consultees. It was the responsibility of the research staff to negotiate with the school districts the actual contracts for the services that would be provided including the consultant's weekly meetings with teachers, the monthly meetings with the site administrator, and ways of resolving any problems that might arise.

The recommendations of the research team (California State Department of Education, 1961) were reported to the Legislature in 1961, ultimately to be adopted during the 1963 session of the Legislature. "Emotionally handicapped" was changed to "educationally handicapped" and services were authorized for reimbursement ranging from consultation to teachers to home and hospital instruction, depending on the nature and severity of the presenting problems of the child. Methods for identifying children in need of services were also made available (Bower, 1960; Lambert, Bower, & Hartsough, 1961, 1974, 1979), and publications pursued the role of education as an agent in the prevention of mental disorders among children. (Bower, 1961, 1965; Bower, Shellhammer, & Daily, 1960; Lambert, 1961, 1965.)

The legislation for educationally handicapped children did not restrict the consultation services to those provided by a mental health professional from the community, but facilitated the expansion of the role of school psychologists to include consultation to teachers as a strategy for discussions about problems with students without having to rely on the results of test administrations and diagnostic services. However, providing consultee-centered consultation required training, whether the consultant was an experienced mental health professional or a school psychologist. The outcome of these early efforts to implement consultation programs consistent with the provisions of the Comprehensive Community Mental Health Services Act of 1963, or the California

State Department of Education legislation for educationally handicapped children in 1963 should be interpreted with respect to the extent to which those who provided consultation received any training in this new method.

CONSULTEE-CENTERED CONSULTATION IN SCHOOLS

In my presidential address to the California Association of School Psychologists (CASP) in 1963, I detailed a vision of school psychology with a primary mission of the promotion of the personal, social, and academic development of children, and the prevention of school failure. School psychologists, in my vision, would gradually become more visible on school sites, by moving out of their offices administering tests and meeting with parents to obtain consent for special education placement, to meeting with teachers to plan for a systematic assessment of children's needs and follow-up consultee-centered consultation. In 1962 when I was responsible for the program for the annual convention, I invited experts to show how learning how to read could promote mental health, how consultee-centered consultation would broaden the service delivery options for school psychologists to assist teachers to be cognizant of and more responsive to the needs of children with problems, how education had preventive power, and examples of primary and secondary prevention efforts already underway in various school settings. Those presentations became a U.S. Public Health Service Monograph (Lambert, 1965) on the "Protection and Promotion of the Mental Health of Children."

Now that consultee-centered consultation had shown its value when provided by community-based consultants and was sanctioned by the State Legislature for school psychological service delivery systems, the task ahead was to inform educational professionals and school psychologists of the preventive agency for consultee-centered consultation, and to develop programs to train those who would provide such services. At the time these important national and local initiatives were underway, those who provided consultee-centered mental health consultation received their consultation training after preparation in their specialty. The issue of whether consultation training could become part of the preparation of the school psychologist as he or she was learning the specialty was debated.

When I went to Berkeley in 1964 to develop a doctoral level school psychology program, I pursued the challenge I laid down as president of CASP, the Berkeley program would provide consultation training (Lambert, 1974, 1986) along with preparation for other school psychological services. Issues pertaining to the novice consultants having to learn consultation skills along with other professional services would have to be resolved with experience. We provided a training consultant for students during their year-long service to teachers as well as a training supervisor who monitored both the process of acquiring consultation skills as well as the professional standards students were to demonstrate in their school placements (Lambert, Sandoval, & Yandell, 1975), and we evaluated the services that the student consultants were offering to the teachers (Lambert, Sandoval, & Corder, 1975; Sandoval & Lambert, 1987.) Once the structure for the training was set up (Lambert, 1983), we focused our energies on the critical challenge of examining more closely the process of our consultation efforts, and the contrasts between services offered by community-based consultants, and those provided by consultants who were school-based.

Several issues facing the school-based consultee-centered consultant had to be addressed squarely. Among these were redefining a request for diagnostic services to a request for consultation before services were to be provided. In those cases where the school-based consultant was seeing only the teacher and not the student, the school-based consultant had to be cautious about the effort being seen as one where the teacher was being evaluated, diagnosed, or treated rather than one of egalitarian information-sharing and joint problem solving about the student.

Still another issue was the extent to which the consultant had an agenda for the consultation, or the teacher had an agenda. The consultant's agenda might be to correct a teacher's way of managing the classroom, or the teacher-consultee might expect that the meeting would result in moving the child to another classroom or to special education or to get counseling services. And finally, the matter of responsibility for follow-up action was expected to be more difficult for the school-based consultant whose salary was being paid from the same source, and who might have problems not being in some way responsible for the well-being of the students. But although these issues were critical to the clarity with which the school-based consultant learned and practiced consultation skills, it became apparent that it was not these parameters that were the most important facets of the successful school-based consultation effort, but rather the process that was taking place. We observed that the student consultees could become proficient at providing consultation services, ameliorating our concern that they would have to be fully trained professionals before consultation training. They became informed and knowledgeable about teacher perspectives, issues in teaching, ways that teachers reacted to particular types of student problems, the challenges that were difficult for all teachers in contrast to idiosyncratic matters affecting only one teacher.

As we were gaining experience in our consultee-centered consultation training efforts, others were promoting new approaches to consultation. Many of these approaches reflected the "adjective" in front of consultee-centered consultation. Consultee-centered mental health consultation was concerned with consultee work problems of a mental health nature invoking the consultant's psychodynamic theoretical framework (James, Kidder, Osberg, & Hunter, 1986). Behavioral consultation, while centering on the teacher, was also an effort to bring a particular theoretical perspective to the consultation process and aimed to shed light on student behavior problems by assisting teachers to develop a more effective management programs to improve student behavior in the classroom (Keys, 1986). Organizational consultation focused on organizational development and systems theory (Vernberg & Repucci, 1986) and viewed presenting problems as reflecting larger problems within the school or district. The espoused theories of the consultant began to drive the consultation process (James, Kidder, Osberg, & Hunter, 1986; Mannino, Trickett, Shore, Kidder, & Levin, 1986). For us at Berkeley, it was obvious that no single theory was sufficient to respond to the many and complex work problems the teachers encountered. And students, like their professors, were not omniscient. But consultants needed a broad theoretical perspective, and could not rely on any single theoretical model if they were to be responsive to the teacher's concerns with students.

These early descriptions of the consultee-centered consultation method were focused on the parameters of consultation—such as inside or outside consultants, responsible for action versus not responsible for action, teacher requests for help versus psychologist suggestions for consultation, and the role of the consultant with respect to teacher evaluations. And foremost among these distinctions was whether the consultation was hierarchical or nonhierarchical and prescriptive versus not prescriptive. At the core of consultee-centered consultation as it evolved at Berkeley, and as it has been developed by Caplan are that it is a nonhierarchical nonprescriptive process and it requires more than one theoretical perspective.

CONCURRENT INTERNATIONAL PERSPECTIVES ON CONSULTEE-CENTERED CONSULTATION

Whereas those of us in the United States were concerned with models, training, and evaluation for consultation services, mental health professionals in other countries were having similar experiences and developing comparable models to what we were trying. On October 17, 1989, three psychologists from Sweden who were in Berkeley to see the late Millie Almy, a professor in early childhood education, came to see us at the suggestion of Eva Johannssen from Norway, who had spent some time earlier at Berkeley studying consultation. We dis-cussed the consultation programs that they were offering and suggested that they share their experiences with our students at a program meeting. When they described their consultation services to Swedish child-care programs, the problems and challenges that they experienced, and the strategies for consulta-tion that they had developed, it was as if they had been in Berkeley working in the same school sites, not thousands of miles away in Sweden. Shortly after, Ing-rid Hylander, Jonathan Sandoval, and I placed in motion the establishment of an International Seminar on Consultee-Centered Consultation. At a first meeting we would invite all of those using consultee-centered consultation methods, which we could identify from personal knowledge or their writings, to attend to share experiences, and to establish a common ground for defining the current status of the consultee-centered consultation method. The initial meeting was held in Stockholm, Sweden in 1995, a second one in Stockholm in 1999, and a third in San Francisco, California in 2001. What seemed obvious on that day in October 1989—the day of the San Francisco Loma Prieta earth-quake—was that a focus on the *processes* of consultee–centered consultation, processes, rather than parameters, would be necessary to describe conceptual changes in the consultee as well as in the consultant. Consultation processes would be the defining principles distinguishing consultee-centered consulta-tion from other consultation methods.

Definition of Consultee-Centered Consultation—
A Consensus From the Seminar Participants

At each meeting of the Seminar on Consultee-centered consultation there were discussions about the need for a definition that would capture the diversity of consultee-centered consultation efforts that were taking place, but one with elements common to all consultee-centered consultation, and a definition that would emphasize process and conceptual change. The result the following:

> Consultee-centered consultation emphasizes a nonhierarchical, nonprescriptive help-ing role relationship between a resource (consultant) and a person or group (consultee) who seeks professional help with a work problem involving a third party (client).

> This work problem is a topic of concern for the consultee who has a direct responsibil-ity for the learning, development, or productivity of the client.

> The primary task of both the consultant and the consultee is to choose and reframe knowledge about well-being, development, intrapersonal, interpersonal and organiza-tional effectiveness appropriate to the consultee's work setting.

The goal of the consultation process is the joint development of a new way of conceptualizing the work problem so that the repertoire of the consultee is expanded and the professional relationship between the consultee and the client is restored or improved.

The chapters in this volume illustrate consultation practice that reflects this definition in a diversity of settings with varying organizational goals, and with consultants and consultees with differing professional responsibilities.

CONCEPTS, PRINCIPLES, AND PRACTICE OF CONSULTEE-CENTERED CONSULTATION

Client-centered consultation, that type of exchange that takes place when a professional seeks information or confirmation from a specialist, is clearly focused on case findings about the client. These findings can include more information about the presenting problems, advice about whether the services provided are appropriate, or clarification of facets of the client's problem that the professional is not in a position to uncover. And usually in this type of consultation, the consultant who accepts the request to provide information has agreed that his or her expertise is appropriate to the request to see or evaluate the client's problem and to offer an evaluation of the problem along with recommendations to the consultee professional.

However, the process changes when the focus of the consultation shifts to the consultee in an effort to assist the consultee with a work problem and the consultant is not expected to see the clients directly. The consultant's focus on the consultee can be seen by the novice consultant as an invitation to assist the consultee with the consultee's problems rather that to assist the consultee with the development of alternatives to help the client. Or the novice consultant who has developed diagnostic and intervention theories may see the consultee as the consultant's agent in serving client needs as perceived by the consultant within his particular theoretical framework.

The shift from the consultant's focus on the client with assessments, diagnoses, and recommendations for plans of action, to a focus on the consultee's presentation of the client's problems is a major shift in the roles of the consultant and consultee. The process of discussion also differs substantially between client-centered and consultee-centered consultation from hierarchical and prescriptive to nonhierarchical and nonprescriptive. Consultee-centered consultation is nonhierarchical because both the consultant and the consultee are considered to have expert knowledge about the problem, shared knowledge that is highlighted in the problem solving process. Consultee-centered consultation is not prescriptive because the consultant does not determine or advise on the course of action for the consultee, but facilitates consultee consideration of relevant follow-up courses of action. The literature on consultee-centered consultation provides a variety of strategies to assist the consultant to maintain a professional egalitarian relationship with the consultee. In doing so, the consultant avoids treating the client's problem as a function of the consultee's inadequacy or unresolved problems. As well, the consultant does not apply his or her expertise directly in an effort to improve the performance of the consultee.

Possibly, it is the this feature of consultee-centered consultation—that of the joint problem solving relationship between the consultant and the consultee with the focus on the client—that invites the inexperienced consultant to attempt to resolve the consultee's dilemma by shifting from an egalitarian and reciprocal problem solving relationship to one where the consultant is the expert and the consultee becomes the trainee or the client. And it is this context of the shared expertise, and shared theoretical perspectives, in the discourse between the consultant and consultee where the *process* of consultee-centered consultation becomes differentiated from the type of consultation where the consultant applies his theories to the solution of the consultee's work problem. This critical distinction between consultation approaches is also a central factor in promoting a problem solving process in consultee-centered consultation.

The three elements of the consultee-centered consultation process—the work problem presented by the client, the consultee, and the consultant—provide three ways to examine the process and the relevance or appropriateness of selected theoretical applications.

The Client

The nature of the case, the setting in which the client resides or works, the resources of the environment, and the people in it, and the consultee's hoped for change; all offer ways to explore the underlying explanations of the problem the client presents. Many theories in the behavioral science literature can be applicable to any of these questions. If the consultant is seeing the client directly, and is expected to take responsibility for the client as in client-centered consultation, the consultant would likely select from among his expert theoretical perspectives the one that offers the most robust explanation of the problem. And, of course, we would expect an expert consultant to seek additional information if the client's presenting problems were beyond the scope of his or her expertise. But when the consultant is in a consultee-centered consultation relationship, the consultee's observations and information about the client are processed through the consultee's professional theories and particular biases and perspectives. During the reciprocal consultation exchange, the consultant encourages the consultee to offer relevant explanations and information about the work problems, and the consultant's questions, observations, and hypotheses about it are processed jointly to result in a set of strategies for resolution of the problem.

The Consultee

The process of consultee-centered consultation illuminates the professional expertise of the consultee, his or her role in the case, the goals the consultee wishes to achieve or for which help is requested, and the range of alternatives available to the consultee in resolving the problem. A novice consultant is tempted to understand the client's problem as a function of the consultee's underlying psychological make-up, unconscious or conscious biases in the consultee's attitudes, such as those that might be reflected in working with culturally different clients, incompetence, or the strategies the consultees use to cope with certain types of clients. Indeed, the consultee issues discussed in the consultation literature—such as lack of knowledge, lack of objectivity, theme interference—can call the consultant's attention to, and invite the application of, various direct approaches to assist the consultee to resolve the presenting problem, rather than a problem-solving process in which the consultant encourages consultees to share their professional expertise in a dialogue or conversation. In consultee-centered consultation the consultant offers relevant comments on the client's problem from his or her theoretical perspectives, reflects on explanations of the client's behavior, the consultee offers her perspectives and the process promotes the consultee's development of an appropriate resolution of the problem.

The objectives of consultee-centered consultation are compromised when the consultee is not on an equal footing with the consultant in their discussions about the client. Shared expertise would be sacrificed when the consultant is a passive listener to the consultee's problem, or when the consultee's information about the case and hunches about possible solutions are not highlighted. Without shared expertise in a reciprocal dialogue about the case, the consultee-centered consultation goals would fail to be realized.

The Consultant

The professional expertise of the consultant is assumed and often not considered to be related directly to the consultation process. Moreover, in the examination of the success and failure of consultation efforts, whether or not the consultant has been trained in the method he or she espouses is often not considered. Both issues of professional background, as well as training and experience should be resolved before the consultation begins. The consultee-centered consultant could be a mental health professional, a health professional, an education professional, or from some other background. Therefore, consultant expertise will be a function of his or her professional training and experience. Consultee-centered consultation skills would be common to all.

The experienced consultant has developed a keen sense of the importance of recognizing the expertise of the consultee. This would be reflected in types of questions asked, redirection of requests for advice, clarification of what has been attempted, and exploration of the resources available. In such interactions, the consultant aims to clarify the consultee's presentation of the work problem and to understand the ways the consultee thinks about or represents the problem. But as the consultation proceeds, the questions the consultant asks reflect his or her developing understanding and presentation of the problem. And during the interaction, the consultant searches his or her theoretical repertoire for appropriate representations of the problem. A joint solution of the consultee's work problem results from the reciprocal nature of the consultee-centered process.

We have removed the adjectives in our definition of "consultee-centered consultation" to assert its applicability for consultants with differing backgrounds and to many types of consultees with varying work problems. An essential feature of the method is the process of shared perspectives that promote conceptual change by clarifying the nature of the client's problem, understanding the forces in the environment that must be accounted for, and interpreting and applying professional perspectives and scientific theories to the development of strategies to resolve the consultee's work problem with the client.

Principles of Consultee-Centered Consultation

The following principles epitomize the ways consultee-centered consultation differs from professional consultation in general:

Principles for professional consultation methods in general

1. Consultation is a way to work with other professionals to solve work problems.

2. All consultation programs have a consultant, consultee, and clients and take into account the ecological or organizational system in which the presenting problems arise.
3. All consultation efforts are guided by explicit or implicit agreements about the role of consultant and consultee in relation to the clients' work problems.
4. The types of outcomes of consultation result from the alternative solutions that are generated in the consultation process.
5. There are always cognitive, affective, and motivational components in the consultation effort.
6. Consultees are always free to accept or reject results of consultation either explicitly, or by failing to implement changes.
7. Consultation centers attention on the professional work problems of the consultee.
8. Consultants encourage consultees to consider work problems from the consultee, client, or system perspective.
9. Consultants need to have both didactic and experiential training and supervision.

Additional Principles Underlying Consultee-Centered Consultation

1. Consultee-Centered Consultation is a problem-solving interaction in which the consultant assists another professional to develop new ways of conceptualizing client/organizational problems and interventions.
2. In Consultee-Centered Consultation, the "client" may be a single case discussed by one or many consultees, many cases discussed by many consultees in a group setting, or an organization or system discussed by a single or many consultees.
3. In Consultee-Centered Consultation the focus is on the client and not on the consultee's affective and motivational responses to challenging work problems.
4. The attention given to the "client" in Consultee-Centered Consultation enables the process to center on the ways the consultees conceptualize client or organizational problems and enables the consultant and consultee to discuss alternative explanations and interventions for the client suitable to the consultee's mode of professional practice.
5. Active reflection on the part of both consultee and consultant is necessary for the successful resolution of the consultee's problem with clients.

6. The interaction between consultant and consultee and between consultee and client must be understood from the perspective of more than one theory.
7. Conceptual change in Consultee-Centered Consultation results from discussion of and reflection on the interaction between consultee and client.
8. Consultee-Centered Consultation promotes conceptual change when the consultee's interaction with the client (and future clients) changes and when there is a change in the consultee's, and often the consultant's, representation of the consultation work problem.

EVIDENCE TO SUPPORT CONSULTEE-CENTERED CONSULTATION AS A PREVENTIVE INTERVENTION

Consultee-centered consultation has been promoted since its introduction into the repertoire of mental health professionals a half century ago as a major primary prevention intervention. As a primary prevention intervention, consultants meet with consultees who have responsibility for the development and welfare of a segment of the population. Consultants and consultees carry on a professional discourse to resolve the problems the consultee confronts with clients, and the consultees, in turn, generalize these solutions to similar client problems confronted in the future. Consultee-centered consultation is, therefore, an indirect, not a direct, service to the clients. The outcome of the process, when effective, goes beyond changes in the client's presenting problem. The consultation process promotes conceptual changes in the consultee that restore the professional relationship between the consultee and the client. This comes about because the consultee will understand the relationship with the client in the context of a more comprehensive view of the client and the client's individual differences. The evidence for this primary prevention intervention should be based on conceptual changes in the consultees, and secondarily on changes in client behavior. It is understood that when conceptual changes about the consultee's professional work problems occur, more effective and favorable interactions with clients will ensue. The evidence to be sought in assessing the effectiveness of consultee-centered consultation is first centered on evaluating conceptual change in the consultees, and second, on evidence that the quality of the client's experience has improved.

In the chapters that follow in this volume, we hope to show that the process of conceptual change is mutual—both consultees and consultants adopt new perspectives from the consultation exchange. The consultation process, not the theoretical perspective of the consultant, nor the work problem of the consultee, defines consultee-centered consultation.

REFERENCES

Bower, E. M. (1958). The emotionally disturbed child—A challenge to public education. *California Schools, 29.*

Bower, E. M. (1959–1960) The emotionally handicapped child and the school. *Exceptional Children, 26,* 6–11, 182–188, 232–242.

Bower, E. M. (1960). *Early identification of emotionally-handicapped children.* Springfield, IL: Charles C. Thomas.

Bower, E. M. (1961). Primary prevention in a school setting. In G. Caplan (Ed.), *Possibilities for prevention of mental disorders in children.* New York: Basic Books.

Bower, E. M., Shellhammer, T. A., & Daily, J. M. (1960) School characteristics of male adolescents who later became schizophrenic. *American Journal of Orthopsychiatry, 30,* 712–729.

Bower, E. M. (1965). Primary prevention of emotional and mental disorders: A frame of reference. In N. M. Lambert (Ed.), *The protection and promotion of mental health in schools, monographs.* Washington, DC: U.S. Department of Health, Education and Welfare.

California State Department of Education (1961). *The education of emotionally handicapped children.* A report to the California Legislature prepared pursuant to Section 1 of Chapter 2385, Statues of 1957. Sacramento, CA: California State Department of Education.

Caplan, G. (1956). Mental health consultation in schools. In *The elements of a community mental health program.* New York: Milbank Memorial Fund.

Caplan, G. (1963). Types of mental health consultation. *American Journal of Orthopsychiatry, 33,* 470–481.

Caplan, G. (1970). *Theory and practice of mental health consultation.* New York: Basic Books.

Caplan, G. (1980). *Population-oriented psychiatry.* New York: Human Sciences Press.

Caplan, R. B. (1993). *Helping the helpers to help.* New York: Seabury Press.

Caplan, G., & Caplan, R. B. (1993). *Mental health consultation and collaboration.* San Francisco: Jossey Bass.

Caplan, R. B., & Caplan, G. (2001). *Helping the helpers not to harm: Iatrogenic damage and community mental health.* New York: Brunner-Routledge.

James, B. E., Kidder, M. G., Osberg, J. W., & Hunter, W. B. (1986). *Traditional mental health consultation: The Psychodynamic perspective.* In F. V. Mannino, E. J. Trickett, M. F. Shore, M. G. Kidder, & G. Levin (Eds.), *Handbook of Mental Health Consultation* (pp. 31–48). Washington, DC: U.S. Public Health Service.

Joint Interim Committee on the Education and Rehabilitation of Handicapped Children and Adults Report. (1959). Sacramento, CA: California State Department of Education.

Keys, C. B. (1986). Organization development: An approach to mental health consultation. In F. V. Mannino, E. J. Trickett, M. F. Shore, M. G. Kidder, & G. Levin (Eds.), *Handbook of Mental Health Consultation* (pp. 31–48.) Washington, DC: U.S. Public Health Service.

Lambert, N. M. (1961). How to introduce mental health consultation in a school. In *Programming consultation services to schools by mental health specialists* (pp. 23–27). Sacramento, CA: California State Department of Mental Hygiene.

Lambert, N. M. (1963, March). School psychology: A search for identity. Presidential address in conference proceedings, California Association of School Psychologists and Psychometrists. Lakeport, CA.

Lambert, N. M. (1965). *The protection and promotion of mental health in schools*. USPHS Mental Health Monograph, No. 5. Washington, DC: U.S. Government Printing Office.

Lambert, N. M. (1974). A school-based consultation model. *Professional Psychology, 5*, 267–275.

Lambert, N. M. (1983). Perspectives on training school-based consultants. In J. Meyers & J. Alpert (Eds.), *Training in consultation: Perspectives from behavioral, mental health, and organizational consultation* (pp. 29–47). Springfield, IL: Charles C. Thomas.

Lambert, N. M. (1986). Conceptual foundations for school psychology: Perspectives from the development of the school psychology program at Berkeley. *Professional School Psychology, 4*, 215–224.

Lambert, N. M., Bower, E. M., and Hartsough, C. S. (1961, 1974, 1979). *A Process for the Assessment of Effective Student Functioning*. (Formerly A process for Screening of Emotionally Handicapped Children.) Stanford, CA: Consulting Psychologists Press.

Lambert, N. M., Sandoval, J. H., & Corder, R. A. (1975). Teacher perceptions of school-based consultants. *Professional Psychology, 6*, 204–216.

Lambert, N. M., Sandoval, J. H., & Yandell, G. W. (1975). Preparation of school psychologists for school-based consultation: A training activity and a service to community schools. *Journal of School Psychology, 13*, 68–75.

Mannino, F. V., Trickett, E. J., Shore, M. F., Kidder, M. G., & Levin, G. (Eds.). (1986). *Handbook of mental health consultation*. Washington, DC: U.S. Public Health Service.

Sandoval, J., & Lambert, N. M. (1987). Evaluating school psychologists and school psychological services. In B. A. Edelstein & E. S. Berler (Eds.), *Evaluation and accountability in clinical training* (pp. 151–182). New York: Plenum Press.

Schein, E. H. (1990). Models of consultation: What do organizations of the 1990s need? *Consultation, 9* (4), 261–275.

U.S. Public Health Service, National Institute of Mental Health (1963). *The Community Mental Health Centers Act*. Publication No. 1298. Washington, DC: U.S. GPO.

Vernberg, E. M., & Repucci, N. D. (1986). Behavioral consultation. In F. V. Mannino, E. J. Trickett, M. F. Shore, M. G. Kidder, & G. Levin (Eds.), *Handbook of Mental Health consultation* (49–80). Washington, DC: U.S. Public Health Service.

2

Recent Advances in Mental Health Consultation and Mental Health Collaboration

Gerald Caplan

Ruth B. Caplan-Moskovich

THE EVOLUTION OF CONSULTEE-CENTERED MENTAL HEALTH CONSULTATION

The time is ripe for key practitioners who have been using our type of consultation in different settings to exchange information about their field experiences, to compare notes on methodological modifications they have found useful, and to seek consensus about basic principles and conceptual models that apply across national and organizational boundaries.

We consider ourselves to be thoughtful enquiring practitioners rather than rigorous researchers and theoreticians. Over many years we have been working as mental health consultants. We and our colleagues at Harvard University and later at the Hebrew University of Jerusalem and at the Jerusalem Family Center have pioneered a variety of techniques to suit the different situations that we have encountered in health, education, welfare, and religious settings in the United States and in Israel. We have described these techniques in our writings (Caplan, 1956, 1963, 1970, 1989; Caplan, R., 1972; Caplan & Caplan, 1993.)

We have sought conceptual formulations to explain practices that we have found to be successful, and we have deduced a body of basic principles that we

21

have communicated to our students and to our colleagues. We have done this partly in the hope of stimulating others to explore analogous techniques, to modify these to suit their own settings, and then to consider on their own, as we have done, the reasons for the relative success or failure of these efforts.

Of the concepts and techniques that we have formulated over the years, some have been discarded because they did not appear to help us deal with the challenges of new practice settings, and some have been kept and refined, not in a doctrinaire way as "correct," but as guidelines to be modified, in turn, by the empirical test of their usefulness in guiding our practice.

In contrast to prescriptions for action that we might have derived from an accepted theory, this empirical pragmatic approach has necessarily led to our developing techniques and concepts that have been heavily influenced by characteristics of our own personality and inclinations; by our philosophical background and past work experience, as well as by chance features of the settings in which we have worked. For instance, the emphasis we used to place on techniques of theme interference reduction, as formulated in the *Theory and Practice of Mental Health Consultation* (Caplan, 1970) was a product of my own psychoanalytic training and also of the realities of our main consultee institution at that period, the Boston Visiting Nurses Association, whose staff were carefully selected, highly trained, and well supervised public health nurses. These nurses were likely to seek consultation when personal or interpersonal problems interfered with their usually effective daily professional operations. The culture of that public health organization placed great emphasis on the value of disciplined hierarchical relationships between nurses and physicians and between nursing practitioners and their expert advisors. This meant that the nonhierarchical consultant-consultee relationship that we advocated had to be achieved by overcoming significant obstacles, and this represented a major innovation in supporting the professional autonomy of staff who were thus enabled quickly to learn new ways of working when we approached them noncoercively and gave them the freedom to actively choose and utilize those elements in our formulations that made sense to them. For the nurses, this was a welcome contrast to the tradition of passively accepting the prescriptions of an authority figure.

What led us to incorporate theme interference reduction in the accumulating body of our accepted methodology was our experience that many consultants who had not been trained in psychoanalysis or dynamic psychotherapy were nevertheless able to appreciate the significance of possible distortion of professional judgement by intrusion of personal problems. The consultants could learn to help consultees overcome such distortions by the tactful use of consultant-consultee influence without discussing explicitly the personal problems of the consultee.

On the other hand, an increasing number of consultants using our method, who have had no training in dynamic psychotherapy, have not felt comfortable using theme interference reduction, or the consultee work problems they confronted required other theoretical frameworks, and they found other effective ways of handling the work problems of consultees linked with subjective distortions. So we have lately come to the realization that theme interference reduction, although useful, is not an obligatory element in our consultation method. In our recent book (Caplan & Caplan, 1993), we have also pointed out that the nonhierarchical noncoercive type of consultant-consultee relationship, and its associated nonacceptance of case responsibility by the consultant that we once believed to be the cornerstone of our type of consultation, may usefully be modified in certain settings where the consultant has been hired as an expert member of a service team.

Two factors have influenced significant changes in our techniques and concepts in recent years:

First, from the start our staff of consultants at Harvard was recruited from both clinical and non-clinical professions. Particularly in the last 25 years, colleagues like Ruth Caplan have played an important role in shaping our methodology. Although Ruth Caplan is widely recognized as a community psychologist and has taught university courses on the psychological aspects of literature, her original academic background and training were in the field of the History of Ideas and her special expertise was in textual analysis. She has exerted a major influence on the development of our consultation model, particularly in her emphasis on historical and socio-cultural factors in shaping the behavior of consultees and consultants and of their institutions and also in helping us focus on cognitive aspects of interpersonal operations.

Our approach to consultation became popular in the United States in the 1960s and 1970s, becoming an integral part of community mental health centers supported financially by the Federal Government. This popularity spread later to other countries such as Norway, Sweden, Denmark, and the Netherlands. Of particular importance was the widespread use of our type of consultation by school psychologists working in school districts in the United States. Our 1970 book (Caplan, 1970) became a basic textbook in many university Departments of Education that organized training in mental health consultation, as documented by Erchul (1993). The result has been that what has been tried in the United States as "Caplanian consultation" has been taken over and molded to conform to the ideas and expertise of a large number of professionals, many of whom have had little or no psychodynamic training and experience.

Second, we originally developed mental health consultation as a method of primary prevention of mental disorders for use by psychiatrists, clinical psychologists, and psychiatric social workers who utilized it outside their home base at their psychiatric clinic or hospital. The clinicians sought to influence the daily operations of caregiving professionals in community institutions such as well-baby clinics and schools so that the consultees would assist their clients to cope with life crises in a mentally healthy way. Our Harvard group extended our operations along similar lines when we offered mental health consultation to parish priests in the Episcopal Church (Caplan, R., 1972). But this then led us in an unexpected direction, when we began to train Episcopal bishops as consultants to their fellow bishops and this led to modifications in the operations of the House of Bishops of the Episcopal Church. We moved along a similar path in the Peace Corps, the Job Corps, and in the armed services of the United States. Our focus widened to the training of consultants whose mission was to improve interpersonal relations and efficiency in the members of these organizations.

When I moved to Israel in 1977, I returned to my clinical preventive psychiatry style of operations, this time as a psychiatrist working as a specialist inside the pediatric, medical, and surgical wards of a general hospital. During the past 10 years, Ruth Caplan and I have worked as mental health specialists in the Jerusalem community with the mission of preventing mental disorder in children of disrupted families as part of which we have offered consultation to the judges of divorce courts and to other court officials. Our latest books (Caplan, 1989; Caplan & Caplan, 1993) have described activities and the techniques and conceptual models we pioneered to fulfil our preventive mission.

Each of these moves led us to modify and to develop further our body of mental health consultation techniques and concepts, a process that was analogous to what was being done by other practitioners in the expanding field, and to what the authors of the sections of this volume have been doing in recent years. We wish to share our recent tentative ideas about two issues.

First, we used to think that the mental health consultation method was characterized by a coherent body of techniques that would be used with minor variations, in most cases. Novel techniques that were developed to deal with new situations were regarded as additions that enriched the traditional method. But the cumulative effect of the developments just discussed raises another possibility. Perhaps we have to move to a pluralistic model of our consultation method, namely to conceptualize our increasing range of techniques as a pool of alternatives from which consultants draw particular methods for use in specific circumstances, much as a physician chooses medicines from his or her medicine cabinet and uses them with different patients to suit their individual needs.

The second issue is more complicated. If mental health consultation includes a wide array of alternative techniques utilized in different patterns by different consultants in accordance with their own personal idiosyncracies and in response to variations in their work setting and theoretical perspectives, how can we define *Caplanian consultation* or *consultee-centered consultation*, or whatever name we affix to this style of consultation? Unless we can circumscribe our method, we will not be able to teach it or to evaluate it. Our avoidance of dogma and doctrine, although liberal and flexible, raises the danger that every consultant may behave as comes naturally to him or her, and this method will degenerate into *laissez faire* eclecticism. One goal of this volume is to offer that definition, to identify the principles on which is it based, and to lay out the characteristics and boundaries of the method.

It would be a useful contribution to our field, however, if those practising mental health consultation or consultee-centered consultation were to pool their ideas in order to define consultee-centered consultation so that the method can be circumscribed and identified. We would like to start such a discussion by proposing the following list of its essential elements:

Consultee-centered consultation incorporates concepts and techniques that our consultants acquire through training that enables them:

1. To identify appropriate caregiving institutions and individual caregivers in the community and to involve these in joint action that achieves the goal of reducing rates of mental disorder in the population, and which also furthers the mission of the other caregivers.

2. To obtain and maintain the sanction of community leaders and institutional administrators for consultants to enter and operate in the nonmental health institution.

3. To negotiate explicit agreements that define our roles as experts who will help consultees, individually or in groups, to improve services that promote the mental health of their clients. Our role may be restricted to providing generalized diagnostic and remedial information to consultees about particular clients, or it may extend to assessing and remedying possible shortcomings of consultees in fulfilling mental health aspects of their mission—shortcomings that may be linked with lack of knowledge, skill, confidence, or professional objectivity in dealing with particular clients. A basic principle of our method is its insistence that in consultation discussions, the boundary between the private life and personal problems of consultees and their professional roles will be respected, and that personal problems of consultees will not be discussed, even when these may

be reducing the efficacy of their professional functioning. Our method provides consultants with various techniques for dealing with this issue.

The consultation agreements may restrict the roles of our consultant experts to those of enabling the consultees to improve their professional functioning, in which event the consultants will accept *no* responsibility for case outcome. Or our experts *will* accept responsibility for mental health aspects of case outcome, in which event the experts will be obliged also to take a direct part in planning and implementing diagnostic, remedial, and evaluation action in the cases, in addition to acting as enablers to improve the professional performance of consultees.

Our method may extend its focus beyond particular cases to improving the policies and programs of the caregiving institution that deal with prevention and remediation of mental disorders in its client population. The consultation agreement will then deal with the administrative issues in analogous ways as just mentioned.

4. Our method has two other essential characteristics:

a. Our cornerstone or fulcrum is the consultant's influence on the consultee, mediated by the content of the consultant's communications and the leverage of the consultant-consultee relationship. The consultant seeks to support the professional autonomy of the consultees so that they will realize that it is their own increased sensitivity and understanding and their own actions that have resolved the work impasse that led to their first invoking intervention by the consultant. This enables the consultees to incorporate quickly the lessons they have learnt from their success in the current case into their future patterns of functioning.

In the purely enabling forms of consultation, our consultants seek to foster the autonomy of consultees while increasing the influence of their theoretical perspectives on consultees through promoting a coordinate noncoercive approach. The latter is made possible by the consultants not accepting responsibility and accountability for the consultee's actions and for case outcome. They also maintain strict confidentiality, so that consultees may feel free to speak frankly without fear that leakage of information by the consultant may lead to their being forced by their supervisors to modify their professional behavior, or that may lead to sanctions against them.

When the necessities of the work setting demand that the consultants do accept responsibility for certain aspects of case outcome, our method calls for the consultants to explicitly delimit significant parts of the case for which the consultees may be assigned full responsibility, and also for consultants to avoid sharing information with the supervisors of the consultees.

b. In collecting information as a basis for assessing the nature of the client's problems, the work difficulties of the consultees, and the reasons why this particular case has been selected at this time for consultation help, as well as in planning and implementing consultation intervention, our consultants use an open-systems conceptual map of interpenetrating fields of psychosocial forces. Every situation is analyzed as being the outcome of forces that influence one another reverberatively. These forces originate in the conscious and unconscious mind of individuals, in interpersonal and family influences, in forces inside the consultee institution and in traditional values and practices, as well as in current events in the community. Our consultants are not required to commit themselves to any particular model of psychology, sociology, ecology, or cultural anthropology, but they must view any current aspect of a case within the framework of a pluralistic dynamic interplay of all these theoretical forces.

MENTAL HEALTH COLLABORATION

In a recent review of our book, *Mental Health Consultation and Collaboration* (Caplan & Caplan, 1993), the reviewer complained that we had given inadequate attention to collaboration because we had devoted only 55 pages to this method compared to the 264 pages on consultation in earlier chapters. We first felt that he had missed the point because most of the earlier part of the book applied just as much to collaboration as to consultation. But in thinking the matter over, we realize that his criticism was influenced by our own lack of clarity. At the time we wrote that book, we had conceptualized collaboration as a method separate from consultation, and not as a type of consultation with specific features that differentiate it from the purely enabling types we had practiced hitherto.

We began to explore collaboration techniques in 1977, when I moved back to Israel to work in a university general hospital where I was directing a department of child psychiatry. The preventive challenge in that setting was to reach out and offer consultation to our medical and nursing colleagues in other departments, particularly to those who were working in the inpatient wards with children suffering from bodily illnesses that were complicated by mental disorders and by emotional reactions to the stress of the illness.

Our mental health approach led us to conceptualize the other hospital departments as potential consultee institutions, and our colleagues as caregivers whose work placed them in a salient position to deal preventively with a population of children at risk. When we began to offer our consultation services to the other departments, some of our colleagues received us with open arms. After discovering what we had to offer in the form of intermittent case consultation, they invited us to attach a mental health consultant to their wards on a regular basis, because they felt that almost all their cases had a mental health component. In consequence, I joined the diagnostic and remedial team in two departments of pediatrics, and a senior colleague joined the staff team in the department of pediatric surgery.

In these settings, we soon discovered that our traditional mental health consultation approach of offering consultation intermittently to help a colleagues do a better mental health job was of value, but was less than what they needed and less than some of their leaders wanted. My colleague and I found that many of the cases we encountered were too complicated to be handled effectively by nonmental health specialist professionals on their own, even if they were optimally supported by enabling types of mental health consultation. Handling such cases jointly on the hospital wards by a partnership of the mental health specialist and the medical, surgical, and nursing staffs did seem feasible. The experience could also provide an opportunity for these caregivers to increase their mental health knowledge and skills, and this could have an important carryover effect on their future functioning.

Within this framework we pioneered our method of mental health collaboration. in which a mental health consultant becomes a member of a team of specialists. As in mental health consultation, we paid much attention to developing an appropriate relationship with our colleagues that would provide the leverage for us to influence their actions in the current case and thus help them acquire new sensitivities, understandings, and skills to enrich their future operations. We were particularly interested in the issue of our relative power vis-à-vis our colleagues. As in enabling forms of consultation, we tried to keep our relationship with them as nonhierarchical as possible, in order to maximize our influence. Such a coordinate status was facilitated by our all being members of the diagnostic and treatment multidisciplinary team, and as such none of us had the power to coerce any other team member to do as we wished. This power was kept in the hands of the team leader, who had responsibility for case outcome. He or she was a senior pediatrician or pediatric surgeon, and because our patients were often seriously ill, all team members accepted the authority of the team leader in making decisions that might deal with issues of life and death. Except in rare cases, such issues involved physical and not psychological factors.

We were invited to join the ward team as specialists responsible for the effect of medical and surgical treatment on mental health aspects of cases, and we had accepted this assignment with the understanding that this would be accomplished by joint action in the pediatric or pediatric surgery department settings, and not by removal of the cases for treatment to our own specialized department. We agreed to be held accountable for the case outcome in regard to the mental health of the patients. We were therefore faced by the dilemma of not, in fact, being free to allow our fellow team members to act as they liked while working in partnership with us.

In pioneering techniques of mental health collaboration, much of our effort has focused on resolving this dilemma. We had to work out ways of involving our fellow team members in joint action in diagnosing and treating the mental health aspects of our cases which would afford them the opportunity to be active in ways which they could feel to be their own, and at the same time we had to get them to accept ways that we judged effective in promoting the mental health of our patients.

We have accomplished this through fostering mutual trust and respect between us and the team leaders and team members, so that they would allow us to exert direction and control through their authority. During team discussions, we have drawn their attention to relevant issues, and persuaded them to allot appropriate tasks to us and to other team members in jointly serving the needs of patients, and then to require feedback reports from all of us about how we have fulfilled these assignments. This has enabled us to modify and replan in the light of the group's evaluation of the information we have collected.

Relative success in such an endeavor depends basically on the personal capacity of the team leader to evoke the participation of the team members in sharing his or her leadership role, on the quality of his or her authority, on the communication system of the team, and on the administrative efficiency and effectiveness of the host department as a problem solving organization. Our 1993 book described techniques to help integrate ourselves in a range of administrative settings. Whereas in enabling forms of consultee-centered mental health consultation we accept as a given the administrative setting of the consultee institution, in mental health collaboration we often act as change agents in order to stimulate improvements in the administrative framework of the host institution that will allow us to accomplish the mission of safeguarding the mental health of our clients.

Mental health collaboration demands not only that we should influence colleagues to enlarge their professional domain by accepting added responsibility for mental health matters and by learning new conceptual skills, but it also involves learning new ways of approaching and understanding the work problem. In order to integrate in the host department, we must learn enough about its ways of working and its professional language to operate inside its framework without upsetting its routines. And we must work out new techniques for achieving our own specialized goals not in the privacy and freedom of our own offices, but in full view in the workspace of the host department. We must constantly keep in mind to act as role models for nonmental health specialist coworkers, so that they may learn by identifying with us. We must also learn to divide up diagnostic and treatment tasks in order to provide meaningful elements that can be shared out among team members, who can be given a relatively free hand in deciding how to accomplish them. Our colleagues will increase their mental health sophistication both by identifying with us and also by actively working out their own ways of accomplishing the tasks that have been allotted to them.

CONSULTANTS AS OUTSIDERS AND AS INSIDERS

When we developed the systematic foundations of our consultation methods forty years ago at Harvard School of Public Health, we were operating as outside specialists in the well-baby clinics and public schools which we had chosen as our main consultee institutions. This outsider status was even more marked in our later work in the Episcopal Church (Caplan, R., 1972). Many of our techniques were developed in order to obtain entry and to gain sanction in the host institutions, and to learn enough about their ways of working to be able to understand and deal with the organizational reasons for the work difficulties of our consultees. Our outsider status made it relatively easy to develop our nonhierarchical approach of not accepting administrative power over our consultees and responsibility for the welfare of their clients. This allowed us to operate as purely enabling consultants. Because we were not part of the consultee organization, we also had little difficulty in maintaining strict confidentiality for our consultation discussions, and in fending off requests from their supervisors for our evaluation of the professional performance of our consultees. And because it was clear that we had entered the consultee institution on behalf of our mental health specialist agency, it was natural for us to negotiate a written agreement between the two organizations that would define the nature of the consultant and the consultee roles and explicate the relationships.

In 1977, when I moved to Jerusalem and joined the staff of its university general hospital, my status as a consultant became less clear. To some extent I and my colleagues in our autonomous department of child psychiatry could operate as relative outsiders when we entered other departments of the hospital, which was so large that there was usually little regular contact between the workers of different departments. Thus, although we were all colleagues in the same hospital and therefore our staff should be received in other departments as insiders, so long as we only occasionally came in to offer consultation we could still profit from an outsider status and operate nonhierarchically in our relationships with consultees. But it was less easy for us to disclaim all responsibility for the welfare of the clients who were patients to whose welfare all hospital staff are expected to contribute.

On the other hand, in departments such as pediatrics and pediatric surgery, our status was that of insiders as soon as we had become integrated in their ward teams. But however effective our integration and assimilation in the life of the consultee departments, we have always been perceived as being somewhat different from the doctors, nurses, and auxiliary staff on their own payroll.

For instance, the senior psychiatrist who was working on the pediatric surgery ward was subordinate to her team leader; but if she felt that his decision about a case would seriously endanger a patient's mental health, and if she was not able to persuade him to change his decision, she could appeal the matter to me as the head of her own department. If I agreed with her, I could bring pressure to bear on the team leader by requesting the intervention of his administrative superior, the chief pediatric surgeon. We organized an administrative mechanism for dealing smoothly and without personal friction with such situations by establishing a steering committee of heads of our two departments that met regularly, and could also be convened quickly in case of a need to discuss and remedy urgent issues that our consultant might feel would otherwise endanger the mental health of the patient, whom she could not adequately protect because of her subordination to the team leader.

In our book (Caplan & Caplan, 1993) we described another example that has a bearing on the outsider–insider status issue in consultation. We signed a consultation agreement with a child rehabilitation institution, partly with the mission of helping improve its organizational efficiency. This was poor because of longstanding ineffective administrative direction and because of intra-staff conflicts linked with competing vested interests among the chiefs of professional disciplines, whose power could not be curbed by the institution's director. We deployed a team of six specialist staff in the institution. In our book, we described the techniques worked out to try and overcome the difficulties encountered in developing a viable program of mental health consultation and collaboration, and our efforts to help a new medical director improve the efficiency of his organization. After 3 years, we withdrew when the medical director resigned, and we realized that apart from the entrenched disciplinary chiefs, turnover of staff was so high that those whom we influenced to improve their mental health skills stayed only a short time in the institution

We did, however, succeed in persuading members of its lay Board of Directors to appreciate the importance of mental health matters. When they appointed a new medical director, they also recruited a junior psychiatrist from our team to take a staff position in the institution. This psychiatrist's duties were defined mainly in terms of giving direct service to patients; and he was able to build up a quite successful program to accomplish this. He involved junior staff of other disciplines as coworkers on behalf of his patients, and he was active in increasing their mental health knowledge and skills by using a variety of educational methods. He was careful to avoid open confrontations with their supervisors, who in any case did not feel threatened by him because of his youth. His program was actively supported by the new medical director who had played a key role in appointing him. The psychiatrist became an accepted member of staff of the institution in which he continued to work for several years before moving on to develop other aspects of his career.

This psychiatrist was able to make use of the mental health consultation and collaboration methods that he had learned from us not only in furthering the interests of the patients under his care, but also in enriching the mental health skills of other members of staff which had a carryover to patients with whom he had no contact. Due to his efforts and those of the new director, staff turnover was reduced, particularly among those workers who were involved in his program. He showed that mental health consultation and collaboration techniques can be an accepted part of the role of a specialist working as an insider, even in an inauspicious setting, as long as these techniques are included as a modest component in a service program that is supported by the authority figures of the institution.

Over the past 15 years, our method of mental health consultation has been utilized on a widespread scale in the United States by school psychologists, who have adapted it for use with teachers and other education professionals. A dominant trend in school psychology in recent years has moved the profession away from direct guidance of problem children in the psychologists' offices, and from the psychologists being required to spend most of their time testing children suffering from learning disorders in order to plan methods of remedial education, to offering consultation to the teaching staff to help them deal, themselves, more effectively with children in difficulty. The relative proportion of the psychologist's time spent on directly diagnosing and treating children in the psychologist's offices in contrast to offering consultation to teachers, has varied from school to school. But it is our impression that in the United States, psychologists are spending time in some form of indirect work outside their offices, and have used various approaches to consultation, including what has been called *Caplanian consultation* (Caplan, Caplan, & Erchul, 1994).

An essential characteristic of insider consultation is that the specialists are not free agents in working out their own programs, but are very much constrained by the nature of their roles as defined by the administrators of their institutions. It is therefore likely that consultation techniques will form only one component in the sum total of their operations, in contrast to outsider consultants who enter the consultee institution with the relatively specific purpose of fulfilling the preventive mission of their home agency, insofar as this may be compatible with the programs of the consultee institution.

The terms of the job descriptions of school psychologists have meant that, like the young psychiatrist in the rehabilitation institution, they have not used consultation techniques exclusively, but have mixed them with other techniques in carrying out their duties. Thus, the psychologists often have been called on to take part in *ad hoc* task forces or teams together with teachers and special education staff in investigating and remedying the problems of particular children, or in planning school policies to deal with widespread problems such as bullying, alcoholism, stealing, and so forth. In such situations, they have usually been called on to use mental health collaboration techniques. But when they have been given the freedom to choose, rather than being asked by other staff to play their part in joint actions, they also have been able to make use of enabling consultation techniques.

When they provide consultee-centered consultation, they have had to modify techniques described in our publications. For instance, they have had to find ways of building a nonhierarchical relationship with consultees whom they may outrank in the formal status hierarchy of the school. Their own training in psychology and education may have equipped them with more pedagogical knowledge than the classroom teachers, which challenge efforts to maintain a nonhierarchical relationships with the consultees.

School psychologists may have been hired as members of the school management team, responsible for monitoring the professional level of teachers and training them in advanced educational techniques. These psychologists may thus be expected to share information about the teachers with other members of the school management team. So how can they maintain confidentiality and not divulge information about their consultees to the supervisory staff? These psychologists may not be able to refuse to be administratively responsible for their consultee's performance, and they may not be able to reject responsibility for the mental health of the students who are the clients of their consultees.

Psychologists may also establish an understanding with classroom teachers, who come to them for consultation, to treat their remarks about the work situation as "privileged communication," and they may negotiate with their school management to be allowed to do this in order to maximize their educational influence on their consultees. The use of such maneouvers may allow insider consultants to overcome some of the main obstacles to providing our basic techniques of enabling consultation.

It is our impression that many school psychologists concentrate most of their consultation effort on remedying not lack of professional objectivity, but lack of knowledge and skills in their consultees that require a focus on theories from psychology and pedagogy. Moreover, since they work continuously in the schools and do not just come and go intermittently for short periods, they are better able than outsiders to develop long term consultation services to promote the mental health status of the student–clients of the teacher–consultees.

How can we differentiate such consultation from in-service training or educational supervision? And what do we gain by considering these operations within the conceptual framework of consultee-centered consultation? The consultation approach emphasizes intervention of specialists in a current situation of disequilibrium and arousal of need for help in teachers involved in a temporarily insoluble work problem. Its basic idea is that by helping the line workers to find a solution to their current work impasse, the experience will have a long term carryover in improving their professional effectiveness. But is this consultation approach really different from that of problem-centered in-service training? Our consultation approach emphasizes the benefits of maintaining the professional autonomy of our consultees, whereas traditional education requires a certain level of continuing dependency of teachers on their professional mentors, from which they can eventually free themselves only after the in-service training program has ended.

Another difference between consultation and training is that the latter usually seeks to impart a predetermined body of information, even when this information may be communicated piecemeal in problem-centered seminars. Consultants on the other hand, deal only with current problems that are raised by consultees, the rationale being that the tension of the disequilibrium motivates the consultees to involve themselves actively in the learning situation.

Circumscribing the appropriate techniques to achieve specific goals does not imply that insider consultation restricts the choice of techniques by consultants. School psychologists, unlike outsider consultants, will probably not sign contracts that sanction only certain forms of consultation. They will not be expected to confine themselves to client-centered, consultee-centered case, or administrative consultation. They will usually be more free than outside consultants to decide how to handle a current work problem. They are likely to make concurrent use of a combination of techniques. Because they have probably been trained in developmental, social, ecological, and behavioral theories, as well as in counseling, assessment, and teaching methodology, and in the techniques of the consultation communication process, they should be equipped to combine methods derived from all these fields in dealing with problem students.

During the course of their professional and post-graduate training, they will probably have learned and practiced each technique in isolation. But as mature practitioners, they should be able to combine them in a package that they tailor to the needs of the moment. For instance, they may accept referrals of problem cases, diagnose the students in their classrooms or in their own offices, counsel the students themselves, and collaborate with other school staff in organising joint diagnostic and remedial action. At the same time, they may exploit this opportunity to enrich the mental health understanding and skills of their nonspecialist colleagues by employing consultee-centered consultation and other forms of in-service education to help their colleagues deal with these and similar cases on their own as an integral part of their daily work.

REFERENCES

Caplan, G. (1956). Mental health consultation in schools. In the elements of a community mental health program. New York: Milbank Memorial Fund.

Caplan, G. (1963). Types of mental health consultation. American Journal of Orthopsychiatry, 33, 470–481.

Caplan, G. (1970). Theory and practice of mental health consultation. New York: Basic Books.

Caplan, G. (1989). Population oriented psychiatry. New York: Human Sciences Press.

Caplan, G., & Caplan R. B. (1993). Mental health consultation and collaboration. San Francisco: Jossey-Bass.

Caplan, G., Caplan, R. B., & Erchul, W. P. (1994). Caplanian mental health consultation: Historical background and current status. Consulting Psychology, 46, 4, 2–13.

Caplan, R. B. (1972). Helping the helpers to help. New York: Seabury Press.

Erchul, W. P. (Ed.). (1993). Consultation in community, school, and organizational practice. Washington, DC: Taylor & Francis.

3

Conceptual Change in Consultee-Centered Consultation

Jonathan H. Sandoval
University of California at Davis

Consultation is a process that involves learning on the part of the consultee and the consultant. Ideally, the consultee learns new ways of thinking and behaving as a professional, and the consultant learns more about the work world of the consultee, and about the vicissitudes of human behavior. One view of the learning process that is increasingly popular in educational circles is constructivism. The central tenant in the constructivist perspective is that the learner is always an active agent in the learning process, not a passive participant receiving transmitted information (Cobern, 1993). Piaget, for one, advocated this view of the learner. Translated into instructional theory, the classroom must be organized to permit students to explore and discuss different explanations of phenomena and to build their own understandings. This facet of constructivist theory has much to offer thoughtful consultants, particularly those who are consultee centered (cf. Caplan & Caplan, 1993). Translated into consultation theory, the consultee must be an active participant in the process, and we must recognize that in consultation both participants will be constructing new understandings of the consultation dilemma.

Another aspect of constructivist learning theory is the notion of the development of cognitive constructions, or schema, over time. This aspect emphasizes conceptual change as an important phenomenon. As individuals grow older and gain more experience solving problems in the external world, they develop or construct their own theories about how things work. These theories or conceptions of the physical and interpersonal world are influenced by what they observe, are told, or deduce from their interactions at home, in the neighborhood, in the community, and in formal educational settings. Developmentalists, such as Piaget or Vygotsky, have documented qualitative changes in thinking over time in children. Young children's explanations of phenomena are often quite different from adults' explanations.

However, there is no reason to believe that conceptual shifting does not continue, at least in some domains, throughout adulthood and across historical time. Scholars in the history of science have noticed that the progression of ideas about the physical world in the history of science is remarkably like the progression of ideas about the physical world held by children. For example, young children believe that the world is flat, as did many scientists in ancient times. As a result, constructivist scholars in science education have tended to focus on conceptual change, acknowledging that scientific understandings may always be under construction or open to reconstruction. In science, as research and theory progress, there may be paradigm shifts that lead to important changes the way in which everyone understands the world (Kuhn, 1962).

As consultants, we also see paradigm shifts in our consultees. We hope that as an outcome of consultation, our consultees come to understand their clients in a new way, one that enables them to be helpful in their professional roles. In a sense, consultation can be an important tool for professional development, although consultees do not come with this goal in mind.

Consultants are no less immune to conceptual change than are consultees. When one hears the first descriptions (presentations) of the consultation dilemma from the consultee, one or several notions (representations) of what may be the underlying dynamics come to mind. As consultation proceeds, however, others may replace these initial ideas, as more information is revealed. And, of course, over time, the consultant may come to develop more and more complex understandings of human behavior.

CONCEPTUAL CHANGE IN SCIENCE EDUCATION

It is well documented that children come to a science lesson with naive conceptualizations and theories for how the world works. Moreover, these preconceptions are remarkably difficult to change. For example, children come to believe that heavier objects will fall faster than lighter ones and, as a result, the abstract notions of gravity—which predict a different outcome for two dropped objects differing in mass—are difficult to teach. Science teachers and researchers have found that for change and new learning to occur, four conditions identified by Posner, Strike, Hewson, and Gertzog (1982) must be present:

1. A dissatisfaction with existing conceptions.
2. A new conception that is intelligible.
3. A new conception that is initially plausible.
4. A new conception that if fruitful, suggests the possibility of solving additional problems.

If these conditions are part of an instructional program, students will accommodate, in the Piagetian sense, and change conceptual schema rather than assimilate new information into their old ones.

CONCEPTUAL CHANGE IN CONSULTATION

For the consultant focusing on the consultee, the task is similar to, although by no means identical to, teaching science. In consultation we must accept that a consultee, on entering consultation, often has a conception of why a client is behaving the way he or she does. However, acting on this conception, the consultee has not been successful. This lack of success often is what brings the consultee to consultation: the consultee's construction of the situation. This conception, if not naive, is at least not working to suggest interventions that allow the consultee to be effective with the client. The task facing the consultant is to explore with the consultee new ways of theorizing about the problems and puzzles facing the consultee that will lead to productive ways for the consultee to serve the client. The consultant must begin by determining the consultee's understanding of the client's situation and the consultee's theory about why the problem exists.

Questions and Conceptual Change

A critical early step in the consultation process is problem identification, following relationship building and maintaining rapport through empathic listening. Typically the consultant helps in the problem identification process by asking questions to elicit the consultee's view of the consultation dilemma. Gunilla Guvå (1999) suggested a number of questions to use to help:

Focus on the client's problem.

What is the problem with x? How old is x? What you mean is that x.

Focus on the history of the client and problem.

When did it start? What were some critical past incidents? What had you heard about x before you met him or her?

Focus on the concrete here and now.

Can you tell me when during the school day the client is at his or her worst? What did he or she do and how did others react?

Focus on the consultee's explanations.

Why do you think this is so? Is there something than can help us understand the client. What do you think is going on?

Focus on the consultee's picture of the client.

What does the client look like?

Focus on the consultee's fantasies about the future.

What do you think will happen if nothing is done?

Focus on other imaginations (ghosts) of importance.

Have you met similar problems before?

Focus on the consultee's expectations of the consultant.

What did you expect me to do for you when you asked for my assistance?

Questions such as these are very helpful in illuminating the consultee's initial theory (or theories) of human behavior in general, and specific theory of what is causing the consultation predicament. Most of the consultant's questions are open-ended (questions requiring an elaborated response) as opposed to closed questions (questions that can be answered yes or no) (Benjamin, 1969). Open-ended questions, along with responses such as reflection and restatement, allow the consultee to explore the problem more easily, and communicate that the consultant is listening carefully to what is being said. The answers to all of these questions permit the consultant to view the consultee's understanding of the problem and the underlying theories of behavior. An important goal of consultation is to understand the consultee's initial representation of the problem. Equally important to the process, the answer to questions such as these will also provide the consultant with information to be used in also forming his or her own conceptualization of situation. The consultant's construction of the problem frequently may be different from the consultee's.

Another useful question to ask of all consultees is "What have you tried to address the problem?" This question has several virtues. It permits the consultant to understand how the consultee has translated her or his theory into action. Often the consultee's action reveals theories that are not explicitly stated. Of course this question also permits the consultant to avoid the trap of suggesting an action that has already been tried. It also permits statements of one-downsmanship, as advocated by Caplan.

Consultant Leads in Consultation

The consultant does not just ask questions and reflect on or restate what the consultee has said. At some point, the consultant will be able to define the problem from the consultee's point of view in a way that the consultee agrees is accurate. However, the consultant does offer other observations coming from her or his point of view or perspective. The statements may be termed consultation leads.

Leads may have many purposes. They may be designed to create cognitive dissonance, to reframe the facts presented, or to offer another conceptualization to the consultee. When the purpose is to create dissonance, the comments may be to point out or search for anomalous data, to comment on what is missing or unexplained in the consultee's statements of the problem, or to note contradictions in what has been said.

Consultant comments or observations, as leads, come from the consultant's point of view. In addition to creating dissonance, they may also reframe the problem by reorganizing the information presented by the consultee. The reorganization using the same facts, may reorder cause and effect, or introduce new ideas to be discussed and verified.

Accessible Reasoning and Conceptual Change

Argyris and Schön (1996) argue that in interpersonal problem solving, a key skill of the consultant, is making explicit to the consultee their own conceptualization of the problem drawn from the information that has emerged from the consultation interview. That is, the consultant makes his or her reasoning accessible to the consultee (Monsen & Frederickson, 2002), and, more importantly, offers up the conceptualization for discussion and debate. Conceptions must be openly examined, tested, and falsified, if need be. To be tested, however, the conceptions must first be organized in hypothetical form. The testing may range from recollections, thought experiments, and actual trials of interventions with the client. The information used must be valid and objective. The discussion and testing must done in a way that does not put the consultee or consultant on the defensive. Such a discussion requires great interpersonal skill, needless to say.

The Change Process

As the process proceeds, the consultant and consultee will likely explore how the consultee's construction is inadequate to explain this and other cases. By the presentation of anomalous data—pointing out where the theory does not work and by highlighting dissonant evidence not predicted by the consultee's framework—the consultant helps build dissatisfaction with the current explanatory theory. When a new theory is generated during consultation, it must be an understandable substitute. It must be intelligible, coherent, and internally consistent and seem like a plausible explanation. Finally, the new idea must seem to have widespread applicability—it should be elegant, parsimonious, and efficacious in working with future clients and problems as well as the current client and problem. It should explain more of the observed facts of the case than the previous theory. As with science instruction, the focus will be on anomalies—that is, how existing notions about the problem fail to explain the situation or produce interventions.

Eventually a new theory will be produced by the consultation. It may be proposed by the consultant or the consultee (or consultees, if it is a group consultation). Often analogies and metaphors will be used to introduce the new ideas and conceptualization and make them intelligible to both the consultant and consultee. Although analogies may be useful initially, it is important to be sure that the correct features are abstracted from the analogy and transferred to the new theory.

Unlike the teaching of science, where there is a goal to bring the learner to the point of thinking like a scientist, the goal in consultation is not necessarily to have the consultee adopt the theories of the consultant. Instead the intent is for there to be a mutual construction of a conceptualization that fits the situation and permits action. This openness makes the understanding that is the outcome of consultation unknown and unpredictable, but also makes the process more enjoyable and challenging.

Theme Interference and Conceptual Change

Caplan (1963) identified four major categories of difficulty that bring a consultee to consultation:

(a) lack of understanding of the psychological factors in the case;
(b) lack of skill or resources to deal with the problems involved;
(c) lack of professional objectivity in handling the case; and
(d) lack of confidence and self-esteem due to fatigue, illness, inexperience, youth or old age.

Category (a) may indicate a missing conceptualization or a naive idea about the causes of the problem with a client, and category (c) may indicate a conceptualization (or theme) that is mistaken, is emotionally charged, and in need of changing. Caplan recommended that theme interference reduction be used to address consultee problems of type (c) but acknowledged that this technique has not been endorsed by may consultants, particularly school-based practitioners (Caplan, Caplan, & Erchul, 1995).

Themes are " A conflict related to actual life experience or to fantasies that has not been satisfactorily resolved (and that) is apt to persist in a consultee's preconscious or unconscious as an emotionally toned cognitive constellation" (Caplan & Caplan, 1993, p. 122). Caplan suggested that in many cases, themes, like neutrally toned schema, interfere with effective problem solving but are even more difficult to address because of the negative affect. He described how themes may be understood as syllogisms the consultee has constructed consisting of an initial category and an inevitable outcome. In consultation, these themes must be shown to be inadequate before new ways of working with and conceptualizing the client will emerge. Theme interference techniques include demonstrating that the inevitable outcome is only one logical possibility and that other outcomes are more likely than the dreaded one, and avoiding giving nonverbal validation to the theme outcome. These techniques of theme interference reduction may be viewed as attempts at conceptual change inasmuch as they attempt to change syllogisms constructed by the consultee. Perhaps considering theme interference reduction as a process of conceptual change, as well as recognizing the possibility that consultees do have *some sort* of theory about client behavior when they seem to lack understanding, will be a fruitful way of viewing collaborative work.

Instead of offering a different conceptualization, however, the attempt with themes is to elaborate them to make them more plausible and fruitful for working with other clients. Anomalous data may be brought in to indicate how the initial category did not lead to the inevitable outcome. As Caplan suggested, the emphasis should be on how the theory is inadequate, not on how the theory is inapplicable to the particular client. There will be no motive to change the theory if it is perceived as not applying to the client.

It must be pointed out that sometimes consultee's difficulties of Caplan type (a) really are because the consultee has no theory or conception, although this seems unlikely, given the prevalence of folk psychology. However, some consultees may be a *tabala rasa* and need to be helped to gain knowledge. Whether or not the consultant supplies the needed knowledge or refers the consultee to other sources depends on many factors having to do with the organizational structure of the institution in which the consultee works.

IMPLICATIONS FOR RESEARCH

I wish to join Henning-Stout (1994) in a call for more research on the discourse of expert consultants, particularly those who are consultee centered. Hylander (2000), for example, documented several examples of conceptual shifts in consultees in what she called *turning processes*. I believe that effective consultants will be found to be engaged with their consultees in a process of conceptual change. Looking for conceptual change may, in fact become a useful outcome variable for evaluating the consultation process. Conceptual change can be assessed by examining the transcripts of the consultation dialogue, by asking consultees explicitly to describe their theory of the client's behavior at different times, by asking them to think aloud about a similar client, and even by asking them to make pictorial models of the systems surrounding the consultation problem (Sandoval, 1999). If this were to be done, I believe consultees would shift, as do novices when they become experts, to more complex, deep, and differentiated models of the phenomena they encounter. Deep and complex thinking should be a goal of the consultation process.

REFERENCES

Argyris, C., & Schön, D. A. (1996). *Organizational Learning II: Theory, method and Practice.* Reading, MA: Addison-Wesley.

Benjamin, A. (1969). *The helping interview.* Boston: Houghton Mifflin.

Caplan, G. (1963). Types of mental health consultation. *American Journal of Orthopsychiatry, 33,* 470–481.

Caplan, G., & Caplan, R. (1993). The theory and practice of mental health consultation. (2nd ed.). San Francisco: Josey Bass.

Caplan, G., Caplan, R. B., & Erchul, W. P. (1995). A contemporary view of mental health consultation: Comments on "Types of mental Health consultation" by Gerald Caplan (1963). *Journal of Educational and Psychological Consultation, 6,* 23–30.

Cobern, W. W. (1993). Constructivism. *Journal of Educational and Psychological Consultation, 4,* 105–112.

Guvå, G. (1999). Teachers ask for help, not for consultation. In *Explorations in process in practice* (Seminar proceedings). Stockholm: 2nd International Seminar on Consultee-centered consultation.

Henning-Stout, M. (1994). Consultation and connected knowing: What we know is determined by the questions we ask. *Journal of Educational and Psychological Consultation, 5,* 5–21.

Hylander, I. (2000). *Turning processes: The change of representations in consultee-centered case consultation.* Linköping, Sweden: Linköping Studies in Education and Psychology No. 74.

Kuhn, T. (1962). *The structure of scientific revolutions.* Chicago: Chicago University Press.

Monsen, J. J., & Frederickson, N. (2002). Consultant problem understanding as a function of training in interviewing to promote accessible reasoning. *Journal of School Psychology, 40,* 197–212.

Posner, G. P., Strike, K. A., Hewson, P. W., & Gertzog, W. A. (1982). Accommodation of a scientific conception: Toward a theory of conceptual change. *Science Education, 66,* 211–227.

Sandoval, J. (1999). Evaluation issues and strategies in consultee-centered consultation. In *Explorations in process in practice* (Seminar proceedings). Stockholm: 2nd International Seminar on Consultee-centered consultation.

4

Analysis of Conceptual Change in Consultee-Centered Consultation

Ingrid Hylander
University of Linköping, Sweden

The expected outcome of a consultee-centered consultation is a conceptual change in the consultee (Sandoval, 1996, 1999). In other words, a successful consultation process ends with a different *representation of the problem* as the consultee has apprehended it. Such a change in representation will be called a conceptual shift or *turning*. When a turning has occurred, the consultee claims that the problem he or she brought to consultation is now solved or can be handled. He or she has framed the problem in another way. Most probably, this turning has been followed by a change in his or her way of encountering and understanding the student, which in turn brings about a change in the student. But as a consultee-centered consultant one may never be sure. The only thing one will know for certain is whether the consultee's way of presenting his or her own representation of the problem has changed.

Many consultees, such as teachers in school-based consultation, would be quite upset to think that the result of a consultation process is their conceptual change. Who wants to change his or her mind while being worn out by a student who does not follow the rules or is not successful in the classroom? Teachers ask for help when they want someone else to do something about the problem—they want the student to change or be removed. They don't want to change their own minds. In this chapter, I argue that the key factor that makes consultee-centered consultation successful—that is, helpful for teachers—is the ability not of the consultee but of the consultant to constantly change *his or her own representation of the problem*. The consultant has to change his or her own way of framing the problem, to start with, to the point where he or she totally accepts and understands the teacher's representation of the case. This is a starting point for subsequent conceptual shifts. The only process that is within the control of the consultant is one's own conceptual change.

This chapter focuses on the process of change of representations (internal conceptualizations) and presentations (verbal statements and nonverbal behavior)—the consultee's as well as the consultant's—and the interplay between them. I report some findings from a grounded theory study of consultee-centered consultation, in school, preschool and child day care settings. A full account may be found elsewhere (Hylander, 1999, 2000).

The beginning point is a nonprescriptive model of consultation. Being *nonprescriptive* (as in consultee-centered consultation) means leaving the responsibility to accept or reject suggestions to the consultee. That is, the consultee is in charge of the solution to the problem and all the interventions subsequently implemented. Being *prescriptive* as a consultant, on the other hand, (as in behavioral consultation) means being an expert generating a solution to the problem. Being nonprescriptive as a consultant means being ready to change one's own representation of the problem and the way to solve it. Being prescriptive means keeping to one's own representation of the problem and wanting the teacher to adopt it.

In Swedish schools, preschools and child care the most common consultation model is consultee-centered consultation, based on and evolved from Gerald Caplan's early writings (Caplan, 1970) and the interview guide developed by Gunilla Guvå (1989, 1992, 1995, 1999). Consultee-centered consultation is well established as a practice, but almost no research on consultation has been done in Sweden. I wanted a method that could explore this consultation practice but was not bound to a particular psychological theory of behavior. Most consultants used psychodynamic theory to frame understandings when consultation came into use in Sweden 20 to 25 years ago and many do today. However, there are several other theories that influence consultation practice today. Most important are systemic theory (Bateson, 1979), constructivistic theory (Anderson & Goolishian, 1998; Berger & Luckman, 1967), including ecological conceptualizations (Bronfenbrenner, 1979), different kinds of object-relation theories (Winnicott, 1971) self-psychology (Brodin & Hylander, 1995, 1997; Stern, 1985) and developmental theories such as Piaget and Vygotsky (1970). Lately other cognitive theories have had an influence. Organizational theories (Argyris & Schön, 1974, 1978), and theories of reflective thinking (Andersen, 1994) have also had an impact on the thinking of the consultants. Starting with one theory would thus have restricted the outcome of the study. Instead, I elected to start with empirical data in order to describe patterns and possibly generate a new theoretical model of change in the consultation process. I selected *Grounded Theory* (Glaser & Strauss, 1967), which is a theory-generating method particularly suitable when a researcher wants to explore a new field or give a new perspective on an old field. The method and its applicability to consultation research are described in the last section of this book, while this chapter focuses on the theory of change in consultation, which is the result of the study.

The question I started out to explore was what has happened *when a teacher (consultee) tells the consultant (psychologist) that the child he or she worried so much about, now is doing much better and that now he or she apprehends the problem in a different way than previously.* What has changed? The child, the mind of the teacher, or the mind of the consultee-centered consultant?

What can be studied are the changes of the verbal presentation of the problem and the change of the inner representation of the problem. As a result of the teacher's changed conception and changed attitude, in the end, we believe that the child changes as well. The theory presented here focuses on the relation between the consultee and the consultant although the relation between the consultee and the client has also been explored.

EVIDENTIARY BASES FOR CONCEPTUAL CHANGE

Method

Participants

The data for this study were drawn from 23 experienced Swedish consultants trained in consultee centered consultation.

Data Sources

The theory in the study is based on data from audiotaped consultation sessions, interviews and responses to questionnaires with consultants and consultees in schools and preschool and child day care.

The samples consisted of the following data sources:

- Six focus groups (three groups meeting twice) with 17 consultants.
- Six audio taped consultation cases (altogether 19 sessions) from six consultants.
- 12 interviews with consultants and consultees from the taped cases.
- Open ended responses to questionnaires from 102 consultees having completed consultation (with a 98% return rate).

Analysis

Transcripts were prepared of all of the audio-taped data and the responses to interview questions and responses to open-ended questions. The data were repeatedly coded and sorted by computer. Every indicator, category, and subcategory was given letters and numbers. Every new code was compared to all other codes and categories of codes by constant comparison (Glaser, 1978). The emerging concepts, patterns, and theory were elaborated in memos, which also were sorted at the end of the process. The analysis was performed in four steps, which is an elaboration (Guvå & Hylander, 1998) of the more common three-step model (Hallberg, 1992, 1994; Strauss & Corbin, 1990):

1. From data to labeled indicators.
2. From labeled indicators to concepts.
3. From concepts to search for patterns.
4. Arriving at a theory.

GROUNDED THEORY RESULTS—THE EVIDENCE

The process of consultation constitutes of interplay between the following four entities: the consultee's presentation and representation, and the consultant's presentation and representation. When there is a group of consultees, this turns the consultation process into a rather multifaceted interaction, as complex to describe as most human activities. Describing it with just these four entities is an oversimplification to make some points more clear.

Representations and presentations have an *emotional*, a *cognitive*, and a *motivational* aspect. The outcome of a consultation process ideally is a turning of all these aspects. Several types of turnings were observed in the data. In a *distinct turning* the teacher feels different about the child, he or she regards the child in a different way, and he or she is prepared to act in an alternative way. Both representations and presentations have shifted and the change is emotional, cognitive, and motivational. Consultation that results in a distinct turning appears to be most successful.

There are examples, however, of successful turnings where there is no change in motivation or conscious teacher behavior. The teacher is not aware that he or she has done something differently. These turnings seem to occur in very specific cases, where the teachers have been very close to the child, over involved emotionally. When the teachers relax and let go of their anxiety, something happens in the relationship with the child and the child's behavior changes. This has been the case in several consultations where the problem has been a child who does not speak in school, although he or she knows how and speaks at home. After one or two consultation sessions the child starts to talk, usually right after the teacher saw the consultant. Consultants have expressed that it seems like magic, thus, those turnings have been labeled *magic turnings*.

If, however, the teacher is much too distant from the child to start with, wanting to get rid of him or her, a turning in presentation and representation without a change in motivation or action tendency will reverse and become a *weather-cock turning*. There will seem to be change on the cognitive level, but in time the new representation of the problem will revert back to the original. If the teacher does not approach the child there is no durable change.

If there is only a change in the presentation but not the internal representation it is a *false turning*. That is when the teacher wants to get rid of the consultant or wants to focus on another child. As a result, the teacher will say that things are fine when they are not, or change the subject to another child without reference to the first.

MODES OF INTERACTION—THE PROCESS

What is on the table for the consultant to begin with is the consultee's presentation of the problem. The consultant starts from the teacher's description of the case and his or her ways of describing possible solutions to the problem, which is the teacher's *presentation* of the problem. From there on there is a joint problem solving between the consultant and the consultee, a problem solving, which the consultant starts from scratch. For the consultant there is no preconceived solution to the problem. The consultant's readiness to constantly change his or her own representation of the problem is the critical part of this process. Even if the consultant has preconceptions—which most consultants have—those must be challenged continuously. Otherwise the interaction between the consultant and the consultee will become stuck, in a similar way as the teachers are stuck in relation to the students. That is the essence of this theory. The consultant oscillates between *confirming* and *challenging* the consultee's presentation of the case, but he or she also oscillates between confirming and challenging his or her own representation of the problem. Through the interplay between these presentations and representations, a conceptual change takes place.

In the beginning of the consultation process the consultant starts where the teacher is and keeps very close to the consultee's presentation, *confirming* his or her story, trying to understand what the representation behind the presentation is like. Thus, the consultant is trying to see the problem the way the consultee does, almost turning the consultee's representation into his or her own. If the consultee feels that the consultant understands his or her problem and is willing to listen to

his or her way of framing it, the consultee will start to *discharge* feelings and negative descriptions of the case. Thus, the teacher's presentation will also come very
much closer to his or her own representation of the problem. The teacher may tell
the consultant how provoked he or she is by the girl who always obstructs. The
consultant only presents very confirming statements, such as, "I understand, uh
huh." This is the approaching position, the *interaction mode of approach.* The consultant is *confirming* and the consultee is *discharging.* This only works, however, if it
is authentic. That is why the consultant has to work constantly on his or her own
representation. If the consultee does not, his or her presentation will be very far
from his or her representation and the presentation will sound false, which the
consultee will discover and feel uncomfortable (Fig. 4.1).

By questions, many of which are part of an interview guide (Guvå, 1989), the
process oscillates from this *approaching position* to a *free neutral position* characterized by an *interaction mode of attention.* In this mode, the consultant *asks neutral questions* and the consultee gives balanced and *neutral descriptions* of the
problem. The consultant mirrors what the consultee is saying, but giving back
both positive and negative statements. In this way, the consultee starts to see his
or her own presentations.

Achieving a *distance* from the consultee's own presentation where he or she
can view them anew, the consultee might discover some new aspects and the
process *moves away* from the original framing of the problem to a new representation and presentation. This interaction mode has been labeled the *mode of autonomy.* In this mode, the consultant *challenges* the way the original problem is

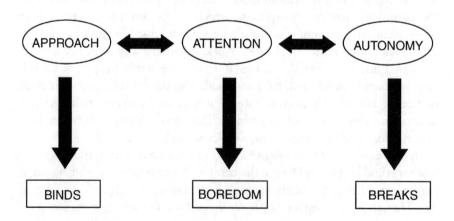

FIG. 4.1.   Modes of interaction in the process of consultation.

described, introducing new thoughts to facilitate new discoveries. The consultee reflects and *discovers* new aspects of the problem.

The consultation process can thus be described as a process constantly oscillating between closeness and distance concerning the presentation and representation of the original problem. The consultant confirms and challenges, always going through the free neutral position by putting a neutral question before switching over. It does not seem possible to go directly from confirming to challenging without a neutral question or statement in between.

At the end, there is a common and *joint description* of the case. The discoveries are such that it is often the case that neither the consultee nor the consultant knows who actually made the discovery. The consultation process is not seen as a set of stages, even though it is more common that the process oscillates between approaching and the free neutral position in the beginning and between the free neutral position and moving away in the end. The process might very well return to approach and discharge of feelings almost to the end of the consultation, particularly after the process has become stuck.

The consultant's way of acting varies immensely in the different modes of interaction. There has been a discussion in consultation literature, whether the consultant should be *directive or nondirective* (Erchul, 1987, 1992; Duncan, Hughes, & Jackson, 1994). Being *directive* means to be in charge of the consultation process by structuring, asking question, giving proposals, and so on. Being nondirective means listening and following the process of the consultee. It is important to emphasize the difference between being prescriptive and being directive. This distinction is often confused when these terms are not clearly defined. Being *prescriptive* means knowing the answer to the question, being in charge of the solution to the problem, and not ready to question one's own representation of the problem. Being *directive,* on the other hand, means that the consultant is in charge of the process but not of the solution and the implementations. In the research program, it has been apparent that it is impossible to categorize the studied model of consultation as either directive or nondirective. It all depends on the mode of interaction for the moment. In the approaching mode, the consultant is nondirective almost in the Rogerian sense—the consultee talks much more than the consultant and the consultant listens and confirms. In the mode of attention, in the free neutral position, the consultant may talk more than the consultee and is directive in the sense of asking questions, focusing, changing focus, and summarizing. In the mode of autonomy, while moving away from the original presentation of the problem, the consultant may be either directive, coming with proposals or nondirective, listening to the proposals of the consultee. The dialogue is very free. There is considerable give and take and the consultant may come with proposals, which he or she would never do in the mode of approach. All three modes of interaction are necessary, which means that the consultant also has to switch between being directive and nondirective. But if the consultant ever becomes prescriptive to the point of believing that he or she has the truth, he or she will become stuck in a blind alley according to this theory.

Blind Alleys in the Consultation Process

When the consultant does not challenge his or her own representations enough, he or she is stuck in a blind alley. When stuck, the consultant is not able to change mode of interaction and not prepared to change his or her representation. The consultant feels bad, overwhelmed by negative feelings, either before or after the session. There are three major forms of blind alleys each connected with one mode of interaction. Each constitutes a particular constellation of the interplay between consultee's presentation and representation and the consultant's presentation and representation, either being too close or too far away from each other.

Binds

In binds, the presentations are always close. The consultant keeps on confirming and the consultee discharges. The consultant is much too close to the consulate's representation, presentation, or both. Even if the consultant tries to move away by asking neutral questions or by challenging, the consultee objects. The consultee's presentation and representation are very far apart. For some reason, the consultee does not want to present his or her representation to the consultant, there is no approach between the consultee's presentation and representation. Still, the presentations are very close. A prerequisite for bind may be a case where the consultee has a representation of a relation to the client that is emotionally involved and entangled, being very worried or angry. The following three binds have been identified.

The Nice Party

Here, the consultant shares the consultee's negative picture and the notion that the solution to the problem does not seem to be within the consultee's control. The social welfare agency is not doing what they should. The group of children is so large that it is impossible to change the troublesome case. As long as the consultant stays in the mode of approach, confirming the consultee's presentation, the interaction is very nice and friendly. The consultant may, for a long while, think that the process is going very well. The consultee is discharging wanting to be confirmed, not listening to neutral questions and strongly objecting to challenges. The consultee's presentation however does not correspond to her representation. The consultee may feel ashamed because the difficult situation makes her behave in a way she does not like in herself and therefore will not admit publicly. The consultant is aware of the situation and has a representation of how teachers relate to children in such difficult situations, but cannot present any of these notions, as that would be regarded as criticism. This may happen most often in classes with many difficult students, in poverty-stricken areas, or in special education, with competent teachers. Even when the consultee says that a case has turned, the process may be stuck. The consultee wants to please the consultant in order not to be blamed, and the consultant wants to be pleased to feel competent. This may be a prerequisite for a *false turning* (Fig. 4.2).

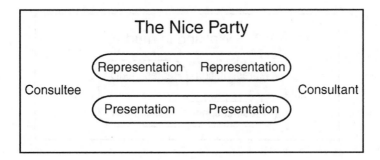

FIG. 4.2. The nice party.

Walking in Mud

The difference between walking in mud and being stuck in a nice party is the feeling of the consultant. While walking in mud, the consultant may say that he or she is stuck, feels heavy, and cannot move. The consultant may get sad; feeling there is no hope. He or she may identify very strongly with the consultee. The consultee is discharging, giving a negative picture of the situation, but still not presenting what's really on his or her mind. If the consultant tries to ask neutral questions or challenges the presentation, this is met by still heavier discharge. The consultee's presentation and representation are still far apart, like in the nice party, whereas the presentations of the consultant and the consultee are very close and stuck.

The consultee may feel ashamed not wanting to present what has actually happened and the consultant has taken over the consultee's presentation and is not aware of the difficulty. A teacher talks about a child as being a bully–victim but is still disgusted with the child. If the consultant accepts the presentation—a child, who should be pitied—there is no space for the teacher's negative feelings. Thus, the distance between the consultee's representation and the presentation may increase. If the consultant is persistent in approaching the consultee's presentation and eventually taking it over completely, the process is stuck.

If the consultant on the other hand starts to challenge his or her own representation he or she might ask: What is this child doing? Is it possible for a child to provoke other children without knowing it? The consultant might even ask: Is it a child who grown-ups sometimes find a bit provoking? Thus, there is a possibility for the teacher's representation to be presented and a new and more authentic discharge may take place, and subsequently the process can move forward (Fig. 4.3).

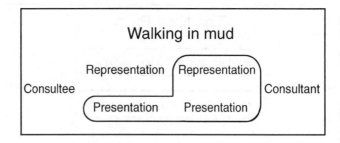

FIG. 4.3.   Walking in mud.

The Hidden Fight

In the hidden fight, the consultant's presentation is close to the consultee's presentation and representation, but the *consultant's representation* is far away—that is, the consultant is not saying what he or she is thinking and feeling. The consultant is afraid that if he or she presented the representation in an honest way, this would result in a *break*. Here is an example of a hidden fight: A teacher presents a child as being very obstructive. The teacher's representation of the relation is that the child gets away too easily, and needs more constraints and demands. The consultant discusses those demands, but actually believes that the teacher should instead approach the child trying to understand him or her. Not until the consultant starts to challenge his or her own representation of a teacher not approaching enough could there be a change. There are many ways of approaching children. Putting demands is one way that could be discussed and tried out and consequently changed and adapted to the ability and the need of the child. Once the consultant gives up his or her view, and secretly attempts to convince the teacher, the process moves on (Fig. 4.4).

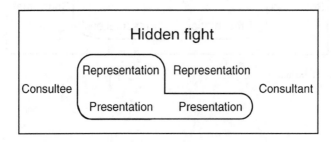

FIG. 4.4. Hidden fight.

Boredom

Boredom may be the undesired outcome of the Free Neutral mode of interaction in consultation. The consultee presents what's in his or her mind, his or her representation. This representation and presentation are very close. The consultant also presents his or her representation, which is in agreement with the consultee's; thus, there is no way for development. It is very stuck and closed. It may be a special education class, a very competent teacher knowing the diagnoses of the children, the consultant agrees on her interpretations. They focus on one child after the other, but nothing really happens, there are no turnings, no changes of representations and the process becomes very boring. The following example illustrates boredom along with an escape.

> The consultee is describing a problem of a girl having toilet problems. The problem is described as very problematic but the consultee shows no signs of affective arousal. The girl's parents are described in a very positive manner. The consultant feels uneasy and the dialogue is awkward until the consultant asks: Is it possible to make a joke with these parents? The consultee answers with emphasis. No, they are definitely lacking all sense of humor. From this point, there is a discharge, about these overly correct parents. The consultant concludes that it was taboo to criticize these parents, because they were so nice and correct. The consultant's theory is that she has intuitively picked up what had blocked the consultee. Through a discharge, an approach from a different angle was followed by a startle reaction that unlocked the hindrance.

The consultant got an idea, a new representation and on presenting it, suddenly the teacher could change his or her representation too (Fig. 4.5).

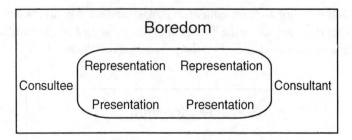

FIG. 4.5.   Boredom.

Break

A break may occur during the mode of interaction of autonomy when the consultant is much too far away from the consultee's presentation (and representation). He or she has challenged the consultee too much, while not challenging
his or her own conception of the problem.

The consultee meets every challenge from the consultant, by moving her
own presentation further away from the consultant's presentation. The
consultee may end the consultation in a *total break*. Perhaps the consultee says
that they need some other kind of help, for example, moving the client, having
more extra hours or getting a special aide.

In the *interaction break*, the consultant is experiencing a great variety of negative feelings. He or she may be very angry, disgusted, or fearful that something
terrible will happen to the client. The consultant is assessing and judging the
consultee. The consultant more easily arrives in this position if the consultee
has a distant and alienated relation to the client, perhaps wanting to get rid of
the client. Three kinds of breaks have been identified: *tug of wars, missions impossible, interpretive relationships*.

Tug of War

In the tug of war, the consultant tries to force his or her opinion and representation on to the consultee by constantly presenting it. Also, the consultee presents his or her view, trying to convince the consultant about the righteousness
in his or her representation of the problem. This is common when a consultee
wants to refer a child somewhere else or get an extra aide to take care of the
problem. It may also be the case when teachers are convinced that a child has a
special kind of diagnosis, which the consultant does not agree to. The following
is an example with a positive outcome:

The consultant feels very pessimistic when the consultees talk about a two-and a half-year old boy as being mean. She concludes that there is no attachment between the boy and his teachers and believes that the solution to the problem is that the teachers approach the boy. The consultees think that the solution is a special aide or any other kind of specific treatment. The consultant asks the teachers to single out one of the teachers to give him more attention. Next time they meet they said it was impossible because the other children became jealous. Other parents are complaining, as they can see how this boy is running around in the hall bumping into the other children when parents come to pick them up. The consultant proposes that they take him away from the hall, when the other parents come. Next time they say it was impossible because he felt as if it was a punishment. The consultant realizes that she gave advice much too early and feels like she is becoming the boy's attorney. She is stuck in a tug of war. There is a break. But teachers consult the psychologist again several months later. Now they have listened to a lecture about attention deficit disorders (ADHD), and they think that this is what is wrong with the boy. The consultant again gets into a tug of war challenging their presentation by saying that it is very unusual to diagnose such a young child for ADHD. However, she gives up her presentation and representation, starting to think that something really is the matter with this boy which needs to be investigated. When discussing the different symptoms of ADHD, the consultant for the first time experiences that the teachers are interested and focused on the boy. The consultation process has escaped from break to attention, the free neutral position. The consultant asks the consultees to observe the boy concerning the symptoms of ADHD. In the *next session*, the consultees say, "it has turned, the boy has calmed down, even if he still has problems and he really needs to be close to adults." The consultant believed that talking about ADHD made them curious about the boy for the first time. The turning is confirmed in the following session. The boy still has problems but the consultees have approached the boy and there is a working alliance between the consultant and the consultees (Fig. 4.6).

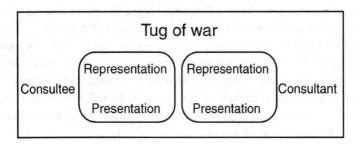

FIG. 4.6.   Tug of war.

Mission Impossible

The consultant's representation is close to the consultee's presentation and representation, but the consultant's presentation is different. An example is a consultee who believes that a child has severe psychiatric difficulties and needs something else than what they have to offer. The consultant actually agrees, believing that what the consultees do and could do is not enough but still insists in discussing how they could relate to the child and keep him or her in the group. In this case the only thing the consultant can do is to give up his or her presentation, or change his or her own representation (Fig. 4.7).

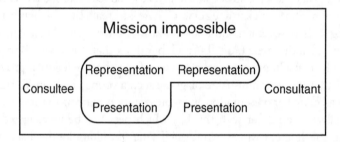

FIG. 4.7.   Mission impossible.

Interpretative Relation

In the interpretative relation, the consultant is "listening" to the consultee's representation instead of his or her presentation. The consultant also presents his or her own interpretation of it. This may lead to a break if the consultant is not flexible but continues to interpret even though the consultee objects to it. Borus (1982) addressed this phenomenon when describing early years of consultation in Boston. Consultants trained in psychoanalytical therapy but not so well trained in consultation methods started to interpret the consultee's representation and treated teachers as clients and not as equal colleagues. This led to a break and the consultation program ceased. Interpretation is not so often described within consultee-centered consultation. Organizational consultants, however, have described breaks as result of interpretations (Fig. 4.8).

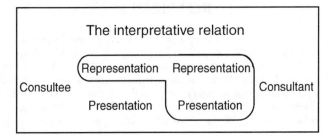

FIG. 4.8. The interpretative relation.

The consultants in the present study are very clever in avoiding the blind alleys. On the other hand, it was discovered that dramatic changes were often linked to being stuck in a blind alley and coming out of it. This resulted in a sudden shift in mode of interaction, an increase or decrease in affective state. Thus, there is no reason for consultants to be afraid of the blind alleys. They just have to know how to get out of them. They have to learn the feeling of "Oh dear now I am there again! What should I do to get out of this?" A consultant who never gets stuck in a blind alley is probably a little too scared to challenge the consultee's presentation enough or too scared to get real close to it. But once stuck in a blind alley, there is no way out for the consultant other than to challenge his or her own representation of the way the problem should be solved. Consultant flexibility of representation is a key to consultation and conceptual change.

CONCLUSION

The grounded theory of consultation reported in this chapter is a substantive theory, limited to the substance (consultee-centered consultations) from which it was inferred. As a model, however, it may have broader applications. The general discovery of an approaching, a free neutral, and a moving away position during consultation, seems to be quite robust. These concepts may be used in different settings, also with different approaches to consultation as long as the approaches are nonprescriptive. They have been discussed and tried out with professional consultants within child care, schools, rehabilitation child-health care, and other clinical settings as well as within organizational consultation.

REFERENCES

Argyris, C., & Schön, D. (1974). *Theory in practice.* San Francisco: Jossey Bass.

Argyris, C., & Schön, D. (1978). *Organisational Learning.* Reading, MA: Addison-Wesley.

Andersen, T. (1994). *Reflekterande processer. Samtal om samtalen.* Stockholm: Mareld.

Anderson, H., Goolishian, H. (1998). Human systems as linguistic systems: Preliminary and evoking ideas about the implication for clinical theory. *Family Process, 27,* 371–394.

Bateson, G. (1979). *Mind and nature. A necessary unity.* Toronto: Bantam Books.

Berger, P. L., & Luckman, T. (1967). *The social construction of reality.* Garden City, NY: Anchor Books.

Brodin, M., & Hylander, I. (1995). *Utvärdering av konsultationsärenden.* Lidingö: Lidingö Stad.

Brodin, M., & Hylander, I. (1997). *Att bli sig själv. Daniel Sterns teori i förskolans vardag.* Stockholm: Liber.

Bronfenbrenner, U. (1979). Contexts of child rearing contexts and prospects. *American Psychologist, 34,* 844–850.

Caplan , G. (1970). *The theory and practice of mental health consultation.* New York: Basic Books.

Dunson, R., Hughes, J., & Jacksson, T. (1994). Effect of behavioral consultation on student and teacher behavior. *Journal of School Psychology, 32,* 247–266.

Erchul, W. P. (1987). A relational communication analysis of control in school consultation. *Professional School Psychology, 2,* 113–124.

Erchul, W. P. (1992). On domination, cooperation, teamwork, and collaboration in school-based consultation. *Journal of Educational and Psychological Consultation, 3,* 363–366.

Erchul, W. P., & Martens, B. K. (1997). *School Consultation. Conceptual and empirical bases of practice.* New York: Plenum Press.

Glaser, B. (1977). *Theoretical sensitivity. Advances in the methodology of Grounded Theory.* San Francisco: The Sociology Press.

Glaser, B., & Strauss, A. (1967). *The discovery of Grounded Theory.* Chicago: Aldine.

Guvå, G. (1989). *Klientmysteriet. Ett fall för förskolepsykologen. Om personalinriktad fallkonsultation.* (Sfph:s monografiserie nr 32.)

Guvå, G. (1992). Om mellanområdet i konsultation. *Psykisk Hälsa 3,* 205–210.

Guvå, G. (1995). *Professionsutveckling hos konsulter. Om konsultativ handledning och självutveckling.* (FOG-Rapport No. 25). Linköpings universitet, Institutionen för Pedagogik och Psykologi.

Guvå, G. (1999). The first consultation session. How to meet a teacher who asks for help but not for consultation. In *Explorations in process in practice. (Seminar proceedings).* Stockholm: 2nd International Seminar on Consultee-Centered Consultation.

Guvå, G., & Hylander, I. (1998). *Att tillägna sig grounded theory* (FOG-rapport nr 43). Linköping: Linköpings universitet. Institutionen för pedagogik och psykologi.

Hallberg, L. (1992). *Hearing impairment, coping and perceived handicap, in middle-aged individuals with acquired hearing loss: An interactional perspective.* (Doktorsavhandling). Göteborg: Göteborgs universitet, Psykologiska institutionen.

Hallberg, L. (1994). *En kvalitativ metod influerad av grounded theory-traditionen.* Göteborg: Göteborgs universitet. Psykologiska institutionen.

Hylander, I. (1995). *Evolvement of consultee-centered case consultation in Sweden.* Paper presented at The International seminar on Consultee-Centered Case Consultation May 5–7. Stockholm: Hasselbacken.

Hylander, I. (1999). Identifying change in the consultation process. Turnings and turning points. In *Explorations in process in practice (Seminar proceedings)*. Stockholm: 2nd International Seminar on Consultee-Centered Consultation.

Hylander, I. (2000). *Turning processes. The change of representations in consultee-centered case consultation* (Dissertation). Linköping: Linköping University. Department of Behavioural Science.

Meade, C. J., Hamilton, M. K., & Yen, R. K. W. (1982). Consultation research: the time has come the walrus said. *The Counseling Psychologist, 10,* 39–51.

Sandoval, J. (1996). Constructivism, consultee-centered consultation, and conceptual change. *Journal of Educational and Psychological Consultation, 7,* 89–97.

Sandoval, J. (1999). Evaluation issues and strategies on consultee-centered consultation. In *Explorations in Process and Practice* (Seminar proceedings). Stockholm 2nd International Seminar on Consultee-Centered Consultation.

Stern, D. (1985). *The interpersonal world of the infant.* New York: Basic Books.

Strauss, A., & Corbin, J. (1990). *Basics of qualitative research. Grounded Theory procedures and techniques.* Newbury Park: Sage.

Winnicott, D. (1971). *Playing and reality.* New York: Basic books. Svensk översättning (1981). *Lek och verklighet.* Stockholm: Natur och kultur.

Vygotsky, L. S. (1970). *Thought and language.* Cambridge MA: The M.I.T. Press.

II

Consultee-Centered Consultation With Schools and Community Organizations

This part is divided into sections focused on the following settings: Preschool and Child Care, School, Health and Welfare, Corporate settings, and Evaluation Practice. In each of the sections, the authors address the following:

A. The key factors that support the consultation process including: the general structure of the organization; the culture of the organization; how consultation is initiated; entry approaches into the organization and the individuals responsible for the consultation agreement; clients of the organization; specific features and description of the consultation process in the particular system; evaluation of consultation in ongoing or short-term relationships.

B. Ways that the interaction between consultant and consultee promote conceptual change as evidenced by: changes in the ways that the problem is presented by the consultee and consultant; and, changes in the ways that the problem is represented or understood by the consultant and the consultee.

5

Development of Consultee-Centered Consultation in Sweden

Ingrid Hylander

Gunilla Guvå

The way consultation as a professional psychological practice has evolved in Swedish human service agencies is closely linked to how programs for mental health prevention have been developed and organized. This is particularly true regarding services for children in preschool, child day care, child physical and mental health care, and school-based health and psychological care. This chapter provides a brief overview of Swedish services for children where psychologists have been and currently are employed to work as consultants. Within the context of Swedish human service agencies consultee-centered consultation has developed particularly within child day care and preschools, but also in schools and health care settings. The following sections describe the development of consultee-centered consultation and identify the prerequisites for its development within these different institutions.

SERVICES FOR CHILDREN IN SWEDEN

School Services

Schools have mental and physical health care teams including a school nurse, a visiting doctor and access to school social worker and school psychologist. The particular services of school psychologists vary among the different schools, different cities, and different parts of the country. Typically, the school psychologist is expected to conduct assessments and to provide consultation to teachers.

All municipalities provide preschool and child day care programs for all children in need (a statutory requirement since 1995). Presently, a majority of all children over the age of one are enrolled in some kind of preschool program and 83% of the Swedish municipalities offer psychological consultation services to child care and preschool personnel (Frygner, 1997.) There are a few special programs for young children with special care needs, most of whom are children with physical or emotional handicaps. Often these disabled children are enrolled in the general child-care program, although some with special assistance from a special resource person. The results of Frygner's survey showed that the majority of child-care special education directors believe that they have enough resources within their district to handle children with special needs.

Health Care

Health care for children under the age of six is provided by public well-baby and health care clinics. Around 98% of parents attend those clinics with their children during the child's first year, returning for shots and check ups, about once a year until the children are six when school starts. At that time school health care takes over. The ultimate goal of these clinics is to promote psychological and physical well-being among all Swedish children. Psychologists are employed to provide consultation to the nurses as well as to provide counseling services for parents. In every school district or city there is also a child guidance clinic, with psychologists, social workers, and doctors—usually with a degree in therapy—offering counseling, assessment, and therapy. Psychologists from these child-guidance clinics are expected to provide consultation services to, among others, child welfare agency staff.

THE EMERGENCE
OF CONSULTEE-CENTERED CONSULTATION

During the 1960s and the 1970s in Sweden mental health professionals began to foster programs for the prevention of mental disorders supported by community psychiatry, community psychology, and psychiatric outpatient clinics. Caplan's (1970) *The Theory and Practice of Mental Health Consultation* was introduced into Sweden in the mid 1970s. Caplan's work was influential in mental health centers, (Forsman & Överholm, 1978; Szecsödy, 1981), in child day care (Carlberg, Guvå, & Teurnell, 1977), and in child health-care centers (Gustafsson & Kaplan-Goldman, 1980). At that time child guidance centers, where psychologists were employed, were established in different parts of the country, but very few well-baby clinics, child health-care centers, and child day care had access to psychologists. In the municipality of Stockholm, within the organization of child guidance clinics, two consultation teams were established, one to serve the well-baby clinics and child health-care, and one to serve child day care and preschool. Gustafsson and Kaplan-Goldman (1980) described Caplan's model of mental health consultation and how it could be used in the well-baby clinics and child health-care. Carlberg, Guvå, and Teurnell (1977) advocated the use of psychologists within child day care and proposed that Caplan's model of consultee-centered case consultation would be a useful method of psychological service delivery in child day care.

A few years later after the establishment of the first consultee-centered consultation programs, Janson, Waldor and Waleij (1983) investigated the need for psychological consultative, collaborative, and referral services to child day care from the child guidance clinics. Those interviewed were positive about the potential for consultation services. Janseon et al. also found no difference among organizational settings in the way consultation services were delivered. The interviewees (teachers, managers, and psychologists) favored the consultation services they were used to, the consultee-centered consultation model in all instances. The investigators recommended that the preventive mental health function should not be independent of the referral service of the child-guidance clinic. According to the investigators, referral services and consultee-centered consultation should both be available from the child-guidance clinics. There was, however, a notable difference of opinion between the head of the child-guidance clinics and the head of the team of consultants. The head of the child-guidance clinic wanted the consultants to have a closer link with the clinic and an emphasis on the referral service, whereas the head of the team of consultants wanted more autonomy with an emphasis on the preventive services.

Very soon different local municipalities and their school districts started to hire their own preschool /child day care psychologists. In the middle of the 1980s the consultation team employed by the central municipality in charge of mental health in the Stockholm area was dissolved, and the city took over. The majority of psychologists and a few social workers who were employed as consultants, as a result, came from a clinical mental health background, familiar with psychodynamic theory, the dominant theoretical orientation at the time. This background, in addition to the educational and developmental approach from early childhood education and the dialogical and student-oriented pedagogy promoted by two important governmental reports (SOU,

1972; 26, 27; SOU, 1981; 25) combined with the every day encounters with the child day-care environment, may to some extent, account for the promotion of Caplanian consultee-centered case consultation (Caplan & Caplan, 1993) in Swedish Child day care.

Consultation practice has developed differently within different settings. In child health care, the preventive aspect of Caplan's work has been emphasized (Gustafsson, 1996; Gustafsson & Kaplan-Goldman, 1980). The psychological teams for the well-baby clinics and child health-care centers remained clinical consultation teams, and in these clinics, client-centered consultation and collaboration has become dominant models, whereas the consultee-centered model has been dominant in child day care and preschool.

Psychologists in schools, typically work in multiprofessional teams in a problem solving collaborative way, like the psychologists in child health-care. Client-centered consultation is common, but consultee-centered consultation is becoming more prominent also among school-psychological services.

The psychological teams for the well-baby clinics and child health-care centers remain clinical consultation teams, and in these clinics, client-centered consultation and collaboration has become dominant model, whereas the consultee-centered model has been dominant in child day-care and preschool settings.

Consultation practice has thus developed differently within different settings. In child health-care, the preventive aspect of Caplan's work has been emphasized (Gustafsson, 1996; Gustafsson & Kaplan-Goldman, 1980). Psychologists in schools, typically work in multiprofessional teams in a problem solving collaborative way, like the psychologists in child health-care. Client-centered consultation and consultee-centered consultation are becoming more prominent among school-psychological services. Over the last few decades, based on practice in these settings in Sweden, the consultee-centered model has been further developed and elaborated (Carlberg, Guvå, & Teurnell, 1981; Falck-Järnberg, Janson, & Orrenius-Andersson, 1980; Janson, Walsor, & Waleij, 1983; Guvå, 1989, 1992, 1995, 1999; Thörn, 1999; Brodin, 1995, 1999; Hylander, 1995a, 1995b, 2000), and is described next.

A Consultee-Centered Model for Case Consultation

The content of the consultee-centered model of consultation, developed in Sweden, is described in several sections of this volume. In this chapter the model is outlined as it has developed and been elaborated by Guvå (1989, 1992, 1995, 1999). Three different phases in the consultation process can be discerned.

The First Interview

The initial consultation session consists of a set of questions to explore the problem and to enhance the process of expanding the consultee's thoughts and feelings around the troublesome situation. Usually the consultant asks the consultee to make unstructured observations of the client. The questions and answers outline the phenomena of the work problem, and can be modified to suit different settings and ages of clients (Guvå, 1999.) The interview is finished with the question "What do you expect me to do for you?" resulting in a contract or consultation agreement.

Interactive Analysis

Having followed up by making observations of the client, the consultee typically has seen new aspects of the work problem or has attended to the client in a new way. The observations (possibly interviews of the client) are used as basis for a joint discussion of what is happening between the client and other clients and between the client and the consultee. In this analysis, the consultant does not ask directly about the feelings of the consultee, but rather asks questions, such as, "What happens when he is behaving like this? What kind of feelings does he evoke in grown-ups, and how does it end?" This analysis will eventually result in a shared reflection regarding the consultee's practice and interaction with the client, and what he or she alternatively could do. Using Winnicot's (1971) terminology, an *intermediate area*, or a *playground* is constructed in consultation where new perspectives and understandings develop. When the consultee subsequently tries out his or her ideas in real life these actions may lead to a favorable outcome, and the consultation is finished.

Identifying the Psychological Dilemma

When a case does not turn in a positive way or seems to become worse, the consultant tries to explore what he or she has not understood. The consultee may be ashamed of his or her own behavior or not believe that the consultant has understood his or her problem. Or the client may be very difficult or hard to understand. At this point, the consultant must challenge his or her own representations in such a way that he or she is truly open for the consultee's feelings and way of thinking. *Almost* feeling and thinking the same as the consultee feels and thinks will promote a new understanding. Communicating this understanding to the consultee makes it possible for the consultee to ventilate forbidden feelings and unwanted ideas, such as wanting to get rid of the client. The consultant creates a secure but open dialogue space. Not until there is trust and understanding is it possible for the consultant to ask for observations and receive them, and the process can continue with interactive analysis.

Training and Education

Training in consultee-centered consultation has been provided in Stockholm by the central municipality (district) and by the national association for the local municipalities. For the last 8 years, courses have been given to psychologist at the university level. An important part of the training has been supervision and reflection groups that meet regularly. As consultation is a psychological relational method, it has to be learned in relational practice. Without supervised practice this is not easily done.

Many students of consultation have had to start their very first consultation in a difficult setting, offering a consultation approach in an organization, or in the schools, with a long tradition of other methods of psychological services. This difficulty was, however, not in evidence for most psychologists within child day care and preschool programs, who were employed during the time when many new day-care centers were being established. Still, introducing consultee-centered consultation was not always easily accomplished, but the significant features of child day care helped to promote consultee-centered consultation in these settings.

Links Between Organizational Factors and Consultation Services

Even if the background of several different theoretical approaches can account for differences in the consultation processes of those providing consultee-centered consultation in child day care in contrast to those providing consultation in other settings, there are also important organizational and contextual factors that must be considered. Hylander (1995a, 1995b) studied the correspondence between contextual factors in different organizations and feasible approaches to consultation. She identified four different organizational features that affected the outcome of consultee-centered consultation services:

1. Organizational objective and culture.
2. Consultee responsibility for client problem.
3. Involvement between client and consultee.
4. Difference between area of competence and area of responsibility.

Organizational Objective and Culture

Every human service organization has a main objective, linked to a core process, and in turn linked to a core relation, between a professional and a client (Crafoord, 1992; Klein, Bernard, & Singer, 1992). The goal of child day care is to care and to educate, in school the goal is to educate; and, in the medical system, the organizational pursuit is to cure and prevent illnesses.

In preschool and child day-care programs, the goal is twofold, to care and to educate, *educare*. The culture is characterized by a psychosocial educational and developmental approach. Thus, there is a fit between the culture of the organization and the theoretical background of many of the consultants working with a consultee-centered consultation approach. It may be easier to work as a consultant when using a professional language that is familiar to the consultee. The challenge for the consultant, on the other hand, is learning the cultural languages of the different organizations. There is also a danger of being too close when the consultee's conception of the problem is similar to that of the consultant. In such instances, the consultee may not be challenged enough to explore the features of the work problem, because the consultant may share the same misconceptions with the consultee.

The main objective in the school system is to educate the students, but education as the primary task of schools can be defined in many different ways (Wiström et al., 1995). Organizational cultures vary among different schools in Sweden and across age levels, education being very prescriptive and curriculum-centered in some schools and more student-centered in others. Teachers, who see their task as knowledge conveyed from the knowledgeable to the ignorant, are less eager to ask for consultation than teachers who pay more attention to educational relations and interactions as prerequisites for the learning process.

The paradigm of the culture in medical systems is mainly a natural science paradigm. Medicine and instruments characterize the process between doctor and patient. The client-centered consultation model has its roots in this clinical world, and is therefore well suited to it. A prescription can be handed over from one doctor to another and executed just the way it is prescribed.

In health care, on the other hand, the main objective is prevention; still the culture is mostly medical, with psychosocial and developmental aspects. The main objective of child healthcare and well-baby clinics is the promotion of physical and psychological health among all children. Nurses, however, being trained in a medical model, are thus given the quite different task of performing in a psychosocial-medical health model. Psychologists, working as consultants to the nurses have expert knowledge in and experience with the psychosocial model and mother–infant relations, knowledge which administrators expect the consultants to teach the nurses. For the nurses, however, this new knowledge calls for extra work and more involvement. The situation is very much like the one described by Jonathan Borus (1982), referring to early years of mental health consultation in Boston. Community Mental Health Centers were required to provide consultation as a service, to promote mental health in the population for whose well being they were responsible. Because of this responsibility, the need for consultation arose from the consultants rather than from the consultees. The consultants could, in some cases, be regarded by the nurses as "strangers bearing gifts" and thus regarded with suspicion. It seems natural, therefore, that psychologists in child health care have developed work methods other than consultee-centered consultation, such as advocacy, client-centered consultation, collaboration, and parent counseling.

Involvement Between Consultee and Client

For the consultation process to proceed, there needs to be a certain degree of involvement between consultee and client based on how frequently the consultee sees his or her clients, for how long a time, how close their physical contact is, and how emotional the relation is. If there is very little involvement, it may be difficult for the consultant to understand what really is the work problem, as the consultee may not seem very troubled by the case. The challenge for the consultant, however, is to identify the consultee's work dilemma. There is always a work dilemma or the consultee would not have turned to the consultant.

Preschool teachers are experts on interacting with children, knowing that this is their professional base. Their involvement is intense, teachers and children being together every day for several hours and for at least a couple of years, the younger the children, the greater the amount of physical contact. When they are stuck in their relationship to a child, it impedes their total work situation and motivates them to ask for help to restore the relationship again.

Teachers' involvement in students varies throughout the grades, being more intense during lower grades. School psychologists have pointed out that requests for consultation are more frequent in the lower grades than in the higher grades (Wiström et al., 1995).

Involvement between a nurse and parent–child in health care is usually not very high. The visit is short and there are months between the times that they see each other. Typically, nurses ask for consultation when they have more continuous contact, as is the case with a newborn child and in the late stage of pregnancy.

Responsibility for the Client

In order for a professional to ask for consultation, he or she must feel that the case is causing him or her a great deal of trouble, and that it is within his or her responsibility to attend to it. In medical settings, a typical strategy is to refer problems to someone with more responsibility, or to a specialist. If a child has serious problems or a mother is extremely worried, the contact with the nurse may be intense. In such cases, however, many nurses also may simply refer the child to a specialist.

Schools also have a tradition of referring to special units with expert knowledge. Originally in Sweden, school psychologists assessed and identified children with special needs for placement in remedial classes or special schools *outside* the regular school. Since 1960, children with special needs more often have been placed in special learning groups *within* the regular school system. Psychologists were employed to help find out in which way these children could be educated. In the 1980s the national curriculum was changed and since then children with special needs have been integrated in a 9-year compulsory school where *all* children (except for the intellectually retarded) are supposed to be educated according to their special needs or abilities. Special education and regular education is organized in *one* unitary system. Today schoolteachers are supposed to be organized in the same way as the personnel in preschools and day-care centers, where a team of teachers work with and have a joint responsibility for a group of children. Even if teachers and school leaders have the primary responsibility for the education of students with special needs, they typically have handed over such problems to psychologists, especially when they perceive a problem not as a primary learning difficulty, but as social or emotional disturbances, i.e., problems that fall within the psychologist's area of specialized competence.

Preschools and child day care are usually organized in small units. Child day care is a young institution without a history of referral to specialists. Teachers work in teams with cooperative responsibility for the children. The culture of these programs encourages professionals to ask for psychological consultation services. Teachers in preschools regard themselves as responsible for the children's well being during the time parents have left them in the institution. If they ask a psychologist for help, preschool teachers usually do not wish to hand over the child or the responsibility for the child to the psychologist. They only want to know how to relate to a child who behaves in a way they cannot really understand. The task of the psychologists in child care is neither to take care of or help the client directly, nor to take over a work problem from the teachers.

Area of Responsibility Versus Area of Competence

For a consultee-centered consultation approach to be accepted and promoted in an organization, it is of vital importance that all parties are aware of and accept the difference between a professional person's area of competence and area of responsibility. This implies that the solution of a work problem is not considered to be within the consultant's area of responsibility just because it is within his or her area of competence. Furthermore, in a consultee-centered consultation approach, the consultant accepts no direct responsibility for implementing remedial action for the client and expects that the professional responsibility for the client remains with the consultee, just as much as it did before he or she asked the consultant for help. It is necessary for the consultee, for the consultant, and for the head of the organization to all agree on this state of affairs and share the same view concerning the primary task of the organization and the consultee's undertaking in the organization. Then, the following question becomes important: Who had the responsibility before the consultee asked for help?

There seems to be a similarity between the agreement about responsibility that is negotiated between different professionals in an organization and the one that is negotiated between a child's family and the school or day-care center. In preschools and day-care centers, the family does not only hand over the child to the teachers, but also the responsibility for the child's welfare, as long as the child stays in the school or in the center. Preschool teachers ask for help when they have come to a critical point where they do not know how to relate to the child. Typically, they are stuck in their relation to the child. More often than schoolteachers they are in a crisis when they contact a psychologist. They may feel that they are not capable of solving the problem and would have liked the psychologist to take it over. If the psychologist encounters this kind of request, it is possible to handle the request as a consultant, because the teachers, the organization, and the psychologist generally accept that the responsibility for the clients remains with the consultee.

In the school system, the teachers' responsibility for the child's education and well being seems more vague and is less well negotiated in relation to the parents' responsibility for the child. This vagueness is also reflected in the negotiation of role responsibilities between teachers and psychologists. Thus it is difficult for the consultant to know when a teacher asks for help, if an attempt to place a problem outside his or her area of responsibility and/or competence is a crises as result of the present problem, or his or her usual way of regarding his or her role responsibility.

Many school psychologists working as collaborative team-members in Swedish schools have been dissatisfied because they have been over burdened by work with individual children and at the same time felt that they were unable to help when the problem is in the classroom and within the domain of the teachers. That is why, they have seen consultation as a way in which they can find a more productive way of using their competence to help children and teachers.

Guvå's (2001) Swedish study found that teachers hand over a problem to school psychologists differently, depending on how they foresee that it should be solved, and who should be responsible for solving it. They may see it as a *work problem of their own*, as a *joint work problem*, or as *the psychologist's work problem*. Only in the first case was the request treated as a consultation question. It was also true, however, that the psychologist's view of the teacher's ability to solve the problem in a successful way, is of vital importance for the psychologist's action. If the psychologist thinks that the teacher is able to solve the problem, the psychologist meets him or her as a consultee (responsible for the client). But, if the psychologist does not trust the teacher, the psychologist typically takes over and tries to solve the problem him or herself. One psychologist said: "It is the same thing as making the beds, I know it is faster and better done if I make them myself, than if I leave them to my children." When a teacher is in crisis, however, he or she might not trust him or herself to solve the problem, feeling that it is not within one's area of competence, which makes him or her inclined to hand over the problem to the psychologist with the demand: "Solve the problem because I am not capable." If the school psychologist accepts this view and takes over the problem, this communicates to the teacher that he or she is not capable. But, as the responsibility of the student's education still is within the teacher's domain of responsibility he or she will not be able to solve the problem without the teacher taking his or her responsibility.

School teachers also hand over a problem, when they have come to a point when they regard the problem as being outside their area of responsibility. In this situation, the teachers are not in crises and do not feel very helpless. When they ask for help, they do not ask a question, but they hand over a task, which they regard is not only within the psychologist's area of competence, but also within his or her area of responsibility.

This brings us to the question: Is it possible to establish a consultant - consultee relationship if the psychologist is expected to be directly responsible for the client's welfare. Our view is that only when consultation is restricted to professional interactions where the psychologist accepts no direct responsibility for implementing remedial action for the client and when the professional responsibility for the client remains with the teacher, is a consultee-centered consultation approach possible. The psychologist's responsibility for the clients is then restricted to a responsibility to use their competence in such a way that teachers may be helped in solving problems in relation to students.

As educational goals are set in the current Swedish school-system (SOU, 1997, 21) the interactive approach is stressed and teachers are looked upon as facilitators of the students' learning processes, rather than as teachers bearing knowledge. Consequently, school-directors and principals, today, may see the point of, and want to promote consultee-centered consultation as a way of empowering teachers to empower students. Also, many teachers ask for opportunities to sit down and reflect with someone coming from outside their own school. Other teachers, however, may be so overwhelmed by work, that the only solution they see to a problem is to get rid of it, hoping that someone else will solve it or take care of it. The challenge for many schools is to negotiate responsibilities and the challenge for many school psychologists is to meet the teachers, helping them with their dilemmas without trying to take their responsibilities away.

REFERENCES

Borus, J. (1982). Retrospective look at the early years of community mental health center consultation. *American Journal of Psychiatry, 141*, 868–871.

Brodin, M. (1995). *Bilden av barnet I konsultationsprocessen. Bilden av ärendet I handledningsprocessen.* (Uppsats för Ericastiftelsens handledarutbildning i konsultation 1993-1995). Stockholm: Ericastiftelsen.

Brodin, M. (1999). An affect-theoretical approach to the consultation process, focused on the consultee's expression of what the client looks like. In *Explorations in process in practice.* (Seminar proceedings). Stockholm: 2nd International Seminar on Consultee-Centered Consultation.

Caplan, G. (1970). *The theory and practice of mental health consultation.* New York: Basic Books.

Caplan, G., & Caplan, R. (1993). *Mental health consultation and collaboration.* San Francisco: Jossey-Bass.

Carlberg, M., Guvå, G., & Teurnell, L. (1977). *Konsultation i förskolan.* (Rapport från förskoleteamet). Stockholm: Stockholms läns landsting, Sociala nämnden.

Carlberg, M., Guvå, G., & Teurnell, L. (1981). *Psykosocial konsultation inom förskolan.* Malmö: Natur och Kultur.

Crafoord, C. (1994). *Människan är en berättelse. Tankar om samtalskonst.* Lund: Natur och kultur.

Falck-Järnberg, B., Janson, U., Olsson, S., & Orrenius-Andersson, A. M. (1980). *Konsultationsprocessen.* (Rapport 2 från förskoleteamet). Stockholm: Stockholms läns landsting, Sociala nämnden.

Forsman, G., & Överholm, C. (1978). *Mentalhälsokonsultation med socialbyråerna i Nacka och Värmdö kommuner.* Stockholm: Stockholms universitet, Psykologiska institutionen.

Frygner, K. (1997). *Barn som behöver särskilt stöd i barnomsorgen. (Socialstyrelsen följer upp och utvärderar 1977:7).* Stockholm: Socialstyrelsen.

Gustafsson, I. (1996). *Handlingsprogram for det förebyggande arbetet inom PBU.* Stockholm: Omsorgsnämnden, PBU.

Gustafsson, I., & Kaplan-Goldman, S. (1980). *Konsultation—Att utveckla ett psykosocialt arbetssätt inom mödra och barnhälsovården.* Stockholm: Stockholms läns landsting.

Guvå, G. (1989). *Klientmysteriet. Ett fall för förskolepsykologen.* Om personalinriktad fallkonsultation. (Sfph:s monografiserie nr 32.) Stockholm: Sfph.

Guvå, G. (1992). Om mellanområdet i konsultation. *Psykisk Hälsa 3,* 205–210.

Guvå, G. (1995). *Professionsutveckling hos konsulter. Om konsultativ handledning och självutveckling. (FOG-Rapport No. 25).* Linköpings universitet, Institutionen för Pedagogik och Psykologi.

Guvå, G. (1999). The first consultation session. How to meet a teacher who asks for help but not for consultation. In *Explorations in process in practice.* (Seminar proceedings). Stockholm: 2nd International Seminar on Consultee-Centered Consultation.

Guvå, G. (2001). *Skolpsykologers rolltagande. Överlämning och hantering av elevvårdsfrågor.* (Dissertation). Linköping: Linköping University.

Hylander, I. (1995a). *Konsultation och handledning. En jämförelse mellan två professionella, psykologiska processer. (FOG-rapport 23.)* Linköping: Linköpings universitet, Institutionen för Pedagogik och Psykologi.

Hylander, I. (1995b). *Evolvement of consultee-centered case consultation in Sweden.* Paper presented at The International seminar on Consultee-Centered Case Consultation May 5-7. Stockholm: Hasselbacken.

Hylander, I. (1999). *Identifying change in the consultation process. Turnings and turning points.* In Explorations in process in practice. (Seminar proceedings). Stockholm: 2nd International Seminar on Consultee-Centered Consultation.

Janson, U., Waldor, S., & Waleij, A. (1983). *Förskolans behov av konsultation och samverkan i psykosocialt arbete. Utredning av förutsättningar för utbyggnad av PBU:s konsultveerksamhet vid förskolor.* Stockholms läns landsting. Sociala nämnden.

Klein, R., Bernard, H., & Singer, D. (1992). *Handbook of contemporary group psychotherapy. Contribution from self-psychology, object relation theory and social system theory.* New York: International University Press.

SOU (1972, 26, 27). Förskolan, del1.Barnstugeutredningen. Stockholm: Socialdepartementet.

SOU (1981, 25). *Bra daghem för små barn.* Betänkande från familjestödsutredningen.

SOU (1997, 21). *Växa i lärande.* Förslag till läroplan för barn och unga 6-16 år. Stockholm: Utbildningsförlaget.

Szecsödy, I. (1981). *Mentalhälsokonsultation.* Sfph`s monografiserie, 14. Stockholm: Sfph.

Thörn, S. (1999). Listen to the contradictory and emphasize the ambiguous. On change and development. In *Explorations in process in practice.* (Seminar proceedings). Stockholm: 2nd International Seminar on Consultee-Centered Consultation.

Wiström, C., Hanson, M., Qvarnström, G., & Westerlund, S. (1995). *Psykologisk konsultation i pedagogisk verksamhet. Analys och utvärdering av konsultationsarbete i barnomsorg och skola.* Östersund: Östersunds kommun, Konsult & Service, Pedagogica.

Winnicott, D. (1971). *Playing and reality.* New York: Basic Books. Svensk översättning (1981). *Lek och verklighet.* Stockholm: Natur och kultur.

6

School Psychologists as Consultee-Centered Consultants Within a System-of-Care Framework: Service Delivery and Training Challenges*

Brent B. Duncan

THE SYSTEM OF CARE FRAMEWORK

Given societal changes taking place in the United States, professionals in many fields related to child and family mental health have developed models of service delivery that emphasize the provision of support services within schools in a multidisciplinary and coordinated fashion. Terms such as *school-family-community collaborative* (Ysseldyke, Dawson, Lehr, Reschley, Reynolds & Telzrow, 1997), *service integration* (APA, 1993) school-linked services (Morrill, 1992), *wrap-around services* (Burchard, 1990), and *system-of care* (Stroul & Friedman, 1986), all argue for a model of service delivery where pro-

*The author would like to thank the many students who have enrolled in Psychology 607 at Humboldt State University, Arcata, CA from 1990 to 2002 for their assistance with the development of this training model. In particular, the participation of Meggan Blanks, Rita Buisson, Carie Dudley, Chris Hill, Teresa Knapp, Danielle Martucci, Suzanne Merideth, Amy Pentel, Patricia Sorci, and Kristin Yoshimoto was instrumental in completion of this chapter. Appreciation is also expressed to Amy Pentel for her helpful comments on an earlier version of this chapter, and to Kristin Yoshimoto for her adaptation of the consultation log format that is presented in this chapter as Table 6.2.

fessionals, parents, and nonprofessionals share responsibility for the design and delivery of services in a cooperative fashion. Literature regarding service delivery to particularly difficult school populations such as children living in extreme poverty, violent youth, homeless families, children with emotional and behavioral disabilities, and abusive families are replete with calls for a shift to these models of service delivery. Attempting to assist teachers, children and parents who are living in a troubled and troubling world will tax the resources of even the most highly trained professional. Many have come to believe that attempting to do so from within a fragmented, categorical, and hierarchically organized social service system is not feasible.

In the United States, the role of the school psychologist working within a system-of-care framework involves a multitude of functions and complex responsibilities. On a daily basis, school psychologists practicing in the United States can be expected to provide:

1. direct supervision for professional or paraprofessional providers of school-based mental health service;
2. direct assessment of children with learning and behavior problems;
3. remedial or crisis oriented counseling or other forms of mental health treatment for children and parents;
4. collaborative problem-solving with school and agency staff regarding a specific client;
5. collaboration with others on a school-based team with specific responsibility for diagnosis, placement or interventions; and
6. consultee-centered individual or group consultation.

Collaborative Problem Solving

Collaboration and consultation are essential components of psychological service in a comprehensive and school-linked approach. A review of the system-of-care literature reveals a tremendous emphasis on collaboration, with less appreciation for consultation. In this literature, collaboration usually refers to efforts at coordinating services to reduce fragmentation, or to improve the coordination of services. For example, Adelman and Taylor (1994) wrote extensively about the need for collaboration, defined as follows: "Simply stated, the purpose of collaboration is to counter inappropriate fragmentation of intervention efforts. Varying degrees of collaboration are accomplished through cooperation, coordination, or integration" (pp. #). A text on school-based collaboration is even simpler in the definition of *collaboration*, referring to a dictionary definition of "working together," or of "cooperative efforts between mainstream teachers, between mainstream and special education teachers, or among workers in several disciplines in a school" (O'Callaghan, 1993, p. 19). In a team approach to collaboration, the school psychologist represents one voice among many regarding the mental health outcome of the case. In cases involving problems of social, emotional, or behavioral adjustment, the school psychologist is naturally expected to play a leading role in terms of both diagnosis and service delivery for children and families. In this type of collaborative model, there is often no opportunity to address appropriately the consultee-related issues that may be playing a significant role in the case. In literature regarding collaboration within schools, Caplan and Caplan (1993) provided perhaps the only clear conceptual model for collaboration that allows the consultant to assume some responsibility for the case, while also addressing the problems faced by the teacher, parent, or other care provider from a consultee-centered stance. For Caplan (2002), collaboration for the school psychologist involves employing techniques for building trust in the consultee, "enabling" the consultee to be more effective with their clients, and serving as a supportive and helpful role model, as opposed to an expert, for the non-mental health members of the team.

A review of the consultation literature in school psychology within the United States reveals a similar trend. The models, tools, and specific methods that are most often used for consultation training and practice are well designed for work within a collaborative framework, where collaboration simply means working together to solve problems. If the focus in the collaboration literature is on working together to reduce fragmentation, the emphasis in the consultation literature frequently concerns the adoption and implementation of a formal problem-solving model, with the emphasis on expert problem solving. In a search for a generic definition of consultation that school psychology as a field could accept, Gutkin and Curtis (1999) relied on a 1979 definition of consultation used by Medway, where *consultation* is defined simply as collaborative problem-solving between a school psychologist or mental health specialist (the consultant) and one or more persons (the consultees) who are responsible for providing some form of psychological assistance to another (the client). In most generic models, consultants are trained to be expert problem-solvers, or facilitators of a problem-solving process. I would argue that the shift toward models of collaborative problem solving and away from a consultee-centered or process-focused framework for consultation has received nearly universal acceptance within the school psychological literature during the past 15 years. Regardless of whether it is called behavioral consultation (Sheridan, 2000), problem-solving consultation (Kratochwill, Elliot, & Callan-Stoiber, 2002) instructional consultation (Rosenfield, 2002), or ecobehavioral consultation (Zins & Erchul, 2002), bringing a expert-driven problem-solving methodology to bear to assist the consultee to more accurately diagnose and solve the problems presented by clients is the overarching goal of each of these models. Despite increasing recognition of the importance of the consultee, and the relationship between the consultant and the consultee, these expert models view consultee change as a preventive bonus or byproduct of an approach that is predominantly behavioral, directive, and prescriptive.

Ecobehavioral consultation (Zins & Erchul, 2002) is perhaps the most popular model in the current school psychology literature that is consistent with a coordinated and system-of-care approach to service delivery. In most versions of this model, the behavioral specialist is not only an expert problem-solver, but is responsible for bringing the vast educational and psychological literature to bear on the problems teachers face with different types of clients. In a recent web-based conference and discussion regarding the future of school psychology, Sheridan makes the following observation about the role of the school psychologist working within a collaborative framework:

> To accomplish these various linkages, effective collaboration and problem solving skills must be present. Consultation and collaboration beyond that which occurs with individual teachers or parents are also necessary. Within the context of collaboration, school psychologists are in a position to bring psychoeducational, developmental, and educational knowledge bases to the table. Furthermore, we are in a strong position to take a leadership role in conceptualizing and conducting research to determine what works for which families and schools under what conditions. Thus, school psychologists in the future may be instrumental in (a) developing collaborative, problem solving processes, (b) providing structure to the strategies to be implemented within coordinated programs, and (c) framing a research agenda around the needs, strategies, and outcomes for children and families for whom integrated services are developed. (Sheridan, 2002).

If the consultant is successful in identifying the client's problems and can generate solutions that are acceptable to the consultee, the consultation is deemed successful. In this model, conceptual change for the consultee may occur through the recognition of the superiority of the behavioral or instructional solutions generated through the consultation process, not through the process of consultation as the consultee experiences it. Although at least some attention is given to the importance of choosing interventions that are acceptable to the consultee, and can be implemented within the consultee's work setting, it is still the responsibility of the consultant to recommend the most efficacious interventions, see to it that they are implemented, and collect follow-up data to assess intervention effectiveness. The movement toward evidence-based interventions (Kratochwill & Callan-Stoiber, 2002), is perhaps the most comprehensive and ambitious effort at moving the practice of school psychology in the direction of expert-problem solving, by cataloging the research-supported interventions for all possible problems, and linking researchers with practitioners in an attempt to assure that the interventions implemented are those supported through accepted standards of scientific evidence.

Consultee-Centered Consultation

As the chapters in this volume make abundantly clear, consultee-centered consultation stands in stark contrast to models of collaboration defined as simply working together to coordinate mutual efforts, or of consultation as expert problem solving. Conceptual change, for both the consultee and the consultant, and social support of the consultee are the goal of consultee-centered consultation (Sandoval, 1996). In this model, the preventive goal of assisting the consultee to see the client and the client's problem in a new way is the primary goal. Solving the consultee's immediate work problem is also a principal concern, but it is accomplished through the cooperative and joint resolution of the problem between the consultant and the consultee.

Consultee-centered consultation is as important a methodology for working within overburdened social systems as it was nearly 50 years ago when Caplan developed his original conceptual model for assisting teachers and caregivers of immigrant children during the post-war settlement of Israel (Caplan & Caplan, 1993). Teachers, school administrators, and others working in systems that are characterized by violence, poverty, and declining resources with which to deal with the severity of problems faced by children and families are at high risk for failure and burn-out. Individuals working in such systems undoubtedly need additional resources, and the coordinated case management that a well functioning system-of-care can provide. They also need what Caplan (1970) defined as social support or enabling consultation. In this model, consultees benefit from the opportunity to reflect on their personal theories, representations, and options for handling problems with a consultant skilled in a consultee-centered framework. In contrast to a purely collaborative problem solving approach, a school psychologist adopting a consultee-centered approach allows teachers the opportunity to reflect deeply about their understanding or management of an individual child or classroom situation, without the consultant assuming responsibility for the welfare of the client, arranging for additional mental health services, or cataloging the recent literature on effective interventions for a particular type of child. In a collaborative system-of-care model, the consultee and consultant share responsibility for assessment, treatment and many other aspects of case management. The solutions that most readily present themselves have to do with increasing resources, decreasing the responsibility for the consultee, or altering some aspect of the consultee's handling of the case. For a child with classroom behavioral problems, a referral to a medical clinic for medication, or cognitive-behavioral counseling offered by the school psychologist focusing on impulse control are interventions that the team may develop. Establishing a contingency management system within the classroom to attempt to control the child's behavior is another obvious solution.

In a consultee-centered approach within a comprehensive system of care, the emphasis is less on obtaining resources, coordinating services, or offering solutions, and more on helping the consultee obtain a clearer and more accurate picture of the multiple elements involved in the client's situation and behavior. Out of this more objective understanding, new ways of understanding and managing the situation that will work best for the consultee can emerge. These solutions are based on the consultee's improved understanding of their particular classroom ecology and the available resources. The consultant is able to offer expertise, hopefully involving effective interventions, but only when suggestions do not undermine the consultee's authority for the case.

In terms of all of the possible roles of the school psychologist, consultee-centered consultation is the most indirect and nonprescriptive of all activities. In his revised text, Caplan referred to this form of consultation as "the purest form of indirect action" (Caplan & Caplan, 1993, p. 339). Unlike many theorists, Caplan clearly differentiates between consultation and collaboration, and cautiously suggests that the school psychologist can work out methods or techniques of providing consultee-centered consultation while also collaborating with other members of the school mental health team, and delivering direct service to children, teachers and parents. Richard Parsons agreed, and in his model for training school-based consultants stated, "the operational model to be employed here encourages the consultant to be flexible in the form and focus of consultation, allowing for technical and process expertise, crisis and developmental focus, and varying modes of collaboration" (Parsons, 1996, p. 40).

MODELS FOR TRAINING
THE CONSULTEE-CENTERED CONSULTANT

Unfortunately, there are few clear road maps and training tools for assisting a school psychologist practicing in the United States to move beyond the role of collaborating expert, and to assume a process and consultee-focused stance. This makes it exceptionally difficult for school psychologists in training to learn how to practice from a consultee-centered framework. Didactic and experiential methods are needed to assist neophyte consultants to understand and assess the changes taking place in their understanding of the problems presented by consultees, and in the dynamics of their relationship, and subsequently to achieve a deeper understanding of the process of consultee-centered consultation. The example that follows comes from several years of experience in preparing school psychologists in training to work in comprehensive systems of care. An abbreviated version of the model has also been used for training in-service school psychologists through workshops offered by the California Association of School Psychologists.

For the past 10 years, faculty and school-based professionals at Humboldt State University have been working to develop a collaborative training program for graduate students in school psychology in cooperation with local school districts. In this program, practicing school psychologists and graduate student trainees are responsible for delivering comprehensive school psychological services in rural and suburban schools on the northern coast of California. We are attempting to support settings where psychological services and all of the activities encompassing the role of the school psychologist can be modeled and practiced, including psychoeducational and socioemotional assessment, in-service training for school personnel, the delivery of direct mental health services, and consultation with school staff, parents, and community-based professionals. Our goal is to implement a preventive and system-of-care approach to delivering psychological services to all children and staff, and to train school psychologists to adopt an ecological and preventive frame of reference for their work (Adelman, 1993; Adelman & Taylor, 1998; Baker, Terry, Bridger, & Winsor, 1997; Duncan, Burns, & Robertson, 1996; Quinn & McDougal, 1998).

In the early days of this collaboration, student trainees, working under the supervision of district school psychologists or university faculty, were free to move between activities involving direct action (assessment, counseling), collaborative action (participating on a student-study team to discuss a child with whom a teacher needs help), and consultee-centered consultation. Using this framework, faculty supervision involved helping trainees to determine the most appropriate focus for their work given a careful analysis of the children, teachers, other specialists, and system-level forces in play at any given point in time.

Over time, I observed that student consultants in certain schools routinely experienced great difficulty moving outside of an expert or collaborative mode to establish a consultee-centered relationship. Consistent with the literature, in several schools collaboration was defined primarily as teamwork or shared decision making, and this was the only common philosophy of collaboration or consultation within the school. In addition, some supervising school psychologists had received training in more expert models of consultation, and expected graduate students to assist in the problem-solving process by providing advice and expertise. Teachers in these schools expected the school psychologist to function as an expert, and expressed confusion when advice was not forthcoming. In these settings, providing consultee-centered consultation became virtually impossible, and the training experience led to considerable confusion, even for highly skilled graduate students.

Gradually, the training in consultee-centered consultation has moved to a more circumscribed and purposefully artificial or contrived context. Student psychologists are required to have at least one consultee with whom to practice consultee-centered consultation as part of their practicum placement during the second year of graduate training. The consultation experience is explained in a letter to supervisors, principals, and potential consultees. Consultee-centered consultation is conceptualized as a flexible, semi-structured conversation that is designed to focus the attention of the consultant and the consultee on carefully defining a work related problem that the consultee is experiencing. Students participate in a didactic seminar, where theories and methods of collaboration, problem solving, and consultee-centered consultation are discussed. Students review the consultation literature in school psychology in order to be able to carefully differentiate expert from enabling models of consultation. Although students are still encouraged to move into consultee-centered relationships during other times in their fieldwork placements, they are required to practice this method with their one consultee, who has explicitly agreed to enter into this relationship with the graduate student.

In the seminar, students are provided with training in methods of consultee-centered consultation following what has come to be known as the "Berkeley Model," developed by Nadine Lambert and colleagues in the doctoral training program at the University of California, Berkeley (Lambert, 1983, 1986). Students discuss their consultee-centered experiences in the schools, present cases as consultees in order to observe and experience the process of consultee-centered consultation from the point of view of the consultee, and write weekly logs of their experiences with their consultees. By observing, participating, and analyzing conversations taking place in a small group consultation, students expand their repertoire of ideas for understanding problems and their strategies for constructing consultation relationships. By listening to colleagues discuss problems they are encountering with their consultees, the seminar also allows students to expand their experience with consultation beyond the conversation they are having with their consultee, and understand that the process of consultation varies with each consultee-consultant dyad.

Consultation Logs: Recording Interactions in the Consultation Process

The dialogue established between the instructor and the graduate student consultants through the consultation logs has gradually become a more critical aspect of the training. A method for recording the consultation experience has evolved that attempts to reflect the model of consultation that is taught, and draws heavily from the work, not only of Lambert (1983, 1986) and Caplan (1970, 1993), but also of Ingrid Hylander (2000, 2002), and Edgar Schein (1999). Hylander's model for examining the *presentations* and *representations* of both the consultee and consultant are blended with Caplan and Lambert's method for evaluating the manifest and latent content in a consultation conversation. Schein's model of *process consultation*, although developed from an organizational consultation and organizational development framework, is consistent with a consultee-centered approach. Students are free to adapt the log template to suit their own writing and conceptual style, but the log must contain the following essential sections, as outlined in the log template contained in Table 6.1.

Students develop individual strategies for taking notes and recording the conversation in sufficient detail to be written up for their log. Occasionally, students have tried tape recording consultation sessions, to transcribe or study at a later time, but this has not proven to be necessary or feasible. Instead, students typically take notes during the conversation that they elaborate on immediately following the session, and write up completely as soon as possible.

Using the log, each consultation conversation or interaction is recorded by the student consultant. The log provides a framework for reflecting on a careful and detailed description of the *manifest and latent content* of the conversation, contains an analysis of the *developmental features* of the session and the consultation relationship over time, and a reflection on the *process themes* that are evident in the dialogue, utilizing questions derived from Schein's (1999) principles of process consultation. It is this active reflection on the details of the conversation that allows the consultant-in-training to attend to their understanding of the problem from the perspective of the consultee, to consciously attend to their own representation of the problem, and to not be drawn into premature problem solving or advice giving.

The content description portion of the log provides the opportunity to record in detail the substance of the consultation conversation. Descriptions of the setting, the participants, background regarding the initiation of the request for help, and the subject of consultation are typically recorded briefly in one or two sentences. This provides a context for how and why the conversation took place, who was present, and the topic of the conversation in very general terms.

TABLE 6.1
Template and Content for Recording Consultation Logs

A. Content Description and Analysis

1. Setting

2. Participants

3. Initiator

4. Subject of consultation—In general terms. What is the topic that is discussed?

5. Manifest content/Presentation—In as much detail as possible. What are the verbal statements and nonverbal behaviors that make up this conversation? ("She said—He said.") How is the problem presented by the consultee, and what understanding is communicated by the verbal and nonverbal behavior of the consultant?

6. Latent content/Representation—What are the unstated or assumed conceptual models or themes that guide the consultee and consultant in this interaction?

   a. Analysis of unstated issues, themes or conceptual frameworks

   b. Perceived need of the consultee (e.g., skill, knowledge, objectivity, emotional support)

   c. Perceived role and needs of the consultant in interaction (e.g., authority, student, resource, professional peer)

   d. Area of consultant expertise being tapped (e.g., knowledge of development, illness, curriculum, learning)

B. Developmental Description and Analysis—(Primary phase of consultation reached, and focal point for THIS consultation)

1. Relationship building (Level of trust, quality of relationship between consultant and consultee

2. Establishing or maintaining rapport (Consultee and consultant affect, and affective tone of relationship)

3. Problem definition

4. Gathering data on what has already transpired, or reviewing previous actions

5. Formulation of interventions or plans for data collection

   a. Who generates ideas?

   b. When are consultant ideas offered?

   c. How is consultee anxiety reduced

   d. Are pitfalls avoided: defining problem for the consultee, defining problem too soon, making suggestions too soon, confronting resistance, knowing the answer?

6. Sharing information

7. Generating interventions

8. Supporting interventions

9. Follow-up and disengagement—assumption of responsibility for outcome (Plans for future consultation with this consultee)

C. Process Description—As you progress in the consultation, pay particular attention to changes in the conceptual framework surrounding consultation, and your relationship with the consultee. What is it that is developing, emerging, or inhibiting change in the relationship? If you are stuck, why and where are you stuck? If there is development in the relationship, where are you going? What evidence do you have for the changes in the conceptual framework for either the consultant or the consultee? In this section, use Schein's (1999) model to reflect on the following questions as you describe and interpret change in the process themes in this consultation session:

1. Was this session helpful?

2. What is the current reality for this consultee regarding this problem?

3. What is my ignorance/bias regarding this problem/situation?

4. What "interventions" occurred?

5. Does the consultee still own the problem and the solution?

6. How, where or when did I go with the flow?

7. Timing errors or opportunities taken?

8. Was I (positively, constructively, and cautiously) opportunistic with confrontive interventions?

9. What were my errors? What did I learn?

10. Did I share the problem?

The description of the manifest content is the first essential section of the log, which I refer to as "She said—He said." This is synonymous with Hylander's (2002) use of the term *presentation*. Following the methods developed by Lambert and Hylander, I ask students to record in great detail the substance of the conversation. Who said what, what questions were asked, and how did the conversation progress from the initial "hello" to the concluding remarks? What nonverbal behavior or communication takes place? How is the problem presented by the consultee, and what is communicated by the verbal and nonverbal behavior of the consultant? It is through a careful analysis of what was actually said and communicated during the consultation session that an understanding of the process of the conversation can take place.

Alongside or parallel to the manifest content description, students address a series of questions regarding their ongoing understanding of the meaning of the consultation. Using Caplan's (1970) original framework for understanding consultee requests for help, and Hylander's (2002) use of the term *representation*, how does the consultant understand the problem being presented? What are the conceptual models or themes that guide *both* the consultee and consultant in this interaction? What is it that the consultee seems to need in order to solve their problem (e.g., skill, knowledge, objectivity, emotional support)? What is the consultant's understanding regarding the relative power in the relationship during this conversation, and what role (e.g., authority, student, resource, professional peer) have they assumed or have they been asked to take on? Finally, what is the area of expertise that the consultant brings to the conversation, or what areas of expertise is the consultee requesting or assuming that the consultant will provide? Using Hylander's framework, this is the place for the consultant to attend to their understanding of the internal *representations* of the problem. By carefully analyzing their own ideas or theories about the nature of the underlying problem and what they are being asked to provide, and their understanding of the consultee's current representation of the problem, the consultant can learn how to ask questions designed to clarify or shed light upon the definition of the problem, from the consultee's perspective.

The next main section of the log allows the consultant to reflect carefully on the developmental aspects of the consultation. By considering a series of detailed questions regarding the dynamics of each conversation, consultants develop a conceptual model for understanding what is taking place during the conversation. This understanding typically changes rather dramatically over time as the consultation progresses, and as the consultant-in-training gains experience with the model. Although the primary focus of this model is on the process aspects of the conversation, consultee-centered consultation is also a problem solving methodology and typically progresses through a series of stages within each session, and over time as the relationship develops. Students are asked to reflect on each of these stages after each consultation conversation, in order to consider how each separate conversation progresses, and how the relationship changes over time. As students gain experience with the model, it becomes more of an internalized guide that lends structure to their consultation conversations.

In the early phases of a relationship, more attention is typically spent attending to building a trusting relationship, establishing proximity, and defining the problem(s) that the consultee wants to address. The initial presentation of the problem made by the consultee is usually acknowledged and supported by the consultant. Later sessions emphasize a greater emphasis on sharing information, exploring alternative theoretical frameworks for understanding the consultee's problem, generating interventions, or setting up data collection systems to monitor intervention effectiveness. Students are encouraged to adopt a flexible approach to building the conversation, and to allow the conversation to move through each of the stages during one session, and over several sessions taking place over several weeks or months. By forcing novice consultants to reflect in such detail regarding their initial consultation conversations, a deeper awareness is developed regarding the complex dynamics of change involved in helping relationships.

Focusing on Process and Representations

The final section of the log forces the consultant to think specifically about a different set of process variables, distinct from the descriptive or developmental dimensions just described. Schein's (1999) principles of process consultation, described in detail in his seminal text, provide another lens for the consultant to carefully review and reflect on their understanding of what is taking place during the consultation session.

For Schein, *process consultation* is defined as the process that is involved whenever one person tries to help another person. "Whether a therapist is helping a patient or working with a group, a parent is helping a child, a friend is helping another friend, or an organizational consultant is working with managers to improve some aspects of the organization, the same fundamental dynamics are involved" (Schein, 1999, p. 3). Although consultee-centered consultation is a more carefully defined and circumscribed process involving a professional conversation, Schein's definition of the dynamics involved in all helping relationships, listed as ten principles, provide a useful conceptual guide for the consultee-centered consultant as she reflects on the details of the consultation conversation and relationship. As summarized by Schein (1999), they are defined as follows:

Always Try to Be Helpful

Consultee-centered consultation is concerned with providing help to the consultee, and only indirectly assisting the client. Consultants are encouraged to remember that, whenever possible, every contact with the consultee should be perceived by the consultee as being helpful. This involves an intentional and conscious effort on the part of the consultant to define carefully what will be helpful for this consultee, given the current presentation of the problem, at this point in the consultation relationship.

Always Stay in Touch With the Current Reality

A consultant operating from a consultee-centered framework must be intimately aware of the details regarding the current work situation facing the consultee. He or she needs to know a great deal about what is taking place in the consultee's work environment, and with the consultee's clients. A consultee-centered consultant must become trusted enough to be able to access this often sensitive and confidential information in an ongoing, unobtrusive and open manner.

Access Your Ignorance

The consultant must be able to distinguish what they know about a situation from what they think they know, from what they truly do not know. All consultants enter a consultation relationship with certain theories and assumptions about human behavior, organizational and systemic contributors to well-being, and problem solving. As mentioned earlier, consultants must be able to distinguish between the *presentations* of the consultee and their own *presentations* (what is actually said about the problem), from the *representations*, (what the consultee and consultant actually believe is going on) (Hylander, 2002). Schein reminds us that we can never know everything about the current reality for this consultee. In addition, one needs to be careful not to make unwarranted assumptions regarding the consultee's representation of a problem. This rule suggests that in addition to asking "what do I know about this situation that will help me provide the consultee with helpful ideas," one must also ask, "*what do I not know,* about which I need to learn more in order to be helpful?" Reflecting on areas of ignorance encourages the consultant to attend to multiple theoretical frameworks that might be helpful in reframing the consultee's problem, rather than trying to resolve all consultee dilemmas by utilizing the theory held by the consultant. A consultee-centered consultant is concerned with understanding what the consultee is thinking. What does the consultee know and not know about a problem, and what theories for action does he or she have?

Everything You Do Is an Intervention

Most expert models of problem solving involve a four or five stage problem-solving process that dictates the type of questions that are asked at particular points in the conversation. Interventions typically occur toward the end of a problem-solving conversation, after all background information has been collected, as solutions are being proposed or developed. Schein believes that every action in a conversation has consequences for the consultation and for the consultee, and every aspect of the conversation should be guided by the goal of furthering to develop a helping relationship, and not dictated by an artificial or stage dependent model or style. Diagnostic questions, for example, may be appropriate throughout a conversation, not just at the outset. Hylander's analysis is particularly useful in understanding critical "turning points" in a conversation, as moments where a conceptual shift has occurred regarding the consultee's understanding of a child or a problem, and as moments when interventions are especially helpful (Hylander, 2002).

It Is the Consultee Who Owns the Problem and the Solution

In contrast to expert models, which Schein refers to as models of "selling and telling" (1999, p. 7) in a consultee-centered model, it is not the consultant's job to solve the problem or take the problem off of the consultee's hands. The task for consultation is to create a relationship between the consultant and the consultee where the consultee can receive help. Genuine help in consultation often occurs when the consultee discovers a new way to view or to understand the client's problem, not when the consultee provides an expert diagnosis or prescribed intervention.

Go With the Flow

This rule implies that there is a natural flow in relationships that varies from one consultation relationship to another. Conversations that occur within a relationship must respect certain rules that have been developed regarding how conversations take place. Imposing a four step or highly sequenced problem-solving framework around the problem may work at some points in some relationships, but it is an overly constricted and controlling view of human relationships to serve as the basis for consultee-centered relationships.

Timing is Crucial

An intervention or a suggestion that a consultant may attempt might succeed at one moment and fail at another. As with the previous rule, this principle implies that there is a flow in the relationship and a consultant must pay attention to opportunities as they present themselves. In particular, the consultee must be receptive to receiving a suggestion or considering an alternative in order for it to be perceived as being helpful.

Be Constructively Opportunistic With Confrontive Interventions

This rule implies that within the consultation relationship there are moments for silence, and moments where a consultant may be verbally more direct or suggestive. The consultant must be alert for moments of thoughtfulness, openness to alternative explanations, reflection, or strength on the part of the consultee, and use these moments to be more directive, or gently confrontive.

Everything Is a Source of Data. Errors Are Inevitable, Learn From Them

A consultant operating from a consultee-centered framework must avoid being defensive, and be able to accept the reality that there will always be errors in consultation. It is never possible to know enough about the situation facing a consultee to be certain of one correct course of action. Errors in consultation provide invaluable information about what is actually going on in the consultation relationship, or with the consultee's problem.

When in Doubt, Share the Problem

In Schein's model, when the consultant is stuck or unsure of where to turn, he or she is free to involve the consultee in a conversation regarding the consultation in an effort to engage the consultee in active reflection regarding both the problem of the client, and the process of consultation. I would agree with many of the proponents of consultee-centered consultation that are represented in the present volume, and argue that the consultant must find a way to engage the consultee in defining and sharing responsibility for the problem from the very beginning of the interaction, not just when the consultant is stuck.

Clearly, these themes relate to one another, and are not meant to be mutually exclusive. In fact, Schein proposes that all of the principles must be taken as a whole, and thought of as slightly different perspectives on the essence of a nonhierarchical helping relationship. In their logs, students answer questions related to each of the above principles in order to foster the development of a process-focused map of their understanding of the relationship with the consultee, to evaluate their thought processes and strategies utilized during each session, and to plan for subsequent sessions.

Recently, Kristin Yoshimoto, a graduate student consultant, designed a particularly useful format for recording the information contained in the consultation log that allows for side-by-side recording of the manifest (presentation), latent (representation) and developmental aspects of the consultation session. It has been my experience that this format has improved student consultant's understanding of the relationship between each of these dimensions, as well as the interaction between them. Although student consultants are free to design their own log format, current students have all chosen to use Yoshimoto's format, which is included as Table 6.2.

During training, student consultants work on their logs on a weekly basis over at least 10 weeks. The instructor provides ongoing feedback regarding each log, posing questions to help clarify each student's understanding of the descriptive, developmental and process related aspects of their relationship. Over time, understanding of the process deepens, encouraged by the interaction in the seminar, and many students experience qualitative shifts at some point in their logs, mirroring a heightened appreciation of the process in which they are engaged with their consultee. A method for coding these conceptual changes is currently being developed, using a method for cognitive mapping suggested by Sandoval (1996).

Practicing Consultee-Centered Consultation
With a Comprehensive School-Based Delivery System

In order to move successfully between different types of complex professional activities within a school, it is crucial that school psychologists have very clear definitions for each of their tasks, and tools for signaling the rules and processes involved to themselves and others. Helping relationships that foster more efficient coordination of services, improved problem solving and access to the literature on effective interventions are obviously valuable. My experience in over-burdened school settings has led me to conclude that consultee-centered consultation is an even more essential service, but it has been more difficult to establish within some school settings. As noted at the beginning of this chapter, in many of our training sites, consultee-centered consultation remains a novel approach, and site supervision and modeling of this method is not always available. My understanding of this training experience as articulated by graduate students in these schools has led me to conclude that in order to move beyond problem solving and learn a consultee-centered role, students must have tools for conceptualizing the dynamics of the conversation between the consultant and consultee, and at least one extended and ongoing relationship in which to practice these new skills. I believe that the log described in this chapter, combined with the didactic training methods pioneered by Nadine Lambert fulfill these criteria. They have allowed me to begin to train a small number of school psychologists who are able to continue to develop their skills during their internship and early careers.

Table 6.2

Suggested Format for Recording Consultation Logs

Consultation Log

Consultant: _____   Consultee: _____   Date: _____

Initiator (who/how): _____   Setting: _____

Subject: _____

(Refer to the Template for Recording Consultation Logs for Detailed instructions regarding each of the following sections)

Manifest Content/Presentation (Detailed description of the conversation)	Latent content/Representation (What are the conceptual models that guide both the consultee and consultant in this interaction?)	Developmental Description
In as much detail as possible. What are the verbal statements and nonverbal behaviors that make up this conversation? ("She said — He said.") How is the problem presented by the consultee, and what is communicated by the verbal and nonverbal behavior of the consultant?	In as much detail as appropriate. What are the internal assumptions and conceptual models or themes that guide the behavior of both consultee and consultant in this interaction?	Primary phase of consultation reached, and focal point for THIS consultation. I. Relationship Building II. Establishing or maintaining rapport III. Problem Definition IV. Gathering data on what has already transpired, or reviewing previous actions V. Formulation of interventions or plans for data collection VI. Sharing Information VII. Generating interventions VIII. Supporting Interventions IX. Follow-up and disengagement

Table 6.2 (continued)

Process Description								
1. Was this session helpful								
2. What is the current reality for this consultee regarding this problem								
3. What is my ignorance/bias for this problem/situation								
4. What "interventions" occured?								
5. Does the consultee still own the own the problem and the solution?								
6. How, where or when did I go with the flow?								
7. Timing erros or opportunities taken?								
8. Was I opportunistic with confrontive interventions?								
9. What were my erros? What did I learn?								
10. Did I share the problem?								

In analyzing program evaluation data and in ongoing conversations with recent graduates who have received this training, several themes have emerged regarding critical system variables that influence how successfully the school-based consultant is able to move freely between consultee-centered consultation, collaboration, and the provision of direct services. These variables include:

1. the skill, training, and degree of sophistication regarding consultation and collaboration among members of the team;
2. the quality of the relationships among members of the school-based mental health team, particularly with regard to levels of trust and mutual respect;
3. the overall organizational health of the institution;
4. the leadership ability of the site administrator (principal);
5. the seriousness of the problems referred to the school mental health team;
6. the availability of resources appropriate for meeting the needs of the children; and
7. the skill, experience, and reputation of the consultant.

In supportive settings where a consultee-centered approach is understood and valued, virtually all of our recent graduates are able to build these types of relationships with teachers and administrators. In overwhelmed environments with weak site leadership, or where psychologists are expected to provide advice and expert problem solving, even our most skilled graduates have struggled.

Program evaluation data provide conclusive evidence that our recent graduates are able to assess child problems comprehensively, collaborate with others, develop comprehensive services, and work effectively and cooperatively within the school environment. Longitudinal data regarding their understanding and performance as consultee-centered consultants will also be necessary in order to determine whether graduates can continue to provide this most essential service as well. Methods for ongoing post-graduate support for early career school psychologists must be explored, particularly for those individuals working in settings where prescriptive methods of consultation are well established.

REFERENCES

Adelman, H. (1993). School-linked mental health interventions: Toward mechanisms for service coordination and integration. *Journal of Community Psychology, 21,* 309–319.
Adelman, H. S., & Taylor, L. (1994). *On understanding intervention in psychology and education.* Westport, CT: Praeger.

Adelman H. S., & Taylor, L. (1998). Mental health in schools: Moving forward. *School Psychology Review, 27*(2), 175–190.

American Psychological Association. (1993). *Violence and youth: Psychology's response. Volume I.* Washington DC: Author.

Baker, J. A., Terry, T., Bridger, R., & Winsor, A. (1997). Schools as caring communities: A relational approach to school reform. *School Psychology Review, 26*(4), 586–602.

Burchard, J. (1990). *The mainstream revisited: The need for community-based wraparound services for children with severe emotional disturbance.* Paper presented at the 24th annual U.C. Berkeley School Psychology Conference, April 1990. Unpublished manuscript.

Caplan, G. (1970). *The theory and practice of mental health consultation.* New York: Basic Books.

Caplan, G. (2002). Recent advances mental health consultation and collaboration. In N. M. Lambert, I. Hylander, & J. Sandoval (Eds.), *Consultee-centered consultation: Improving the quality of professional services in schools and community organizations.* Mahwah, NJ: Lawrence Erlbaum.

Caplan, G., & Caplan, R. B. (1993). *Mental health consultation and collaboration.* San Francisco: Jossey Bass.

Duncan, B., Burns, S., & Robertson, L. (1996). *Providing quality services to emotionally disturbed students and their families in California: Recommended program standards for community-based programs.* Sacramento: California Department of Education, Resources in Special Education.

Gutkin, T. B., & Curtis, M. J. (1999). School-based consultation theory and practice: The art and science of indirect service delivery. In C. R. Reynolds & T. B. Gutkin, (Eds.), *The handbook of school psychology.* New York: John Wiley & Sons Inc.

Hylander, I. (2000). *Turning processes. The change of representations in consultee-centered case consultation.* (Dissertation). Linköping: Linköping University. Department of Behavioural Science.

Hylander, I. (2002). Analysis of conceptual change in consultee-centered consultation. In N. M. Lambert, I. Hylander, & J. Sandoval (Eds.), *Consultee-centered consultation: Improving the quality of professional services in schools and community organizations.* Mahwah, NJ: Lawrence Erlbaum Associates.

Kratochwill, T. R., & Callan-Stoiber, K. (2002). Evidence-based interventions in school Psychology: Conceptual foundations of the procedural and coding manual of Division 16 and the Society for the Study of School Psychology Task Force. *School Psychology Quarterly, 17*(4), 341–389.

Kratochwill, T. R., Elliot, S. N., & Callan-Stoiber, K. (2002). Best practices in school-based problem-solving consultation. In A. Thomas & J. Grimes (Eds.), *Best practices in school psychology-IV.* Bethesda, MD: National Association of School Psychologists.

Lambert, N. M. (1983). Perspectives on training school-based consultants. In J. Meyers & J. Alpert (Eds.), *Training in Consultation: Perspectives from behavioral, mental health, and organizational consultation* (pp. 29–47). Springfield, IL: Charles C. Thomas.

Lambert, N. M. (1986). Conceptual foundations for school psychology: Perspectives from the development of the school psychology program at Berkeley. *Professional School Psychology, 4,* 215–224.

Morrill, W. A. (1992). Overview of service delivery to children. *The Future of Children-School-Linked Services, 2*(1), 32–43. (Available from Center for the Future of Children, David and Lucile Packard Foundation, 300 Second Street, Suite 102, Los Altos, CA 94022).

O'Callaghan, J. B. (1993). *School-based collaboration with families.* San Francisco: Jossey-Bass.

Parsons, R. D. (1996). *The skilled consultant: A systematic approach to the theory and practice of consultation.* Boston: Allyn and Bacon.

Quinn, K. P., & McDougal, J. L. (1998). A mile wide and a mile deep: Comprehensive interventions for children and youth with emotional and behavioral disorders and their families. *School Psychology Review, 27*(2), 191–203.

Rosenfield, S. (2002). Best practices in instructional consultation. In A. Thomas & J. Grimes (Eds.), *Best practices in school psychology-IV*. Bethesda, MD: National Association of School Psychologists.

Sandoval, J. (1996). Constructivism, consultee-centered consultation, and conceptual change. *Journal of Educational and Psychological Consultation, 7*, 89–97.

Schein, E. H. (1999). *Process consultation revisited: Building the helping relationship*. Reading, MA: Addison-Wesley.

Sheridan, S. M. (2000). Considerations of multiculturalism and diversity in behavioral consultation with parents and teachers. *School Psychology Review, 29*(3), 344–353.

Sheridan, S. M. (2002). Selected essays on the future of school psychology. *http://education.indiana.edu/~futures/essays.html. futures@indiana.edu.*

Stroul, B. A., & Friedman, R. M. (1986). *A system of care for seriously emotionally disturbed children and youth*. Washington, DC: CASSP Technical Assistance Center at Georgetown University.

Ysseldyke, J., Dawson, P., Lehr, C., Reschley, D., Reynolds, M., & Telzrow, C. (1997). *School psychology: A blueprint for training and practice II*. Bethesda, MD: National Association of School Psychologists.

Zins, J. E., & Erchul, W. P. (2002). Best practices in school consultation. In A. Thomas & J. Grimes (Eds.) *Best practices in school psychology-IV*. Bethesda, MD: National Association of School Psychologists.

7

Facilitating Conceptual Change in New Teacher Consultation Groups[1]

Leslie M. Babinski
Educational Consultation and Development, Inc., Chapel Hill, NC

Steven E. Knotek
Dwight L. Rogers
University of North Carolina at Chapel Hill

Research on teacher induction makes a strong case for the need to provide first-year teachers with frequent opportunities to share experiences and solve problems collaboratively (Huling-Austin, 1992; Rogers & Babinski, 2002). The value of engaging in problem solving within a community of peers has been supported by the work of several scholars (Bakhtin, 1981; Brufee, 1993; Harris, 1995; Hollingsworth, 1992; Vygotsky, 1978). Brufee argued that learning is a collaborative enterprise where knowledge is constructed by negotiation through conversations in communities of peers. Vygotsky (1978) claimed that dialogue provides a powerful vehicle for learning and development. Vygotsky further asserted that individuals learn and develop from the outside in, or in other words, individual development moves from the interpersonal to the intrapersonal.

[1]Portions of this chapter first appeared in Rogers, D. L., & Babinski, L. M. (2002). *From isolation to conversation: Supporting new teachers' development.* Albany: State University of New York Press.

Like Vygotsky, Bakhtin (1981) wrote persuasively about the power of community in stimulating individual growth. Bakhtin maintained that the personal, or "inside," voice(s) and the social, or "outside," voice(s) exist simultaneously as a result of and at the expense of each other. As one engages in dialogue, one calls on and responds to both "the others without" and "the others embedded within." It is this tension between the personal and the social that Bakhtin believes stimulates the conversations that are essential for intellectual growth.

According to Meyer (1999), "in order to learn from experience, teachers must have access not only to a community that engages in inquiry but to a community that has the capacity to talk in certain productive ways" (p. 7). Sandoval (this volume) emphasized the role of the teacher as an "active agent in the learning process." In this constructivist view, the dialogue among professionals within consultation serves as a catalyst for conceptual change. Cissna and Anderson (1994) suggested that dialogue is much more than a simple back-and-forth exchange of information through verbal interaction. In fact, they insist that dialogue "points to a particular process and quality of communication in which the participants 'meet,' which allows for changing and being changed" (p. 10). They contend that participating in dialogue can stimulate change both among and within individuals, because in dialogue "we have not 'planned' what we will say or who we will be" (p. 24).

Other researchers make equally strong claims for the power of dialogue in supporting the professional growth of teachers. According to Cochran-Smith and Lytle (1993), teachers construct fresh insights into their practice through engaging in deep discussions centered around the thoughtful analyses and interpretations of events experienced in their schools and classrooms. Hollingsworth (1992) contended that collaborative conversations contain the social interaction and intellectual stimulation that encourage new teachers to gain "power to think and act within an uncertain framework," and to "create and analyze broader knowledge about teaching" (pp. 398-399). Sergiovanni (1994) and Shulman (1988) claimed that teachers' roles as learners in collaborative discussions with their peers seem to inspire them to teach in more innovative and sophisticated ways. More generally, Corcoran (1995) stated that teacher engagement in genuine dialogue around such issues as teaching, curriculum, evaluation, and assessment fosters professional development. Richert (1992) asserted that it is critical that beginning teachers are provided with opportunities to converse with other teachers because they:

> learn to think as they talk, and they become conscious of what they know and believe as they hear themselves speak (and examine what they've spoken) .... Listening to yourself as an authority on your own experience ... is an important part of learning. In

fact listening to your own words and attempted explanations is fundamental to reflective practice that results in learning to teach. (p. 193)

In this chapter we describe our New Teacher Consultation Groups that are designed to facilitate professional dialogue and problem solving among beginning teachers. The chapter concludes with an example of the dialogue from one of our groups that illustrates the process of conceptual change within a group session.

OUR NEW TEACHER CONSULTATION GROUPS

In an attempt to provide a structure that facilitated collaborative discussions among new teachers, we adapted the problem-solving process from Caplan and Caplan's (1993) consultation theory. This consultation process provided a framework for our discussions that helped the new teachers cope with their situations in a way that would foster personal and professional learning and growth.

Our New Teacher Consultation Groups created professional relationships that were unlike most others that teachers encountered in their schools. The group facilitators had no supervisory or evaluative power over the teachers, nor did they have any responsibility for the students in the teachers' classrooms. Because of the unique nature of this relationship, we decided to follow a consultee-centered consultation approach that focused on the teacher's professional development. The primary focus of consultee-centered consultation is on helping the teacher become a more effective professional. In this approach, the main objective is to improve the teacher's capacity to deal with a current problem and future similar problems (Caplan & Caplan, 1993). Because it was clear from the research literature that the initial focus of the teacher is inward (i.e., on his or herself as a teacher) (Levin & Ammon, 1992), we felt that a consultee-centered model was an appropriate choice to guide our New Teacher Consultation Groups.

Caplan's model of consultation has been used to support professional development in a number of diverse disciplines; Caplan described his use of consultee-centered consultation with nurses, rabbis, social workers, and judges (Caplan & Caplan, 1993). The benefits of this type of approach for educators have been described (Caplan, Caplan, & Erchul, 1995), although our work is the first that we know of that systematically uses Caplan's consultation framework for supporting beginning teachers during the induction phase (Rogers & Babinski, 2002).

Given the difficulties faced by beginning teachers and the lack of a collaborative culture in many schools, Caplan's model of consultation is an effective way to address these needs. According to this consultation approach, learning, and generalization are more likely to occur when the teachers retain ownership of the problem (Brown, Pryzwansky, & Schulte, 1998). Furthermore, consultation has been found to improve teachers' problem-solving skills, facilitate teachers' understanding of and attitude about children's problems, and promote gains in long-term academic achievement (Meyers, 1995). We hoped that helping the new teachers become more effective professionals would positively impact their students, not only in current classrooms, but also for years to come.

Important Features of New Teacher Consultation Groups

Caplan's model of consultation is ideal for supporting new teachers because it focuses on the noncoercive nature of the consultant-consultee relationship and the need for a collaborative dialogue to foster orderly reflection, and it provides the opportunity to listen to others as they reflect on their teaching experiences (Caplan, Caplan, & Erchul, 1995). The first of these elements, the noncoercive relationship, is especially important in a group setting with beginning teachers who are in a vulnerable position and very sensitive to evaluative comments by parents, administrators, and other teachers. By establishing a coordinate, nonhierarchical power relationship with teachers, we were able to encourage a more open and honest exploration of the issues presented. Second, "unhurried, systematic reflection" (Caplan et al., 1995, p. 26) during the teacher's first year creates a unique opportunity to increase the teacher's awareness of possible solutions available to address her or his concerns. In fact, Schön (1987) believes that providing teachers with opportunities to formally and informally reflect on their practice is one of the most critical methods for helping teachers develop into thoughtful and effective practitioners. Furthermore, consultee-centered consultation groups appear to promote what Reiman and others term *relaxed reflection*, which they believe is critical for assisting novice teachers to "make meaning from their new complex roles" (Reiman, Bostick, Lassiter, & Cooper, 1995, p. 109).

Another critical feature of many consultation groups (e.g., Bergan & Kratochwill, 1990; Caplan & Caplan, 1993) is the importance placed on the problem-solving process. In this form of group consultation, it is essential that the facilitator engages in a dialogue that helps the teacher view the problem from multiple perspectives, reframe the problem if necessary, and generate hypotheses about the problem that will lead to possible strategies or solutions to address the concern. According to Zins (1993), "the consultation process may be facilitated through *overt cognitive modeling of the problem-solving process*," (p. 188) and consultants can explicitly emphasize the stages of the problem-solving process to help teachers better understand the goals of consultation. In our New Teacher Consultation Groups, we explicitly described the problem-solving process we followed to provide the participating teachers with a framework for thinking about the issues they were encountering in the classroom.

Providing new teachers with opportunities to talk about teaching is critical to enhancing their professional growth and listening to their peers talk about their experiences in schools may be equally valuable. Listening is also salient to the process of gaining a voice—in short, fostering a sense of identity as a teacher. Coles (1989) claimed that when we listen to someone else's story one can share their lives by experiencing their joys, their pain, their perceptions—almost as if one were seeing it through their eyes. By talking together, teachers can overcome the limits of bounded rationality and become better able to process the infinite complexity of teaching and learning to teach. Part of this process involves listening to the ideas of their colleagues and comparing those ideas with their own (Richert, 1992).

Structure of the New Teacher Consultation Groups

Participation in the New Teacher Consultation Groups encourages the development of teachers' ability to reflect on issues central to successful teaching through the use of problem-based discussions. Problem-based discussions are those in which each beginning teacher shares issues and concerns with the entire group; in turn, the group, under the guidance of the facilitator, works to help the teacher better understand and resolve the problem. The group facilitators used the following structure to guide the problem-solving discussions at the meetings:

- A teacher presents his or her problem to the group.
- The facilitators and the group members work together to help the presenting teacher gain a clearer conception of the problem and generate alternative interpretations by asking questions and pushing for clarification and further refinement of the definition of the problem.
- Once the problem is defined, the group assists the presenting teacher by either discussing additional information needed to understand the problem or brainstorming possible solutions, and developing an initial plan of action.
- At subsequent meetings the teacher provides follow-up reports on the implementation of the plan, which allows for further exploration and collaborative assistance from the group members.

The Problem-Solving Process

Through teachers' participation in the New Teacher Consultation Groups in general, and in the problem-solving process in particular, they were encouraged to define themselves as teachers more clearly. As Schwab (1976) noted, educators learn more about themselves "through involvement with others—involvement in problems, involvement with elements of the culture" (p. 5). The problem-solving process in our groups prompted teachers to reflect and learn more about their teaching and themselves as teachers by allowing them to talk about their issues with their peers for extended periods of time. This problem-solving process permitted new teachers to "think out loud" and publicly reflect on their teaching by presenting their problems to the group. As the group explored multiple perspectives on the problem, the teachers were encouraged to reconstruct their understanding of the problems and to generate possible solutions. This process also encouraged those who were not presenting to really listen and contribute to the discussion by asking sensitive and responsive questions. Such careful listening and thoughtful questioning invited participants to analyze their own teaching as well as their colleagues' practices.

Jointly participating in problem-solving discussions is crucial to developing a sense of oneself as a teacher. Novices learn much about teaching, and about themselves as teachers, through engaging in collaborative conversations focusing on their practices (Hollingsworth, 1992). The stories that teachers tell each other about their teaching experiences provide them with a "sense of coherence" about their work (Friedman, 1994, p. 201). It is the *process* that is important, rather than simply hearing about how to address a problem. According to Corey and Corey (1997), "people learn more from hearing how others are engaged in a struggle than from hearing their solutions to their problems" (p. 144).

Data from our end-of-the-year interviews with teachers provide further support for the importance of talking and listening. (For a more detailed description of the New Teacher Consultation Groups, our research methods, and analyses of the teacher interviews, see Rogers & Babinski, 2002.) Craig, a fifth-grade teacher in one of our groups, claimed that he and the other teachers acquired new insights into their teaching and greater knowledge of themselves as teachers because they felt like they were *invited to talk* about their problems in the group. Craig believed that the group meetings provided him and others with the chance to "verbalize what you are doing and think out loud [about] what you could have done differently and what you are going to do next time." Marilyn, a K-1 special education teacher in another group, also felt that she was more reflective about her teaching as a result of her participation in the group. She said

"[I became] a little more self aware and also more willing to probe my thoughts and feelings about what was going on in school and what was going on with my kids in the classroom ... it helped me clarify my own thoughts." In the following, Victoria, another fifth-grade teacher, described how the problem-solving process helped her think about how to deal with the day-to-day issues she confronted in her classroom:

> If I am having a specific problem with a specific child ... it is very hard to step away from it and look at it objectively. The group is really good at saying, "Okay, have you thought about this?" Or asking questions you haven't asked yourself ... maybe things you haven't taken time to think through yourself ... [and] that gets you thinking more about the problem. We all have different philosophies of teaching .... [So you get] suggestions and ideas from people who teach differently and who do things differently. It is always helpful. I might think [to myself], "No, it doesn't really sound like me." [But then] I might think, "Well, that part of it is good and I can take it and adapt it to what I want it to be."

As Victoria explained, the opportunity to hear the other teachers' perspectives is a critical piece of learning to teach. The teachers just quoted illustrate that the New Teacher Consultation Groups provided novices with a chance to understand themselves as teachers by offering them a forum for discussing their experiences in schools. Richert (1992) explains the importance of teachers getting the chance to seriously discuss teaching with each other in the following:

> As teachers talk about their work and "name" their experiences, they learn about what they know and what they believe. They also learn what they do not know. Such knowledge empowers the individual by providing a source for action that is generated from within rather than imposed from without. In Dewey's (1933) terms, teachers who know in this way can act with intent; they are empowered to draw from the center of their own knowing and act as critics and creators of their world rather than solely respondents to it, or worse, victims of it. (pp. 196, 197)

The beginning teachers in our groups felt that they were able to talk, listen to others, and reflect on their own teaching by engaging in the problem-solving process. The problem-solving process became a mechanism for structuring the conversation so that teachers were able to actively construct new conceptions of the students and their teaching.

One of the best ways to identify and understand the process of conceptual change within consultation is to examine transcripts of the actual consultation process to identify themes and patterns. Below is an excerpt from one of our New Teacher Consultation Groups that illustrates the process of conceptual change for one teacher (for further analysis of the consultation process, see Babinski & Rogers, 1998 or Rogers & Babinski, 2002).

AN ILLUSTRATION OF THE PROCESS
OF CONCEPTUAL CHANGE[2]

The following discussion took place in a group of four new teachers and one consultant early in the school year. The teachers had already reviewed the problem-solving process and felt comfortable with the other members of the group.

Initial Concerns

During one of the first meetings of group the teachers discussed some of their most immediate frustrations and problems. Because these initial sessions dealt with issues the teachers had found unmanageable their initial images of the children and themselves tended to be pessimistic. The students were portrayed in an undifferentiated state, as an aggregated assembly. Annette is a new teacher of a combination 3rd and 4th grade class who has just said that much of her day was, "children being mean—not good to each other all day."

Annette: They just sit there and yell at each other and do whatever they want to do.

Leslie: (consultant) It is more of [a problem with] the younger kids or more personality [conflict]?

Annette: No, it's all of them. It's just constant.

In this exchange the new teacher, Annette, presents an image of the students that is undifferentiated, and in which the students are combative, inconsistent, and persistently frustrating. The students in her class are described as a generalized group ("They just sit there" and "No, it's all of them") who are a continual problem ("it's just constant"). Annette's representation of children was also intertwined with her representation of herself as a teacher—not only did she not differentiate among the children, but also she did not initially differentiate herself from the students. The mood and tone of her descriptions of the students were mirrored in the mood and tone of her description of herself. Correspondingly, in these next utterances, which were continued from the previous quote, Annette goes on to present an image of herself that reflects a sense of inadequacy and of falling short of her own expectations.

Leslie: Has anything helped?

---

[2]Portions of this case study first appeared in Knotek, S. E., Babinski, L. M., & Rogers, D. L. (2002). Consultation in new teacher groups: School psychologists facilitate collaboration among new teachers. *The California School Psychologist, 7*, pp. 39–50.

Annette: We have great mornings [in my class]. I just can't figure out what makes the difference between a great morning and a horrible afternoon. We have a good time, which is usually good, and bad times which are usually bad, but can't figure out what the difference is. I don't feel like there is a difference in me.

Annette: [The bickering is] just constant. If it's not his fault, it's that one, and not that one, it's this one, etc ....
Leslie: Do you feel like you are putting out fires?
Annette: Yes

Annette's description of the issue is phrased in personal speech in which she is powerless to stop these difficult children from acting out, "but I can't figure out what the difference is. I don't feel like there is a difference in me." On further questioning about the situation in the classroom, Annette then describes how this image is tied to her understanding of the situation.

Active Problem Solving Begins

At this point early in the session, Annette has done most of the talking and she has painted a picture of herself as a concerned, frustrated teacher who has yet to effectively respond to children who are being mean to each other. Next the facilitator begins to ask the other teachers for their point of view, "How do you handle it?" And, as other teachers contribute to the process, Annette's images show their first evidence of change.

Annette: It seems to me like it's *a whole bunch* [of students who are acting out in line], maybe it's just an *overbearing situation*. (Conversation continues.)
Craig: Like when are the *certain situations* when it actually happens?
Annette: Like I said, we have 75% of our day, which is really good, and then it's just one part of the day. It could be a horrible morning and a terrific afternoon; it could be a terrific morning and a horrible afternoon.
Craig: It is not consistent, right?
Annette: No, maybe I'm not consistent in *methods*, but it's not consistent. I don't know, I really can't figure it out. Some days would be perfect and the next day ... and really I am just sorry but praise does not work with this group.

Craig: I *purposely* think with things like that it is best to *change the environment* before anything else. Always try to *focus on a kid* or whatever *situation*, and try to *alter* that.

   Although Annette continues to use potent generalizations such as "overbearing situation" to portray the scene in her classroom, her image of herself and the students begins to shift. The other teachers in the group, Craig and Victoria, engage in problem solving with Annette and use professional speech to press her to get specific ("When are the certain situations?") and her speech changes from describing her internal states to instead identifying some external skills, "No, maybe I'm not consistent in *methods*." Annette has begun to unpack her gloomy images and her explanation of the problem has changed.

   With the narrowing of her focus and an adjustment of the description of the problem to learnable skills (methods) comes an opportunity for new images of the children and their teacher to emerge. Craig illustrated just such a connection when he says, "change the environment" and "focus on a kid." Craig uses words that present an image of a teacher who has agency, "I purposely think," and "alter that," as well one who portrays a value neutral issue "environment," "situation," and "a [single] kid."

Multiple Perspectives

As the session continues, the focus of the discussion shifts toward a co-construction of alternative explanations for the problems in Annette's class. The interpersonal, social space of the New Teacher Group is providing a forum for "dialectical constructivism" or interpersonal bootstrapping (Marshall, 1992; Vygotsky, 1978). The facilitator begins to pose questions that call on Annette and the group to interpret and explain the process in Annette's class from multiple perspectives. Consequently, the images of students and teachers continue to evolve. (The teachers begin to take a more active part in later sessions.)

Annette: It's really *my younger ones*. The "not fair thing" is coming from the 8-year-olds. We need rules.
Leslie: It is so typical that things have to be black and white for these kids and that's the way they think.
Annette: It has to be a wrong or a right.
            (Intervening conversation.)
Annette: I think they know, they know [when they are being mean]. Especially, my fourth graders know when they have done something wrong and it is almost, okay you're right [and] I'll deal

with the consequences sort of thing. But, my *third graders, it's just that it's different.*

Leslie: It is interesting because that is that *developmental change* you know. Seven and 8-years-old, and then older kids. So do it. [Understand] that *it is not you.* It is 8-year-olds.

Annette: It is a very *transitional* age, they are very *different.*

In this transcript professional discourse, in the form of developmental explanations for differences in the students' functioning, saturate the conversation ("don't know if the third graders would get it," "developmental change," and "transitional age") and Annette incorporates this outlook into her speech. The representation of children presented here is one of students who have different needs to which the teacher must try different approaches.

In summary, even within the first session there was a pronounced shift in the images of children and images of self as teacher that were expressed in the group. The images of children have moved from undifferentiated to more differentiated, and the teachers' image of self has moved away from frustrated and powerless to thoughtful and insightful. This initial discussion has allowed the group discourse to move from monolithic and single-dimensional images to slightly more open and multi-faceted representations. This example provides support for the notion that group consultation can help teachers change perceptions and reconstruct their understanding of school-related issues.

CONCLUSIONS

The New Teacher Consultation Group offered a context for professional dialogue in which the new teachers solved problems in a constructive setting. The group was, in essence, a situated context in which facilitators and peers were engaged in the process of cognitive apprenticeship (Rogoff, 1990). The collaborative dialogue within the group allowed the teachers to explore multiple perspectives and to reframe their problems with the help of the group. The process of consultee-centered consultation provides teachers with the opportunity to talk, listen, discuss, and develop as professionals within a community of learners.

REFERENCES

Babinski, L. M., & Rogers, D. L. (1998). Supporting new teachers through consultee-centered group consultation. *Journal of Educational and Psychological Consultation, 9*(4), 285–308.

Bakhtin, M. M. (1981). *The dialogic imagination.* Austin: University of Texas Press.

Bergan, J. R., & Kratochwill, T. R. (1990). *Behavioral consultation and therapy*. New York: Plenum.

Brown, D., Pryzwansky, W., & Shulte, A. (1998). *Psychological consultation: An introduction to theory and practice* (4th ed.). Boston: Allyn & Bacon.

Brufee, K. (1993). *Collaborative learning: Higher education, interdependence, and the authority of knowledge*. Baltimore, MD: Johns Hopkins University Press.

Caplan, G., & Caplan, R. B. (1993). *Mental health consultation and collaboration*. San Francisco: Jossey-Bass.

Caplan, G., Caplan, R. B., & Erchul, W. P. (1995). A contemporary view of mental health consultation: Comments on "Types of mental health consultation" by Gerald Caplan (1963). *Journal of Educational and Psychological Consultation, 6*(1), 23–30.

Cissna, K. N., & Anderson, R. (1994). In Anderson, R., Cissna, K. N., & Arnett, R. C. (Eds.), *The reach of dialogue: Confirmation, voice, and community* (pp. 9–30). Cresskill, NJ: Hampton Press.

Cochran-Smith, M., & Lytle, S. (1993). *Inside/outside: Teacher research and knowledge*. New York: Teachers College Press.

Coles, R. (1989). *The call of stories: Teaching and the moral imagination*. Boston: Houghton Mifflin.

Corcoran, E. (1981). Transition shock: The beginning teacher's paradox. *Journal of Teacher Education, 36*(6), 49–53.

Corey, M. S., & Corey, G. (1997). *Groups: Process and practice* (5th Ed.). Boston: Brooks/Cole.

Dewey, J. (1933). *How we think: A restatement of the relation of reflective thinking to the educative process*. Chicago: Henry Regnery.

Friedman, M. (1994). The partnership of existence. In R. Anderson, K. N. Cissna, & R. C. Arnett (Eds.), *The reach of dialogue: Confirmation, voice, and community* (pp. 79–88). Cresskill, NJ: Hampton Press.

Harris, D. L. (1995). *Composing a life as a teacher: The role of conversation and community in teachers' formation of their identities as professionals*. Unpublished doctoral dissertation, Michigan State University. UMI Dissertation Abstracts, UMI Number 9605874.

Hollingsworth, S. (1992). Learning to teach through collaborative conversation: A feminist approach. *American Educational Research Journal, 29*(2), 373–404.

Huling-Austin, L. (1992). Research on learning to teach: Implications for teacher induction and mentoring programs. *Journal of Teacher Education, 43*(3), 173–180.

Knotek, S. E., Babinski, L. M., & Rogers, D. L. (2002). Consultation in new teacher groups: School psychologists facilitate collaboration among new teachers. *The California School Psychologist, 7*, pp. 39–50.

Levin, B., & Ammon, P. (1992). The development of beginning teachers' pedagogical thinking: A longitudinal analysis of four case studies. *Teacher Education Quarterly, Fall*, 19–37.

Marshall, H. M. (1992, April). *Reconceptualizing learning for restructured schools*. Paper presented at the annual meeting of the American Educational Research Association, San Francisco, CA.

Meyer, T. (1999). *Conversational learning: The role of talk in a novice teacher learning community*. Unpublished doctoral dissertation: Stanford University.

Meyers, J. (1995). A consultation model for school psychological services: Twenty years later. *Journal of Educational and Psychological Consultation, 6*(1), 73–81.

Reiman, A. J., Bostick, D., Lassiter, J., & Cooper, J. (1995). Counselor- and teacher-led support groups for beginning teachers: A cognitive-developmental perspective. *Elementary School Guidance and Counseling, 30*(2), 105–117.

Richert, A. (1992). Voice and power. In L. Valli (Ed.), *Reflective teacher education: Cases and critiques* (pp. 187–197). Albany: State University of New York Press.

Rogers, D. L., & Babinski, L. M. (2002). *From isolation to conversation: Supporting new teachers' development*. Albany: State University of New York Press.

Rogoff, B. (1990). *Apprenticeship in thinking: Cognitive development in social context*. New York: Oxford University Press.

Sandoval, J. (2003). Conceptual change in consultee-centered consultation. In N. Lambert, I. Hylander, & J. Sandoval (Eds.). *Consultee-centered consultation: Improving the quality of professional services in schools and community organizations*. Mahwah, NJ: Lawrence Erlbaum.

Schön, D. A. (1987). *Educating the reflective practitioner*. San Francisco: Jossey-Bass.

Schwab, J. J. (1976). Education and the state: Learning Community. *The great ideas today*. Chicago: Encyclopedia Britannica.

Sergiovanni, T. J. (1994). *Building community in schools*. San Francisco: Jossey-Bass Publishers.

Shulman, L. S. (1988). Teaching alone, learning together: Needed agendas for the new reforms. In T. J. Sergiovanni & J. H. Moore (Eds.), *Schooling for tomorrow: Directing reforms to issues that count*. Boston: Allyn and Bacon.

Vygotsky, L. S. (1978). *Mind and society: The development of higher psychological processes*. Cambridge, MA: Harvard University Press.

Zins, J. E. (1993). Enhancing consultee problem-solving skills in consultation interactions. *Journal of Counseling and Development, 72*, 185–190.

8

Alternative School Psychological Services: Development of a Model Linking Theory, Research and Service Delivery

Chryse Hatzichristou

BACKGROUND

A number of studies during the last 2 decades, examining the status of children's mental health in various countries, have yielded similar findings and correspondingly similar recommendations (Costello, 1989; Hatzichristou, 2000; Koyanagi, 1995; Pfeiffer & Reddy, 1998; Rog, 1995; Wardle, 1991) that only a low percentage (20–30 %) of those children identified as needing mental health services actually receive any care, while the great majority of students in need remain untreated. Moreover, the services provided are often inappropriate, inadequate, and lack coordination across multiple providers and systems (e.g., health care, educational, juvenile justice, and child welfare systems).

There has been growing concern in many countries regarding the limitations of traditional direct psychoeducational services provided to children. This has reflected a growing emphasis on the importance of broadening the array of services delivered in school psychology (Lambert, 1993) and a growing interest in consultation theory, practice and research, mainly in the United States. Several models of consultation have been developed reflecting the theoretical prefer-

115

ence of the consultant, such as the "mental health", "behavioral" and the "Adlerian" model, in an effort to cover the different needs and requests of a wide range of children (Brown, Pryzwansky, & Schulte, 2001). Findings from several studies have shown that all professionals in a school setting value consultation as one of the major and preferable job functions of school psychologists and the research evidence has further supported the efficacy of consultation interventions (Hughes, 1979; Kratochwill, Elliott, & Busse, 1995; Lambert, Sandoval, & Corder, 1975; Medway & Updyke, 1985; Reschly & Wilson, 1995).

There is considerable variability among different countries regarding the role, function, and training of school psychologists, the types of school psychological services offered (Oakland & Saigh, 1989), and the utilization of consultation services. Even in countries with a history of public support for psychological services, consultation in schools has been developed only in the last few years in England and Wales (Lambram, 1993) or there is no clear differentiation between consultation and counseling services such as in the Federal Republic of Germany (Mason, Mietzel, & Höfler, 1989). Despite the variability in professional practice, a conceptual framework has been proposed with specific components for examining and comparing the evolution of school psychology in different countries (Hatzichristou, 2002). Common phases and considerable similarities in the most important areas that define the specialty of school psychology show that a similar dynamic process of change that differs in pace is followed in different countries.

It is noteworthy that cross-cultural issues may affect not only the attitudes, the expectations and the needs of teachers and other school professionals when acting as consultees, but even the successful outcome of the consultation process (Brown, Pryzwansky, & Schulte, 2001). Nastasi, Varjas, Bernstein, and Jayasena (2000) pointed out that "effective consultation is dependent on our understanding of the diverse population we serve, our ability to work with individuals from varied cultures, and our capacity for conducting assessments and developing interventions that can fulfill the diverse needs of clients (e.g., students), consultees (e.g., parents, teachers) and systems (e.g., schools, communities)" (p. 401). Ingraham (2000) emphasized the need for a comprehensive framework that considers diversity issues in the structures, processes, context, and their interaction for practice especially within schools.

Cultural differences can become a barrier to effective consultation and as Henning-Stout and Meyers (2000) reported, research and practice in consultation will be well served by looking first to culturally based assumptions that limit the effectiveness of the proposed theories and models of application. Cross cultural perspectives can frame and guide consultation practice and consultation efforts must address the role of culture in promoting and sustaining the behavior of individuals (Nastasi et al., 2000). It is vital to take into account the cultural context from which theory and interpretation arise. All researchers who aim to achieve cultural understanding can contribute to developing a knowledge base that can support relevant and responsive service delivery across cultures (Henning-Stout & Meyers, 2000).

Based on the concerns described in the relevant literature, a conceptual framework was presented incorporating relevant science, and professional practice competences influencing school psychological services (Hatzichristou, 1998). The proposed integrative framework synthesizes and expands the following conceptual domains:

1. the scientist–practitioner specialty in school psychology;
2. the systemic (social, cultural–ethnic–national, ecological) approach in assessment and intervention practices;
3. the evolving roles and functions of school psychologists in research, practice, and training; and
4. the systemic approach of personal and professional development and identity of school psychologists.

This chapter describes how this integrative conceptual framework led to the development of a data-based model of alternative school psychological services addressing developmental competencies and needs of culturally diverse populations within one country. The application of the model in a specific educational and cultural context—the Greek context—is presented. The model attempts to provide guidelines for understanding the culture of individual students, the country, and the school system to determine the service delivery model and the specific school psychology services, including consultee-centered consultation, that are likely to be most useful.

Greece is a country with limited provision of school psychological services. The educational system is centralized, and the curriculum is fully prescribed for every grade and every school in the country. Since 1989, the first 50 psychologists were employed and have worked in special education public schools. Recently, the foundation of Centers for Diagnosis, Assessment and Intervention in various school districts has been announced. School psychological services operate in many private schools in the big cities. For the most part, psychological services involve a focus on individual cases following a "clinical" direct service model. The lack of school psychological services in the Greek public schools, presented a unique opportunity and a great challenge for the development of alternative service delivery models with the goal of filling the system's vacuum.

A MODEL FOR THE DEVELOPMENT OF A SCHOOL
PSYCHOLOGICAL SERVICE DELIVERY SYSTEM

Based on the integration of the domains of the proposed framework the data-based model of alternative school psychological services was developed (Hatzichristou, 1998.) There are four evolving and interrelated phases (Figure 8.1) each of which contributed to widening the "presentation" of the needs of Greek children, and understanding the current "representations" of the professionals in the system.

1. examination of the patterns of psychosocial and academic functioning of the average students.
2. examination of the profiles of at risk groups of students with unmet needs.
3. school and community based needs assessment.
4. development of a service delivery model and provision of specific services.

The four phases of the model emphasize the necessity of a systematic examination of needs at multiple levels (individual, school, culture, community, country) with multiple measures for the development of prevention and inter-

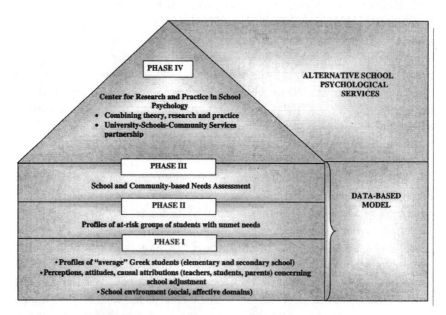

FIG. 8.1.   Model of Alternative School Psychological Services: Connecting Theory, Research and Interventions.

vention programs taking into consideration the ways the social, ethnic, and ecological validity constructs are represented in problem identification and intervention procedures.

The application of the model in the Greek school system was developed over many years when the author had different positions at Max-Planck Institute for Human Development and Education in Berlin, Germany and later at the University of Thessaly. The development of the model continued over the last several years at the Department of Psychology, University of Athens during which the development of the model was extended by examining, determining, and understanding basic educational and cultural factors in order to promote all students' psychological well-being and academic competence in the regular Greek schools.

The project explored the patterns of *school-based competence* of primary- and secondary-school students using a multifaceted, multicomponent assessment. Available evidence suggests the importance of using a multimethod assessment approach of children's behavioral patterns and competence across various domains (Coie & Dodge, 1988; Hatzichristou, 1987). The use of the term *school-based competence* implies and includes several *domains of adaptive behavior* of children in a specific *cultural context*—the *Greek context*—as determined by the standards of *significant others* (teachers, peers, and self) in a specific situational context—the *school* setting.

The development and application of the model constituted a dynamic process of adaptation, change, and evolution being enriched by several new research domains and service components. The evolution of the model included organizational and resource development and a strategic planning perspective and resulted in the foundation of the Center for Research and Practice of School Psychology at the Department of Psychology, University of Athens.

The lack of traditional direct school psychological services in Greek public educational system provided a unique opportunity for the introduction of indirect services, like consultee-centered consultation. Indirect service delivery constitutes the core concept of almost all consultation models. In consultee-centered consultation in schools, the consultation triad can be defined flexibly to include different constellations of consultant, consultee(s), and the contexts in which they work. Both consultees and clients may consist of multiple parties or systems (i.e. consultees may be teachers, administrators, parents and clients may be an individual student, group, classroom, or system). Furthermore, it has been increasingly recognized that a successful consultation leads to a different conceptualization of the problem on behalf of the teacher consultee. Although teachers expect the child to change, the real success for the consultation process is to help the teacher change his or her presentation and representation (understanding of the problem as Hylander and Sandoval have proposed in this volume).

The origin and evolution of the model in the Greek schools included a synthetic consultation approach consisting of several basic components designed to support a broad understanding of the theory and practice of consultee-centered consultation. Key factors that support the consultation process taking into account cultural, educational, and systemic aspects, and promote conceptual change between consultant(s) and consultee(s) are addressed in the following brief description of the *development* and *evolution* periods of the model.

Phase I: Profiles of "Average" Greek Students

Development Period

The lack of systematic research data on children's functioning in the Greek schools led to the need for a systematic examination of the adaptive behavior and school-based competence of "average" Greek students. Therefore, the aims of the first phase of the model included the following:

1. Examination of the profiles and normative patterns of competence across several domains of the "average" Greek students in childhood and adolescence based on the perceptions of teachers, peers and self.
2. Examination of the types, prevalence and developmental trends of psychosocial and academic problems in the general school population.
3. Examination of the association between psychosocial problems and academic performance.
4. Examination of the effects of several independent variables on children's functioning in school.

The sample consisted of two age groups: elementary school pupils (10- to 12-year-old, N=1041) and secondary school students (13- to 16-year-old, N=862). The students attended public schools in various towns and cities in Greece. The instruments of the study included a teacher rating, a peer nomination assessment, and a self rating. Achievement data were also obtained. Detailed descriptions and discussion of the findings and comparisons with published results from relevant studies in different countries are included in various papers (Hatzichristou & Hopf, 1991, 1992a, 1992c, 1996; Hopf & Hatzichristou, 1994, 1999) and are beyond the scope of this chapter. The types, prevalence and developmental trends of psychosocial and academic problems in the student population were identified. A high percentage of Greek students experience problems in various domains of competence in school underlining the urgent need to develop prevention and intervention programs to address the academic and mental health needs of Greek youth.

The importance of distinctive educational and cultural factors affecting students' adjustment in the Greek schools, based on empirically derived data, identified specific needs in the general school population and constituted a solid knowledge base for school-based consultative services in the Greek educational setting. For example, strong gender-related differences were found in every aspect of children's functioning in school reflecting the greater gender-role differentiation of the Greek society as compared to other countries.

School achievement also was clearly related to almost every domain of children's competence, reflecting the strong emphasis of the Greek parents on the education of their children and the intense pressure for academic success in the Greek society. The most maladaptive children, based on the combination of the perceptions of all raters, had substantially lower achievement in all subjects underscoring the importance of prevention and early intervention, and of finding ways to promote social and emotional growth of children as well.

Evolution Period

The developing course of the model led to the enrichment of phase I including new research domains with additional goals. The first research domain aimed at exploring the perceptions and causal attributions regarding academic achievement and students' psychosocial adjustment based on teacher, parent, and student questionnaires. The other research domain aimed at exploring; aspects of interpersonal relationships and communication between teachers and students; classroom environment / school climate aspects; support systems in the school context and the family; and, school-family partnership and collaboration. Furthermore, the examination of various dimensions of students' school-based competence was extended.

These data resulted in the identification of teachers', parents', and students' personal theories of several aspects of children's school and psychosocial adjustment. Furthermore, the data facilitated a better understanding of the presentations and representations of various problems during the consultation process, which are key factors in promoting conceptual change of both the consultant and the consultee.

Phase II: Profiles of at Risk Groups of Students With Unmet Needs

Development Period

A synthetic model for defining risk was adopted including risk factors at macro-, family-, and individual-levels (Resnick & Burt, 1996). Following the first phase, at risk groups of students in the sample were identified based on psychosocial and academic factors (peer sociometric status groups and students with learning difficulties), and sociodemographic factors (remigration and parental status). The psychosocial and academic patterns of competence of the following groups of students were examined:

1. *Peer sociometric status groups* (popular, rejected, neglected, controversial, average).
2. *Students with learning difficulties.*
3. *Remigrant students.*
4. *Children from divorced families.*

The profiles of these groups of students with unmet special needs were explored in comparison to all their classmates using teacher, peer, and self ratings.

Detailed descriptions and discussion of these findings are included in various papers (Hatzichristou, 1993; Hatzichristou & Hopf, 1992b, 1993; Hopf & Hatzichristou, 1994). Children with identified needs (learning problems, children from divorced families, rejected elementary school students) were clearly overrepresented in the most maladaptive group of children based on the combination of the perceptions of all raters. Specific difficulties in several domains of academic and psychosocial competence of the various at-risk groups of students in the Greek schools provided the basis for understanding their functioning and needs, and for effective consultation and intervention programs.

Evolution Period

The research domains were extended including two basic projects: school and psychosocial adjustment of children of divorced families begun by exploring teachers,' parents,' and children's attitudes about divorce and perceptions of divorced-family children's adjustment (Hatzichristou, Gari, Milonas, Giavrimis, Karitsa, & Tsiovolou, in press); and, school adjustment of migrant students (coming from Albania and the former Soviet Union countries; Hatzichristou, Gari, Milonas, Georgouleas, Likitsakou, Mpafiti, Vaitsi, Bakopoulou, 2001a). Additionally, special issues were addressed and explored such as children's rights, health issues at school and sex education programs.

Phase III: School- and Community-Based Needs Assessment

Development Period

The initial development period of the third phase of the model included the exploration of the particular needs of specific school districts in a community. Community information was collected through multiple sources and using various techniques (survey, interviews, observations) in order to identify specific characteristics and needs. The multicomponent and multiperspective needs assessment procedure of this phase was not only important for gathering information in order to determine the specific services that are likely to be most useful in the particular community and its schools, but also for establishing cooperation and involvement of members of the organizations (schools, children's institutions, community services) in the change process (Curtis & Metz,1986).

A teacher questionnaire was designed to identify teachers' perceptions of the most important student-related problems in their schools and community. The sample consisted of 142 elementary school teachers. Findings indicated the types of problems that most concerned teachers and presented difficulties in terms of management (Hatzichristou, Vaitsi, Dimitropoulou, & Falki, 2000). Teachers lacked precision in their identification of student problems, and they conceptualized a few general rather than several specific alternative interventions. Results indicated that academic achievement remained the basic and most important concern of Greek teachers. Problems in the processes involved in the understanding and/or in using language, written or spoken, constituted the most frequently reported problems and the types of problems that concerned teachers most and were considered resistant to solutions. Furthermore, Greek teachers regarded the family environment as strongly related to most of the students' problems.

Teachers' causal attributions for most types of problems included causes that are less subject to volitional influence or control and implied less teacher personal efficacy. Perceptions about control influence behavior toward others through the mediating influences of responsibility. When a student's need state is perceived as uncontrollable, the professional is not held responsible and the absence of a sense of responsibility tends to elicit pity and prosocial actions. Furthermore, the lack of perceived personal responsibility by teachers seems to be consistent with self-serving bias notions, but also may exert an influence on their intention to change teaching style and employ alternative intervention strategies.

The exploration of teachers' perceptions and implicit theories of children's problems is important for the efficacy of the consultee-centered consultation process in the next developmental phase of the model and teachers' perceptions exert a critical influence on parental decisions to seek professional help for their disturbed children. Thus, these results have extensive implications for consultee-centered consultation.

Evolution Period

The evolution of the third phase included a needs assessment at a systemic level in schools, institutions and community, where intervention programs take place (Hatzichristou, et al., 2001a; Hatzichristou, et al., 2001b).

A new research domain was included aimed at exploring teachers', students', and parents' perceptions regarding the delivery of psychological services in schools and the role of school psychologists (Hatzichristou, Dimitropoulou, Konstantinou, & Lampropoulou, 2002). Teacher, student, and parent questionnaires were used. Data were collected in the following schools: schools without school psychological services; schools having school-linked psychological services; and, schools having school-based psychological services. All participants expressed an intense need for an increase in the delivery of psychological services and the importance of the active presence of a school psychologist was further stressed.

Phase IV: Service Delivery Model

The empirically-based data of the previous three phases have been integrated into a comprehensive prevention-consultation approach. To overcome the lack of school psychological services in the Greek schools, this phase of the model included a proposal and the eventual foundation of University Centers, the *Center for School and Family Consultation and Research* in the Department of Education at the University of Thessaly (when the author was a faculty member at the University of Thessaly) and later the foundation of the *Center for Research and Practice of School Psychology* in the Department of Psychology at the University of Athens (where the author is a faculty member at the University of Athens). The foundation of the Center was necessary not only for the development of the proposed model, but also for the coordination of services. Based on the findings of the first three phases, priorities for intervention were determined and prevention programs were developed.

During all these years, several primary and secondary prevention programs have been developed and implemented as a result of our effort to apply a model that will link theory, research, and practice and that will cover the particular needs of the Greek educational system (Figure 8.2). The members of the teams, who cooperated and participated in the implementation of the programs mostly on a volunteer basis, were the author (being the Scientific Director of the Center), school psychologists, graduate and undergraduate students, teachers, and other volunteers. The graduate students were responsible for the coordination of the groups. During the implementation of the programs, the participants were trained through seminars and courses and were supervised by the members of the scientific team.

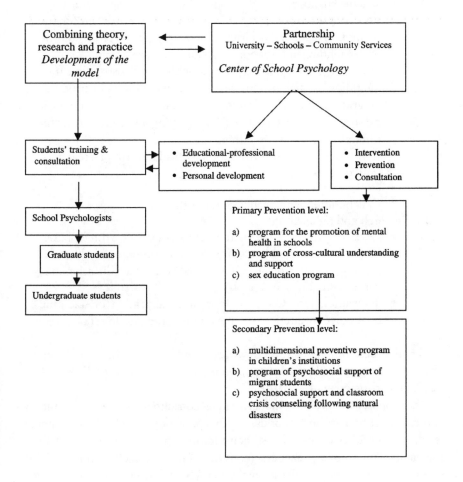

FIG. 8.2.   Integrative Framework: Combination of Theory, Research, and Practice.

The goals of the Center are based on three interrelated axes:

1. Education, preservice and in-service training (students, school psychologists, teachers, parents)
    - New courses at the University (consultee-centered consultation, intervention programs in the schools)
    - Seminars with specific topics (i.e., promotion of mental health in schools, prevention programs, support of children of divorced families)
2. University–Schools–Community Services partnership and collaboration
    - School-linked services: development of partnership models with schools, institutions and school-based psychological services
    - Primary prevention programs in schools (i.e., program for the promotion of mental health in schools, program of cross-cultural understanding and support, sex education programs)
    - Secondary prevention programs in schools and institutions (i.e., multidimensional preventive program in children's institutions, program of psychosocial support of migrant students, psychological support and classroom crisis counseling following natural disasters—earthquake in Athens area)
    - Consultee-centered consultation with administrators, teachers, staff, parents
    - Crisis intervention
    - Collaboration with agencies and institutions
3. Research and publications
    - Research projects have been described in the first three phases
    - Preparation and publication of education-training booklets regarding several issues (i.e., emotional and social education prevention programs in schools)
    - Translation into Greek, editing and publication of scientific books on consultation and prevention programs in schools

Detailed descriptions of several programs are included in various papers (Hatzichristou, 2000; Hatzichristou, Vaitsi, Dimitropoulou, & Falki, 1999, 2000; Hatzichristou et al., 2001a).

The proposed intervention model includes consultee-centered consultation approaches at primary and secondary school prevention levels. At the primary level, the consultee-centered case consultation approach (Caplan, 1970) is used aimed at improving teachers' (consultees) professional functioning. This consultation phase targets all the teachers of school districts in the context of a series of workshops and presentations and have the following goals:

1. To increase teachers' knowledge of various factors relevant to children school functioning in the Greek educational and cultural context and the nature and function of home-school-community linkages.
2. To broaden teachers' understanding of the multiplicity of factors influencing children at various ages and their relation to the development, maintenance and correction of children's problems.
3. To increase teachers' knowledge about the utility of school research and systematic analyses in order to ameliorate students' difficulties.

At the same time, graduate school psychology students attend similar presentations in the context of school psychology and consultation courses at the University and seminars at the Center and are trained to conduct classroom-based primary prevention programs in the schools (i.e., increasing effective communication, enhancing self-esteem, building inner control, reducing stress, etc). This way the University students help to establish cooperation and especially to maintain linkages between the schools and the University.

At the secondary level, consultation services are being offered to groups of teachers, who have identified common difficulties with specific problems exhibited by some of their students. The primary goal of the consultation is to improve teachers' capacity to deal effectively with these students' difficulties. The consultation services can also include discussion about students who need to be referred to community mental health agencies.

The multidimensional preventive program is an example of the model applied at a secondary prevention level. The specific program was developed for and implemented in three children's institutions (Hatzichristou et al., 1999, 2000). The development of the program was based on the results of a systemic needs assessment in the institutions, which included environmental parameters and children's academic and psychosocial competence. The results highlighted children's poor academic performance and various interpersonal difficulties. Differences among the three institutions were identified and were taken into consideration as the program was implemented in each institution. The Intervention–Consultation phase included three interrelated domains: an academic domain, a psychosocial domain, and creative activities.

A synthetic approach of consultee-centered consultation in children's institutions was used : a combination of consultee-centered administrative consultation, program-centered administrative consultation and consultee-centered case consultation (Caplan, 1970; Caplan & Caplan, 1993; Hatzichristou, 2003). The *consultee-centered administrative consultation* required an active role on the part of the consultant in understanding the consultees–staff members of the institutions and the organization–institutions, in identifying organizational problems, in looking for barriers to effective consultee functioning at many different levels, and building relationships and approaching consultees to discuss issues and problems. The *program-centered administrative consultation* involved the assessment, development, and implementation of the intervention program in the institutions and was aimed at improving children's academic and psychosocial problems. University teams implemented the program in collaboration with staff members of the institutions. The *consultee-centered case consultation* offered the consultee's (mainly graduate and undergraduate students) opportunities to discuss professional functioning concerning several dimensions of program development and implementation: goal identification, assessment, design of material, construction of achievement tests, implementation of the program, and dealing with difficulties.

More specifically, a multilevel approach to professional development of future school psychologists included the following stages of skill acquisition in consultation process.

- *Education–teaching* regarding consultation theory and practice at the context of new courses at the University.
- *Training* of graduate students as consultants and undergraduate students as consultees (pre-service training). The students were trained by the Scientific Director through seminars at the Center. Group consultation and consultee-centered consultation processes were used.
- *Research* regarding needs assessment at a system-level-institution and assessment-identification of children's academic and psychosocial problems.
- *Supervision* of graduate students as "consultants" and undergraduate students as "consultees."
- *Modeling-* facilitating skill learning in consultation promoted by the consultees' identification with the consultant. A strong, positive relationship made it more likely that the consultant will serve as a role model to consultants. Due to lack of other professionals and colleagures being knowledgeable and trained in consultation theory and practice, there was a necessity to combine all these aspects as interrelated stages of the consultation process.

Our initial experience shows that indirect services and consultee-centered school-based consultation could be the basic model for future school psychological services in the Greek educational system. It is assumed that the core elements of school-based consultative services (Gutkin & Curtis, 1990) would facilitate the initial stage of cooperation and collaboration between teachers and psychologists in the Greek schools. The research findings of the three phases of the model will facilitate further the understanding of the consultees' presentation and representation of problems and theories by the consultants, which in turn will promote conceptual change. Also, it should be pointed out that the training in consultee-centered school-based consultation and indirect service delivery should be included in the core program of university psychology and education departments. It is indicative that in Greek there was only one common word for translating the English words "counseling" and "consultation." A new term for consultation has been already proposed in Greek, namely, διαλεκτικη συμβουλευτικη (Hatzichristou, 2003).

The framework incorporates a parallel conceptualization of evolving phases at different system levels. A number of advantages attend the use of this framework as a basis for a gradual change process in the Greek schools. First, much emphasis has been placed on the combination of theory, research and practice at the context of a partnership-based framework. This further reflects the long-standing efforts in other countries for the application of the scientist-practitioner model in school psychology (Lambert, 1993). Second, information is collected across methods, sources, and settings using large sample designs. Empirically derived data provided a comprehensive picture of the patterns of school adjustment of Greek students and determined target need areas of a specifically high risk population. Third, cultural factors and community idiosyncratic characteristics have been explored providing the basis for an ideal assessment x treatment model. It is our strong conviction that systematic research is essential for effective practice.

This comprehensive and integrated approach to enhance mental health in children and to address barriers to learning and psychosocial functioning of students in the Greek schools further underscores an emerging possible role of the school psychologist promoting organizational change at a system level in Greece. Similarly, the role of school psychologist as influential in school reform efforts across the United States and as critical in facilitating organizational change has been pointed out (Curtis & Stollar, 1996; Short & Talley, 1997). Consultative services in the Greek schools have been proposed as a pragmatic and effective alternative to direct psychological services. The proposed school-based consultation model has complexity and flexibility and requires the cooperation between university, schools, and community. The challenge neces-

sitates training of investigators, professionals, and university students to carry
out the work required in the community context.

REFERENCES

Brown, D., Pryzwansky, W., & Schulte, A. (2001). *Psychological consultation. Introduction to theory and practice* (5th ed.). Boston: Allyn & Bacon.

Caplan, G. (1970). *The theory and practice of mental health consultation*. New York: Basic Books.

Caplan, G., & Caplan, R. B. (1993). *Mental health consultation and collaboration*. San Francisco: Jossey-Bass.

Coie, J. D., & Dodge, K. A. (1988). Multiple sources of data on social behavior and social status in the school: A cross-age comparison. *Child Development, 59*, 815–829.

Costello, E. J. (1989). Development in child psychiatric epidemiology. *Journal of the American Academy of Child and Adolescent Psychiatry, 28*, 836–841.

Curtis, M. J. & Metz, L. (1986). System level intervention in a school for handicapped children. *School Psychology Review, 63*, 510–518.

Curtis, M. J., & Stollar, S. A. (1996). Applying principles and practices of organizational change to school reform. *School Psychology Review, 25*, 409–417.

Gutkin, T. B., & Curtis, M. J. (1990). School-based consultation: Theory, techniques, and research. In T. B. Gutkin & C. R. Reynolds (Eds), *The handbook of school psychology* (pp. 577–611). New York: John Wiley & Sons.

Hatzichristou, C. (1987). *Classification and differentiation of socially isolated children*. Doctoral dissertation, University of California, Berkeley.

Hatzichristou, C. (1993). Children's adjustment after parental separation: Teacher, peer and self report in a Greek sample: a research note. *Journal of Child Psychology and Psychiatry, 34* (8), 1469–1478.

Hatzichristou, C. (1998). Alternative school psychological services: Development of a data-based model in the Greek schools. *School Psychology Review, 27* (2), 246–259.

Hatzichristou, C. (2000). Programs of psychosocial support of students. The Greek experience. In A. Kalantzi & E. Bezevegis (Eds.), *Mental health issues regarding children and adolescents*, [Themata psihikis igeias paidion kai efivon] (pp. 35–56). Athens: Ellinika Grammata.

Hatzichristou, C. (2002). A conceptual framework of the evolution of school psychology: Transnational considerations of common phases and future perspectives. *School Psychology International, 23* (3), 266–282.

Hatzichristou, C. (2003). Consultation in the school context. *Psychology* (Psychologia), 10 (2–3), 343–361.

Hatzichristou, C., Dimitropoulou, P., Konstantinou, E., & Lampropoulou, A. (2002). School psychological services in the Greek schools: Teachers', students' and parents' perceptions. *Symposium at 25th Annual International School Psychology Colloquium*, Nyborg-Denmark, July 24th-30th.

Hatzichristou, C., Gari, A., Milonas, K., Georgouleas, G., Likitsakou, N., Mpafiti, T., Vaitsi, A., & Bakopoulou, A., (2001a). Immigrant and remigrant students adaptation: I. Application of an intervention program. II. Evaluation of the program. *Nea Paideia, 99*, 13–36.

Hatzichristou, C., Gari, A., Milonas, K., Giavrimis, P., Karitsa, V., & Tsiovolou, A. (in press). Perceptions regarding divorce in the school community: Linking theory and practice. *Proceedings of the 8th Greek Conference of Psychological Research*. Demokretio University of Thrace, Alexandroupoli.

Hatzichristou, C., & Hopf, D. (1991). Behavior problems and school performance of primary and secondary school students based on teachers' evaluation. *Educational Review* (Paedagogiki Epitheorisi), *14–15*, 107–143.

Hatzichristou, C., & Hopf, D. (1992a). Behavior patterns of elementary and secondary school students based on peer evaluation. *Educational Review* [Paedagogiki Epitheorisi], *16*, 141–164.

Hatzichristou, C., & Hopf, D. (1992b). School performance and adjustment of the Greek remigrant students in the schools of their home country. *Applied Psycholinguistics, 13*(3), 279–294.

Hatzichristou, C., & Hopf, D. (1992c). Dimensions of self-concept of primary and secondary school students. *Educational Review* [Paedagogiki Epitheorisi], *17*, 253–277.

Hatzichristou, C., & Hopf, D. (1993). Students with learning disabilities. Academic and psychosocial aspects of adaptation. *School Psychology International, 14*(1), 43–56.

Hatzichristou, C., & Hopf, D. (1996). A multiperspective comparison of peer sociometric status groups in childhood and adolescence. *Child Development, 67*, 1085–1102.

Hatzichristou, C., Karadimas, E., Giavrimis, P., Dimitropoulou, P., & Vaitsi, A., (2001b). Linking assessment and intervention at a systemic level: The example of cooperation of the University Center of School Psychology with a children's Institution of Athens. *Counseling and Guidance Review*, [Epitheorisi Simvouleftikis kai Prosanatolismou], *58–59*, 193–212.

Hatzichristou, C., Vaitsi, A, Dimitropoulou, P., & Falki, B. (1999). An intervention program of multidimensional counseling support: The experience of the Center of School and Family Consultation and Research of the University of Thessaly. *Scientific Annual Journal "Alexandros Delmouzos" of the School of Human Sciences, University of Thessaly,* [Epistimoniki Epetirida «Alexandros Delmouzos»], (pp. 45–64). Volos: University of Thessaly.

Hatzichristou, C., Vaitsi, A., Dimitropoulou, P., & Falki, B. (2000). Learning difficulties and adaptation problems of children in school: Teachers' perceptions. *Child and Adolescent. Mental Health and Psychopathology* [Paidi kai Efivos. Psihiki Ygeia kai Psychopathologia], *2*(1), 32–47.

Henning-Stout, M., & Meyers, J. (2000). Consultation and human diversity: First things first. *School Psychology Review, 29*(3), 419–425.

Hopf, D., & Hatzichristou, C. (1994). Die Rückkehr in die Heimat: Zur schulischen und sozialpsychologischen Situation der griechischer Schüller nach der Remigration. [The return home: The educational and socio-psychological situation of Greek pupils after remigration] *Zeitschrift für Pädagogik, 40*(1), 147–170.

Hopf, D., & Hatzichristou, C. (1999). Teacher gender-related influences in Greek schools. *British Journal of Educational Psychology, 69*, 1–18.

Hughes, J. N. (1979). Consistency of administrators' and psychologists' actual and ideal perceptions of school psychologists' activities. *Psychology in the Schools, 16*, 234–239.

Ingraham, C. (2000). Consultation through a multicultural lens: Multicultural and cross-cultural consultation in schools. *School Psychology Review, 29*(3), 320–343.

Kohn, M. (1977). *Social competence, symptoms and underachievement in childhood: A longitudinal perspective*. Washington, DC: Winston & Sons.

Koyanagi, C. (1995). Systems change: Moving beyond reports. In L. Bickman, & J. Rog (Eds.), *Children's mental health services. Research, policy, and evaluation* (pp. 42–63). Thousand Oaks, CA: Sage.

Kratochwill, T. R., Elliott, S. N., & Busse, R. T. (1995). *Behavior consultation*. Rockville, MD: Aspen.

Lambert, N. M. (1993). Historical perspective on school psychology as a scientist-practitioner specialization in school psychology. *Journal of School Psychology, 31*(1), 163–194.

Lambert, N. M., Sandoval, J., & Corder, R. (1975). Teacher perceptions of school-based consultants. *Professional Psychology*, 6, 204–216.

Labram, A. (1993). The educational psychologist as consultant. In S. Wolfendale, T. Bryans, M. Fox, A. Labram & A. Sigston (Eds.), *The profession and practice of educational psychology* (pp. 71–85). London.

Mason, E. J., Mietzel, G., & Hoffler, K. W. (1989). Research in school psychology in the Federal Republic of Germany. *Professional School Psychology*, 4(3), 219–226.

Medway, F. J., & Updyke, J. F. (1985). Meta-analysis of consultation outcome studies. *American Journal of Community Psychology*, 13, 489–505.

Nastasi, B., Varjas, K., Bernstein, R., & Jayasena, A. (2000). Conducting participatory culture-specific consultation: A global perspective on multicultural consultation. *School Psychology Review*, 29(3), 401–413.

Oakland, T., & Saigh, P. A. (1989). Psychology in the schools: An introduction to international perspectives. In P. A. Saigh & T. Oakland (Eds.), *International perspectives on psychology in the schools* (pp. 1–22). Hillsdale, NJ: Lawrence Erlbaum Associates.

Pfeiffer, S. I., & Reddy, L. A. (1998). School-based mental health programs in the United States: Present status and a blueprint for the future. *School Psychology Review*, 27(1), 84–96.

Reschly, D. J. & Wilson, M. S. (1995). School psychology practitioners and faculty: 1986 to 1991-92 trends in demographics roles, satisfaction and system reform. *School Psychology Review*, 24, 62–80.

Resnick, G., & Burt, M. (1996). Youth at risk: Definitions and implications for services delivery. *American Journal of Orthopsychiatry*, 66(2), 172–188.

Rog, D. J. (1995). The status of children's mental health services: An overview. In L. Bickman & J. Rog (Eds.), *Children's mental health services. Research, policy, and evaluation* (pp. 3–18). Thousand Oaks, CA: Sage.

Short, R. J. & Talley, R. C. (1997). Rethinking psychology and the schools: Implications of recent national policy. *American Psychologist*, 52(3), 234–240.

Wardle, C. J. (1991). Twentieth-century influences on the development in Britain of services for child and adolescent psychiatry. *British Journal of Psychiatry*, 159, 53–68.

9

Multicultural Consultee-Centered Consultation: Supporting Consultees in the Development of Cultural Competence

Colette L. Ingraham

When consultation is viewed through a multicultural lens (Ingraham, 2000), opportunities for conceptual change abound. Multicultural consultee-centered consultation provides an array of possibilities for supporting consultees in the development of cultural competence and new understandings about problem situations (Ingraham, 2000, 2001, 2002). Cross-cultural (Ingraham 1995) and multicultural perspectives (Ingraham, 2000) have extended Caplan and Caplan's (1993) work to address consultee needs for knowledge, skill, confidence, and perspective (Ingraham, 2002).

Multicultural consultation has emerged as a new model for consultation where cultural issues are brought to the forefront and adjustments in traditional consultation processes are made (Ingraham, 2000; Ingraham & Tarver Behring, 1998a, 1998b; Tarver Behring & Ingraham, 1998; Tarver Behring et al., 1997). Multicultural consultation is well suited to promote conceptual change in consultees and is ideal for the co-construction (e.g., Sandoval, 2001) of new understandings through consultation (Ingraham, 2001, 2002).

BLENDING CONSULTEE-CENTERED CONSULTATION WITH CROSS-CULTURAL ISSUES IN CONSUL TATION: EMERGENCE OF THE MULTICULTURAL CONSULTATION MODEL

Multicultural consultation is defined as, "a culturally sensitive, indirect service in which the consultant adjusts the consultation services to address the needs and cultural values of either the consultee or the client, or both." (Tarver Behring & Ingraham, 1998, p. 58). Consultants must be carefully attuned to the needs of the consultee and client, often finding ways to reframe the consultee's understanding of the problem situation in ways that support the consultee's development of increased knowledge, skill, confidence and/or perspective[1] (Ingraham, 2000). Multicultural consultation (Ingraham, 2000) encompasses situations where members of the consultation triad (consultant, consultee/teacher and client/student) share the same culture (e.g., Tarver Behring & Gelinas, 1996), as well as cross-cultural diversity among members of the consultation triad (Ingraham, 1995, 2000). Multicultural consultation draws from work in multicultural counseling (e.g., Ponterotto & Pedersen, 1993; Sue, Ivey, & Pedersen, 1996; Sue & Sue, 1990) and is grounded in theories of mental health consultation (e.g., Caplan & Caplan, 1993), school-based consultation (e.g., Conoley & Conoley, 1992; Gutkin & Curtis, 1982), multicultural collaboration (Harris, 1996), and cross-cultural consultation (Brown, 1997; Duncan, 1995; Gibbs, 1985; Ingraham, 1995, 2000).

Analysis of authentic case studies in which members of the consultation triad represent differing cultures has revealed a variety of consultation issues and processes that emerge in culturally diverse settings (Ingraham, 2000, 2002; Ingraham & Tarver Behring, 1998a, 1998b; Tarver Behring, Cabello, Kushida, & Murguia, 2000). The cross-cultural consultation triad can consist of four combinations of cultural similarity and difference (Ingraham, 1995, 2000). Each of the four combinations can elicit different issues that can interfere with effective problem-solving efforts, and I (Ingraham, 1995, 2000) identified specific strategies the consultant can use to rebuild the effectiveness of the teacher–student relationship. For example, the consultant can model for the teacher how to learn about the student's culture, reflect on the potential for culturally-loaded perceptions clouding judgment (need for perspective), and empathize or express feelings often associated with cross-cul-

---

[1]Ingraham (2002) suggested changing the term from Caplan & Caplan's (1993) *professional objectivity* to *perspective* to signify the notion that no individual is truly objective, consistent with a more socially constructed paradigm.

tural work as a means to develop conceptualization and consultee confidence. When teacher and student are of the same culture, the teacher may tend to overidentify with the student, making it difficult to see the unique circumstances of the student's situation. Conversely, the teacher may overcompensate for the apparent cultural similarities by being extra hard on the student in an attempt to dispel accusations of cultural favoritism. (See Ingraham, 2000 for a more thorough discussion of the techniques for the consultant to use with each of these triad variations.)

In addition to consultee needs for development of knowledge and skill in working with culturally diverse students and their families, I proposed that multicultural consultation often involves some specific types of threats to objectivity and confidence (Ingraham, 1995, 2000). I described resulting processes such as intervention paralysis, cultural blunders, walking on eggshells, and color blindness that can lead to ineffective problem solving on the part of the consultee. *Intervention paralysis* is when the consultee is aware of cultural differences but is afraid to intervene for fear of being culturally inappropriate. A *cultural blunder* is when a person thinks or acts in a way that is culturally insensitive or even offensive to the other person. *Walking on eggshells*, the feeling that one must be very careful not to say or do anything that might be perceived as a cultural blunder, racist or inappropriate, often leads to hypersensitivity, defensiveness, and/or lack of confidence. *Color blindness* occurs when a person is trying to "treat all people the same" and not attend to cultural diversity or race, often leading to a denial of cultural identity and heritage. I believe (Ingraham, 2000) that these processes are particularly common in the early stages of development of cultural competence among consultees. Consultants can use multicultural consultee-centered consultation (Ingraham, 1995, 2000, 2001) to support consultees in regaining their problem-solving capacity and expanding their understanding of cultural issues at play within diverse classrooms, often leading to shifts or turnings (Hylander, 2001; Ingraham, 2002) in their conceptualization of problems.

SUMMARY OF THE MULTICULTURAL CONSULTATION MODEL

In brief, the multicultural consultation approach (Ingraham, 2000, 2002; Ingraham & Tarver Behring, 1998a, 1998b, 1999; Tarver Behring & Ingraham, 1998) considers the potential influence of culture on the entire consultation process and the individuals involved in the consultation triad. Culture is broadly perceived to include an organized set of thoughts, beliefs, and norms for interaction and communication, all of which may influence thoughts, behaviors, and perceptions. I stress that it is important for the consultant to *explore cultural issues, as well as individual differences*, so as not to overgeneralize about the cultural underpinnings at play, and to remain cognizant that culture is far more complex than the color of one's skin or the language one speaks (Ingraham, 2000). It is *imperative* that the consultant vigilantly works to examine his or her own stereotypes and biases to reduce interpretations or hypotheses developed out of the consultant's own lack of knowledge, perspective, or professional objectivity. The consultant works to understand the influences of culture on the thoughts, expectations, and behaviors for each party in the consultation process (e.g., the consultation triad with consultant, consultee, and client; or the consultation team in terms of the culture of the school, community, client's family, etc.) and adjusts the consultation process to develop rapport with the consultee(s) and understanding of the client(s).

Table 9.1[2] shows the five areas of knowledge and skill I identified (Ingraham, 2000) as important in successful multicultural consultation:

1. Consultant development in multicultural consultation (understanding of own culture, other cultures, cross-cultural consultation skills).
2. Understanding of consultee needs for development (knowledge, skill, self-confidence, and professional objectivity).
3. Cultural variations in consultation triads and consultation approaches typically successful for each.
4. Issues of context and power.
5. Methods to support consultees in increasing their capacity to work with diversity.

Since 1995, Shari Tarver Behring and I have collaborated in the development of the multicultural consultation model and its application within culturally diverse school settings. The model evolved through our work teaching consultation and supervising culturally diverse graduate students and practicing school psychologists and counselors. Our design for developing knowledge and skill in multicultural consultation involves three components, all of which are crucial in developing understanding regarding cultural issues and the application of this knowledge through the consultation process: basic consultation models and processes; excellent foundation in multicultural issues related to human development and psychological service delivery; and specific training in

TABLE 9.1
The Five Components of the Multicultural School Consultation Framework

1. Domains of Conultant Learning and Development
   a. Understanding one's own culture
   b. Understanding the impact of one's own culture on others
   c. Respecting and valuing other cultures
   d. Understanding individual differences within cultural groups and multiple identities
   e. Cross-cultural communication and multicultural consultation approaches for rapport development and maintenance
   f. Understanding cultural saliency and how to build bridges across salient differences
   g. Understanding the cultural context for consultation
   h. Multicultural consultation and interventions appropriate for the consultee(s) and client(s)

2. Domains of Consultee Learning and Development
   a. Knowledge
   b. Skill
   c. Objectivity and decreasing:
      1. Filtering perceptions through stereotypes
      2. Overemphasizing culture
      3. Taking a "color-blind" approach
      4. Fear of being called a racist
   d. Confidence
      1. Preventing intervention paralysis
      2. Avoiding reactive dominance

3. Cultural Variations in the Consultation Constellation
   a. Consultant-consultee similarity
   b. Consultant-client similarity
   c. Consultee-client similarity
   d. Three-way diversity: Tri-cultural consultation

4. Contextual and Power Influences
   a. Cultural similarity within a differing cultural system
   b. Influences by the larger society

(continued on next page)

137

TABLE 9.1 (*continued*)

c. Disruptions in the balance of power

5. Methods for Supporting Consultee and Client Success

   a. Framing the problem and the consultation process

      1. Value multiple perspectives

      2. Create emotional safety and motivational support

      3. Balance affective support with new learning

      4. Build on principles for adult learning

      5. Seek systems interventions to support learning and development

   b. Potential multicultural consultation strategies for working with the consultees

      1. Support cross-cultural learning and motivation

      2. Model bridging and processes for cross-cultural learning

      3. Use consultation methods matched with the consultee's style

      4. Work to build consultee confidence and self-efficacy

      5. Work to increase knowledge, skill, and objectivity

   c. Continue one's professional development and reflective thinking

      1. Continue to learn

      2. Engage in formal and informal continuing professional development

      3. Seek feedback

      4. Seek cultural guides and teachers

multicultural consultation techniques (Ingraham & Tarver Behring, 1998a,1998b; Tarver Behring et al., 1997.)

RECENT INNOVATIONS

Through analysis of authentic case studies in which members of the consultation triad (consultant, consultee, and client) represent differing cultures, we are examining a variety of consultation issues and processes that emerge in culturally diverse settings (Ingraham, 2002; Ingraham & Tarver Behring, 1998a, 1998b, 1999; Tarver Behring et al., 2000). We are finding predictable patterns in the communication styles and relationships formed when the cultures and psychological needs of the consultant, consultee, and client are identified. We have reported cases where consultants have modified traditional consultation approaches to address the specific cultures of the consultees or clients (Ingraham, 2002; Tarver Behring et al., 2000). The emphasis of this work is on developing methods for supporting teachers that lead to openness and an increase in teacher inclusiveness for diverse learners, as opposed to increasing teacher defensiveness or stereotypes. Issues of trust, rapport, cultural knowledge, and communication styles are all significant in the implementation of multicultural consultation. Through this model, teachers develop the necessary knowledge, skill, confidence, and perspective to successfully build learning bridges with students of diverse cultures.

A special issue on "Multicultural and Cross-Cultural Consultation: Cultural Diversity Issues in School Consultation" in the *School Psychology Review* (Ingraham & Meyers, 2000) focused on cultural influences in consultation. The issue featured conceptual articles and empirical studies on the processes of consultation with diverse consultees, clients, and within diverse school and community contexts in different regions of the United States, and overseas in Sri Lanka. In this special issue, I presented (Ingraham, 2000) a comprehensive framework for multicultural school consultation that delineates cross-cultural variations in the consultation constellation and domains for consultant and consultee learning and development. Table 9.1 summarizes the key components of this framework.

I use Multicultural School Consultation (MSC) (Ingraham, 2000) in pre-service and in-service teaching for school support professionals. I explain that by focusing the consultant's attention to some of the multicultural issues discussed in the article, such as communication style, power, empowerment, development of cultural competence, and dimensions of diversity, greater success is achieved in furthering the cultural competence of both consultee and consultant. Consultee-centered multicultural consultation that involves co-constructing a new conceptualization of the problem situation offers a non-threatening, supportive approach that is particularly sensitive to the consultee's affect and evolving cultural knowledge. The two cases in the next section are illustrations of how these notions can be used in multicultural consultation with teachers.

ILLUSTRATION OF THE CONSULTEE-CENTERED FOCUS WITHIN MULTICULTURAL CONSULTATION

Perhaps a useful way to demonstrate the application of multicultural consultation, with specific attention to consultee-centered consultation, is to critique cases between consultant trainees of different cultural backgrounds and teacher consultees. Two cases are summarized here. In each case, the consultant worked to increase the teacher consultee's cultural competence. Case One[3] demonstrates how Lynda Nguyen, a consultant trained in my multicultural school consultation framework (Ingraham, 2000), expanded the cultural competence of a teacher consultee. The consultant used multicultural consultee-centered consultation, including self-disclosure and reframing, to increase teacher knowledge, confidence and perspective. It involves a European-American[4] teacher who asked for consultation regarding a Vietnamese immigrant student in her class. In this case, the consultant and student are of similar ethnic backgrounds but have different levels of acculturation in the United States.

Cases Two[5] illustrates how a European-American consultant worked to increase the cultural competence of a European-American teacher consultee. In this case, the multicultural consultation model was used to provide the teacher with information about the student's culture, build the teacher's skills in developing culturally appropriate intervention strategies, and educate the teacher in a supportive way regarding issues of second language acquisition and cultural adaptation. Case Two demonstrates how trust, established through individual multicultural consultation, can lead to organizational consultation and change. We presented aspects of the second case in Tarver Behring and Ingraham (1998) and Ingraham and Tarver Behring (1998a).

---

[3]Lynda Nguyen was the consultant for this case during her enrollment in my school psychology practicum and consultation courses at SDSU. She is now practicing school psychology in the San Francisco Bay Area. She has given permission to report this case here.

[4]The term *European American* is a self-referent term used in the United States by people of European-American decent who are typically racially white/Caucasian. Their cultural heritage may come from any one or a combination of European cultures and regions. In situations where people delineate the origins of their culture and ethnicity, they may identify the specific countries and/or regions in Europe from which their ancestors came to the United States. The term "European American," instead of the term "White," is preferred by many U.S. multicultural advocates because it refers to the continent of cultural origin, not the color of one's skin. In a similar way, other ethnic groups are referred to their as their continent of origin as a descriptor of "American," such as African American or Asian American. There is much cultural diversity within the group called European American, just as there is much diversity within Asian Americans and other culturally grouped peoples. It is important to learn of the specific cultural identity of a person, when possible, so as not to stereotype and diminish the rich diversity that exists within people given a particular ethnic label. When known, a specific country or culture of origin is preferred to general groupings by continent, such as an American of Irish, Scotch, and English Protestant heritage rather than the term "European American" or "White."

[5]Portions of Case Two are reprinted with permission from Lawrence Erlbaum and Dr. Tarver Behring. Elements of the case were used in a scenario originally published in Tarver Behring, S., & Ingraham, C. L. (1998). Culture as a central component of consultation: A call to the field. *Journal of Educational and Psychological Consultation*, 9(1), 57–72. Parts of this analysis were presented in Ingraham, C. L. & Tarver Behring, S. (1998a, April).

Case One: Conceptual Change Through Increasing Cultural Awareness and Perspective of An European American Teacher Toward A Vietnamese American Student

Point of Entry and Presenting Problem

The student (S) is a 12-year-old boy who just came to the United States from Vietnam. Due to his limited proficiency in English, he was placed in an English immersion class (that functioned as a Spanish-English bilingual class) class in a Southern California school. The teacher, a European American in her mid-40s who has learned Spanish and techniques for supporting Spanish-speakers in learning English, requested consultation with a Vietnamese-American school psychology trainee. The teacher (T) was concerned about the student's adjustment to her class, stating that he rarely sought help, was quiet and shy in class, and hesitated to speak English aloud. T was concerned that S had not yet done much work for a major history project. T wanted the consultant, a 24-year-old bilingual (Vietnamese/English) Vietnamese American whose parents immigrated to the United States a few years before her birth, to work with the student. The consultant (C) used multicultural consultee-centered consultation to address the teacher's concerns.

The Consultation Process and Problem Analysis

Initially, C was concerned that the teacher, "would use me as a crutch in supporting [the student] and therefore would not develop her own skills in working with students of different cultural and linguistic backgrounds." C believed the teacher felt insecure about her ability to relate to the student and lacked knowledge of the student's cultural background. C initially hypothesized that the student's timid and shy behavior in class was culturally based, given that respect in the Vietnamese culture is shown by listening and being quiet, which is sometimes interpreted by Americans as shyness and timidity. Based on her observation in the classroom and additional time in consultation, C revised her initial hypotheses to reflect her awareness that T may need to increase her objectivity/perspective and skills as well. C observed T giving oral directions to students first in Spanish, then in English. T referred to several cultural stereotypes, such as the student's excellent abilities in math, as related to his ethnicity, but seemed unaware of how his interpersonal style might relate to his culture. T, experienced in Spanish-English bilingual education, did not seem to realize that her teaching methods were not meeting the needs of this Vietnamese-American student and possibly the Filipino student in the classroom. The lesson was a historical unit about the covered wagons and explorations of the western United States during the 1800s. The classroom activities built on the students' understanding of the era of cowboys and rustic American history, a history with which this student from Vietnam was very unfamiliar. Because many of T's students were excited about the unit, T did not understand why the referred student was not enthusiastic and participating.

Creating Conceptual Change in the Consultee

C worked first to develop T's empathy for this student's unique cultural and linguistic background, and his experience as an immigrant to a new continent. She worked to *expand the teacher's frame of reference* to better attend to the student's perspective. C hypothesized that by helping T see the student's perspective, C would support the teacher–student relationship and better use instructional methods to meet S's needs. This is where the paradigm shift and conceptual change (Sandoval, 2001) or the turning (Hylander, 2001) occurred. Once the teacher understood the experience through the eyes of a newly immigrated English learner surrounded by unfamiliar languages and cultures, a new representation of the student was possible. Through this intervention, T saw that she needed to use more contextual cues, gestures, visual aides, and nonverbal communication tools to support S's understanding of her instructions. Some of this involved helping T access her previously learned strategies for supporting second language development of students. Additionally, T recognized her need for knowledge of the student's culture, and she obtained resources about Vietnamese culture, such as books, an English–Vietnamese dictionary, thus diminishing her feelings of helplessness and increasing her confidence in her ability to work with S. C provided additional cultural information to help contextualize T's interpretation of S's classroom behaviors. Then C worked to find way to create better inclusion of this student's experiences with the class activities and classmates.

Consultee Interventions With the Student

T used the strategies just described to provide more meaningful instruction for the student. C supported T in implementing some activities that would allow S to share about his culture, thereby furthering the cultural learning of T and other students in the class and giving S an opportunity to share his knowledge, rather than his lack of English skills. The students were eager to learn more about S's experiences and culture.

Outcomes

Instead of falling victim to T's initial quest for the consultant to intervene directly with the student and "fix the problem," C used one downsmanship and multicultural consultee-centered consultation to support T's learning about how to work with S. The teacher greatly expanded her understanding of S's life experiences and culture, other students in the class learned about Vietnamese culture and immigration from a distant continent, and S benefited. In T's comments and C's own observations in the class, S increased his level of interaction and participation in class activities, increased his social interactions with peers, and was more comfortable answering questions in English, but not usually in front of the class. He remained "timid" and rarely sought help, but overall, T reported that S improved. S's peers were extremely excited to hear the stories of Vietnamese folklore and were more accepting of S and his culture. C learned that by helping the consultee explore the situation from the perspective of the client, much conceptual change could occur.

Analysis of Case One: Building Consultee Perspective, Confidence, and Knowledge

When C elected to work towards *increasing T's capacity to relate to S*, rather than using her expertise and cultural understanding to intervene directly herself, positive outcomes resulted for the teacher, student, peers, and consultant. Both consultant and consultee reported that they *increased their knowledge, skills, and confidence* through working on this case. The consultant's use of *empathy* helped set a nonjudgmental tone with comments such as, "It must be difficult for you to be in a situation where you are so willing to support this student but don't know how to communicate with him." The consultant used *onedownsmanship* and *self-disclosure* of her own experience being Vietnamese American to help see the situation from the child's perspective without threatening T's feelings of competence. C shared with T how quiet and uncomfortable she herself was as a child when she was the only Vietnamese-American child in a class. She shared with the teacher her hesitance to speak out in a group, even now as an adult. The consultant also reflected comments such as, "I can see how your bilingual skills in Spanish are much more useful, considering the population at this school [many Spanish speakers.] Your bilingual skills and awareness will help with this case too." The empathy, self-disclosure, onedownsmanship, and hypothesizing about what the student might be feeling *shifted the attention* from the teacher's feelings of helplessness and cultural incompetence toward increased empathy for the student and a focus on his emotional, social, and learning needs. This shift *empow-*

ered T to access her knowledge and skill for working with English learners, restore her feelings of competence, and engage in some new strategies with S. C also worked to modify cultural stereotyping by T. When T stated, "They're just so strong in math," the consultant *reframed this stereotype* that Asians are good at math and said, "Yes, he is strong in math, but unfortunately my math skills are not as well developed," seeking to help T see that S's math strengths were individual strengths rather than a culturally endowed strength. C used *tentative suggestions* to support T in thinking of a way to address S's needs to move ahead in math, along with another student in the class. T mentioned that S worked well with another student who also had advanced math skills. C tentatively shared, "Gosh, since they both have strengths in math, I wonder how … " and the teacher completed her sentence by suggesting that they place both students in the same (English instruction) math class so they could support each other. C's use of empathy, respect, and recognition of the teachers' areas of expertise helped her support the teacher in taking responsibility for the intervention, rather than having C draw on her cultural expertise to engage in direct interventions with the student. This further enhanced T's cultural learning, feelings of efficacy, and competence.

Case Two: Increasing Culturally Specific Classroom Skills (as well as Cultural Awareness) of a European American Teacher with a Latino Student

Point of Entry and Presenting Problem

A European-American elementary teacher (T) approached a European-American consultant for help with a bilingual Mexican-American 10-year-old girl who the teacher reported as experiencing academic difficulty, not interacting with peers, and showing low self-esteem. Early in their work together, C indicated that it was safe for the teacher to discuss knowledge and feelings about the Mexican-American culture. The C encouraged T to also examine T's own cultural background and beliefs and those of the school as a whole to better understand cultural differences and structures, both personal and in the school context. C acted as a role model for cultural inclusiveness by disclosing her changing awareness about her own culture, the Mexican-American culture, and her associated feelings of understanding and acceptance. T, frustrated with the number of children in her class with similar problems as the identified child, said she did not understand "how to reach these kids." T felt that education was not a high priority for parents from this background. This information all contributed to C's understanding of the problem situation and the hypotheses C developed.

The Consultation Process and Problem Analysis

The consultant, who was aware of the cultural differences between the predominately European-American teaching staff and school culture, and the large number of Mexican-American students and community members, hypothesized that this teacher was lacking knowledge and skills for working with a portion of her class. C also hypothesized that T needed greater professional objectivity. C knew that a systemic intervention was most desirable, but decided to build credibility within the school by starting with the individual with whom the teacher was concerned, gradually leading into a more comprehensive systemic intervention with the school.

Developing Culturally Relevant Interventions

C provided the teacher with literature on the Mexican-American culture and language and educational issues and strategies specific to children from this background. She introduced T, with her permission, to a Spanish-speaking interpreter at the school. C knew that the interpreter understood the beliefs and characteristics of many Mexican Americans within this community, including the economic struggles of many families, the high priority placed on work, and the respect for educators and their role in teaching children. T was put in contact with a bilingual language specialist in the school who could screen this child in language and/or academic areas, if needed, and recommend classroom curriculum and instruction appropriate for this and other children in the class. The specialist introduced T to general first grade curricula that included Mexican history and culture, because the composition of T's class was half from Mexican-American backgrounds and half from European-American backgrounds. This inclusive curriculum was intended to make children from the two backgrounds feel equally valued as they were introduced to beginning academic concepts. T and C developed a peer pairing strategy for the girl to work cooperatively in class with another child who was bilingual and doing well academically. Cooperative and culturally mixed groups were created with the entire class for classroom activities and the playground.

The parents were contacted via a note in Spanish and C arranged a home visit because it was difficult for the parents to come to school for a conference due to work and childcare demands. Additionally, the family seemed apprehensive of the school system, and C thought an initial visit to the home might be a way to build trust and to learn of the child's behavior and communication patterns within the home context. The interpreter also came on the home visit. C, in adhering to culturally specific patterns, addressed the parents by their formal names and asked permission for the school to build a program with them to help their child improve academically. The parents agreed and shared more information about their child, family history, and current home situation. The mother was interested in a new program for parents to learn English using computers while at the same time receiving an introduction to the reading curriculum at the school. Opportunities to read together after school and to finish homework with a tutor were provided in the computer room. The father gave his permission for the family to participate and the mother made baby-sitting arrangements in order to work with her daughter twice a week in this program.

Outcomes

The parents came to the school a few weeks later during an early evening meeting with the teacher, interpreter teacher, consultant, and language specialist to continue to build a strong home–school relationship and to review progress. The child was showing more initiative and confidence in class, was developing play groups at recess, and was completing work (that was set at appropriate levels by T, with the help of the consultant, interpreter, and language specialist). The language specialist assisted T in modifications for the identified child; in addition, she helped to locate a bilingual classroom aid and bilingual room parents who were present in the classroom throughout the day to help any child with academic activities.

At the conclusion of the case, T reported a great reduction in her own frustration and stress at work, a better understanding of the Mexican-American culture, and acquisition of skills and resources to involve parents and to work with children in social, academic, and language areas from the Mexican-American background. T was already seeing ways to generalize her learning from this case to her organization of the curriculum and instruction for all students in her class. C began to dialogue with the administration at the organizational level of consultation. The emerging goals were: to promote teacher cultural awareness (of self and others) of the European-American/ Mexican-American school and community, and to educate teachers regarding instructional approaches appropriate for the cultural populations served.

Analysis of Case Two: Increasing Consultee Skills and Knowledge and Expanding the Scope of the Identified Problem

This case illustrates how the consultant used the multicultural consultation model to increase the teacher's *cultural-specific knowledge, skills, and cultural awareness* and to develop a more *systemic intervention* to the problem situation. Instead of just focusing on building the teacher's knowledge about bilingual issues and skills in teaching students for whom English is the second language, C also *expanded the scope of attention* to include the curriculum, instructional methods, and involvement of parents and community. C used the multicultural consultation techniques (Ingraham, 2000) of *self-disclosure* and *modeling for cultural learning* to support the teacher in exploring her own and the school's cultural assumptions, perspectives, and approaches. Also, C *exposed T to resources* within the school that could provide T with curricula and methods more culturally appropriate for the students in her class, thus the *expanding T's repertoire* of curricula, methodologies, and available support systems to help her apply her new learning in her school. The outcomes for the teacher, student, classroom, parents, and school are numerous and profound.

Application of Multicultural Consultation in Diverse Settings

Multicultural consultation has the potential to be useful in situations where the experiences, cultures, expectations, and/or cultures of the parties differ in some ways. I have written (Ingraham, 1995, 2000, 2001) about a variety of dimensions of diversity that could influence the communication and relationships among people. In consultation, the members of the consultation party may hold differing cultural norms, expectations for communication styles, languages, levels of professional experience and/or education, or frames of reference due to differing settings. In these situations, multicultural consultation may allow the consultant to better develop and maintain rapport with the consultee and collaborate with the consultee in developing effective interventions for use with the client(s). When members of different nations, cultures, or perspectives are coming together for consultation, this model may help the consultant to reframe the problem situation as a consultee need for knowledge, skill, perspective, or self-confidence rather than a client deficit.

REFERENCES

Brown, D. (1997). Implications of cultural values for cross-cultural consultation with families. *Journal of Counseling & Development, 76*, 29–35.

Caplan, G., & Caplan, R. B. (1993). *Mental health consultation and collaboration*. San Francisco: Jossey-Bass.

Conoley, J. C., & Conoley, C. W. (1992). *School consultation: Practice and training* (2nd ed.) Boston: Allyn & Bacon.

Duncan, C. F. (1995). Cross-cultural school consultation. In C. Lee (Ed.), *Counseling for diversity* (pp. 129–139). Boston: Allyn & Bacon.

Gibbs, J. T. (1985). Can we continue to be color-blind and class-bound? *The Counseling Psychologist, 13*(3), 426–435.

Gutkin, T. B., & Curtis, M. J. (1982). School-based consultation: Theory and techniques. In C. R. Reynolds & T. B. Gutkin (Eds.), *The handbook of school psychology* (pp. 796–828). New York: John Wiley & Sons.

Harris, K. C. (1996). Collaboration within a multicultural society. *Remedial and Special Education, 17*, 2–10.

Hylander, I. (2001, August). A grounded theory of the conceptual change process in consultee-centered consultation: Successful turnings in representations and blind alleys. In Explorations in process in practice. (Seminar proceedings). San Francisco: 3rd International Seminar on Consultee-Centered Consultation.

Ingraham, C. L. (1995, May). *Cross-cultural applications of consultee centered case consultation.* Paper presented at the invitational international seminar on Consultee-Centered Case Consultation, Stockholm, Sweden.

Ingraham, C. L. (2000). Consultation through a multicultural lens: Multicultural and cross-cultural consultation in schools. *School Psychology Review, 29*(3), 320–343.

Ingraham, C. L. (2001, August). Multicultural consultee-centered consultation: A model for supporting consultees in the development of cultural competence. In *Explorations in process in practice.* (Seminar proceedings.) Third International Seminar on Consultee-Centered Consultation, San Francisco, CA.

Ingraham, C. L. (2002, February). *Multicultural consultation in schools to support teacher and student success.* Invited workshop at the annual meeting of the National Association for School Psychologists, Chicago, IL. Audiotapes available (# WS 16) from NASP and Gaylor MultiMedia, Inc. www.GaylorOnline.com.

Ingraham, C. L., & Meyers, J. (Eds.). (2000). Multicultural and cross-cultural consultation in schools: Cultural diversity issues in school consultation. [Special issue]. *School Psychology Review, 29*(3).

Ingraham, C. L., & Tarver Behring, S. (1998a, April). *Developing teachers' capacity to work effectively with diverse learners.* Paper presented at the annual conference of the American Educational Research Association, San Diego, CA.

Ingraham, C. L., & Tarver Behring, S. (1998b, August). *Multicultural consultation: A model for consultation in culturally diverse schools and communities.* Paper presented at the International Congress of Applied Psychology, San Francisco.

Ingraham, C. L., & Tarver Behring, S. (1999, April). *Multicultural consultation: A blueprint for school consultation in diverse school settings.* Presentation at the annual meeting of the National Association of School Psychologists, Las Vegas, NV.

Ponterotto, J. G., & Pedersen, P. B. (1993). *Preventing prejudice.* Newbury Park, CA: Sage.

Sandoval, J. (2001, August). Conceptual change in consultee-centered consultation. In *Explorations in process in practice.* (Seminar proceedings). San Francisco: 3rd International Seminar on Consultee-Centered Consultation.

Sue, D. W., Ivey, A. E., & Pedersen, P. B. (Eds.). (1996). *A theory of multicultural counseling and therapy.* San Francisco: Brooks/Cole.

Sue, D. W., & Sue, D. (1990). *Counseling the culturally different: Theory and practice.* New York: John Wiley & Sons.

Tarver Behring, S., Cabello, B., Kushida, D., & Murguia, A. (2000). Cultural modifications to current school-based consultation approaches reported by culturally diverse beginning consultants. *School Psychology Review, 29*(3), 354–367.

Tarver Behring, S., & Gelinas, R. T. (1996). School consultation with Asian American children and families. *The California School Psychologist, 1*, 13–20.

Tarver Behring, S., & Ingraham, C. L. (1998). Culture as a central component of consultation: A call to the field. *Journal of Educational and Psychological Consultation, 9*(1), 57–72.

Tarver Behring, S., Ingraham, C. L., Peyton, T., Kushida, Gelinas, R. T., Johnson, & Murguia, A. (1997, April). *Training school psychologists to be culturally competent consultants: Changing the system in diverse school and community settings.* Presentation at the National Association of School Psychologists/California Association of School Psychologists joint conference, Anaheim, CA.

10

Thirty Years of Consulting to Child Welfare

Paul D. Steinhauer[1]

1962–1963: BAPTISM UNDER FIRE

In 1962 b.c.—that is, before Caplan—I finished my residency in child psychiatry and began my first job, as psychiatrist in charge of two inpatient wards of what was then the only children's psychiatric hospital providing long-term in-patient care for severely disturbed children and adolescents in the Province of Ontario. During my training, I had never been exposed to residential treatment, and I approached my new job wondering whether my newfound charges had much in common with the constricted and primarily neurotic children that I had treated during my residency. Nor was I convinced that the play therapy and family therapy that were the major weapons in my therapeutic arsenal during my training would have much relevance to this radically different group of patients who, at times, seemed to have more in common with wild animals than with the only other child psychiatric patients I had ever known. Right from the start I was very much aware that something very different was expected of me. But what?

On my first day on the ward, the head nurse said to me, "Well, I certainly hope that you aren't going to hide in your office the way the last psychiatrist did!" From that I learned that she—who clearly knew much more about this dif-

---

[1]Dr. Paul Steinhauer died sadly after post-operative complications. His wife, Estelle Steinhauer appointed Dr. Steinhauer's colleague, Dr. James Wilkes to review the manuscript.

ferent breed of children than I did—thought I should be out on the ward min-
gling with the children and the staff. So I mingled and I observed. In fact, I
mingled so much that after about a week, the same head nurse said to me, "Why
don't you go back to your office, and start acting like a psychiatrist, instead of
like a child care worker! " Well, I never withdrew from the ward as much as she
would have liked me to, but, by that time, I was already beginning to get oriented to the ward milieu. I had observed that the child care workers, with their
two year diploma from a community college, were far more skilled than I was in
dealing with the children when they were misbehaving or out of control, which
was most of the time. Intuitively, they managed the children quite effectively on
an hour by hour basis, but nothing very therapeutic seemed to be going on. Also,
although they were fine observers of the children's behavior, I learned that they
had little real understanding of what the behavior they were observing meant,
and even less of an idea as to how to intervene in order to bring about change.

Realizing this helped me begin to define our respective roles. The child care
workers would be my eyes and ears, my major sources of information about the
largely nonverbal, behavior-oriented and impulse-ridden children on the ward.
But even after I had defined their role fairly clearly, I still had to struggle to determine my contribution to the therapeutic mix. Again, it was the child care
workers who showed me the way. They gradually let me know that what they
needed from me was help in understanding the meaning of the children's behavior, and help in formulating strategies and developing a repertoire of responses that would lead to lasting and internalized change, to improvement.

We worked well together and enjoyed each other, the child care workers and
I. I greatly respected their expertise in observation and in the hour-to-hour
management of the children. Although I enjoyed being the primary strategist,
intuitively I sensed that the less hierarchical our relationship, the better we
functioned as a team. For that reason, I tried wherever possible to avoid telling
the staff what to do, preferring instead to use Socratic questioning and analogies
to help them understand the underlying themes of a particular child's
psychopathology, to relate the behavior they were observing to those themes,
and to come up with appropriate therapeutic strategies on their own wherever
possible. The more they understood, the keener their observations, the more
puzzles there were for us to work on together. If I learned nothing else that year, I
learned that sometimes a child psychiatrist could achieve far more as part of a
team than when one tried to do everything oneself.

Another thing I learned that year was that almost 80% of the ward's children
were wards of a Children's Aid Society, and that many of them had been
shunted from one foster home to another. It was obvious that most of these children were so mistrustful of close relationships that they strenuously resisted any

attempt to engage them in a therapeutic alliance. They had elevated their ability to distance adults to the level of an art form, and were adept at provoking
staff to reinforce their self-fulfilling prophecy that adults only appeared to be
caring and concerned. Sooner or later, they were sure, the staff would show their
true colors and become just as rejecting and abusive as the adults who had trau-
matized them repeatedly in the past. It gradually became clear to me over the
years that many of these children—some of whom had been through more than
a dozen foster homes and experienced repeated rejections, abuse, and disruption of their attachment relationships—were so lacking in basic trust and so
tightly defended that trying to "treat" them after so many years of maltreatment
was like locking the barn door after the horse was out. This sparked my interest
in the child welfare system. I became intrigued by the task of finding ways to
help Children's Aid Society workers intervene earlier and more effectively, before children coming into care were so irreparably damaged that it was too late
to interrupt the far too common drift into sociopathy.

1963–1979: CONSULTING TO THE CHILDREN'S
AID SOCIETY OF HALTON COUNTY

Three of the children on my ward were served by the same Children's Aid Society, located in a mixed urban and rural area just west of Toronto. This Society
appreciated the importance of continuity of key relationships to children in
care. Children were visited by their caseworker once every other week without
fail. After getting to know the worker, I began to learn something about the
pressures and problems of working in child welfare, and when I expressed an interest, I was invited to become that agency's psychiatric consultant.

I was invited to devote a full half-day each week to help the director up-
grade the knowledge and clinical skills of his staff. We were both convinced
that I had more to offer the agency through a consultee-centered consultation
than with one that remained client-centered. It was about this time, in the
early 1960s, that I had discovered the work of John Bowlby (1960; 1969;
1973) and Gerald Caplan (1963; 1970) who, between them, provided the two
major theoretical structures around which I organized my understanding of
children in care. It was from Bowlby that I first learned about attachment and
loss, and began to understand how much of the behavior of children in care is
distorted by disorders of attachment and their inability to complete the work
of mourning. From Caplan, I learned to refine my skills as a consultant, which
had begun to develop during my work at the hospital, and his recommendations around the handling of theme interference were useful in helping us
draw up a consultation contract.

The contract specified that during the half day of consultation, the first hour and a half of each consultation would be used for a training session for the total staff, usually based on a theme that would be developed over four to ten sessions. This would typically begin with the interviewing of a case, or with a role-playing exercise—for example, one of the staff or I would interview a simulated family chosen to illustrate a particular problem with which the staff was having difficulty—or, occasionally, with either the staff or myself would make a brief initial presentation on a topic about which the staff felt uninformed, followed by a discussion or role-playing exercise designed to help them apply the material to improve their practice skills. The next hour would be spent differently on alternate weeks. One week, I would consult to the home-maker and staff of a group home in which the Society placed the most disturbed and hardest to manage children in its care. On the alternate week, I would consult in turn to the staff of the Society's three departments—family service (i.e., protection, and work with natural families); child care (i.e., service for children in care); and adoption. The last hour, I would also devote to the group home, meeting either just with the staff or with the staff and the children, depending on whether I had already seen the staff earlier that day.

The group home was, to my knowledge, the first staffed group home in Ontario. It was opened in 1964, when the Society's director was forced to decide what to do with four children, several of them with dual diagnoses who, despite having spent up to 3 years in residential care, remained so unmanageable that they could not be cared for in any foster home the agency had to offer. The director was so appalled at their having, among them, managed to act their way out of ten foster homes within a year that he determined to buy a house that would remain constant for them as long as they needed it. We decided that we had the best chance of providing continuity for these children if we adopted a staffed model. That way, even if one staff member were to leave, the children would be left with other familiar figures with whom to form and sustain an affiliation. The group home later expanded to accommodate up to six children, and was able to manage in its milieu the most difficult and disturbed children that the agency had in its care.

Children remained in the group home until it was in their best interests to leave. Most stayed three to five years. Our experience was consistent with Balbernie's—which we only learned of years later—that for a permanently detached child's first 2 years in residential care he or she can only be contained, supported with, possibly, some behavior modification. We found, as Balbernie did, that it is well into the second year, or even later, that some permanently detached children select out one of their caregivers, act as if they consider that person special and behave differently with that person, as they begin to form a tentative attachment. It is only after that has occurred that one can move beyond mere containment and behavior control in order to treat the underlying attachment disorder. (Balbernie 1966; 1974). Thus, it is usually just around the point where most such children are at their most vulnerable that most treatment institutions discharge them. Most respond with renewed distrust and hostility because, once again, they have been ripped away from that "good enough" caregiver whom they have, despite their fears, allowed to become important to their security and well-being (Steinhauer, 1991).

My role in relation to the staff of the group home was rather similar to my previous one in relation to the ward staff the hospital. The staff—and the milieu of the group home—were the primary therapists. My role was that of the staff's consultant. My direct contact with the children, however, advanced our goals in several important ways. It allowed me, through direct interaction with the children, to confirm or extend hypotheses derived from the staff's reports. It also regularly confronted me with how difficult and resistant these children really were. This kept me from underestimating the staff's frustrations and from developing unrealistic expectations—as I might have done had I not had the direct contact. It also showed the staff that I was prepared to roll up my sleeves and get right into the trenches with them, while helping them see that I, too, sometimes failed in my attempts to deal with the children. This helped them feel less inadequate personally during those periods when their own efforts were repeatedly frustrated.

Over the 17 years that I consulted to this one Children's Aid Society, the director and I worked closely together to improve the staff's understanding of what was known in the child welfare, attachment, and treatment literatures, and to apply what they learned to improve the quality of the agency's response to children and families in its care. During the later years of my work with the agency, statistics collected comparing the performance of all Children's Aid Societies across the Province by the (then) Ministry of Social Services revealed that one agency: had the lowest cost (per 100,000 population) of any agency in the province; took many fewer children into care, spent more money on those children whom it did take into care, devoted more casework time to children in care, moved children in care far less than any other agency, spent more on administration (largely because of its spending on the consultee-centered consultation) than any other agency.

Thus, this agency, despite spending more on consultation than any agency in the province, was more efficient (i.e., lowest cost), more effective at prevention (taking fewer children into care) and worked more intensely with children in care (devoting more money and casework time to them; exposing them to far fewer breakdowns and replacements). For these reasons, the agency considered its spending on consultation a good investment.

1979–1982: THE FOSTER CARE RESEARCH PROJECT

In 1979, I became involved in a research project comparing two models of care. The Foster Care Research Project (Steinhauer et al., 1988, 1989) was a 2-year prospective study comparing individual and group models of support for foster parents. It randomly assigned parents either to a control group, which received all the training and services usually provided by the Children's Aid Society of Metropolitan Toronto, or to an experimental group. Foster parents in the experimental group were assigned to one of four foster parent support groups, each of which was jointly led by an experienced foster parent couple—the foster parent co-leaders (FPCLs) and a social worker (SWCL) with special training and experience in group dynamics. Each set of co-leaders was supervised together. The groups provided basic orientation, guidance, and support and contributed to foster parent development so that the group performed most of the duties usually assumed by individual caseworkers. To meet provincial regulations, families in the experimental group also were assigned a caseworker, but he or she visited only once every 3 months—the minimum requirement under provincial law—so that, in effect, the support group took the place of and did the work of the social worker.

As director of the project, I met for 2 hours with the operational team—that is, the co-leaders of the four groups (all FPCLs and SWCLs) and their supervisors, along with the research coordinator and her supervisor. Almost the entire 2 hours was regularly devoted to a consultee-centered consultation for the group leaders and their supervisors. Over the 2½ years that I met with the operational team, we gradually identified nine repeating group processes from the consultee-centered consultation approach that contributed to the foster parent support group members' almost universal perception that their groups were both instructive and supportive. Many of these processes were paralleled within the operational team. These processes included:

Helping Members Feel Understood

Some foster parents felt that only someone who had been a foster parent could truly understand how hard it is to foster such difficult children. The groups helped them share and learn from the experiences of other foster parents, which diminished their feelings of isolation, loneliness, excessive responsibility and alienation.

Cognitive Reframing

Issues which were initially overwhelming were discussed in ways that identified the problem, analyzed it, partialized, and reframed it in a way that made it understandable. This gave the group members a sense of being far less out of control and, at least, a strategy for addressing the problem that made it easier to cope.

Teaching

This occurred when either group members or co-leaders introduced new information that provided fresh ways of understanding and/or responding to previously overwhelming situations.

Ventilation

At most meetings, one or more members were feeling so anxious, angry, guilty, discouraged, or depressed that their capacity for problem solving was paralyzed by the intensity of their feelings. At such times, the opportunity for ventilation in the safety of the group was essential before they could utilize the cognitive reframing or teaching. They would need to go back and confront the situation that had been immobilizing them. It was essential, however, that the leaders—recognizing when tension had been sufficiently reduced—help the group make the shift from ventilation to creative problem solving. Group leaders learned to shift foster parents' feelings and attitudes through reframing their understanding and refocusing them on the needs of the child.

Support

Group members had access to support at a number of different levels. They supported and felt supported by each other, and by the co-leaders of their groups.

Relief (Respite)

There were far fewer formal requests for relief than had been anticipated, and those that occurred were usually informally negotiated among group members.

Sense of Shared Responsibility

Both group members and the co-leaders expressed intense relief at the opportunity to share with their group the stress resulting from feeling responsible for coping with such difficult children, rather than having to deal with it on their own. The same was true of their sense of relief at the opportunity to share periodically their negative feelings with the group.

Increased Sensitivity to the Needs and Feelings of Foster Children

Group members developed greater sensitivity to the needs and feelings of their foster children. Largely through the processes just listed. Increasingly over time, this increased their ability to provide "good enough fostering" for even the most difficult children, by helping them perceive more accurately and respond more appropriately to their needs.

Increased Motivation and Commitment to Fostering

The processes listed previously contributed to higher morale, a greater sense of accomplishment, a persistent striving to remain therapeutic despite multiple frustrations.

In the analysis of the research data, group members unanimously reported that the support groups had increased their skills as foster parents, and they were far more satisfied with the support they had received from their social workers, the Society, and from other foster parents than those in the comparison group who were fostering within the individual service model. Those assigned to the group service model felt much more included and listened to by the Society, were significantly more satisfied with how the agency helped them deal with their feelings around upsetting decisions, and were far more satisfied with their relationship with their social workers—that is, the SWCLs—than were participants in the individual service model (Wilkes, 1979a, 1979b; Johnston, 1989). The increased trust developed within the group service model allowed members to ask their SWCL to form a natural children's group to help their own children deal with the considerable stress of fostering such difficult children. Group model foster parents were far likelier to feel that their fostering was of real benefit for their foster children. As a result, 75% of the group model parents—compared to only 40% of those receiving individual service—planned to continue fostering (Santa-Barbara & Kane, 1982a, 1982b).

In summary, through the operational team, it was possible, in only 2 hours monthly, to contribute indirectly—through the FPCLs, SWCLs and their supervisors who were my consultees—to the further development of the foster parents of 59 foster children, most of whom were seriously disturbed. In over 33 years of practice as a child psychiatrist, no project in which I was involved has been a better use of my time or provided a more effective and efficient service to the community.

1988–PRESENT—THE TORONTO PARENTING CAPACITY ASSESSMENT PROJECT (TPCAP)

In recent years, I have used the product of some of my research activities to provide consultee-centered consultations of a different kind. Between 1988 and

1994, I chaired a research group consisting of staff from two Children's Aid Societies and the local Family Court Clinic in a project to develop Guidelines for Assessing Parenting Capacity (Steinhauer et al., 1995a, 1995b). Rather than focus on the development of the guidelines themselves, I show how I used them to increase judges' and Children's Aid Society workers' understanding of:

1. The developmental needs of children, and how they are affected by decisions in child welfare court;
2. What constitutes a balanced assessment of parenting capacity;
3. Ways of predicting the capacity for significant improvement in response to counseling and/or treatment;
4. How the guidelines promoted permanency planning by protection workers;
5. How the guidelines could be used to help workers testify more effectively and confidently in court.

Guidelines for Assessing Parenting Capacity

An accurate assessment of parenting capacity is the key to permanency planning and to optimal developmental protection for children in care. But with the increasing complexity and difficulty of the cases being seen by child welfare agencies—and with the tendency of the courts to overrate mental health professionals' time-limited assessments of parenting capacity while often failing to appreciate case workers' superior knowledge and understanding of families they have worked with for years—many child protection workers are losing confidence in the credibility of their assessments and are turning to an insufficient supply of child psychiatrists and clinical psychologists to do the parenting assessments that child welfare workers have been doing for years.

The TPCAP Guidelines and the accompanying Manual (Steinhauer et al., 1995) were developed between 1988 and 1993 through a critical review of the child welfare, parent assessment risk assessment scales, and child well-being literature. The guidelines provide a detailed map of the nine critical variables that define the crucial parameters of parenting capacity. Taken together, the scales illuminate the social context of the assessment, characteristics of the child, child/parent interactions, characteristics of the parents, and their respective contributions to both current parenting ability and the capacity for change in response to intervention (see Table 10.1.). Unlike risk scales or child well-being scales the TPCAP Guidelines are *not* quantified. This was a deliberate decision. All such scales, like the guidelines, are only as good as the clinical assessment on which they are based. Workers using such scales are expected to make impor-

TABLE 10.1
Guidelines for Assessing Parenting Capacity

Section A—Focus on the context

    Guideline 1. Current stressors

Section B—Focus on the child

    Guideline 2. Child's developmental progress

Section C—Focus on parent–child inter-relationships

    Guideline 3. Attachment status

    Guideline 4. Observations of current parenting ability

Section D—Focus on the parent

    Guideline 5. Impulse control

    Guideline 6. Parental acceptance of responsibility

    Guideline 7. Behaviors affecting parenting ability and capacity

    Guideline 8. Parent's manner of relating to society

    Guideline 9. Parent's use of clinical interventions

---

tant and sensitive clinical judgments with little or no direction despite wide discrepancies in training and expertise. If one then proceeded to objectify those judgments by quantifying them and basing decisions on preset cut-off scores, one would risk inept clinical judgments leading to faulty decision-making and inappropriate case planning.

Use of the TPCAP Guidelines for Assessing Parenting Capacity to Improve the Quality of Service in Child Welfare in Ontario

Training Seminars for Child Welfare and Children's Mental Health Professionals in the Use of the Guidelines

Over the past 3 years, the authors of the TCPAP guidelines have conducted over 20 full-day workshops in seven of Canada's ten provinces to groups of 60 to 150 workers, consultants, and lawyers from one or a group of neighboring Children's Aid Societies to familiarize the participants with the content and use of the guidelines. In each such workshop, potential uses of the guidelines are explored such as: orienting new workers; improving assessments by experienced workers; guiding decision making and case planning within child welfare; estimating sooner and more accurately the prospect for change in response to intervention; monitoring change in response to intervention; structuring the case record; and organizing clinical and historical data for optimally effective presentation in court. Then, each guideline, in turn, is introduced by a focused discussion of the theoretical and empirical issues related to its design, inclusion, and use.

Participants are then given a clinical vignette to apply to that guideline, after which they compare results and problems in the use or interpretation of the guideline first with each other, and then with the workshop leader. Although, in general, interrater reliability is extremely high, invariably some discrepancies in ratings are found resulting from the participant's lack of familiarity with the concepts related to that guideline, or to problems using the rating system for that particular scale. Other discrepancies arise from different evaluations of the data contained in the vignette. These usually reflect different levels of experience and theoretical sophistication, and are used to demonstrate that, in spite of the apparent objectivity of the guidelines, subjective factors still influence individual ratings. This makes the point that the guidelines are a tool for the worker—who remains the assessor—and that the usefulness of any rating is only as good as the assessment on which it is based.

Use of Guidelines to Inform Judges of Clinical Issues Related to Case Decisions

In Ontario, as no doubt in most other jurisdictions, a proud and fiercely independent judiciary—with wide variations in sensitivity to developmental, clinical, and counter-transference issues—makes the decisions about whether or not to return children to parents, to free them for adoption, to allow visits with natural family, and so on. Most judges are caring, conscientious, and committed, but almost all lack clinical training, and they vary widely in psychological sophistication, although they are making what are essentially complex clinical decisions. Many tend to rely on time-limited assessments by psychologists and psychiatrists far more than they do on the importance of the historical record, which is typically presented by social workers from agencies that have often been following and trying to work with the family for years. But judges frequently complain when experts introduce as evidence the results of psychological tests with whose reliability and limitations they are unfamiliar. Judges frequently express a preference for expert evidence that allows them to review the database, and the theoretical underpinnings of the reasoning process used by expert witnesses to arrive at their conclusions. This allows judges more opportunity to assess the credibility of the expert witness, because it enables them to follow the process that the witness used in arriving at conclusions and recommendations.

The essential process in consultee-centered consultation is that the consultant uses the request for consultation as an opportunity to extend the understanding of the consultee. In such cases, the consultant's specific recommendations for the management of the case are less important to the primary purpose of the consultation than that the consultee recognize the salient facts, the underlying principles, and the thinking process the consultant uses to arrive at the resolution of the work problem. The less consultees, in this case the judges, are expected to take on faith and the more they are able to follow, understand, and incorporate the reasoning process of the consultant as an expert witness, the better the consultation. The testimony will prepare them to identify similar themes in their other cases and to generalize and utilize the principles and reasoning of the consultant with other cases presented to them for judicial decisions.

During appearances in court, I am at least as interested in extending the understanding of the judge as I am in gaining acceptance for my recommendations for the particular case. For that reason, I carefully go through a three-step process. First, for each point that I make here, I lay out the facts on which I am basing my opinion. Second, I discuss the significance of those facts, by indicating the theoretical or experimental basis I was using to interpret them. Third, I demonstrate the reasoning process I have used to arrive at my conclusions and recommendations. Thus, just as in consultee-centered consultation, I use the case to demonstrate to the judge how a clinician evaluates the situation, so that the judge can follow this process from start to finish and apply the principles to other cases. If the process requires a recommendation from the consultant, it could be considered client-centered consultation. On the other hand, my focus is more on the learning of the consultee than is usually the case in a client-centered model.

I consistently structure my presentation to the court—the evidence in chief—around the TPCAP Guidelines. This provides an opportunity to discuss the background, the structure around the organization of the guidelines—with the judge following with a set of the guidelines and the manual before him or her—as I list and explain the clinical significance of each guideline in turn the psychological meaning of the key facts and the extent to which my interpretation of them is consistent with the professional literature and key theoretical constructs.

In presenting the guidelines to court, I first present the theoretical basis of each guideline without any mention of the particular case. Next, facts from the specific case are applied to that guideline, thus illustrating the application of those general concepts to the case itself. Finally, in drawing the case together through my conclusions and recommendations, I review and underline the pattern and weight of the clinical evidence. If the first two steps have been done effectively, the judge will be anticipating my conclusions or, at the very least, will understand why they make sense. And, because he or she can see for him or herself the patterns and has been taken through the process, the recommendations will sit more comfortably than if he or she were forced to accept large sections of my evidence on faith. As a result, as has been made clear repeatedly in written judgments, the judges take away with them a pattern of thinking and a greater understanding of the core issues which they have internalized and which have become theirs to apply to similar cases.

The Use of a Response to a Hypothetical Case or Chart Review as a Form of Consultation

One useful variant of this approach, possibly more in line with client-centered or program-centered consultation is the hypothetical case or chart review. The consultant is expected to offer a course of action that takes the form of a written response to a hypothetical case or one based on a review of the chart. In both cases, the child and/or family are not seen. These approaches are useful when the case has been known to the agency for years and has already been assessed by many mental health professionals. In such cases, another time-limited assessment is unnecessary, at times counter-productive and, possibly, intrusive, and upsetting.

In adapting this process by providing a written response to a hypothetical case, I ask the agency and/or its lawyers to present a scenario illustrating the major issues about which the agency is seeking an opinion. In responding to an agency's hypothetical case, I make it clear that I know nothing about the real case, and that it is the responsibility of the agency to satisfy the court that the issues and principles involved in the scenario submitted to me do indeed apply to the case before the court. Having established this point, I proceed through the same three steps outlined previously. I state the major themes and issues illustrated by the hypothetical case and discuss them in terms of theoretical and/or experimental evidence relevant to their significance and implications in determining the needs of the child(ren). This is all done at a general level without any reference to the details of the particular case. I then establish a connection between the themes and the case to demonstrate that the case does, indeed, illustrate the themes and issues discussed in the hypothetical scenario. I explain the reasoning behind my conclusions and recommendations, why they represent the least detrimental alternative for the child. In many cases a consultation on a hypothetical case may be just as effective in outlining the principles that should apply while being far more efficient and economical than plowing through a clinical record of several hundred pages. Obviously, the better the agency and its lawyers are able to focus and capture the essence of their case in the hypothetical scenario, the more brief and focused the response will be, and the more strikingly the relevant principles will stand out.

An alternative to the hypothetical case is the chart review, which could be seen as a client-centered consultation model because the consultant makes recommendations from the information he or she already has. The Society forwards a comprehensive summary of what it sees as the key issues and a statement of how it understands and is dealing with these along with reports of past assessments by collateral agencies or professionals. I may clarify areas of confusion or try to obtain important additional data by an interview with key personnel—either in person or, with cases from geographically distant agencies, by telephone, in order to complete or to clarify areas of confusion in the chart. When I am satisfied that I have the information I need—or as much as I am going to get, I then explain in my report why I am doing a chart review rather than a clinical assessment. This could involve commenting:

1. On the number of assessments that have already been performed.
2. On the relative weight of combined historical factors versus a fresh assessment in informing the decision to be made.
3. On the limited validity of a time-limited assessment of parents who have understandable reasons for withholding and or manipulating the facts in order to influence the result.
4. On the fact that yet another assessment will, in this case, prove intrusive and, possibly, even be clinically contraindicated.

I carefully list the sources of information on which my report is based, indicating that it is for the Society and its collaterals to establish the accuracy and the balance of the facts made available to me but that, if they succeed in doing so, I am prepared to defend my conclusions and recommendations based on that information in court.

Next, I introduce in general terms the guidelines, and go through the same three steps described earlier, just as I would if responding to a hypothetical case. For each guideline that I consider relevant, I first describe what the guideline measures, why that guideline (in general) is relevant to an assessment of parenting capacity in the given case and to the issues at hand. I then select relevant information from the chart and organize it around the guideline. I conclude by summarizing what the chart shows about the adequacy, inadequacy and/or implications of this aspect of parenting. If I become aware of significant information that should be, but is not available, I note this in the preliminary report along with a statement of why this would be useful to know. Then, prior to writing the final report, I contact the agency to see if the missing facts are known to the agency. If they are, I integrate them and modify my report accordingly. If not, and if what is missing could be obtained with agency staff utilizing one or more guidelines, I suggest that the worker obtain the desired information, and report it directly to the court.

When I have completed my review of the relevant guidelines, I turn next to answer any specific questions for which the Society is requesting an opinion. In doing this, I refer back to my summary of the case—along with a review of its relevance to the question I am answering—discussed during my review of each of the guidelines.

I make any additional statements that I considered relevant but that were not specifically asked for, and compare my conclusions and recommendations to those of past consultations, using their reports to bolster mine whenever possible or, if they disagree, explaining why my conclusions differ from those of consultants whose contrary opinions are on the chart. This could be on the basis of the passage of time, new evidence, or and different options being considered given the changed situation. I will state quite openly that the other assessor or consultant and I may evaluate the situation differently, that there is no consensus in the literature as to which interpretation is correct. Because each of us is responding from his or her clinical experience, the judge—given the greater mass of evidence at his or her disposal—will have to decide which of the opinions is the more credible.

I finish with my conclusions and recommendations. As in a court appearance, the way in which the facts, the conclusions drawn from the facts, the evidence on which those conclusions are based, and the way those conclusions lead to the recommendations, have the effect of stripping away any mysticism or demands for a leap of faith by inviting the reader—caseworker, lawyer, parent, and/or judge—to review and understand the entire process that has led to the conclusions and recommendations.

A surprising number of such cases may, after months or even years of adversarial wrangling, agree to settle out of court on the basis of a clear and thorough chart review. There is often a second, and highly useful, result of such consultations. Invariably, staff of the consultee Society are impressed with how the reworking of their own information around the structure of the guidelines makes recurrent patterns of behavior stand out, thus making their case stronger than they would have believed possible. This gives them a model for using the guidelines to increase their workers' effectiveness in court.

At the same time, because I rearranged their data around the framework of the guidelines, it demonstrates that they are just as capable as I am of utilizing the data to make the same points. This is important, because the agency often has more than enough information to complete the guidelines at its disposal already. Such a demonstration shows how using the guidelines can help workers maximize the impact of their information in court. Some agencies conduct their entire examination in chief along the framework of the guidelines.

PUBLIC EDUCATION AND ADVOCACY FOR CHILDREN UTILIZING THE PRINCIPLES OF CONSULTEE-CENTERED CONSULTATION

Since 1989, and overlapping with the use of the Guidelines for Assessing Parenting Capacity to sensitize judges and child welfare agencies toward greater sensitivity to the needs of children and more proactive permanency planning, the author chaired two major voluntary coalitions formed to promote healthier development for all children. The first was the Sparrow Lake Alliance (Novik, 1993), primarily a coalition of professionals who provide services for children, although youth and parent consumer groups and representatives from five government ministries that plan and fund services for children are also members. Their goal is to improve the effectiveness and the efficiency with which available resources are utilized. The second group is the Coalition for Children Families and Communities (CCFC) that was established to increase public awareness of the numbers of children whose development is at risk, the available strategies to deal with their needs, and the changes in families, workplaces, in communities, and in schools that are needed.

A major stimulus for the formation of these coalitions was the publication of the Ontario Child Health Study (Offord, Boyle, & Racine, 1989), a province-wide epidemiological survey that demonstrated: that over 18% of Ontario's children and youth met the criteria for at least one psychiatric disorder (as defined by DSM-IIIR); two-thirds of those with one disorder meet the criteria for two or more disorders; only 1 in 6 of those children with a disorder had, in the preceding 6 months, received any form of remedial intervention (children's mental health; child welfare; corrections) for that disorder; and, in the past 30 years, the suicide rate for adolescent boys in Canada has quadrupled, and it has doubled within the same period for boys aged 10 to 14 years (Harvey et al., 1994).

It is obvious that Canadians will never have, and will never be able to afford, enough mental health professionals to treat all those children whose development and adjustment have been undermined. In addition to being vulnerable to mental health disorders, they are prone to unacceptably high levels of premature school dropout and functional illiteracy. At the same time, Canadian rates of juvenile delinquency and violence while still far short of those in the United States—are unacceptably high and rising (Carrington & Moyer, 1994; Mitchell, 1994; Platiel, 1994; Police, 1993).

The Alliance worked with government to promote among civil servants and politicians, a better understanding of the problems facing young children and their families and to suggest more effective and efficient ways of using existing resources. But, in spite of a virtual consensus on the kind of changes needed among a number of knowledgeable, articulate, high profile, and well respected advocacy groups, the government decision-makers have paid little more than lip service to meeting the needs of children. For this reason, the Sparrow Lake Alliance—realizing that government would not respond until the electorate understood the issues and demanded change—took the lead in 1992 in establishing the Coalition for Children, Families and Communities (CFCFC).

In a relatively short time, CFCFC has captured the attention of some of Ontario's leading journalists and decision makers, and the needs of children, youth, and their families have been given a much higher profile. The number of newspaper articles in the Toronto area child- and family-related issues has approximately tripled in the less than 3 years that the CFCFC has been in existence, and many public addresses on this topic that have been made and televised, and are constantly being rerun in response to a steady demand from the public. Both the Sparrow Lake Alliance and the CFCFC have made strong, clear, well-referenced presentations to Ontario's Royal Commission on Learning, which adopted all their major recommendations in a recently released report that has catalyzed major changes in Ontario's educational system. Also, the Sparrow Lake Alliance has already appeared once—and has been asked to re-appear—before the Standing Committee on Justice and Legal Affairs, the major national parliamentary committee that is currently revising the Young Offenders Act, the statute governing Canada's response to youthful law-breakers. The main thrust of the Alliance's position has been to demonstrate to the parliamentarians—in spite of a public outcry in favor of more and harsher punishments for younger and younger children as the "solution" to youth crime and violence—that tackling the well known precursors of youth violence is the most effective and least costly way of bringing about the safer society that we all desire. In doing so, the Alliance suggests guidelines for more effective sentencing, and has demonstrated that harsher punishments and longer periods of confinement—especially when they consist of little more than warehousing large numbers of children without any serious attempt at rehabilitation—have been repeatedly shown to aggravate aggression, rebellion, and recidivism in adjudicated delinquents. At the same time, rising national and provincial debts have severely curtailed the amounts available for social spending, thereby necessitating a major revision of Canada's social security system. The CFCFC, through its submission to parliamentary Standing Committee on Human Resources Development, has suggested priorities for directing and focusing the necessary cuts in social funding in a persuasive and well-referenced brief. It has recommended basic principles for maximizing effectiveness in human services while minimizing divisiveness and unnecessary dependency.

But, one might ask, what do public education and advocacy have to do with consultee-centered consultation? Consultee-centered consultation is, in its essence, a way of changing how a colleague understands and deals with a work-related problem. Sometimes the consultation is sought because the consultee lacks the basic information needed to understand and to act effectively. At other times, the consultee is unable to appreciate the significance of the information already available or to see its implications for planning and intervention. Not infrequently, different consultees may disagree about case management, and the consultant is, in essence, asked to serve as a mediator. Finally, there are those cases in which consultees, due to their idiosyncratic and often unrecognized reactions to personally emotionally-loaded issues triggered by the case, are unable to think, plan or intervene appropriately. In the process of consultee-centered consultation, consultants establish a trusting relationship with the consultee that they then use to help the consultee transcend the problems in case management. Finally, because the consultation usually occurs at the interface between two or more overlapping areas of expertise, that of the consultant and of the consultee, the entire process is based on mutual respect even in the face of substantial disagreement at times—and on a recognition that, in any good consultation, both partners can learn from the opinions and expertise of the other. How, then, do these features of effective consultee-centered consultation contribute to public education and advocacy?

In both public education and advocacy, one begins with the assumption that if the object of the advocacy had, and could see clearly, information that advocates possess, their awareness of and attitude toward the subject of the advocacy would change. For example, to convince the public as to the cost-effectiveness of home visiting or of high-quality child care, or to help employers see that a family-friendly workplace can improve their company's productivity while increasing the company's social responsibility, one must present the information required to demonstrate the need for and the advantages of such programs sim-

ply, clearly, and succinctly in a way that is interesting, logical, and both intellectually and emotionally persuasive.

For effective public education, one starts with an up-to-date knowledge of relevant areas of research from a variety of fields that are often not considered to be
related to one another (e.g., child development, day care, sociology, economics,
and political science). That done, these are translated and repackaged in a way
that challenges the interest while striking the desired chord in the hearts of the
public. As in a consultation, if too few or too many wrong facts are chosen, or if
these facts are presented in a way that seems irrelevant or bullying, or if theme interference is evoked in those whom one seeks to persuade, one will not succeed. If
what they see as their concerns are not addressed, or if because of miscalculations
those whom one seeks to bring on one's side feel talked down to or manipulated or
overwhelmed and inadequate, the risk being tuned out and people dismissing
what one has to say increases. One must be sensitive to how those whom he or she
is addressing currently see things in order to focus the interaction and to say what
one has to say in a way that will be compelling to them. Also, as in consultation,
for maximum impact, one will have to achieve just the right tone. If one is too
dull, too negative, or overly dramatic, the listeners will tune him or her out. If the
need for action is not conveyed, one's audience will be lost. One will need to create just enough of a sense of crisis to challenge complacency, but not enough of
one to push listeners into denial or overreaction. Still it must be stressed that
there is a vital difference between using principles of consultee-centered consultation in advocacy and consultee-centered consultation. In consultee-centered
consultation the consultant is ready to change his or her representation of the
problem to promote the consultation process, whereas in advocacy, the advocate
wants the public to understand his or her representation of the problem. For that
purpose, the advocate sharpens his or her arguments and tries many different presentations in order to reach the advocacy goals.

The CFCFC truly believes that it can convey to the public the necessary
facts. If the public understands the implications of those facts, then the community will begin to share the CFCFC's concern about the effects on society and on
the economy of continuing to squander the healthy development, competence,
and productivity of almost a third of a generation of our children (Schweinhart,
Barnes, & Weikert, 1993; Weikert et al., 1984).

One of the important roles of the consultant, at times, is to mediate between different professionals who cannot resolve their disagreements as to
what to do. Similarly, at a time of increasing financial constraints, both professionals and the public are confused. How should the limited number of public
dollars be best spent? Clearly, whenever funds available for social spending are

sinking, those who feel that their own interests are threatened—be they bankers, the middle class, seniors, treatment professionals, health care providers, civil servants, and so on—will fight more fiercely to hold onto what they have. Thus, anything that can be done to suggest priorities and an appropriate balance between competing interests will be useful. Just as consultants need to mediate between consultees who hold opposing views, the effective public educator seeks ways to build bridges and reconcile incompatible positions—in an age when strident demands for getting one's way have all but eclipsed the spirit of compromise, thereby making it increasingly possible for those who yell the loudest to get the most.

In order to build a social consensus, it is far more important to suggest scenarios that can simultaneously accommodate the needs of more than one group than it is to indulge in militant claims on behalf of a single interest group at the expense of all others. The effective consultant must, at times, refocus the attention of consultees who have lost sight of the needs of the case away from their rigid commitment to fixed positions and back onto the client. In the same way, the successful advocate for children mobilizes community concern and a commitment to social equity on behalf of those who are most vulnerable and least able to speak for themselves to persuade more affluent groups committed to the defense of the status quo that a commitment to children, rather than imposing a cost on society, benefits the economy, and increases the prospects for future growth and societal well-being (Osberg, 1995).

The ability to establish and maintain a relationship of trust between the advocate and the community is no less important than the relationship that exists between effective consultants and their consultees. The integrity of the advocacy is a key issue here. Even a single inaccurate, exaggerated, or inconsistent statement can seriously undermine credibility over the long haul to the point where nothing that the advocate says will be believed. One must never overstate his or her case or temporarily set aside one's integrity in order to manipulate or score cheap points. Effective advocacy, like successful consultation, is an ongoing and cumulative process. Treating the community (by analogy, the consultee) with meticulous respect is crucial to the credibility of the advocate and, ultimately, to success.

I have presented a series of variations on the theme of consultee-centered consultation, variations that have evolved over 3 decades to meet a number of new and different challenges that have evolved as I have worked in different ways to protect the welfare of Ontario's most vulnerable children. To my mind, the richness of Caplan's seminal work on mental health consultation is confirmed partly by the fact that it is as well-respected and even more heavily utilized today than it was when it was originally presented 30 years ago. But another proof of its vitality is its ability to inspire variations that can help shape our responses 30 years later to challenges related to, but far beyond the clinical situations that Caplan was addressing in *The Theory and Practice of Mental Health Consultation*. Gerald Caplan gave us more than theories and models. He introduced us to a way of looking at things and a pattern of thinking. It is for those that I, personally, thank him most of all.

REFERENCES

Balbernie, R. (1966). *Residential work with children*. Oxford: Pergamon.
Balbernie, R. (1974). Unintegration, integration and level of ego functioning as the determinants planned "cover therapy" of unit task and of placement. *Journal of the Association of Workers for Maladjusted Children, 2*, 6–46.
Bowlby, J. (1960). Grief and mourning in infancy and early childhood. *Psychoanalytic Studies of the Child. 15*, 9–52.
Bowlby, J. (1969). *Attachment and loss. Vol. 1: Attachment*. London: Hogarth.
Bowlby, J. (1973). *Attachment and loss. Vol. 2: Separation, anxiety, and anger*. London: Hogarth.
Caplan, G. (1963). Types of mental health consultation. *American Journal of Orthopsychiatry, 33*, 470–481.
Caplan, G. (1970). *The theory and practice of mental health consultation*. New York: Basic Books.
Carrington, P. J., & Moyer, S. (1994). Trends in youth, crime and police response, pre- and post-YOA. *Canadian Journal of Criminology, 36*(1), 22.
Harvey, L., Avard, D., Graham, I., Underwood, K., Campbell, J., & Kelly, C. (1994a). *The Health of Canada's Children: A CICH Profile (2nd Ed.)*. Ottawa: Canadian Institute of Child Health. Figure 2–12, p. 11; Figure 3–3 & 3–4, p.44; Figure 4–5 & 4 a–6, p. 6 1; Figure 5–3 & 5–4, p.88.
Harvey, L., Avard, D., Graham, I., Underwood, K., Campbell, J., & Kelly, C. (1994b). *The health of Canada's children: A CICH Profile (2nd Ed.)*. Ottawa: Canadian Institute of Child Health. Figure 6–10, p. 119.
Hewlett, S. A. (1991). *When the bough breaks: The cost of neglecting our children*. New York: Harper Perennial.
Johnston, M. (1989). How self-help discussion groups can help natural children cope with the stress of foster children in the family: Two different reports. *Journal of the Ontario Association of Children's Aid Society, 33*(6), 2–9.
Mitchell, A. (1994, November 24). Justice spending soars: Calls for crime protection cited (based on Statistics Canada figures). *The Globe & Mail*, A-12.
Novik, M. (1993, April 3). Presentation on panel on facilitation of change at the Fourth Annual Meeting, Sparrow Lake Alliance, Sparrow Lake, Ontario.
Offord, D. R., Boyle, M. H., & Racine, A. (1989). *The Ontario child health study: Children at risk*. Toronto: Ontario Ministry of Community and Social Services.
Osberg, L. (1995, March 17). Presentation at Conference on Economic Growth and Inequality at Laurentian University. Reported in D. Crane. Reducing inequalities now can only serve us well later. *The Toronto Star, Mar 18, 1995*. Section B-2.
Platiel, R. (1994). Weapons, assaults on the rise. *The Globe & Mail. October 21*. (Includes chart entitled "Weapons Use in Canadian Schools" credited to Ministry of the Solicitor General).

Police Report Data, Centre for Justice Statistics. (1993). Adolescents charged with violent crimes. Youth Update. *Youth for Study of Antisocial Behaviour in Youth, 11* (2), 7.

Santa-Barbara, J., & Kane, B. (1982a). *The foster care research project: A comparison of two models of foster care service.* Unpublished observation.

Santa-Barbara, J., & Kane, B. (1982b). *The foster care research project: Follow-up report.* Unpublished observation.

Schweinhart, L. J., Barnes, H. V., Weikart, D. R., with Barnett, W., & Epstein, A. S. (1993). *Significant benefits: The High Scope Perry Preschool study through age 27.* Ypsilanti, MI: High/Scope Press.

Sigurdson, E., & Reid, G. (1990). *The Manitoba child abuse and neglect scales.* Mimeographed.

Steinhauer, P. D. (1991). The role of psychotherapy and residential treatment within the child welfare system. In P. D. Steinhauer (Ed.), *The least detrimental alternative: A systematic guide to case planning and decision making for children in care.* Toronto: University of Toronto Press.

Steinhauer, P. D., Johnston, M., Snowden, M., Santa-Barbara, J., Kane, B., Barker, P., & Hornick, J. P. (1988). The foster care research project: Summary and analysis. *Canadian Journal of Psychiatry, 33,* 509–516.

Steinhauer, P. D., Johnston, M., Snowden, M., Santa-Barbara, J., Kane, B., Barker, P., & Hornick, J. P. (1989). The foster care research project: Clinical impressions. *American Journal of Orthopsychiatry 59* (3), 430–441.

Steinhauer, P. D., Leitenberger, M., Manglicas, E., Pauker, J. D., Smith, R., & Goncalves, L. (1995a). *The Toronto parenting capacity assessment project: Guidelines for assessing parenting capacity.* Toronto: Institute for the Prevention of Child Abuse.

Steinhauer, P. D., Leitenberger, M., Manglicas, E., Pauker, J.D., Smith, R., & Goncalves, L. (1995b). *Manual, accompanying the Toronto Parenting Capacity Assessment Project Guidelines.* Toronto Institute for the Prevention of Child Abuse.

Weikert, D. P., Berrueta-Clement, J. R., Schweinhart, L. J., Barnett, W. S., Epstein, A. E. (1984). *Changed lives: The effects of the Perry Preschool Program on youth through age 19.* Ypsilanti, MI: High/Scope Press.

Wilkes, J. (1979a). The stresses of fostering. Part 1: On the fostering parents. *Journal of the Ontario Children's Aid Society, 22* (9), 1–8.

Wilkes, J. (1979b). The stresses of fostering. Part II: On the fostering children. *Journal of the Ontario Children's Aid Society, 22* (10), 712.

11

Using Consultee-Centered Consultation in a Network Intervention With Health Providers

José Navarro Góngora

The chapter describes a self-sufficient network created for resolution of medical problems, and the role played by consultee-centered consultation in promoting a resolution of the health crisis. The first part briefly describes the mutual relationships and the roles played by the health professionals in the hematology unit of a clinical hospital, a patient self-help group, and the Medical Family Program of a Masters program in the faculty of psychology. These relationships and the respective roles are understood by those involved in the network as self-sufficient and noncost mutual services and help. The second part of the chapter describes the consultation services provided by the medical family program with both the hematology unit and the patients self-help group. Some examples are offered, and the consultation process is depicted in its various stages and goals. The main goals of the paper are to offer a structural description of the network, describe the consultation intervention, and finally, to present examples of the problems experienced.

CONSULTEE-CENTERED CONSULTATION

In consultee-centered consultation the consultant's primary focus is on eluci-dating and enhancing the consultee's professional functioning. (Caplan &

Caplan, 1993). The discussion is mainly restricted to clarifying the details of the client's situation to increase the consultee's cognitive grasp and emotional mastery of the issues involved in caring for the client. But in consultee-centered consultation, improvement in the client is a side effect, welcome although it may be. The primary goal is to improve the consultee's capacity to function effectively with work problems of the type presented.

Consultee-centered consultants utilize the difficulties being had with the patient in order to understand and resolve the difficulties of the consultee, and not the difficulties of the patient. For this reason the subjectivity of the consultee's experience is what is important and not the objectivity of the patient's history. In this way, enhancing the professional practice of the consultee is defined as the objective of this kind of consultation. Caplan and Caplan (1993) have identified four types of work problems confronted in consultee-centered consultation that typify problems of health professionals in their work with oncology patients; a lack of knowledge about the psychosocial factors involved in handling the patient's case; a lack of skill in finding a solution to the problem, either by the consultee's own efforts or by invoking the help of others; a lack of self confidence related to seniority, ill health, burnout, or inexperience; and, a lack of objectivity that occurs when the consultee is either too close or too distant from others in the patient's life drama, and is not able to perceive the work problem accurately enough to carry out his task. The network intervention described in this chapter reflects the first two types of work problems—lack of knowledge and lack of skill. The network approach is based on the assumption that the social network that engulfs each physically ill patient plays a determining role in the psychological well-being of the patient. The literature regarding this issue is more than abundant. When a person becomes seriously ill, a deeply-committed social network springs up around this person. This social network tends to be made up of the ill person's immediate family and a part of the extended family, concerned friends, and health professionals. All networked health interventions take these resources into account and try to coordinate and maximize them to the benefit of the patient. Such networked interventions have been utilized for several purposes. They can control problems that may extend beyond the threshold where the family and the institution can manage separately, or develop relationships that provide emotional support, functional support, and informational support. The intervention coordinates the resources available in the network and replaces the detrimental relationships with new ones, or creates relationships when none are present. All network interventions should aim to solve the problem that has emerged from somewhere in the social network. Health care professionals are then assured that the locus of control of the change process is displaced from the professionals to the social network.

Many models for social network intervention have been described, but few of them have been applied to health crisis situations. Two distinct strategies may fit such crisis situations: the *network assembly* approach (Rueveni, 1979; Speck & Atnneuve, 1973) and the *session network* approach (Garrison, 1981). The *network assembly* strategy calls for all available family members, friends, acquaintances who are willing to help, volunteers interested in helping, and health care professionals to come together and work as a group. The *session network* strategy also involves the same members of the social group, but it calls on only the most representative of them to gather together. There are noticeable differences between the two in terms of the number of participants, the group dynamics, the intervention procedure to be followed, and the professional's role in the process.

The *network assembly* process consists of a fewer number of interviews because it is almost impossible to involve such a large group of people (which tend to be as many as 50) for more than three interviews. Network assemblies are applicable virtually as a last resort, because they are difficult to convene and arrange from a health professional's point of view because of the high number of people involved and because it is difficult to apply problem-solving procedures based on negotiation and rational discussion.

The *network session* approach is much more manageable from a health professional's point of view, because it gathers together no more than 15 people at a time. This allows the health professional to approach the problem in a much more rational and negotiated way. *Assembly networks* tend to be used for cases where all else has failed, whereas *session networks* ideally might be used as the standard procedure in health crisis situations. Certain adjustments in the procedure are necessary in order to utilize consultee-centered consultation in a *session networks*, always respecting the objective of any network intervention—the social group has to take control of the situation. Also the health professionals have to be trained to use consultee-centered consultation to utilize a session network procedure. This is what the modest innovation that we propose portends to do.

OUR SETTING: THE AUTONOMOUS NETWORK

This network was established following several criteria. There was to be no extra cost to any of the institutions involved. It was to be self-sufficient and not depend on other organizations for its functioning, and its goal was to promote mutually required services. In psychosocial terms, the most important organiza-

tion is ASCOL, the leukemia self-help group that receives the patients who
have gone through the Medical Family Therapy Program (MFTP), run by the
Masters in Mental Health program taught by the faculty of psychology of the
Salamanca University (Spain), as well as those released by the Hematology Service of the University Clinical Hospital. ASCOL carries out several programs.
In the hospital, ASCOL provides respite programs for the primary caretaker,
storytelling for children, and a pairing program for leukemia patients. At its offices it offers the encounter groups, social events, and support activities for the
volunteers. The organizations involved, the Masters program, ASCOL, and the
hospital, have long provided services for each other. Although these services
have varied from time to time, they now consist mainly of care for patients and
their families in critical or crisis situations within the confines of the hospital
and the Masters program. Specific programs such as the program for family
members of bone-marrow transplant patients under ASCOL, training for
health care professionals (primarily for nurses) and for volunteers; and the evaluation of all of these joint programs.

The Medical Family Program

The MFTP, which carries out the network intervention, is a modest unit that
provides health care for patients and their families in our own unit at the Faculty, and consultation to other institutions, the University Hospital, and
ASCOL. This work has resulted in developing a specialization in the area of
psychosocial intervention for health problems and training for professionals
and volunteers. A faculty member from the program serves as a consultee-centered consultant to the network.

The Hematology Unit of the University Clinic Hospital

The Hematology is a large ward of 19 hematologists and 38 nurses, which provides up-to-date care for hematology patients. As many advanced units in its
area of influence is not only the region, but it is a reference hospital for the entire country. As a result of this patients from all the regions, especially from the
north part of Spain, come here. It is a populated, busy, and highly technologi-
cal unit, which provides care for very ill people, who, many times, do not live
in the city of Salamanca. The unit has to face the psychosocial problems that
any other hematology unit faces. As a result of implicit understanding, the
nurses take over the role of attending the psychosocial needs of the patients
and their families. They have been very persistent in implementing these
psychosocial programs to the point of receiving two national awards for "hu-

manistic medicine" and one special national mention for the best program presented at the National Congress of Nurses in the last 3 years. With the permission of the doctors and the supervision of the nurses, the ward has opened its doors to self-help group associations (cancer and leukemia) and to the cooperation with the Faculty of Psychology.

The ASCOL Organization

One of the most important programs of ASCOL reception, and probably of the three cooperating institutions, is undoubtedly the reception group, which, as its name indicates, is the group that receives new patients and works as an encounter for patients who have been in the organization for some time. The weekly meetings have no predetermined topic for discussion and the group leader has only one rule to follow: to encourage the conversation that occurs (whatever its nature) and to get everyone to participate. In addition to the reception group, the ASCOL organization provides psychosocial help for the ill and help for the primary caretaker in the family because that person's well-being has direct repercussions on the quality of care given to the ill person in the respite program. It also gives support for the volunteers provided by periodic meetings with the program coordinators and in meetings of the coordinators with the persons responsible for the program of the association. Periodically, the coordinators, the person responsible for the programs, and any volunteers who wish to do so, consult with the author to discuss how the programs are working and whether or not new ones are needed.

Those situations that ASCOL volunteers cannot handle, are referred to the MFTP. They respond within 24 to 48 hours if the situation is critical, place them on a short waiting list of no more than five patients, or refer them to other institutions if there are already five patients on the waiting list. The family therapy program advises ASCOL on the progress of the services that it is carrying out, as well about any new services begun, and on relations with other units.

NETWORK INTERVENTION WITH HOSPITALIZED PHYSICALLY ILL PATIENTS

The Consultee-Centered Consultation Services Agreement

The consultation contract establishes that the consultant will help the consultees understand problems from a psychosocial perspective and the consultees will be responsible for the follow-up actions that seem most relevant. With this agreement the consultant does not take offense if consultees fail to follow through from the consultation sessions.

Goals of the Consultation Service for the Network

Consultation is sought usually in response to a crisis situation. The crisis can be brought on by the physical condition of the patient, which requires difficult decisions or increased care responsibilities from the family. Because hematology patients are always facing the potential of a life-threatening health crisis, the approach I describe here can be considered a consultee-centered consultation for confronting and solving a health crisis.

The goals of the consultation are: first, to resolve the problems that the patient and his or her family are going through; and second, to teach medical professionals how to increase the effectiveness of the social and professional networks of the patient when the family is having trouble responding or making decisions, and the patient, for whatever reason, is incapable of making them. It is, then, a crisis intervention.

Evaluation and Planning Phase

There are two basic pathways that lead to a network intervention. In the first instance, the services are client-centered. The client is the ill person who schedules and attends the interview, either alone or accompanied by family members. During the course of the interview if the client is judged to have a problem in which his or her doctor could play a decisive role, the client's doctor is contacted, and a joint interview is set up with the patient, his or her family, the doctor, and ourselves. In these instances the situations tend to be critical to some degree, but not yet a full-blown crisis.

In the second instance, the consultee-centered consultation intervention begins at the request of physicians who have come on a situation that they cannot resolve themselves. The consultee is the physician and the patient's crisis is the work problem. The work problem, for example, may include trying to release a terminal cancer patient from the hospital when nothing more can be done for him or her; asking less sacrifice on the part of the parents of a little girl, in the intensive care unit who is in an irreversible coma, who are spending all day in the hospital with their daughter; or asking the family of a multiple sclerosis patient to have the patient at home, with a portable respirator instead of keeping the patient in the intensive care unit. Following the request for consultation, the first step is a meeting with the health professionals, physicians, and nurses who have asked for help. Depending on the case, the head nurse in charge of the customer service also participates. It is also important to invite the head of the ward and the supervising nurse, so that they can participate in the discussion, thereby curtailing any suspicion about what information has been exchanged. Because this is a new kind of intervention, their permission and involvement are needed. Furthermore, in view of the fact that the problem the physicians are facing requires that new knowledge will be shared, their participation will facilitate the utilization of these new perspectives in future situations.

We followed three lines of inquiry in the consultee-centered network session for our evaluation and planning.

The Maximum Level of Crisis Reached

This implies determining what level the impasse, or *tug of war*, between the family and the medical professionals has reached and the number, type, and outcome of other problem-solving attempts.

The Work Problems Faced by the Health Care Professionals

Two types of work problems tend to surface: serious problems with the patient and/or the family, or lack of the skills required to solve the problem.

The Location of the Problem(s)

We try to locate the source(s) of the problem(s). For example, it is important to determine whether it is a problem among hospital professionals (e.g., between the hospital management—which in our country is in the hands of non-health professionals—and the medical team), between the hospital and the family, between the hospital and the patient, or between the patient and his or her family or social network (Doka, 1993; Navarro Góngora, & Beyebach, 1995; Rolland, 1994).

In the example of the patient in the terminal stage, the crisis originated in the hospital. The hospital administration wanted to discharge the patient, who was beyond help, in order to be able to admit patients with more possibilities. Although the physicians agreed with the hospital administration, they found themselves faced with the refusal of both the patient and his family. A second problem was detected between the family and the patient. The patient's wife felt that neither his family nor hers would be able to cope with the demanding care he would require at home, meaning that she would have to leave her job, with no guarantee that she could get it back once her husband had died. Finally, the patient himself, who was aware of being a burden, added that he did not want family and friends to see him in the state he was in. As usually occurs in circumstances such as these, none of these problems had been discussed openly.

Generally, the evaluation takes only one meeting. At this same interview with the medical professionals, the network approach and rules are defined, because it is a new procedure for them. It is very important that the attending physician understands that he or she will lead the network session, and that it would not make sense to have a strange person—the consultant—whom the family has never seen before, taking charge of the network meeting. Then the intervention is planned in detail, assuring the physician that during the network session, he or she will receive the assistance of the consultant when solicited. This is assuming the leadership forces the physician to remain very active and involved during the network session, which will likely facilitate learning more from the experience. Proceeding in this way contributes to the medical personnel learning a new technique to be used in future cases, and perhaps use without consultation.

At the end of the interview, the consultant has a definition of the problem as set out by the attending physician who has requested his or her assistance. The physician's version of the problem is, logically, complemented by the family and the rest of the network during the first part of the network session.

Intervention Phase

On most occasions it is possible to get all those involved in the crisis to meet in a single network session. Yet on a few occasions, the degree of conflict between health care professionals and the family has escalated to such a height that such a meeting between the family and health care professionals is counter-productive, and even dangerous. In this case, the consultant meets each group separately. The consultant meets with the family and loved ones first. The meeting is recorded on video, after consent to being recorded has been granted. Then, the recorded interview is presented and evaluated by the network of health care professionals, who jointly seek a mutually acceptable compromise. We have had to resort to separate sessions in cases where patients suffer from a combination of physical ailments, chemical dependency, and violent tendencies.

The intervention phase is resolved in one or two sessions at the most. The social network of the patient and the network of professionals attending the patient in the hospital, together with a representative of the hospital's social services—who in our case is the head nurse in charge of customer's service and also a psychologist—are called together. The patient is usually not present because of the seriousness of his or her condition, but is invited if his or her condition permits. The basic rule is simple: the network called together depends on the needs imposed by the problem and by the availability of the health care professionals. The duration of each meeting is usually an hour or an hour and a half, and is composed of the following phases:

Setting the Goals

The session begins with a report on the physical condition of the patient given by the attending physician, who answers any questions that the family may have. There are not usually many questions because the family, in the majority of cases, has a very precise knowledge of the patient's condition. Afterwards, the physician presents the specific reason for the meeting, such as the patient's release and the problems this will pose; why some parents of a child in a coma insist on remaining in the hospital against all hope; or the need to have a more humane life at home with a portable respirator once the patient leaves the intensive care unit.

Exchanging Points of View

A discussion follows in which every one of the members of the nuclear and extended family and the professional network gives his or her view of the situation. It is essential that the members of the network express their points of view, first, because they expect (and have a right) to be heard, and second, because the consultant can guide the network to a common set of opinions. When the views expressed become arguments, the consultant may intervene. The consultant, however, keeps in mind that although it is important that network participants discuss their conflicting views of the problem, what is most important is that all segments of the network commit to specific problem-solving measures.

At this stage of the consultation session, when it becomes clear what the discrepancies are, often one of those present, usually a family member, enters into an argument with the physician about the respective views that have been expressed. This stage usually reflects the crisis that originated the consultation. Generally, this conflict is of the sort Hylander (this volume) calls a *tug of war*. The consultant intervenes in order to get over the impasse. Most times the consultant restates the views of both parties in nonbelligerent language. Through these descriptions of the various perspectives, the respective positions of one and all are made comprehensible without repeating the same statements. Expanding on or interpreting them is avoided. It is important that all those involved gain a new understanding of the situation, but this does not determine the outcome of the consultation. What determines the outcome is the fact that each one involved must respond to a dramatic problem. The purpose of the exchange of viewpoints is to accept the discrepancy between the other parties' views and one's own if an agreement cannot be reached, and to go on to next step when the compromises expected of each one will be defined. Ideally, we prefer the compromise to take root in a change in understanding. But in situations of crisis, conceptual changes are possible without agreement, precisely because the situations are so dramatic, because they call for such urgent solutions, and the social network takes on such an active (and pressing) role.

Disclosing a Problem-Solving Procedure

Once the discussion is finished, the physician, or, if needed, the consultant, proposes a way to solve the problem that seems feasible to all. The problem-solving formula generally defines what each part of the network present at the meeting will do. For example, someone should take over the role of primary caretaker, a role generally taken by someone in the nuclear family. The extended family would play a "break-giving" role by standing in for the primary caretaker for a limited time, or taking charge of specific tasks related to the patient. The professional network would commit to tasks concerning the follow-up of the patient's physical health, and psychological help, if necessary, and arranges for public or volunteer social resources. The idea is to create a network that will sustain the patient and his or her primary family caretaker, using first of all the resources of the network itself, and if this failed or was not enough or ineffective, to turn to public or volunteer social services. It is, of course, fundamental that medical attention is assured, and that patient's networks understand that psychological services will be available within 48 hours of the petition. It is essential that the family should not get the idea that the hospital is trying to displace them, but that it is rather offering to establish a new modality of care because it is more humane and more effective for all those involved.

In the case of the terminal patient that the hospital wished to release, his wife refused to have him at home, because it would mean losing a job she would definitely need after her husband's death, and she was also afraid of caring for him in his delicate condition. The patient himself did not want to go home, aware of being a burden on his wife. The scheme proposed by the network was that the Hospital Customer's Service found a local hospital that would treat the patient, who was assured that the Hematology Unit would readmit him should he need special treatment. Tasks were distributed throughout the extended family network. They agreed to support the wife and visit the patient at the new hospital. Their awareness of the patient's terminal condition and imminent death forced them to consider their support a personal responsibility.

The plan for action varies according to the problem. Thus, in the case of the little girl in a coma, the parents and sister of the patient were asked to explain to the doctors why they continued with such an extreme degree of sacrifice. They lived 70 miles away from Salamanca and there was always a member of the family, usually the mother, permanently at the hospital. The consultant was able to communicate the needs of the parents to the physicians, instead of the other way round. The physicians were the ones who changed their minds when they learned the importance of the parent's sacrifice for their future, when their daughter was most likely to be dead. For the parents' mourning it was important for them that their daughter knew that they always provided her with what they thought to be the most meaningful care in the state she was in. Under those circumstances, the physical presence and contact with the daughter helped to console the parents even though the patient was unable to perceive it. The fact that the hospital staff had limited their visits so drastically made the parents feel guilty for not being able to provide their daughter with what she needed. As a result, they were angry with the physicians. The most likely outcome of this network session was for the physician to put the problem within its psychosocial framework. The highly emotional climate of the session ensured that the professionals will remember the "psychosocial lesson," which is one of the most important goals of this type of consultation. Families play the role of ancillary professionals who teach the professionals their own expertise—the psychosocial dimension of the problems they are suffering.

Negotiating and Assigning the New Roles and Functions

The idea proposed by the professionals is discussed in terms of its viability. Once accepted, the "who does what" is negotiated. Negotiation can lead to a variety of results:

1. If the family accepts the plan, the consultant facilitates the definition of problem-solving roles and commitments.
2. If the family only partially accepts the plan, and proposes one of their own, the consultant helps the network to renegotiate problem-solving roles and commitments.
3. If the family rejects the plan and presents no alternative proposals or propose unviable or insensible plans, all those involved are declared to be in disagreement and the experience is brought to a close. If the alternative plan they propose is different from the one proposed by the physicians but sensible and viable, the consultant's role is to support it and forsake the former plan. The consultant's strategy is to support the family, and not to blame them if they do not choose what the professionals propose.

Let us return now to the case of the patient whom the hospital wanted to release with a portable respirator. His wife, who was the person most likely to assume the role of primary caretaker, refused to do so, weakly supported by her own family and criticized by her husband's family even though the intensive care unit (ICU) had promised to train the family in the use of the portable respirator and how to carry out simple procedures, such as aspirating phlegm, which is necessary for the patient's comfort. The wife manifested her inability to learn, her own helplessness (as a chronic patient herself—a previous breast cancer case—she was always cared for by her husband) and how she did not really believe that either her own or her husband's family would really help, despite the fact that her in-laws had already committed themselves to a daily care shift during the session. We later found out that a physician from the very same hospital had advised her not to let the ICU physicians convince her to take her husband back home. In this unfortunate situation, supporting the professionals' decision meant the consultant's role was get the network to focus on improving the contact between the family members and the patient.

In contrast, the negotiations in the case of the little girl in a coma resulted in the physicians' accepting the parents' sacrifice, and in their giving them not only explicit permission to continue, but also their "blessing" for what they were doing, thus improving the relationship of collaboration between the family and the hospital personnel. Paradoxically, once they gained access to their daughter, they stopped spending the entire day at her bedside, but that did not prevent them from filing a suit against the hospital for negligence one year later when their daughter eventually died.

We noted that the presence of the family facilitates the agreement among the professionals soothing the problems they might have among them. Often professionals want neither to exhibit their problems in front of the family members nor in front of other professionals. But with the family in the session, the professionals can present a united front.

Follow-Up Contacts

Once the roles have been negotiated and assigned, the network sessions are brought to an end, with the understanding that the social and professional network will deal with the problem. Frequent follow-up contacts are carried out by the health care professional assigned to the case, who is generally one of the hospital's social workers, and in our case the head nurse in charge of the hospital's customer service. The contacts occur every 2 weeks at first, and at longer intervals later on, for a long period of time, usually as long as the problem precipitating the intervention remains. During these contacts, information is obtained on how the work of the network members is progressing and this information is distributed to the physicians participating in the network session,

It is very important that each of the participants in the network be informed about the outcome of their efforts; likewise, our commitment to help them if needed is reiterated.

The follow-up on the three families revealed that the terminal patient died after 3 months, and his wife said she thought she had behaved better toward her husband than she would have had they stayed in Salamanca. The little girl in a coma died in a year, but while she was alive, her parents visited her, allowing themselves more rest and to be accompanied or substituted by family members. The medical personnel gave them free access to the ICU. The patient connected to the respirator become more and more depressed and died in a year. His wife reminded him constantly who he was and who he is, in a strange kind of ritual that we supposed was meant to encourage him. The relationship with the medical staff, marked by constant complaints over lack of medical attention greatly deteriorated. They refused any psychological help, even though they had expressed interest in it during the network meetings.

CONCLUSIONS AND DISCUSSION

The primary objective of consultee-centered consultation in a network intervention is to solve very critical problems in areas where more simple procedures that have been presented to the physician or to the family have failed. This procedure may be applied in cases of less critical problems that involve the same common denominators, such as the patient's family, friends, and medical professionals.

The secondary objective of the model is to enable medical professionals to use it in cases where they are willing to participate actively during the session. This role enables them to make the learning process more meaningful than if they merely attended the session as a spectator or if they had discussed their problems with the patients in client-centered consultation.

The social network operates as a control and pressure mechanism that channels the conflict in a health care crisis toward a solution. It is difficult to maintain a different opinion when such differences of opinion have to be defended in front of all those involved in the problem. This is an aspect of great importance for both the family network and for the network of health care professionals.

The most imposing obstacle for accepting a network experience is a supportive health-care culture that does not stipulate that critical problems, or problems that involve several different professionals, must be dealt with in a joint consultation session.

The outcome of the intervention depends on the creation of a joint relationship of between the health care institutions and the consultant in which the consultant is obliged to acquire a certain status in order to be permitted to intervene. As in all pioneering work, it is usually necessary that the professionals have become desperate enough with the problems they face daily to be ready to try something new. It was not, then, a matter of chance that our program started in the hematology unit and the ICU. It is difficult to know the amount of knowledge acquired by the medical personnel for treating these kinds of cases. For the time being, the most noticeable result of this kind of intervention in the hospital is not the fact that an increasing number of network interventions are occurring, but the fact that the number of other kinds of programs dealing with the psychosocial care of patients and their families has been increasing. This activity supports our inference that what is learned from a network session for one crisis situation is expanded and generalized to new presenting problems. It is difficult to find a method for evaluating this knowledge. Paradoxically, the success of an intervention of this type would be measured by a reduction in the petitions for intervention, which could be understood as a gain in autonomy of the medical staff.

It is also difficult to establish criteria for measuring success of the network experience on the family, especially if we take into account that the death of the patient is the most likely short term result. For the medical staff, success with a patient is what, in the last instance, justifies the continuation of the intervention.

Following the guidelines laid out by Caplan and Caplan (1993), we believe that networks can become a consultee-centered consultation venue, which is what we have proposed here. The session network consultation can be used by the hospital customer's service because the service is required to patient service units are required to intercede between patient and family members on the one hand and hospital personnel on the other, thus acting in a network fashion. Hospital customer's service intervenes in sensitive cases; therefore, these services would benefit significantly from network procedures in many of the cases that are brought to them. Because much of the work falls to the head nurse of customer's service to look for both public and volunteer services for the family, to attend to the meetings while contriving to attend to his or her own work in the hospital, and so forth, this person should not only be familiar with the procedures of network interventions, but also very committed to networks where responsibility for the patient is negotiated among health care and social support systems.

The whole procedure has to do with the presence of the family in the process of making-decisions. It seems that their presence has the effect of soothing conflicts among professionals, and in doing so facilitate their agreement. They work as ancillary professionals when they provide a vivid and frequently dramatic picture of how the patient's problems are connected with the broader psychosocial framework, a first-hand experience difficult to forget for those professionals involved in the session.

REFERENCES

Caplan, G., & Caplan, R. B. (1993). *Mental health consultation and collaboration*. San Francísco: Jossey-Bass.

Doka, K. J. (1993). *Living with life-threatening illness*. New York: Lexington Books.

Garrison, J. E. (1981, Winter). Clinical construction of action social networks. *International Journal of Family Therapy*, 258–262.

Navarro Góngora, J., & Beyebach, M. (1995). *Avances en terapia familiar*. Barcelona: Ed. Paidós.

Rolland, J. S. (1988). Family systems and chronic illness: A typological model. In F. Walsh & C. Anderson, *Chronic disorders and the family*. New York: The Haworth Press.

Rolland, J. S. (1994). *Families, illness and disability: An integrative treatment model*. New York: Basic Books.

Rueveni, U. (1979). *Networking families in crisis*. New York: Human Science Press.

Speck, R., & Attneuve, C. (1973). *Family networks: Retribalization and healing*. New York: Pantheon.

SUGGESTED READING

Caplan, G. (1989). *Population-oriented psychiatry*. New York: Human Science Press.

Doherty, W. J. (1995). The why's and levels of collaborative family health care. *Family Systems Medicine, 13*, (3–4), 275–281.

Gottlieb, B. (1983). *Social support strategies. Guidelines for mental health practice*. Beverly Hills: Sage.

Hurd, G. S., Mansell Pattison, E., & Llamas, R. (1981). Models of social network intervention. *International Journal of Family Therapy*, 246–257.

McDaniel, S. H., Hepworth, J., & Doherty, W. J. (1992). *Medical family therapy*. New York: Basic Books.

Rolland, J. S. (1994). Working with illness: Clinicians' personal and interface issues. *Family Systems Medicine, 12*(2); 149–170.

Saranson, B. S., Saranson, I., & Pierce, G. R. (1990). *Social support—An interactional view*. New York: John Wiley and Sons.

Seaburn, D. B., Lorenz, A. D., Gunn, W. B., Gawinski, B. A., & Mauksch, L. B. (1996). *Models of collaboration. A guide for the mental health professionals working with health care practitioners*. New York: Basic Books.

Trimble, D. W. (1980, Summer). A guide to the network therapies. *International Journal of Family Psychiatry*, 9–20.

12

Consultee-Centered Consultation in Low Feasibility Settings

Ruth B. Caplan-Moskovich

Gerald Caplan

Until recently, in our thinking and writings about consultee-centered consultation, we felt that two prerequisites were needed to create a viable consultee-centered consultation program for a community agency, The first was *salience*, which meant that the agency was strategically placed to have a high potential for influencing the mental health of its clients by supporting them in the face of stressors that our studies had led us to believe would produce a statistically significant elevation in rates of psychosocial pathology in an exposed population. Second, we felt that entry to the agency must be *feasible*; that is, the administration of the agency would understand the need for our service and would have the capacity to make use of it effectively. Because like every other mental health service provider, we have always been limited by available time and by the number of highly trained staff able to carry out so sophisticated a technique, we did not feel it necessary to expend effort recruiting agencies that might well have had high salience, but also had low feasibility because for various reasons they did not welcome our overtures. Indeed, we could pick and choose readily among institutions that fulfilled our criteria, and occupy all our time providing a service that these welcoming agencies felt was benefiting their clients and staff alike.

Unwittingly, however, we thereby restricted ourselves to a select, and therefore unrepresentative arena of practice. For example, one of the agencies that used our Harvard University consultants and provided practical experience on the basis of which we developed and refined our ideas and techniques was the Boston Visiting Nurse Association, which recruited a select staff, trained them highly, and continued to supervise and educate them throughout their employment. This highly feasible agency provided us with pure laboratory conditions, as it were, to study the intrusion of unconscious, subjective material that distorted professional functioning. Lapses by nurses in expected standards of case management were quickly noted by a supervisory system that demanded a high order of effectiveness so as to safely maintain gravely ill patients out in the community. Supervisors were sensitive to changes in the functioning of their nurses. Sophisticated and self-assured, they had the confidence and pragmatism to absorb whatever help from outsiders would enable their organization to accomplish its mission more efficiently. We met a similar welcome and lack of defensiveness among the bishops and parish clergy of the Episcopalian Church of the United States, and among certain groups of school administrators in Boston.

When we encountered cases of professional malfunctioning among these groups of caregivers, we over-estimated the degree of our understanding and competence to manage it, for we had overlooked the fact that we were operating in privileged circumstances, among a population of agencies and professionals who had been highly selected to fit *our* needs as well as their own. Unwittingly, our operation had become analogous to that of private individual-oriented patient practice, or a traditional mental health clinic where, given the limitations of professional resources and the vast sea of need, it was legitimate to choose to treat only those patients with a good prognosis for benefiting from our services—patients who were interesting, who were clean and civilized, and who were prepared to follow our rules.

When we moved out of Harvard Medical School into the Hadassah Hebrew University Medical school in Jerusalem and the wards of its teaching hospitals, our view of professional malfunctioning and consultation techniques began to change because we were now operating in a qualitatively different sphere. Now we had to deal with an institution with high salience, but whose feasibility was not always optimum because the staff was now heterogeneous and no longer as selective and sophisticated as we had been used to. Our traditional consultation techniques required us to work as outsiders with a recognized mantle of status due to our superior qualifications and our prestigious university affiliation, but at the same time we were to assume the role of equals, deferring to the expertise of the consultee about the issues of that particular case. In Hadassah we became insiders, and fellow members of diagnostic and therapeutic teams in various hospital departments where mental health issues might be secondary to immediate questions of life and death. In this setting, we developed the techniques of *mental health collaboration,* in which we had to set aside certain aspects of the nonhierarchical, noncoercive consultant's role to assert the primacy and authority of our ideas when we saw that the management of a case was endangering a patient's mental health.

In our current setting, where we are operating out in the community to lower the risk of psychosocial disorder in children of disrupted families, we are not only seeing a much wider variety of cases and caregivers, but we are often working among forces of very low feasibility—where entry and sanction to operate at all are major obstacles, and where, unlike the welcome offered by the Boston Visiting Nurses, the local agencies may regard us as interfering interlopers.

We were moved to revise our ideas about the need to work within low-feasibility settings, by our exposure to cases of what we have come to call *iatrogenic harm.* This is a medical term that denotes the damage induced in a patient as a by-product of a therapeutic intervention, such as undesirable side effects of medication, secondary infections caused by invasive procedures, and so on. We have extended the words to refer to the harm that is caused to a patient or client by any caregiver, whether physician, teacher, psychiatrist, school guidance counselor, social worker, or judge, in the course of a professional intervention that has the declared intention of curing or preventing psychosocial pathology.

In reviewing cases that have been referred to our clinic in Jerusalem after passing through local religious and secular courts, the adoption service, the welfare-child protection office, the schools, and other agencies, we have been struck by the irony that community services ostensibly dedicated to preventing psychiatric and social disorders are often prone to generating them. Such damage to individuals and families may be so severe that it dwarfs the client's original problem and leads to more psychological suffering and social maladjustment than could have been expected to emerge from the predicament that first brought the client to the notice of caregivers. Colleagues in a number of countries have privately agreed that harm caused by the caregiving system is a serious and widespread problem, but one on which they have been reluctant to speak out for fear of spoiling relations with colleagues.

In our Jerusalem study of how to prevent psychosocial disorder among children of broken families, we tried to identify high risk target groups within the heterogeneous population of divorcing parents whose children appeared to be at particularly high risk of developing pathology. We looked for identifiable groups with certain common characteristics. We expected that by focusing on these target groups in the divorce courts and community agencies, we might be able to help our colleagues address the special needs of these sub-populations; and this might reduce the rates of damage to their children. We identified one such target population among families that are the victims of harmful intervention by malfunctioning professional care givers. Divorce procedures provide fertile ground for iatrogenic damage because they require the opening of the hitherto private domains of a family's circumstances and relationships to public scrutiny by a range of legal and child welfare professionals, any one of whom may interpret and direct the situation into a potentially pathogenic direction. Because many cases of divorcing parents are characterized by intense conflicts between the parties—each of whom seeks to persuade caregivers to identify with them in condemning the other parent and in helping them to wrest the children from the other—divorce cases are particularly conducive to triggering loss of professional objectivity, allowing unconscious or preconscious biases to invade professional functioning. We soon realized, however, that victims of iatrogenic damage were not confined to divorcing families.

As we began to collect and study these cases, we came to recognize commonly occurring warning signs of immanent professional malfunctioning, and realized that it might be possible, therefore, to forestall this significant hazard that increases the risk of ongoing psychosocial disorder in the population, especially among those families that are already vulnerable because they are disrupted and may be socially marginal.

As a result of our study of cases of iatrogenic harm, salience, for us, has now gained an even more urgent meaning. It includes agencies that are not only positioned to support and help individuals in crisis but also, agencies positioned to do particular harm by mishandling those who are disequilibrated and therefore particularly vulnerable. The fact that our entry into such agencies is usually hard to achieve, challenges our theories as consultants and mental health specialists.

Within long-established caregiving fields, it has been recognized that well-intentioned professionals may harm clients because of a lack of knowledge, skill, empathy, or objectivity, (Caplan & Caplan, 1993). The statistical possibility of malfunctioning taking place has been recognized and has been integrated into the planning of medical, educational, legal, and other human services, and avenues have been provided by custom and statute for clients to protest and seek redress. But supervision of staff performance and avenues of redress for clients may not operate effectively in all such cases because the need for them has not been sufficiently anticipated, or because they have been deliberately blocked.

Moreover, unlike the field of physical medicine, where mistakes are known to produce not only measurable, but also inevitable damage, psychosocial interventions give variable results over a variable time span. What works well in one case may be catastrophic in another. For example, certain children who have been alienated from one parent may, ultimately, be immeasurably relieved when the breach is healed, despite initial reluctance and fears about restoring contact. In other cases, the same situation handled initially at least in an apparently similar way, can lead to considerably less encouraging results.

One source of iatrogenic damage that has long interested us is the normally competent caregiver who unwittingly and repeatedly mismanages particular categories of cases. Within an heterogeneous caseload, these professionals may encounter occasional situations that trigger a loss of professional objectivity and consequent lapses in judgement and performance. Such lapses can also occur systematically, when caregivers compulsively hunt out cases that link onto unresolved unconscious themes or conflicts in their own lives, manipulation clients so as to reenact the caregiver's own inner drama. These professionals typically identify issues in a case that are not necessarily based on observable facts, and they distort the evidence to fit the mold of their own making. They may work compulsively, for example, to "rescue" children whom they erroneously perceive to be at risk, stereotyping the family as degenerate, uncaring, and perverted, and rejecting all evidence that contradicts their conclusions.

The hallmark of this category of damaging professionals is their almost religious zeal and self-righteousness; the repetitiveness with which they discover and pursue "similar" cases; the tenacity with which they cling to a distorted image of the clients; and their resistance to acknowledging any indications that may run counter to their own apocalyptic predictions about the client's fate should the professional's own directives for management not be followed. It is as though these caregivers are being driven by forces outside the case that have little to do with concrete reality.

Among damaging professionals are those who have been drawn to fields like child protection, for example, where they are most likely to meet the category of cases that stimulates them to engage in iatrogenically harmful behavior. Working in such an area endows them with a formal mission that may disguise the irrational quality of their functioning and legitimizes their victimization of certain types of clients; for if child protection workers identify and prosecute many cases of abuse and remove supposedly victimized children from their families, they will be regarded as fulfilling their public mandate in exemplary fashion. Although a proportion of their cases may indeed require extreme forms of intervention, others may be misperceived and may not warrant the draconian measures that are meted out to them.

The situation may be aggravated further if a number of caregivers with a similar compulsive drive to hunt down the cases that excite them come together in the same institution. They may gain control of its policy making and of hiring staff; and this may make it virtually impossible for those who are harmed to gain redress because of the solid front that validates the harmful misinterpretation of a case. Such organizations may have high salience but they have very low feasibility because they tend to deny that they are doing harm and they reject any hints by outsiders that their work is anything but perfect. As the director of one such agency repeatedly told a reporter researching an article on their work, "We are engaged in a sacred mission," which in Hebrew are very strong words with messianic overtones.

Most readers will recognize that we are picking up signs of theme interference. A *theme interference* is an unconscious maneuver engaged in by a caregiver in order to solve an unresolved problem in his or her life. The caregiver projects onto a current work situation his or her own unconscious or pre-conscious constellation that is triggered by an evocative cue in the characteristics of a client or in a feature of a client's case. Theme interference is a psychic defense, whereby, to use psychoanalytic terminology, a displacement is effected so that the caregiver confronts and struggles with his or her own problem *out there*, where it is relatively unthreatening because it is supposedly taking place at a safe distance in someone else's life, not obviously within the life of the caregiver. We now recognize that a theme interference signals the possibility of iatrogenic damage taking place.

This displacement process endangers the client for two reasons: First, the cue linking the reality of the client and the unconscious theme in the caregiver is not totally congruent. In order for the theme to fit, the caregiver cannot permit himself or herself to perceive the client and his or her surround clearly and realistically, because the idiosyncrasies of the client and possible discrepancies in his or her identity would spoil the character of the match. Consequently, the caregiver typically stereotypes the client and figures in the client's life, and hence the caregiver's capacity to gather undistorted information about the realities of the case is blinkered because if he or she permitted himself or herself to scrutinize the facts too closely, the mismatch would be revealed and the displacement would be disrupted.

The second danger to the client comes from the fact that the theme is a complex of thoughts and feelings that are linked in the mind of the caregiver with a past problem that he or she has found *insoluble*. For this reason, when the theme is activated, the caregiver feels helpless and hopeless to deal effectively with the issues. Although he or she may struggle to avert that doom, he or she unconsciously does so in a manipulative way that ensures a bad outcome in real life to match the caregiver's fear of failure in his or her own dilemma.

The particular attributes of unconsciously motivated mismanagement caused by a theme interference are characteristic markers for most instances of iatrogenic damage, whether caused by unconscious or conscious forces, namely the creation of a false picture of the client's situation in order to achieve an ending that is, for whatever reason, determined and rendered inevitable from the very outset of contact between client and caregiver. This then leads to premature cognitive closure because it obviates any felt need in the caregiver to pursue and analyze the client's actual circumstances, because to look at reality might threaten the achievement of a prefigured, inappropriate end toward which the damaging caregiver consciously or unconsciously drives the hapless client.

In our experience working as mental health consultants among school teachers, public health nurses, Episcopalian Parish clergy and bishops, and other professional groups, intrusion of unconscious material into the caregiver's work was regarded by superiors and co-workers as an uncharacteristic and unwelcome lapse in the caregiver's accustomed level of effectiveness. A worker who was usually competent was seen as having inexplicable difficulties in a case, which thereby disturbed the mission of the caregiver's agency. The caregiver himself or herself would also be upset by this apparently mysterious inability to manage a case at his or her usual level of functioning. Thus, client-centered consultation depends on workers or supervisors asking for help from a specialist consultant because they realize that a problem exists and they are disturbed by it. Our recent practice has taken place in a wider and more varied context where many cases of iatrogenic damage have been fueled by unconscious bias and stereotyping that are system-linked and are embedded in the cozy collegiality of an hospitable institutional setting, in which neither the individual caregiver, nor the supervisor, nor the higher echelons of their agency have been able or prepared to acknowledge that they have any problem at all. Thus theme interference may be not merely the handicap of an individual worker, but its irrationality and harmful consequences may become legitimized within the social fabric of the organization, from which fortified position it becomes very difficult to dislodge. To summarize so far: In our Jerusalem program, we took on ourselves the responsibility to set up a population-oriented program of primary prevention, which means, according to our value system, that we cannot pick and choose where we can work most comfortably. Instead, we must go where the major threats to the well-being of the target population are to be found. Because we have determined that one of these threats is iatrogenic damage, the elements involved in its etiology and perpetuation must be considered.

The first issue is the behavior of the individual harming professional. Here we are on relatively familiar ground, because we often recognize characteristic aspects of a theme interference, with whose anatomy and manifestations most of us in this room are familiar. However, the second element may be less familiar—namely, the institutional cocooning of the individual damaging caregiver—the protection and support for what we regard as irrationality. This stems from the fact that it is in line with the prevailing ethos of that system; and the consequent reinforcement of what is, to us, a clearly pathogenic manner of case management, and the concomitant rejection of all questioning by outsiders, which ensures that although such agencies' salience is high, their feasibility is very low indeed.

In considering this situation, two facts must be faced: First, the defensiveness of some leading, highly salient agencies is influenced by their operating with embittered and deprived clients who are prone to complain about whatever treatment they receive. Thus these agencies develop a protective posture and are apt to attack any critic in line with the sentiment expressed by one embattled agency head: "Those who don't act, don't make mistakes."

Second, in Israel, a country of immigration and consequent cultural heterogeneity, there are two main, discrepant, value systems in the field of human services. One of them focuses on the rights and needs of the individual and his or her family, holding that the healthy collective is the product of healthy individuals. The second is a value system that focuses on building and safeguarding the collective, or the State, on the grounds that a healthy society promotes the well-being of its individual members, and therefore its adherents demand conformity with generally accepted norms, and tends to discount the discomfort of individuals.

We follow the former tradition, whereas certain key Israeli agencies, especially in the child welfare field, identify with the second philosophy. Therefore, what we designate as damaging, they tend to discount as the inevitable sacrifices on the path to establishing a better end. It would be important to learn what degree of suffering is caused by each of these systems, but such an evaluation cannot be carried out because the adherents of the two philosophies do not talk to each other, each regarding his or her own position as axiomatic.

In order to adapt consultation to such unfamiliar and unfriendly settings, one must identify and separate the formal role and outer trappings of the consultation system from its essential core elements. The first and most obvious of these is preserving and working inside the displacement, thereby avoiding threatening and endangering the consultee's privacy and the integrity of his or her defenses. In inhospitable settings, this means, by extension, being particularly tactful by avoiding as much as possible engaging in frontal attacks against the hidden agenda and what for us are questionable techniques of other professionals. Because such professional malfunctioning is in part linked with defensive strategies, frontal attacks only exacerbate the need to evade and counter outside scrutiny.

A second core element of consultee-centered consultation is that it should provide a safe, supportive setting in which that which the consultee finds threatening or repugnant can be reflected on in a calm, orderly, and professionally dispassionate way. The consultant conveys the message that human relations are expectedly complex and that it is possible and worthwhile to consider how to disentangle this complexity at length, avoiding the over-simplified and stereotyped view, the intolerance of ambiguity, and the premature cognitive closure that characterize iatrogenically damaging interventions.

A third core element lies behind our placing heavy emphasis on the consultant maintaining a nonhierarchical stance vis-à-vis the consultee. This is not based on a liberal ideology, nor is it a purely manipulative procedure, because a noncoercive approach makes it emotionally easier for a consultee to choose to adopt and internalize the consultant's less inhibited and more hopeful view of the client's situation. The nonhierarchical relationship also encourages free expression without fear of disparagement. In these highly defensive organizations, therefore, this is a significant advantage. This runs counter to another widespread growth-inducing technique practiced in many military and authoritarian educational traditions, in which growth is fostered by first inducing stress and discomfort and by tearing down the subject's personality in order to habituate the subject to enduring discomfort and to reconstitute the personality to fit a predetermined mold. The nonhierarchical, noncoercive aspects of the consultation relationship also encourage and enable the consultee to think freely. Within a setting that is safety insulated from the dogmas and political correctness of the consultee's normal professional framework, he or she is set free to play with ideas, to think heretically and unusually, and to be inventive about solving an unusual problem about which he or she may have felt constricted not only for individual unconscious reasons, but also because of the limitations posed by the ideological bias and covert agenda of his or her colleagues. This is in line with our discoveries about crisis intervention that began in Israel and continued at Harvard. The essence of a crisis is that it is a novel situation that taxes an individual by demanding novel responses that are beyond his or her current capacities. The consultant is supporting the consultee during a crisis induced by a problem at work that may be reverberating with a more personal problem. The process of consultation, therefore, involves supporting the consultee during the disequilibrium and confusion of the crisis to arrive at a novel, mentally healthy solution to the present challenge that will be incorporated into his or her ongoing professional problem-solving repertoire.

When attempting to initiate contact with unwelcoming agencies, we would seek to establish a super-ordinate goal. We operate on the assumption that although they are nonfeasible, most community care systems share our desire to engage in good practice and that they would agree in theory that it is desirable to reduce iatrogenic damage and the misery it causes, although they may deny that they perpetrate it. Most caregivers would also agree on the importance of encouraging reality-based perceptions and opposing premature cognitive closure in situations of ambiguity that then lead to over-simplification and stereotyping that foster iatrogenic harm. Without focusing on their own possible involvement or assigning any blame, we would attempt to gain their participation in a joint community-oriented search for ways of achieving a common objective—by disseminating information about the existence of iatrogenic damage and devising ways to counter it. Such a joint educational venture would aim to foster among veteran professionals and their students the value that is axiomatic in medicine and in psychoanalysis—namely, that despite good intentions everyone is fallible and thus liable to cause damage, even inadvertently. Consequently, one must guard against it, and when it occurs, one should face its reality and not try to brush it aside and deny it.

As in consultation, the issues involved in professional malfunctioning should be discussed tactfully and jointly within the defensive structure, otherwise agencies will increase their withdrawal and evasiveness. This also echoes a well-practiced consultation technique: In consultation, we do not confront the consultee with questions about what he or she has done with the client, but we sit next to him or her, as it were, and together look at the problem from the same side of the table. Similarly, if we all sit on the same committee to examine the problem of iatrogenic damage "out there," we become co-ordinate, mutually supportive partners, where everyone's good will is taken for granted in focusing on reducing damage to clients. Although the actual prevalence of harm in the population is not known, most of us may agree that even one such case is too many, especially if it involves the kind of tragic suffering described in our forthcoming book.

In a non-blaming way, caregivers should be encouraged to develop the self-scrutiny that is drilled into medical personnel. Psychoanalysis accomplishes this by an expensive training procedure that teaches candidate practitioners to constantly engage in self-analysis. Because even this is not an infallible solution, they also use mutual surveillance by colleagues, who by definition share a nonhierarchical relationship. Psychoanalysts have established a mode for dealing with professional lapses in which the fact that damaging behavior can occur is conveyed in neutral, nonstigmatizing terms (boundary issues = sexual involvement with patients) and becomes a professional problem to be treated openly and without shame, like any other counter-transference situation. Psychoanalysts, of course, are hardly typical of the generality of caregivers, being extraordinarily highly trained; closely bound to peers; and reveling in introspection and in a fascination with the various odd ways the libidinous unconscious manifests and disports itself. Nevertheless, the principles governing their efforts to prevent damaging clients and, thereby, scandal and public opprobrium, can serve as models to others in the human services fields.

If we wish to start this procedure in agencies that regard us dubiously, we will not necessarily be believed if we approach them with a direct message about our benevolent intentions and the proven safety of our methods. Instead, we should arrange that they overhear and observe what is taking place in the consultation program in a feasible agency, where the doors and windows have been left open, as it were, so that staffs of neighboring systems can see and hear what we are doing. Influencing by catering to the urge to copy and to identify with the modeling behavior of others is quicker, cheaper, and more effective than direct communication and persuasion. Once again, it involves working obliquely within defenses and establishing proximity so that those who are dubious can see for themselves that we are safe and useful.

What we hope to help these nonfeasible agencies to discover is that it is possible to achieve various mission-related as well as intra-organizational goals by creating an atmosphere of mutual support for their workers. That such an atmosphere is inherently attractive was illustrated for us, many years ago, when, engaged in mental health consultation in the field for the Peace Corps, we explained the purpose of our journey to the local American ambassador—that we were bringing a message to the volunteers from the head of the agency that he wanted them to know that when they encountered inevitable pressures in the field because of differences of culture, he knew that they would become personally upset. This, he wanted them to remember, was expected, and he would arrange to help them to master the discomforts and the resulting inefficiencies in their operations. "I wish we could have a program like that," the ambassador said wistfully. "In the Foreign Service, everyone is watching everyone else for the slightest mistake; and when they find one, they jump on you and it leaves an indelible black mark on your record." One way to control iatrogenic damage is to work with caregivers and their management to build into their agency an atmosphere of intercollegial trust that will enable workers to feel secure in revealing the details of their daily work with clients to fellow workers on an ongoing basis without the fear that any inadequacy in their operations will be dealt with by derogatory criticism.

In the pursuit of this goal, and anticipating probable negative, as well as positive results of our proposal, we must persuade caregivers of the need for tact—to convince them to accept that every one of us is entitled to privacy as regards the workings of our own unconscious. Most people have sensitivities to themes that may intrude without warning into one's conscious world, and many of us may "act out" on occasion when our rational judgment is overwhelmed and our focus is narrowed by ghostly visitations from a mercifully repressed past. It must be stressed to colleagues that such eruptions of unconscious material in a coworker is in no way shameful or bad, nor is it to be explored and prodded. If a supportive atmosphere could be fostered, workers may be encouraged to establish dyads or small groups, in which they may share supportive surveillance over each other's daily work on a mutual basis. Each caregiver then may feel secure that he or she will be alerted by his or her supporter (who is not personally involved in this particular case and is therefore less likely to distort his or her perceptions), whenever the colleague involved with the client seems to be closing his or her thinking about a case prematurely, thereby coming to impulsive or irrational conclusions without being aware of doing so. Because the roles of giver and receiver of helpful surveillance would be rotated regularly in response to alternating needs, there should be no loss of face or feeling of undue dependency in such a mutual support system.

In order to select a professional group to be a model for low-feasibility caregivers and their leaders, we need caregivers who are influential enough to be themselves relatively nondefensive and open to new ideas, and whose role constitutes a leverage point because it controls the path along which many iatrogenic damage cases are carried and who are therefore strategically placed to alter the functioning of other agencies. The profession that fulfills our criteria of status, location, and power is that of judges.

Within the overall system of community caregiving, judges are most strategically placed to affect not only the fate of individual children and their families, but also to discourage the perpetration of iatrogenic damage. If judges are motivated to act and are fully aware of likely patterns of injurious behavior against clients, they are among those wielding the most influence and power to change the situation. In order to identify and interrupt the course of conscious and unconscious falsification of the reality of clients; of chronic harassment; and of the imposition of a pre-existing agenda on superficially likely cases that lead caregivers to engage in misdirected punitive behavior and premature closure, judges may be most effectively placed not only to interrupt damaging activities against an individual who appears before them, but also to force changes in long-entrenched practices that, in general, endanger the interests of children and families, culminating in the distorting of the court process itself. For instance, iatrogenic damage may be caused by false testimony because certain child welfare and protection workers, who may not be bound by the judge to tell the truth on penalty of perjury, are usually not cross-examined because they deliver their statements from the bench of the State Attorneys, and appear in the role of experts although they do not have to detail, as do all expert witnesses, their professional expertise and training (that may, in fact, be inadequate to support the authority they claim). These State employees can further falsify the picture of clients by exploiting their privileged status to object to the clients and their expert witnesses testifying in court. All these practices can be stopped by judges who are on the alert to identify such sources of distortion.

It is therefore important to secure the collaboration of the judges in our campaign to reduce iatrogenic harming. We are doing this in Jerusalem through a program of Joint Study Groups for Judges and Mental Health Specialists. We would have preferred to achieve our aims by the well-tried methods of consultee-centered consultation in order to increase the sensitivity and sophistication of judges about problem cases that they feel overtax their current capacity to understand and master because of their inherent complications. But all our attempts over the past 10 years to establish such a program of consultee-centered consultation in the Rabbinic Courts and the secular Family Courts have failed. This is an interesting example in which low feasibility is caused by the realities of the local legal structure. A judge in the Family Court pointed out that it is illegal for judges to discuss cases with outsiders, but that the need to help them master current problems in the area of mental health of divorcing parents and their children might be satisfied by an educational approach rather than by providing the judges with traditional mental health consultation. Therefore, we have worked out a method of sensitizing judges and increasing their knowledge and skill in the mental health area by a special system of discussion groups that focus on understanding the problems of an anonymous, "fictitious" case prepared by a judge, based on a recently completed real case that he or she has handled with the help of a mental health specialist from our team. The stratagem of using a "fictitious" case seems an auspicious way of overcoming both legal obstacles and also the difficulty posed by the fact that judges are supposed to know everything about a case, so that they do not need to have specialist assistance in conducting their role, but only to use expert witnesses in court in carefully delimited ways to focus on details of the functioning of clients. Incidentally, this method of focusing on the case, not on the judge's handling of it, is very much like our focusing on a discussion of the client and avoiding discussing similar issues in the behavior of the consultee.

The stratagem of the "fictitious" case is a manifestation of the mental health consultation principle of displacement. In the "fictitious" case we discuss the essential problems of the real case. The one thing that is lacking is the immediacy of the sense of helplessness of the judge trying vainly to come to conclusions about an apparently insoluble situation. The consultee's crisis-type upset is what makes our consultation intervention so potent a method for engendering professional growth. We try to mimic this situation artificially in the setting of the judge's presentation to the study group, so that the judge acts the part of him or herself being perplexed and upset by his or her current difficulty in the hope that his or her colleagues will identify with him or her and will be engaged emotionally as they identify with his or her professional predicament. This is similar to the situation in a group consultee-centered consultation, as discussed in our book, *Helping the Helpers to Help*, where we arrange for the other group members to identify personally with the presenting consultee, who is talking about the details of his own case, so that they are not merely observers of the consultation process, but become personally involved in it.

Because no aspect of such programs is free from unanticipated complications, after overcoming the organizational issues involved in bringing together for the first time ever in a joint meeting, secular Family Court judges and Rabbinic Court judges; after apparently working through the tensions and animosities of relationships and ideologies of two different and to some extent competing court systems; and after we had one active discussion of a case presented by a secular Court judge, we found that the Rabbinic judges, for the most part, had been bored. We then discovered that the two groups did not mix well, not because of ideological or political reasons, but because the Rabbis were a far more highly-trained and experienced group, with an average of 15–20 years of divorce court service, while the secular Family Court judges for the most part were recent appointees to the Bench. Thus the issues that interested the two groups did not over-lap.

Despite these obstacles, we believe that we will be able to help individual judges recognize the value of our contribution if we can ensure the continuation of proximity. We will try to achieve this by arranging for a flow of philanthropic funds from outside Israel to our program so that we will not need to charge clients fees for our services. We will then recruit appropriate cases and these will legitimately demand judgement in the various divorce courts where we have the beginnings of collaboration between the judges and ourselves. In the current inflationary situation of rising professional fees in Israel which, as one Family Court judge recently observed, has resulted in the experts pricing themselves out of the market, we will therefore be able to arrange the amount of proximity and interaction we need in order to develop relationships with particular judges. And it is hoped that the neighboring judges as well as other community agencies, will want to share the benefits of a program that they and their peers perceive to be worthwhile.

REFERENCES

Caplan, R. B., & Caplan, G. (2001). *Helping the helpers not to harm*. New York: Brunner-Routledge.

13

Consultation and Administrative Coordination in a Special Day Treatment Setting

Eva Rubin

Marjatta Eladhari

INTRODUCTION

The aim of this chapter is to describe how consultee-centered consultation operates within a system of care that enables children with severe emotional disorders to stay in their own homes and to receive specialized education and treatment in *special day-classes* within the general school system. An important part of this program is the *Child Guidance Consultation Team,* hereafter referred to as the "Consultation team" composed of consultants and coordinators. The team has been in existence for 24 years. The purpose is to support the organization of the classes and to contribute to the teachers' professional skills and well-being in such a way that they remain in the program. It is necessary to guarantee the continuity for children in the classes.

We particularly focus on the difficulties that consultants encounter when staying with a required consultee-centered model. First, we describe the program, the administrative structure and then present four different consultation cases. The first two cases are examples of how the consultant manages to maintain the consultation relationship, without taking steps into the organization, but enhancing the consultee's ability to take the necessary contacts. The third and the fourth cases are examples of severe breakdown among those who cooperate in the program requiring the consultant to ask the coordinator for help. After resolving the impasse, the consultant returns to his or her role as a consultee-centered consultant.

The Special Day Class Program

The special day class program combines psychotherapeutic treatment with educational programs for children ages 7 to 17 years, who are average or functioning slightly below average intellectually, with neuropsychiatric or severe emotional disorders. Two specially trained teachers work with a class of four to six children. There are 19 special day classes integrated in mainstream schools in the Stockholm area. Every child in a special day class and his or her family takes part in treatment at a *Child Guidance Outpatient Clinic*, hereafter referred to as the "Outpatient Clinic."

Many professionals from different organizations are involved with each child. This requires an organizational plan that makes it possible for everyone involved to cooperate. Teachers, therapists and families have regular meetings and teachers meet their consultant once a week. A managerial group, the *County Coordinating Board*, is responsible for administration and cooperation among the professionals associated with the special day class programs in the county. The managerial group includes representatives from each local district that operates special day classes as well as representatives from the Consultation team. At the local district level, the *District Co-ordinating Board* is composed of the leader for special education in the district, the special day class teachers, and representatives from the district level Outpatient Clinic, and from the Consultation team (see Fig. 13.1).

The structure of the Organization enables the professionals to avoid conflicts or to handle them in a constructive manner in order to prevent interprofessional conflicts among those involved with the children that may threaten a child's schooling or the therapeutic treatment.

The Consultation Agreement

The organizational model (Fig. 13.1) dictates the boundaries of the relationship between the teacher and the consultant. But the agreement between the consultant and the consultee establishes the framework for the content of the consultation. Each consultee is free to accept or reject whatever the consultant says. The agreement establishes that the consultation should focus the teach-

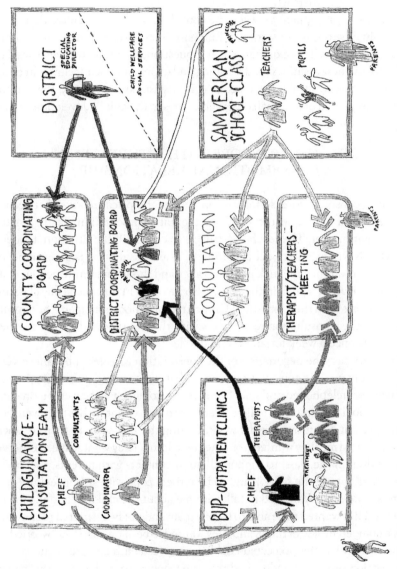

FIG. 13.1. The Administrative Support Structure for the Special Day Classes

ers' difficulties with their professional role (as teachers in a special day class) and their professional boundaries in relation to the work with children and in collaboration with others who are involved with the child.

There is an agreement between the consultant and the consultee that there is no right or wrong in consultation. Emphasis is on the experiences and feelings of the consultees. This experience is not questioned, but freely investigated in order to find new openings for describing and expressing their feelings. In order to support and to sustain the teacher's enthusiasm and creativity, the consultant focuses on all of the small observable steps in the child's development that show progress.

ANN—HOW TO COPE WITH A THREATENING CLOSE EMOTIONAL RELATIONSHIP

This first consultation-case focuses on the psychological relation between a teacher and a child and the teacher's mental representations of the child's home environment. The teacher's struggle to cope with the situation, to identify what is wrong, and to act accordingly. This consultation is an example of how the consultant gets stuck in a blind alley and shows one way to get out of it. The client is Ann, a pupil in the class. Also involved in the special day class are the therapists from the Outpatient Clinic and the school principal. The consultant from the Consultation team meets with the two special day class teacher consultees once a week for an hour and a half.

In Ann's case the negotiation of the consultation agreement became a very important part of the consultation process. Before the very first meeting, one of the teachers telephoned and said: "you are not going to be just a common consultant." So, I was prepared to listen very carefully to what wishes they were going to present about our mutual work. During the first session, I wrote down what they told me they wanted from the consultant. They wanted me to observe the children in the class, to support them in contacts with parents, therapists and others outside the school, and to help them cope with strong feelings and aggressiveness. They wanted to talk with me about the children and the job in general. They wanted to be able to let off steam and not be restricted to showing only a competent side of them, and they wanted to be allowed to feel "worried."

Knowing what they expected enabled me to establish an agreement for our consultation sessions. I understood that the teachers wished to develop "a new way of conceptualizing the work problem so that the repertoire of the consultee is expanded." They also wished something from me that might have turned our consultation-relation into a collaboration-relation instead. That would not promote the deep reflection they wished in the first place, so I made an active choice to keep to the role of a consultee-centered consultant to meet the more complicated and demanding wishes of professional development. In consultation the teachers are expected to present aspects of the work problem about which they are concerned, and to explore possible solutions with the consultant. In a collaborative relationship the teachers would be co-members of a team with the consultant as an additional member. They jointly would discuss the problem and one of the team members would take responsibility for follow-up. In consultation, they could be helped "to cope with strong feelings, not being restricted to show only a competent side and to be allowed to feel worried."

The consultation agreement specified that the object of consultation was to deal with the teacher's professional role and boundaries in relation to the children and in collaboration with others.

Taking this long time to make an agreement had an obvious parallel to the teachers' work with the children. Trust must be developed between consultant and consultees, as it must between teachers and children. I learned that these teachers intended to gain an understanding of the inner world of the child as a basis for their work. They also needed to trust the network of professionals around the child before there was any chance for the children to develop trust in a learning situation.

The Client

The class consisted of two girls and two boys. It was autumn and one of the girls, Ann, had just began her second year in the class. The teachers described her as aggressive and self-destructive. As time went on Ann calmed down and could sit at her desk and work for a while, listen to, and comment about what was happening around her. She began to give short explanations for sores and bruises she had. She related to the teachers mostly in an aggressive and repulsive manner, but could also show trust, asking for help and information, and asking "why" questions.

Other Professionals Involved With Ann

The model of cooperation between the therapists and the parents had been cracked. Therapists told the teachers that the family was withdrawing from contact at the outpatient clinic and they could not help it. They no longer saw Ann. Her parents came rarely to meet the teachers who felt abandoned in their work with Ann and experienced at the same time an increasing emotional closeness to her. Nobody else seemed to care or understand.

The Consultation Process

One of the teachers told the consultant that now Ann had got under her skin. She thought about her all the time. The teachers could not avoid thinking that Ann was a battered child. Ann told about it in her way. Still the teachers were afraid that they were just making up things that did not exist.

The following questions occurred in our consultation sessions from time to time: "How is it possible to endure the deep emotional closeness that is required to succeed in teaching these children?" The need for help from the consultant to endure was expressed in words such as, "we are the only ones to see the child the way she really is with all her difficulties and pain," "we must be nuts doing this kind of job, nobody understands." "We must find a limit inside ourselves so we don't get so close to the child and experience its chaos and pain so much." For me it became clear that these feelings of being alone with so much responsibility originated from disappointments in cooperation with the other professionals as well as a disappointment in the consultant, when I didn't act on behalf of the teachers. The teachers told me at our sessions how their work drained their energy and occupied their whole life. "No one else does anything." They wanted me to do something concrete, or at least to tell them what to do. They told me that they couldn't bear having Ann in the class because of her stories about maltreatment at home and her acting out. But neither could they stand feeling the guilt they would feel if they let her down and tried to get her transferred somewhere else.

As a consultant, I felt incompetent because I did not take the burden away from them. I was tempted to contact other professionals in the organization on the teacher's behalf but I knew that if I did, we could not continue the consultee-centered consultation they initially asked for. The teachers had to carry on their work with Ann and I had to endure meeting with them every week, listening without acting out. Doing so I gained an emotional understanding of the painful situation they lived in every day. I could not take the burden away from the teachers and the teachers could not give up the burden of Ann. The teachers also began to tell me about their own somatic symptoms at the consultation sessions.

I encouraged them to ask for a meeting with their director to describe their difficult situation. They were suspicious—he wouldn't understand them. They met him anyway and he promised them help and support, if they told him what could be of help to them. They still felt misunderstood and I thought they wished a miracle to interfere and unburden their sufferings. I could not become a god, and I understood now that neither could the teachers, but they wanted to have a godlike power to be able to help Ann. The teachers seemed to believe that it was their responsibility to take away the suffering from the child and that they failed as teachers when it was not possible. There was a parallel between the child's powerlessness and incapacity to express it and the teachers' experience of helplessness. I considered the situation to be a professional crisis. According to the principles of consultee-centered consultation, the consultant is not supposed to act to take away the difficult situation but to approach the consultees' representation of the situation. When the consultees feel that it is possible for the consultant to understand (emotionally and cognitively) their situation, they are ready to move towards a more neutral and objective evaluation of the work problem, which opens up consideration of different solutions and the foundation for conceptual change.

As consultant I had to tolerate the feeling of helplessness in order to understand their helplessness. Now, it became possible for the teachers to acknowledge their knowledge of Ann's home situation and ask her more specific questions about it. This questioning led the teachers to understand that they knew enough to proceed and inform the social welfare agency about Ann's situation. They insisted on doing this even if it would result in moving Ann from her home and perhaps also from the class. They expressed a new strength. They knew that they were taking a difficult step for Ann and for themselves and they knew that they were responsible for what they were doing. They did not express anxiety and fear anymore. The teachers, thus, gave up the hope of a miracle-solution without disqualifying themselves and their consultant. At the same time they gained back their professional self-respect. It was possible for them to have feelings of inadequacy and still know that they were working successfully as teachers.

Discussion and Conclusions

The teachers said that they wanted "support in coping with strong feelings," "not being restricted to show only a competent side," "to be allowed to feel worried" said with a little laughter. None of us was conscious at that time when it was said what it actually meant but it opened up a window for reflection.

In this part of our job we touched the very basis of the work of teachers in a special day class—the demanding duality of, on one hand, a deep understanding and sharing of the child's inner world and on the other hand staying back in the role of a teacher. One of the reasons the teachers gave for consultation was to have support to handle the children's strong feelings and aggressiveness, but also support in managing their own feelings in contact with the pupils. When the teachers said that they could hardly bear the feelings the children invoked in them and the consultant realized her inability to help them, a point was reached in consultation that could be a turning point, moving toward conceptual change, a moment of meeting, or a break in the working alliance. It was an ordeal to return as consultant to the consultation without any concrete help for the teachers. This gave me an emotional understanding of what the teachers' experienced everyday with Ann. Anxiety and fear because of their feeling of helplessness prevented the teachers from proceeding to act on Ann's behalf. They felt that they were stuck with her in the classroom and if they removed her they betrayed her. They could not move in any direction, creating a professional crisis that deepened every day. It was up to the consultant to keep focused on Ann so it was possible to understand the feelings behind the crisis and how to handle it.

The incident with the director, whom the teachers did not regard as considerate, although he verbally acknowledged that he understood their problem, gave the consultant a new dimension of understanding. The director probably could not show empathy in the way teachers expected just as the teachers expected magic solutions for Ann. This was a process that paralleled the girl's inability to talk and describe her problems in words to ask for help.

Identifying the problem as the teachers' fear of feeling inadequate gave the consultant a *feeling of capability*. The feeling of danger disappeared from the consultation and, at the same time, the teachers showed that their feeling of danger vanished.

Hylander described this consultation process as going into a *blind alley* (Hylander, 2000). There is a tug of war between the consultees' expectations of the consultant, and the consultant's focus on gaining a clear understanding of the problem. The consultation presents a "mission impossible," neither the consultees nor the consultant actually believe that the teachers will solve the dilemma, but the consultant presents his or her understanding of the problem as if he or she believes that it is possible. Not until the consultant becomes aware of his or her own representations is a move possible; consequently, the teachers can change their way of framing the problem and act accordingly. In the meanwhile, the teachers' and the consultant's relationship is protected by the mutual consultation agreement. They have a strong working alliance created by mutually articulated expectations and they are also protected by boundaries in the organization. They can lean heavily on the contract: consultation once a week with the same consultant and teachers as long as the teachers work in the class, and an agreed on way of working that involves asking, describing, and reflecting.

TEACHERS DENY THEIR OWN DRAWBACKS INSTEAD OF ACKNOWLEDGING THE FACT THAT ONE TEACHER IS COPING WITH DAVID'S ANXIETY

The Client

David, a psychotic boy, started school in a regular classroom when he was seven. The large variety of stimuli made him restless and chaotic. The school tried to solve the problem in different ways. Ultimately he spent the days at home with an assistant and a teacher visiting him each day for one hour of schoolwork. That should give the reader an idea of the agony he awoke in the people surrounding him. He came to the special day class program after having failed completely. He could neither express himself nor give adequate expression to anger, fear, sadness, or happiness in relation to other people. He could not stand still for more than a few minutes not to mention sitting on a chair and focusing on schoolwork. He was frequently too close physically to other children and grownups. They were all afraid of him and could not handle the situation. He was repeating meaningless words and had only very few moments of harmony and calmness in his life.

After one and a half years in the special day class, his anxiety is still there, but it is vanishing in the closeness of a well-known, relaxed teacher and in well-known surroundings. When the situation changes or something unexpected happens, his anxiety increases and David needs an immediate support from one of his teachers to prevent his anxiety from escalating. The teacher support is to hold his shoulders and seek eye contact, and at other times to embrace him and hold him tightly.

The Consultation Process

The problem brought to consultation was a question of David's integration into a regular class. Two semesters passed before one of the four teachers started to plan for David to have a trial integration. She wanted him to be with normal children to see how they acted and also to give him an experience of being with other children without frightening them. The plan was for the teacher to follow the boy into one classroom with children of the same age for one hour. The other three teachers, however, thought that the timing of integration was too early and totally impossible. They thought that he was not ready, and that it would hurt him and damage him even more. The four consultees gave more or less the same description of the boy's behavior in different situations and how he related to other children. But the teachers' descriptions of how they reacted to him were totally different. The teacher who wanted to integrate David was not afraid to correct him whenever it was needed—to shout at him, to hold him, or to embrace him. The other teachers thought that doing this in public was offensive to them and the boy. They had totally different suggestions for giving David necessary boundaries and they varied in their ability to cope with his anxiety and extreme behavior. The only person who was not overwhelmed by his anxiety was the teacher who wanted to integrate him into the regular classroom. A deep trust and confidence had developed between this teacher and the child. She was able to create calm periods with the boy where he also was able to show a capacity to learn. With the support of the teacher he was able to be with other children, which gave him great joy and a sense of reparation. It increased his general capacity and functioning as a schoolboy.

When each of the consultees had the opportunity to describe their work with David, their insight gradually grew. They acknowledged that they all were performing valuable work and that David was making progress. Consequently, when they accepted the fact that they were contributing to David's development, the question of whether he should be integrated in a regular classroom or not was relevant any more. The focus of consultation had moved from the boy's capacity for integration to the consultees' different levels of readiness to meet the boys' anxiety and odd behaviors in public. For the boy the limited integration in a regular classroom with one teacher was possible and now supported by all of the consultees.

Discussion

Through the consultation process the consultees reframed their problem from a question of integrating or not integrating to an issue about how to relate to a difficult child. The cognitive change implied an acknowledgment and acceptance of their different relations to the child.

THE CONSULTATION PROCESS INTIMATELY INFLUENCED BY CONFLICTS IN THE ORGANIZATION

The Work Problem

The teachers have very successfully, for a long period of time, worked intensely to integrate their special day class into the regular school curriculum. Each student has a host class where they participate in classroom activities whenever possible. There is a great deal of collaboration between the special day class teachers and the regular teachers in the school. One day the teachers are informed unexpectedly that their special day class is to be moved to another school because of the shortage of classrooms.

The Consultation Process

Teachers start a consultation session by saying "Do we really have to start all over again?" They are very negative about being moved. The teachers say that the special education director avoids all contact with them, gives no information about how he is going to handle the issue, and has no advice about how the teachers should act in relation to all the people they are cooperating with around the children. What should they do and what should the director do and what should the principal of the local school do to inform parents, therapists, other teachers and the children? They are extremely anxious. The trauma about moving is palpable in the consultation room. They do not talk about the children. Teachers project all their anxiety and become aggressive. They say that they need the consultant to meet their own needs. Their workload is too heavy, parents do not appreciate what they are doing for their children, and the therapists are not doing a good job with the children and the families. The teachers think that they give these children more than they give their own children. Now they have all decided to quit and look for another job.

The consultant makes it clear to the teachers that what they can do together in consultation is to talk about how they can handle their situation at work, how they can meet the principal and the director and what kind of difficulties with them they can expect. They can ventilate their disappointment with how the issue is handled and investigate what kind of responsibility they really have in relation to children and parents. They may also recapitulate the structure of the responsibilities in the program and analyze who, actually, has the power to decide if they are going to move or not. The consultant also comments on their joint decision to quit, which will make them feel united for a short while when they inform the director, but then they have to make their own individual decision for their own futures.

The Reaction of the Consultant

The consultant gets tired and irritated, feeling that the teachers are functioning on a very low level. The consultant wants the teachers to be professional (according to the agreement) toward children and parents. Teachers feel that they are not wanted in the school and that their students are not good enough to be there. The consultant is working intensely to return the discussion to a professional level.

Loss of Professionalism

In this crisis situation theme interferences appear. An excellent teacher, with high standards of performance with a need to control things, starts to talk about awful consequences and paints people in dark colors, people that she usually works with in a productive manner. She just lets go with all her anger. (She is a clever big sister for a brother with a handicap.) Another teacher, who is the mother of a small child, says that she cannot be close to the children in class because she feels she is neglecting her own child because of her job situation. She concludes that this is an impossible way of working.

The Tug of War

During the consultation session the aggression is first turned toward the consultant, but then is redirected and the conversation becomes more constructive. A week later the situation is the same, and the teachers express the same aggressive acting-out behavior. When the consultant arrives teachers talk loudly in the corridor to each other about a message that should be given over the phone to parents and therapists: "Everybody is going to quit and the class is being moved away." They act very powerful toward the consultant and tell her that she has to be their therapist, because that is the kind of need they have. They need someone who cares about them and protects them. They give way to suspicions that the consultant has information that she is not giving them. They start the session by saying that they have many things to talk about and ask the consultant if she has something special that they should know. Later it is evident that there have been rumors about a change of consultant. They think that the consultant is leaving and they want to have information.

The situation becomes critical and the consultant, reflecting on the tug of war she is in with the teachers, decides that she cannot manage this without help from the organization. She informs the chief of the Child Guidance Consultation Team about the teachers' crisis. The consultant wants her chief to talk to the special education director to give her information about the crisis and to tell her how important it is that she takes responsibility for moving the classroom by informing parents and therapists, and by meeting with the teachers throughout the moving process.

At the next consultation session the teachers are much calmer and can talk about the children again. In the sessions that follow teachers talk about quitting and separation but in a more constructive way. Personal choice and wishes have evolved and they are not united anymore in a collective punishment to the program.

Discussion

This case clearly shows that the consultation process is intimately influenced by the conflicts in the organization. The prospect of moving a class exposes a weakness in the organization, in this case an unclear negotiation between the local principal and the special education director. This unclear negotiation infects the consultation and the relationships between all involved: teachers, pupils, parents, and therapists. One objective for the consultant has been to interfere with the teachers' regression, in order for them not to act out but to turn their anger to where it belongs in the organization. The consultant and the consultees discussed their representations of the structure of the program. When the pressure from the consultees became too strong, the consultant focused on the teachers' individual choices and responsibilities and also decided to take action with her administrator about the chaos moving the class has created and to involve a higher level in the organization. This action enables the consultant to return to consultee-centered consultation. The consultation resolved the crisis when the teachers became clear about their own responsibilities and were satisfied with the solution of the crisis, thus being able to make individual professional choices and plan for a good separation from children and parents.

KARIN—CO-OPERATION BETWEEN CONSULTANT AND CO-ORDINATOR IN A CONSULTATION PROCESS—THREATS TO THE ORGANIZATIONAL FRAMEWORK AND BOUNDARIES IN CONSULTATION

The consultant is part of the same organization and is therefore an internal consultant. But the consultant comes to the school only for consultation and her involvement with the other professionals in the program is kept to a minimum. Karin's case is an illustration of circumstances that force the consultant to act in a way she wouldn't intend to and one that threatens the consultee-centered consultation. The responsibilities and boundaries of the professionals in the organization enable the consultant to return to her consultee-centered consultation relationship.

The Client

Karin is a 9-year-old girl beginning her third year in the special day class. Before school starts, her psychiatrist had suggested placing her in a treatment home. Her parents refused to send her to a home. When Karin came to school, she could not play and take roles; for example, she *was* a cat instead of playing cat. She also had a language disability.

Professionals in Other Units in the Organization

Karin's mother had had some contact with a psychiatrist from the Outpatient Clinic, however, Karin received no treatment. The teachers meet the psychiatrist and the psychologist, who had examined Karin before she started school, in teacher-therapist meetings according to the model established by the organization. Karin had a day care assistant before starting school, who followed her to school and Karin stayed with her in her home during the afternoons. At school the teachers meet with Karin and her mother regularly at parent–child conferences. . The coordinator from the Consultation Team became a very important person in this case by coordinating with the professionals from the child guidance organization as well as the principal in the local school, the special education director, and a child welfare assistant.

The Consultation Process

The three main themes in consultation became: how to help Karin to develop; how to create trust between Karin's mother and the teachers; and how to cooperate with the Outpatient Clinic.

Teachers brought to consultation their view of Karin's home situation. Karin's relation with her mother bothered them. Karin's mother made no demands on her because she was "disturbed." In other situations, her mother expected her to be independent and "normal." Karin's mother was described as aggressive, pointing out "enemies" who changed from time to time, such as the school, the social services office, Karin, Karin's father, or the neighbors.

Teachers thought that Karin simply needed explanations of what was expected of her and she could manage demands adequately at school. Karin had temper tantrums at home but not at school. Teachers said that they could manage her, and that she let teachers direct her.

The teachers meet with Karin and her mother regularly at parent–child conferences. Karin and her mother are not able to sit together at these meetings when they are expected to both participate and focus on the school. Instead, they act out their own conflicts in front of the teachers.

Teachers also observed that Karin was anxious in class, rubbing out her writing and drawings. She longed for her mother, made herself impossible, said that she did not want to go to this class, and said insulting things to other children. In consultation it becomes clear that Karin does better at school when she feels that there is contact and good relations between her mother and her teachers. Once the teachers assured Karin's mother, after Karin had been in a fight with other children, that Karin is welcome to come to school even though she fights, her mother's fear of being criticized fades away and she becomes less aggressive. Karin starts to understand that her mother and her teachers act and think differently and neither of them is wrong. She begins to use her energy for playing and for her schoolwork and she starts to tolerate challenges.

Break Between the Outpatient Clinic Staff and the Teachers

According to the teachers, Karin's diagnosis from Outpatient Clinic was "inner chaos, probably brain damage and autism," but the teachers thought that her problems were due to a chaotic home environment with lack of structure and consistency. They wanted Karin to have a new examination, as they did not observe the autism that Karin was expected to have. The teachers try to convince the Outpatient Clinic that Karin has capacity and that she is developing mentally and could profit from therapy.

In consultation the teachers say that they are not going to meet the psychiatrist any more. They feel insulted and lectured to by him and feel that he blames them when they talk about Karin's difficulties. They cannot meet him without arguing and they do not want to fight with a grown-up therapist. They only want to get help for Karin. The teachers refuse to fulfil their work assignment, which includes cooperation with the Clinic. The system of care program is not working as intended.

The Consultant's Considerations During the Session

When the teachers announce their decision to refuse cooperation with the therapists, they also ask the consultant for approval to do so. It is easy to understand their need for acceptance, as the consultant is part of the program that promotes cooperation. But they also threaten the boundaries of consultee-centered consultation as they try to pull the consultant into a hierarchical relationship, where she is supposed to give them approval like a supervisor or head of the organization. To be able to continue to work in the consultee-centered way it is necessary to avoid this role confusion. The teachers need, according to the consultation agreement, freedom to use consultation without judgments about their actions. It is the task of the consultant to guard the consultation agreement and to keep a space of reflection open. The consultant invites the teachers to draw a picture of the organization together with her and to point out where the fight is taking place. This creates a space for reflection and the consultant is free from the teachers' demands to take sides in the conflict. In the picture the teachers draw, the place for the conflict seems to be the therapist/teachers meeting. The situation has reached a crisis there.

The consultant now realizes that the crisis cannot be handled just in consultation with the teachers. The system of care organization is involved. She recommends that the teachers inform their chief, the special education director, about the crisis. The consultant also states that she should inform her coordinator, which the teachers agree to.

Involving the Coordinator

The coordinator's role is to reinforce established organizational patterns, deepen the understanding of the situation for all involved, and let the different pictures of the girl be apparent to everybody. This arrangement gives the consultant freedom to stay within the consultation agreement and to remove herself from the crisis in cooperation among the different professionals involved in the program. She can listen to the presentations of the teachers without questioning their work and the teachers can use the consultation to focus on their work in the classroom, without having to bother with what is going on outside the classroom.

The coordinator now takes the responsibility to call a meeting of the District Coordinating Council. If cooperation between professionals cannot be established, Karin cannot stay in her class. The Outpatient Clinic and the school do not understand each other's way of working. They have different pictures of the girl's problems and the proper treatment. They all have ideas of what other professionals are doing without listening to each other. After a series of meetings, the network around Karin reaches a common understanding of Karin's situation and how exposed she is. A plan for action is created and the participants identify their separate fields of responsibility. For example, the Outpatient Clinic, instead of the County Coordinating Board, decided which child gets a place in a class. Also professionals from the clinic told the teachers how to teach and gave them pedagogical advice. The teachers, on the other hand, told the therapist what kind of clinical treatment the children needed and how to handle parents.

At the meetings, when it becomes apparent that there is a lack of care-taking for Karin at home, an assistant from child welfare joins the network. Network meetings now replace the failing therapist–teachers meetings. The coordinator has created a new forum for cooperation.

During the meetings the coordinator recognizes that the tension is lessening and questions among the professionals start to get more frequent. One obvious sign of a change occurred at a District Coordinating Council meeting when pupils and the special day classes are discussed. The teachers and the principal ask about the treatment the Outpatient Clinic will offer and about the willingness of the parents to cooperate. The chief of the Outpatient Clinic provides deeper explanations about the cases and a fruitful discussion follows.

At the end Karin gets treatment and special schooling, has the support of social welfare and the cooperation among all those involved in her case. The situation is similar to a treatment home, but it is within the organizational frame work for the special day class. The result is that Karin can stay at home and develop together with her mother.

Discussion

The usual organization around a child in a special day class is not enough to contain and secure the work in Karin's case. There was a feeling of insufficiency in the therapist–teacher meetings. In fact, there was a real lack of help for Karin that neither the teachers nor the therapists could prevent. When consultee-centered consultation is threatened by a failure of collaboration in the organization, the coordinator of the Consultation team interferes on behalf of the consultant. This intervention offers the organization the possibility of collaboration on another level permitting the consultant to remain in her consultation role. When the special education director takes responsibility and supports the teachers and the chief of the Outpatient Clinic takes responsibility and supports the therapists, their collaboration secures the framework of the consultation relationship and the teachers can focus on what is going on in class. When all involved have clear areas of responsibility and boundaries, the collaboration in the organization has improved, the network around Karin functions and consultee-centered consultation may achieve its goals of conceptual change to improve the situation for Karin and for other children in the class.

REFERENCES

Hylander, I. (2000). *Turning processes. The change of representations in consultee-centered case consultation.* (Dissertation). Linköping: Linköping University. Department of Behavioural Science.

14

The Consultation Process in Corporate Groups

Margit Ekenbark

This chapter describes consultee-centered consultation to leaders in different kinds of organizations. The prerequisites for the kind of consultee-centered consultation described in this chapter are that consultation is conducted in groups of consultees and within a specific contracted period of time. The consultant may, for example, be hired for a consultation session every fourth week for one year.

The experience reported here was drawn from two different types of corporate groups: groups of leaders and managerial teams. Each type has a differential impact on the consultation process. The groups of leaders do not have a joint work problem to present, but the problems they experience are similar. The leaders in the managerial teams usually have two general goals. They want to develop their role as a member of the managerial team and they want to develop their individual role as a leader of a group of employees. It might be useful to differentiate this kind of consultation from other types of consultee-centered consultation, as there is a difference in the process if the focus is a client of an organization or an employee in the organization. It could simply be labeled leader-centered consultation, which would imply that the focus oscillates between administrative questions and single employees. Two types of leader-centered consultation can be described: group consultation with leaders coming from different parts of the organization or from different organizations and group consultation with managerial teams.

In my work with leaders from different levels in organizations, it has become apparent that the double focus in the definition of consultee-centered consultation—*to enhance the work role of the consultee* and to help him or her *to develop a new way of conceptualizing the work problem*—has more dimensions than I first had thought.

In my practice with different groups of leaders over the these last years, I have noticed that leaders coming for developmental or problem-solving consultation in groups, show a much more complicated, interesting, and creative way of working with their problems than I experienced when my focus in the consultation process was more single-dimensional and individual-focused on problems concerning individual employees. The different roles of the leaders in their day-to-day work, and the varying work problems they encounter in their roles influence the consultation group and the work process in consultation.

THE CONSULTATION PROCESS
IN CORPORATE GROUPS

Experiences from more than 25 corporate groups have given me a picture of the consultation process that I have found useful in my work with leaders in different settings. Many of these consultations were part of an extensive developmental leadership program in which the participants also attended seminars where different themes of leadership were explored.

Every consultee in the group presented his or her specific problem in contrast to a group where a common joint problem would be discussed. Even if the problems of the consultees sometimes are very similar or almost the same, they are presented as individual problems.

The participants were leaders of preschool and school organizations. The objective of the consultation was to develop the leadership competence of the consultees. Sometimes the problem was about their managers and/or colleagues, but the primary focus of attention was on problems concerning their employees, parents, children, or other people. But themes like leadership, strategies, priorities, administration, and organization also came up. Consultee-centered consultation with groups of leaders was characterized by an oscillation in focus between general issues that most consultees were interested in and individual problems concerning relations to one employee or client.

Out of this multiplicity of consultees, groups, and consultations, little by little, a pattern of behaviors and reactions has fallen out. Even if the focus of the presentation is on the consultee, it is indirectly on the consultant, as the process of consultation between the consultant and the consultee develops. The consultant is the guide, but a guide who does not always know where he or she and the group are heading.

In order to describe the process I formulate it as five phases that the consultant and the consultee have to pass through.

Formulating a Problem

If you do not have a problem there is no solution. If you do not have a question there is no answer.

One of my consultees started by saying: "I have no problems to discuss because my employees fit very well together. We are like friends and they all know what to do. But I can listen to the others who need more time." In this short introduction, she gave the group the opportunity to raise a number of questions. Her way of thinking changed from seeing a problem as something that should not exist in a good workplace to a problem as an opportunity for change. Together we also defined two or three themes worth discussing.

Development grows out of conflicts, problems, questions, and dilemmas. Because consultation, in general, aims at development and learning, the first step is formulating the problem. The embryo of change, perhaps even the solution of the problem, lies in the ways the problem is formulated or framed. The formulation of the problem is a process that the consultee begins, helped by the consultant. The solution often consists of reframing the problem.

Another consultee comes to the group saying: "I have a problem. One of my employees cannot cooperate with the others in her group. I don't know what to say to her and how to handle her. Do you have any suggestions?" This consultee offers an unsolved problem and is open to different solutions. He lives in the present with a flexible attitude to the future. He is offering the group his dilemma. He "owns one problem with 100 ways out."

Still another consultee says: "I don't know what is wrong, but I can't work effectively with my vice manager. I have chosen him myself but we don't get on very well together. Can you help me?" This consultee offers an unsolved problem and is open for a gradual reformulation (reframing) of it. In this case, the consultee has an even more flexible attitude to the perspective of time. She has 100 questions and no answers. She is grounded in the present but makes busy journeys both backward and forward in time. She is prepared both to redefine the problem and to look at different solutions. "With 100 questions and no answer" is one way to describe her attitude.

Discussing the Problem From Different Aspects

One of my consultees once said to me: "It would have been much better if you also had experience working as a preschool leader, then you would have understood what it is like." She found it extremely difficult to answer my questions about how she felt and thought and what was special about her work problem.

It is important to promote a feeling of confidence in the group so that the consultees interpret questions as a way of investigating, not as a way of criticizing, or as a way of disciplining. For the consultation process to continue the consultees must have enough confidence and trust in the consultant and the group so as to present their own inner pictures of reality, to verbalize thoughts, perceptions, and feelings. The consultees are involved with their problems. Consequently, they report them in their own subjective way, with all the attendant feelings, imperfect logic and chronology, and necessary blindness. By labeling thoughts and feelings about the work problem in consultation, the consultees get a chance to develop a distance from their own experiences and inner images.

An important part of the consultation process is to understand the difference between one's own inner picture and the outer reality and to dare to take in another person's presentations of their reality. Some of my consultees say: "We think it is an advantage that you don't work in this organization and know all the people we are talking about." To oscillate between inner picture and outer reality, fantasy and reality, and feeling and thought promotes the consultation process. The consultant helps the consultees to take one step backward, look at, differentiate between, and label the different realities. Thus they will be able to discuss themselves as parts in a play, an interaction where their parts influence the whole and the whole influences them. The consultant creates this playground by showing confidence in the consultees. The competence of the consultant to give secure boundaries to the consultation is therefore an essential prerequisite for the play to take place.

To Come to a Decision

This phase is about handling ambivalence. The consultees now have enough tolerance of frustration to stand the chaos created by a decision that still has to be made. They are also able to keep alive the different ideas in their inner space and let them mature before they try them out in reality.

One consultee reported a situation where she had three newly employed preschool teachers who asked so much of her that she could hardly bear it. One of the other consultees described how she had made an introductory program for the first weeks for newly employed teachers. The consultee immediately asked her colleague to send her this program and wanted to finish the consultation. She was not yet ready to investigate the whole problem, but was happy to get a recipe.

One of the difficulties involved in a process of conceptual change is to give room for expression of different kinds of ideas, which consultees often experience as chaos created by an undefined question and no answer. It is a challenge for the consultees to permit themselves to stay in this chaos as long as necessary for different alternatives to be explored and to develop into a new way out. They have to be able to bear the psychological frustration, stay in the creative phase, and not close the circle too early. Of course, the same applies to the consultant. The consultant who can not stand the chaos of expectation, but delivers solutions and alternatives too early in the process will not promote enough confidence in the consultees to enable them to find their own solution. In cooperation with the consultant, the consultees must find solutions that they can accept. Because the consultees are the only ones who have all the details and facts about the background of the problem and likewise are the ones who will carry through the solution the group ends up with, the solution has to be owned by the consultees.

The consultees also must give up perfect solutions on behalf of possible ones. There are always prejudices that have to be abandoned. The need to feel competent paired with our omnipotent childish imaginations, makes us all inclined to reach for the optimal solution instead of inventing one that is realistic.

Implementation

Implementation means to move from thought to action. In consultation, the process is going on, but out in reality, nothing more has happened. One of the risks in consultation is that it can become a pseudo occasion, where nothing comes out of it. The goal of consultee-centered consultation is conceptual change. It is implied that conceptual change is a change of feelings, thoughts, and action-motivation. If there is no change in relation to a client, or in relation to a consultee's work problem, what has happened in consultation is a reversible turning, a conceptual change that changes back again.

In one of my consultation groups, a consultee was discussing a problem she had with her manager. The manager didn't see what and how she was performing as a leader. The consultee wanted her manager to come out to her workplace to visit her and talk about her work, but she never did. The consultant asked the consultee if she had talked to her manager about her wish. She said she hadn't and immediately got the idea that she should go to her manager to tell her. So, she asked for a short break in the consultation. I did not think the break was a good idea, but we used the rest of the time to discuss the things she should think about before she went to her manager.

To many people it is natural to spend a lot of time thinking, reflecting, symbolizing, talking and discussing. To others, it is much more natural to "roll up one's sleeves," go to work, and settle the matter. In other words, act, produce something, or do something. Those who are too much oriented in one direction may become either a dreamer or a visionary and those oriented too much in the other direction may become persons acting out their impulses.

By providing frustration and maintaining boundaries, the consultant gives room for this dance between thought and action.

Following Up and Evaluating Results

In this phase, the competence of the consultees to handle the aspects of time and space in the consultation becomes important. Psychological time has its origin in our perception of time as duration. It consists of a feeling, a perception of order of the inner experiences as continual, simultaneous, and harmonious contrasted with something inconsistent and without rhythm, quick, or slow. Out of this perception of time as duration, *time as perspective*, develops. Time, as a perspective is more conceptual and less intuitive and sensitive than time as duration. Together with time as perspective, the concepts of future time, present time, and past time come up. The experience of time as duration is dependent on the competence to remember and to wait (Hartacollis, 1986).

After having had a long consultation about a child acting out with repeated aggressive outbursts, I met the group after summer. I asked the consultee about the child and she told us that everything was all right. He was getting on well. When I asked why she thought he was getting on so well now, she told me that after a long and fine summer all the children felt and behaved better. This was an example of a consultee experiencing time as duration. The consultants task here is to help her to develop her way of seeing time as perspective by giving her tools to analyze what she had done and what she actually did with the child in question.

In this phase, both the consultant and the consultees have returned to the playground where they were in the phase of discussion in order to be able to connect specific feelings, thoughts, behaviors and ideas discussed to the relevant later actions of the consultee. The consultee has to have access to the two different views of time—time as duration and time as perspective. Lacking this, concepts like planning and projecting become incomprehensible. The relation between cause and effect becomes artificial and hazardous and the weather becomes a stronger determining factor than consciousness and planning.

I want to underline that the presumed phases of development of the consultee are not complete, but rather should be seen as an attempt to put words to the multidimensional process to which the consultee is exposed.

Even after having found a structure, a way of understanding one's experiences, as I have outlined in the phases of consultation, there will always be something new to understand and learn in these multidimensional processes of consultee-, or leader-centered consultation.

I give a few examples in the following:

GROUP CONSULTATION WITH A MULTIDIMENSIONAL PROBLEM IN A MANAGERIAL GROUP

As mentioned earlier, there are two aspects of the professional role of the consultee, leader and member of a managerial team, that have a great impact on the relationship to the client. In this case, the "client" is the staff or a member of the staff. The role of the leader has a more direct impact on the "client" whereas the role as a member of the managerial team has a more indirect impact on the client from an organizational perspective.

In consultation with a managerial group there is a need for an alternating focus in the consultation process between these two roles or work problems. It is impossible to work with one role at a time or to exclude one or the other. The focus of the consultation may oscillate between questions concerning role relations in the managerial team and role relations among the staff of each leader.

The fact that the consultees are members of a managerial team will greatly influence the way the work process is carried out. A managerial team always has a task, more or less well defined. The members of the managerial teams may have different roles but they also may have roles that are very much alike. Being a staff manager or a controller constitute specific and different roles. The consultees, however, may also all share the same role of a leader in an administrative hierarchy. The leader of the managerial team on the other hand has always a specific role.

Managerial teams differ from each other in their routines and work procedures. How often do they meet? For how long? Do they write minutes? What kind of minutes? Every managerial team is also carrier of a culture of their own and of a specific way of communicating. The culture of a group may be described as the personality of the group, and is characterized by its way of building up or failing to build up relevant defense systems for its work, flight from here and now to there and then, projections onto the next hierarchical level of the organization, denying of responsibility, intellectualization, and so forth.

The culture can also be characterized by the way the group focuses on exceptions rather than the rule, and the way that it focuses on history instead of a focus on present or future. Other themes can be about power, responsibility, authority, mandate, and so on.

A managerial group's way of communicating is, on one hand, part of their culture and on the other an obvious sign of its defense system. Do they let questions fall or do they come to a decision? Is talking nothing but just talking? Are the words of the leader more true and important than what other people say? Do they avoid talking about important issues and are they spending a great part of their time on details? Are they outwardly effective, discussing and making decisions only to leave the team and forget all about it? Do they all talk a great deal, but only about their own issues? Do they listen to each other?

This description of a managerial team and its members seems to apply to every working group. This means that the investigation of the questions just mentioned form a platform from which it is possible to scrutinize the individual roles of the leaders and how they relate to their staff, as a group as well as individuals. By understanding their own behavior, their deficiencies as well as competencies, it makes it easier to attend to their own staff and understand their way of functioning.

If the focus is only on the managerial team there is a great risk that the process stops and becomes superficial. Through the emergence of the work problems concerning their individual roles of being leaders or concerning their different staff or staff members, the process accelerates, picks up energy and thereby is better able to attain the goals.

A Frightened Group

A managerial team consisting of ten leaders came for consultation. They wanted to meet once a month during one year, one day each time. Their goal was to develop as leaders and form a way of working together that was good for them and good for the organization. They were working in a service-producing enterprise with a long history of hierarchical and authoritarian thinking. In the last decade, however the agency had undergone extensive changes and a great deal of responsibility had been distributed on to the leaders.

The fourth time we met in the group, one of the leaders, John, arrived declaring that he wanted to bring up his problem as a leader. Before this, the group had spent a great deal of time discussing common questions, "chatting" about similar problems from their different work places. This had mainly become a defensive strategy against focusing on individual work problems and thereby having to reveal one's deficiencies. It had also prevented the group from deepening its questions and finding new ways out of the problems. Now John wanted to discuss his work problem with the rest of the group. John's situation, in short, was as follows. In the surging waves of reorganization, he got the job of taking over and managing two units with rather different characters. He had received a great amount of criticism and complaints from his staff.

The managerial team listening to this story was now alternating between compassion with John and anger against the nonpresent leader who had contributed to this situation. The language used in the group reflected the culture: "As a leader, you were individually responsible for the quality and the economic results of the unit, independent of prerequisites and conditions." This could be seen in their way of giving names to their units, not from where they were located in the country but from the first name of the leader. When they were talking about Stockholm, for instance, they did not call it the region or unit of Stockholm but just "Elisabeth." In the culture of this organization this meant that if one unit did not manage so well, this was handled by getting rid of the manager, Elisabeth, not by looking at all the factors contributing to the problem, among which the leader was only one. The fear and apprehensions of the group that this should be the case made them discuss the possibility of dedicating the whole day's work just to John and his situation. Without the help of the consultant, they would have been caught in the trap they had wanted to avoid, namely to dedicate all their energy and time to caring about John and his problem instead of investigating different prerequisites for framing the problem and finding a constructive strategy for this kind of situation.

The group continued discussing the difficulties of the fusion of two very different units. They discussed the fact that one leader had been taken away, but was to come back later and they connected these facts with the bad economical situation of the unit. They saw the difficulties in leading two staffs, one just for a limited time, and what that meant in terms of more work, frustration of the staffs, and the problems of handling the differences between the two units. Further on, they reflected on what they, as individuals and as a managerial team, could do to make their manager handle the question in an "untraditional" way, that is attend to the difficulties instead of firing John. The result was that John was content with the limited support, (the consultant helped the group to stop talking about John and his unit after 2 hours), and the group's analysis of the situation. He pointed out that he was especially glad that they had not continued this discussion for the whole day.

At the next ordinary meeting of the managerial team, the question was raised in accordance with the plans. After that, the chief manager made a decision that John should be put on the sick list, another leader should fill in for him and after that, John should leave the company.

With a great deal of anxiety, concern, and reflection about their own responsibility in the decision that was taken, the group returned one month later, without John. At that time, they discussed the influence of the bonus system on the work of their teams in their respective units. What should they do when they had a person in a team who did not manage so well and thereby lowered the average bonus of the team? It was easy to understand the frustration of these teams, but what should they do? Should they move the failing person?

The consultant's mirroring of the parallel of the problem with the leader who was later dismissed and their way of thinking of the divergent member of the team helped them to deepen their understanding of the problem and how to handle it. The continued discussion concerned the prerequisites needed to make a good team, focusing on dynamics and cooperation in the team instead of focusing on the possible limits and deficits of the individual members of the team.

The group's resistance to alternating between questions of common character in the managerial team and questions concerning their individual leadership shows up when the group keeps to one or the other dimension. This resistance toward discussing questions concerning their individual leadership often appears in lengthy discussions about how to use this group. In these discussions, the consultees are reflecting their cultural character, in an obvious way, and indirectly expressing the most important problems of the organization. One group for instance can argue endlessly, proposing a number of different proposals but still not coming to a decision, as they are not allowing anybody to put his or her opinion before somebody else's. This is an example of a group that is stuck and is not able to come to a decision as described in the first part of this chapter. This phase of consultee-centered consultation is about handling ambivalence. The consultees must have enough tolerance of frustration to stand the chaos created by a decision that still is not made.

A Defensive Group

Another group had difficulties in separating the consultation session from other situations when the managerial team also met and were inclined to put all-important events in other constellations of the group and thereby reducing the importance of the consultation group. Therefore, there was no room for the dance between thought and action, and the implementation phase did not come about in the consultation process.

A Fight-Flight Group

Still another group performed the conflicts of the organization by, de facto, getting unfriendly toward each other. One case illustrating this situation is a group of staff managers in a big company acting out the conflict of the company's managerial team in the consultation group. Two of the staff managers began accusing each other saying that the other person was talking behind his back and was a liar. In between the group sessions, one of them came to the consultant to slander the other person. Despite the consultant's consciousness of the parallel problems of the managerial team and despite trying in different pedagogical ways, to show, the "cultural" part of the problem, the group denied this and refused to meet again. The group sessions were finished with a session where all of the attempts of the consultant to create a space to reflect over the conflict were refused. This was the first session when the group totally agreed with each other. The flight from the possibility of working with problems they all had come for is sublime, refined, and partly unconscious. It was evident that they did not have enough confidence in the group to present their own inner picture of reality, to verbalize thoughts, perceptions, and feelings, for example to present their representations as has been described in the second phase. They probably interpreted the consultant's or group member's questions as a way of criticizing or transgressing instead of a way of investigating.

A salient question is: Are there defenses and defense systems that make leader-focused consultation impossible by not allowing the oscillation between the two focuses?

When the pendulum has oscillated too far in one direction, when the group keeps talking about other groups outside the actual consultation group, where they report having had a good time and being efficient—that is to say different idealized situations of groups with different conditions from the present one—can the consultant help the group of leaders?

When the pendulum has oscillated too far in the other direction when they attend to the personal problems of one of the consultees in the role of helpers, the other consultees feel effective and professionally healthy, and do not have to expose their own professional shortcomings. The consultee who is exposed to this kind of care taking, may feel that his or her needs are met but also burdened by the energy and projections directed on to him or her. As a result, the consultee becomes more dependent on the consultation group than on his or her own professional judgment. The consultant must be aware of this difficulty and help the consultees, the leaders, to widen the problem, to be aware of some of their defenses and see the problem from two aspects?

THE CHALLENGE FOR THE CONSULTANT
WITH MANAGERIAL GROUPS

When consultees have come to the point, where they can see the parallels between their own behavior in the corporate group, the culture of the whole organization and what is going on within their individual staff, they no longer tend to personify or project the problems to a higher or lower level of the organization.

My experience is that it is important to enhance the two-level focus, working with groups of leaders as well as managerial teams, to promote effectiveness and satisfaction in consultation. Consultation groups of leaders may not come from the same culture or even the same organization, but still they need to reflect over the twofold focus, their role as leaders and their role representing the organization, how to handle these roles and reflect over the parallels in the two systems. They can look at, recognize, and reflect on similarities and differences in their respective organizations but they cannot experience, feel, and act it out in the group as the managerial team.

Due to the consultant's potential for reading the group and using the findings to deepen the process, conceptual change often comes about faster in the managerial teams. The group defenses differ in the way that groups of leaders tend to avoid talking about the management and the organization whereas the managerial groups tend to avoid the individual work problem situations. Most important of all is the consultant's openness to maintaining the double focus of management and leadership, and that it is the consultant's task to help the consultees, in whatever group they are, to augment their flexibility to change focus and give room for the two perspectives in consultation.

REFERENCES

Caplan, G. (1970). *The theory and practice of mental health consultation.* New York: Basic Books.
Hartacollis, P. (1986). *Time and timelessness.* Madison, CT: International Universities Press.

15

The Legacy of Consultee-Centered Consultation for the Process of Collaborative Research

James G. Kelly[1]

The sequence of settings into which you are projected as you go, if not forward at least on-ward, thoroughly uncertain of what awaits, does far more to shape the pattern of your work, to discipline it and give it form, than do theoretical arguments, methodological pronounce-ments, canonized texts, or even, as are these days too much with us, left and right iron com-mitments to intellectual creeds.

—Clifford Geertz (1995, p. 134)

The epigram by Clifford Geertz, expressed a point of view not widely noted by professionals, namely that the particular situations in which we work have sub-stantial impact and meaning on what we do and how we think about what we do. This has certainly been so in carrying out the work I report.

My situation has had a direct impact on the translation of concepts from consultee-centered consultation to conducting collaborative research. How

[1]Appreciation is expressed to L. Sean Azelton, Margaret Bagby, Dan Cervone, Steve Goldston, Charles Izzo, Chris Keys, Lynne Mock, Dan Romer, Darius Tandon, and Marc Alan Zimmerman for their very helpful comments on a previous draft.

the processes of the work and the ways in which trust between participants will affect judgments of truth is a pivotal theme (Schapin, 1994).

When a university research group and a community organization decide to work together, they have selected a marginal activity. Both groups are moving beyond their usual work agenda. Yet this marginality can be a potential resource for both groups and for their mutual efforts at collaboration. This observation is a theme for my comments.

Consultee-centered consultation created new options, in the 1960s, for delivering mental health and community services. The significance of Gerald Caplan's contributions have been well documented (Erchul, 1993). In this chapter, I illustrate the application of consultee-centered consultation to the process of community research, particularly community research that has been designed and implemented as collaborative (Elden & Chisholm, 1993; Hall, 1992; Oja & Smulyan, 1989; Park, Brydon-Miller, Hall, & Jackson, 1993; Reason, 1994; Reason & Bradbury, 2001; Tolman & Brydon-Miller, 2001).

THE EPISTEMOLOGY OF COLLABORATIVE RESEARCH

A dominant point of view for the social sciences has been that the research investigator studies, evaluates, and assesses persons as an object of inquiry. The role of the informant is expected to be passive; it has been restricted to answering or responding to the researcher's predesigned questions or prearranged stimuli. This style of inquiry reflects the dominant influence of logical positivism on the field of psychology and the aspirations of psychologists to be equal in social status to scientific exemplars in the physical sciences (Danziger, 1990; Koch, 1992).

Since the 1970s, alternative points of view have been presented in the social sciences that counter the status of the researcher as the primary source of control and influence in inquiry. Feminist scholars and researchers in sociology and anthropology have independently presented points of view that emphasize the informant as an equal participant in inquiry (Kingry-Westergaard & Kelly, 1990). As investigators have taken seriously this thesis—to redefine the role of the investigator as the primary source for the construction of knowledge—researchers have been more attentive to exploring the actual social processes of doing research (Kelly, 1986). The concepts of consultee-centered consultation are one resource to understand the changing role-relationships between researcher and respondent in a participative enterprise.

I previously cited four ideas from Caplan's writings on consultee-centered consultation (Kelly, 1993). These four ideas have been a source of continuing help in my own work (Kelly & Hess, 1987). In the following comments, I present some examples of how these ideas are also useful in carrying out collaborative research.

The four ideas about consultation are:

1. Obtaining sanction from the top administrator.
2. Dissipating stereotypes of both consultant and consultee.
3. The role of the first consultee as a deviant member of the consultee system.
4. Focusing the consultation on the role requirements of the consultee (see Kelly, 1993 for a more detailed exposition).

THE CHICAGO EXPERIENCE

Between 1989 and 1999, doctoral students at the University of Illinois at Chicago and I worked with a community organization on the south side of Chicago (Kelly, 1992). The purpose of the work was to document the development of community residents who were being trained to become community leaders in a predominantly African-American community. The major goal was to understand more about how community leaders develop and emerge as proactive leaders in behalf of their community. In the initial phase of the collaboration, I requested the executive director of the community organization to convene a panel of citizens to advise on the topics and methods to be used in the documentation (Glidewell, Kelly, Bagby, & Dickerson, 1998; Scheinfeld, 1992).

A panel was convened consisting of a clergyman, an elementary school principal, an elementary school teacher, the president of a local school council, a director of a neighboring community organization, a labor union organizer, and two parents. Eighteen meetings with this eight-person community panel over 1½ years resulted in the choice of four topics that the panel considered salient for exploration. These topics were:

1. Social support systems for the leader.
2. The competence/skills learned by the leader as well as additional skills as needed by the leader.
3. Styles of communication with persons from other organizations.
4. The leader's personal vision.

The process for making these particular choices were the deliberations and dialogue between the panel members and the university research group. We came to grips with what topics and themes were most appropriate for not only the current leaders, but for emerging leaders as well. Because the eight persons on the panel were leaders themselves, the university research group benefitted from the exchange with these expert informants. The panel members translated current research findings and then generated new topics that related to the context of their community.

These four topics formed the basis of an interview schedule. Eighty persons were nominated by the community organization as having potential to be effective community leaders. These eighty persons were interviewed with the interview schedule co-designed with the community panel (Tandon, Azelton, Kelly, & Strickland, 1998).

During the construction of the interview, periodic conversations also took place with members of the panel and with the staff of the community organization. Yearly briefings with the funding agency and six presentations at professional meetings included the executive director and associate director of the community organization and panel members.

I review this collaborative work in terms of the four consultee-centered concepts just identified (additional reports of this work are included in Kelly, 1999; Kelly, Azelton, Lardon, Mock, & Tandon, in press; Kelly, Mock, & Tandon, 2001; Tandon, Kelly, & Mock, 2000).

THE FOUR CONSULTEE-CENTERED CONCEPTS

Effective and Sustained Innovations Require Sanction and Access From the Administrator of the Host Organization.

This principle of receiving sanction from the top administrator, has been essential in this work. This is particularly so because the state staff was the "matchmaker" in bringing the community organization and research group together. I had not met the staff of the community organization before the state staff member initiated the contact. The specific social and political dynamics in this situation are that the community organization was receiving funds from a department of state government—the Illinois Department of Alcoholism and Substance Abuse (DASA)—to generate a community organizing approach to the prevention of alcoholism and substance abuse. Because the state required an evaluation, state personnel recommended me to the community organization as a potential "evaluator."

At an initial meeting in December 1989, I presented a proposal that was accepted by both the state staff and the executive director of the community organization. The two key elements of this proposal were: First, the proposed work would focus on documenting the development of the community leaders, in contrast to identifying explicit indicators of substance abuse in the larger community. This approach refocused the topic of evaluation away from the more conventional assessment of explicit behavioral outcomes to an understanding of the personal and social processes that hinder or help the development of community residents to become community leaders; second, the proposed work would be collaborative—in that the decisions about the topics and methods of documentation would be a product of consultation, advice, and discussion, between the research group and representatives of the community. The goal of this process was to establish explicit co-equal decision making between the university research group and community participants about the content and methods of the interview. To enhance these goals, a board member of the organization was recruited and received a small monthly stipend to serve as liaison between the community organization and the research group. The first board member served until 1997. A second board member served until 2000. Staff of the state government were committed to a community organizing approach to the prevention of alcoholism and substance abuse. My commitment to documenting the impact of organizing efforts of citizen leaders was conceptually and ideologically consistent with the community organization's goals.

I initiated regular meetings with the first executive director of the organization, for example, a breakfast or luncheon meeting once every 3 weeks over a 3-year period. Meetings with the second executive director occurred every 3 to 4 weeks. Meetings with the third executive director occurred about once a month. Meetings with the liaison persons were every 3 weeks. During the interviewing process (August 1993 to March 1995) monthly meetings were held with the interviewers attended by the liaison person. Four presentations to the Board of Directors were made in the early phases of the work. Additionally, the university research group attended the community actions sponsored by the organization. In summary, substantial effort was given to insure that the staff and board of directors had multiple opportunities to comment on and influence the direction of the work. The staff approved the use of the interview schedule as congruent with the organizations' activities.

The understandable anxieties of the community organization about being judged by an outside and unknown university research group were real issues. The university research group also believed that the efforts to maintain communication were even more essential because African-American communities have had a long history of being exploited by White social scientists (Clark, 1973).

The multiple efforts over the course of the 10 years have been made to activate a working level of trust about the intentions and the activities of the university research group. These multiple efforts have been essential to create sanctions for the work to proceed. Obtaining sanction has been essential to create a positive context for the work to proceed. Once it was established that the university group could actually be trusted to work in this community, there were more opportunities to note and report constructive criticisms to the executive directors and liaison persons.

The creation of an Action Research Panel to review the research data in 1997 presented additional opportunities for the organization to use the research group as resources in creating oral histories of selected members of the organization (Kelly, Azelton, Lardon, Mock, & Tandon, in press; Tandon, Kelly, & Mock, 2000). Like entry into the process, sanction to continue is continuously negotiated. This principle was an essential guidepost in keeping at the task of building a working relationship when the odds were that the relationship could not be realized yet alone be productive.

Managing Entry Involves Dissipating Stereotypes

The activities mentioned in the previous section in gaining sanction may have lessened some possible negative judgments often associated with research investigators being "intrusive," "judgmental" and prone to use the community for the researcher's self-interests. At the early meetings of the research panel, several panel members asked the university research group directly what this work was really all about (Scheinfeld, 1992). This created an opportunity for the research group to be explicit about the rationale and long range goals for the work. The statement I prepared to address these issues was perceived by panel members to insure a forthright discussion of the research agenda. The university group was self-conscious about the judgments of our work, particularly since the values and goals of the university research group were as yet unknown to the community panel members.

Most collaborative processes are ambiguous, open-ended, and often without explicit imposed agendas. Being explicit about the values and goals of the documentation was an important step to create a more collaborative relationship. Our premise was that the collaborative style could be a resource to reduce negative and incomplete judgments about the research group as well as about the community.

A topic that was mentioned and continued to be mentioned by community participants was: "What use will all this data be to us?" During the early phases, the university research group was continuously alert to see how any information obtained from the interviews and specific research projects could be a resource to the organization. The Action Task Force was created in 1997 to focus directly on this issue. A catalyst for these discussions was a quote book from the interviews with exact verbatim comments organized by topics so the members of the organization could read their views in their own words (Tandon, 1995).

What about the community's judgments of the university research group? The research group included in the beginning two doctoral students, one African-American woman (Mock), and one Caucasian woman of European heritage (Lardon). Two men joined the group, one Caucasian (Azelton) and one of Middle Eastern descent (Tandon). I had previously worked with African-American high schools in a mid-western city. One issue related to the entry process in this community is discussed in the following:

Differences in the Everyday Currency of Written and Oral Communication

The members of the panel were very responsive in the beginning to the many documents that were sent to them for their review, comments, and recommendations. Most panel members read them and commented on the appropriateness of the various possible methods and findings for their particular interests and needs. This process of preparing documents for the panel members worked very well. They focused on the materials and generated comments and observations that helped to create a unique perspective for our work, namely evaluating current research findings and then reframing the findings in terms of their specific community characteristics.

The process of connecting to the staff was not as smooth. When the university group desired consultation from the staff of the community organization it soon became apparent that written proposals or reports were often unread. The first executive director requested one-page summaries of presented material to help digest the readings. Until an actual face-to-face meeting occurred, the written materials usually were not examined. The apparent norm was that written materials were addressed primarily during face-to-face meetings. The community organizing style was, in fact, to establish working relationships via personal "one on one's," establishing the power of the personal connection between a staff person and a community participant. This preferred work style of the community organization might have made it easier to discuss issues face-to-face, rather than read about them in the absence of an actual personal conversation. The preference for face-to-face meetings, in retrospect, enhanced the working relationship between the university and the community organization because the face-to-face discussions defined the collaborative relationship as primary source of communication, instead of topics to be read and discussed.

The First Consultee Who Agrees to Meet With the Consultant
Is a Deviant Member of the Organization

This very important concept is not as overtly observed as the two previous principles. The fact that I was introduced to the two key staff of the community organization by the state agency, meant that the entry process was not typical;
entry was mediated by the funding organization. Because the funding organization gave the proposed work an initial boost by their approval and endorsement
meant that the university group worked hard to establish credibility with the
community organization.

In this situation, the entry dynamics were reversed; the university group was
the deviant and intruding group. This marginal role required the university
group to commit substantial energy to initiate and establish communication.
This also meant that the university group had to be genuinely committed to receive feedback on proposals and to provide information that was timely and
useful for the staff and board members.

Doing collaborative research generated a dual marginality for the university
group. In this case the university group was not of the community. Additionally,
the very nature of doing collaborative research was atypical with other university colleagues, for example, participatory inquiry with community residents in a
non-White setting. I viewed the responsibility to establish trust as the primary
role of the university group. The university group was more invested in the content and process of documentation than the community organization. The success in completing the interviews with the eighty community leaders can be
attributed to the university group reminding ourselves that this documentation
activity was, in fact, a marginal activity for the community organization. Patience plus persistence paid off in achieving the goal of completing the interviews in a cordial manner (Kelly, Azelton, Lardon, Mock, & Tandon, in press;
Tandon, Azelton, Kelly, & Strickland, 1998).

This situated set of roles and power relationships between researchers
and community informants points to another distinguishing difference between this type of work and previous discussions of consultee-centered consultation relationships. The boundaries between consultant and consultee
are more explicit than between two collaborative partners. The usual premise in consultation is that the consultant, as expert, has some advice, understandings, recommendations to communicate to a less informed, less
knowledgeable person: the consultee. The outsider is the consultant.
Consultees agree at some level to have the outsider establish an opportunity
for the consultant to communicate their expertise. In doing collaborative research on the other hand, all participants are considered to be equally valid

informants and full participants. This very assertion of equality can create confusion and disbelief based on our everyday experiences in working in hierarchical organizations. Making the collaborative enterprise a reality is further emphasized when working with a community organization whose own philosophy explicitly advocates the empowerment of people. The newly redefined power relationship of equality between researcher and citizen creates new role expectations and sets in motion a process that takes longer than a few fiscal years or semesters to realize. When this more equal relationship begins to work, social interactions are not as hierarchical. The "consultees" are certainly not passive and the relationship is continuously reassessed for its potential to be mutually beneficial to both parties. The collaborative process is difficult to realize in a research relationship when the benefits of inquiry can be tenuous, often indefinite and most likely modest. Research relationships of this type require continued reflection and self-awareness about the very social processes of collaboration.

The Success of Collaboration is Measured by the Consultant's Ability to Translate Mental Health Concepts to the On-Going Role Requirements of the Consultee

The efficacy of consultation is expected to be determined directly by the consultant's ability to translate concepts, data, and insights from the consultant's discipline to the needs and role requirements of the consultee. The translation requires the ability of the consultant to understand the culture of the consultee, the conceptual and language traditions of the consultee plus the consultant's ability to translate concepts from one professional domain to another. In this particular case, the university research group clearly expressed efforts to understand the multiple constraints on the community organizing organization so that a common value framework could be established for the collaborative work. One important factor, in retrospect, was the congruent values between community organizing and the ecological perspective that was the philosophical basis for the work. Without this congruence doing the work would not only have been insurmountable but the project could have ended prematurely.

A community organizing organization and a university research group represent very contrasting cultures. These two cultures create different, even contradictory expectations. For example, the community organizing organization is working to identify, involve and sustain citizens' involvement and commitment to community development. Researchers are more contemplative, less action-oriented and espouse a value for neutrality. The community organizing group, with very limited staff, is under constant pressure to locate funds to conduct their work. The research group, although certainly active in seeking grants, usually has no fear of going bankrupt.

The philosophy of community organizing emphasizes personal choice and an egalitarian leadership style to achieve goals. The professor, historically, is often in a privileged position to control, if not dictate to students. The professor works in an elite, more hierarchical culture. Another important but subtle difference is that the community organizing organization is more likely to embrace a variety of different kinds of persons, and then work to form a bond between them in terms of shared goals and aspirations. A university research group, particularly of psychologists, is oriented to clarify the differences between people. If the alternative epistemologies are not addressed the university group can be perceived as nonegalitarian and elite. The continuing challenge for the university group is to deal with these generic differences between the premises of "scientific" activities and the premises of "organizing" activities. The task is to create a new and shared point of view for the work that can validate the aim of both groups. In retrospect, both groups have indeed deviated from their respective host cultures in carrying out this activity. This marginality emerged as a resource for both groups. They each were able to recognize something special in the collaborative enterprise. The collaborative research process is an opportunity for both partners to be validated, thereby reducing their own marginality.

CONCLUSION

The activation of collaborative and participatory research is a potential resource for community organizations. The collaborative style can make inquiry a more genuine, less distant enterprise. Collaborative research means that inquiry is an elaborated series of personal and organizational relationships based on trust and shared power. This essential point was initially presented by Caplan in 1993 (Caplan & Caplan, 1993).

The concepts of consultee-centered consultation stimulated this work carried out over a 10-year period in Chicago. The four consultation concepts illustrated here, and first articulated by Caplan, have been an asset. These concepts take into account the personal and social dynamics of the helping relationship and provide insights about the situation of the consultee. These contributions of consultee-consultation made it less jarring as we traveled from the university into the community.

REFERENCES

Caplan, G., & Caplan, R. (1993). *Mental health consultation and collaboration.* San Francisco: Jossey-Bass.

Clark, C. X. (Ed.). (1973). The white researcher in black society. *Journal of Social Issues, 29*(1), 1–121.

Danziger, K.(1990). *Constructing the subject: Historical origins of psychological research.* Cambridge, England: Cambridge University Press.

Elden, M., & Chisholm, R. F. (Eds.). (1993). Human relations: Towards the integration of the social sciences. *Human Relations, 46*(2), 121–298.

Elden, M., & Chisholm, R. E. (1993). Emerging varieties of action research: Introduction to the special issue. *Human Resources Special Issue: Action Research, 46,* 121–142.

Erchul, W. P. (Ed.). (1993). *Consultation in community, school and organizational practice.* Washington, DC: Taylor & Francis.

Geertz, C. (1995). *After the fact: Two countries, four decades, one anthropologist.* Cambridge, MA: Harvard University Press.

Glidewell, J. C., Kelly, J. G., Bagby, M., & Dickerson, A. (1998). Natural development of community leadership. In R. S. Tindale, I. Heath, J. Edwards, E. J. Posavac, F. B. Bryant, Y. Suarez-Balcazar, E. Henderson-King, & J. Myers (Eds.), *Theory and research on groups* (pp. 61–86). New York: Plenum Press.

Hall, R. H. (Ed.). (1992). Participatory research. *American Sociologist, 23*(4), 15–28.

Kelly, J. G. (1986). Context and process: An ecological view of the interdependence of practice and research: An invited address. *American Journal of Community Psychology, 14*(6), 573–605.

Kelly, J. G. (1992). *Ecological inquiry and a collaborative enterprise: A commentary on "the Chicago experience."* Unpublished manuscript, University of Illinois at Chicago.

Kelly, J. G. (1993). Gerald Caplan's paradigm: Bridging psychotherapy and public health practice. In W. P. Erchul (Ed.), *Consultation in community, school, and organizational practice* (pp. 75–85). Washington, DC: Taylor & Francis.

Kelly, J. G. (1999). Contexts and community leadership: Inquiry as an ecological expedition. *American Psychologist, 54,* 953–961.

Kelly, J. G., & Hess, R. E. (Eds.). (1987). *The ecology of prevention: Illustrating mental health consultation.* New York: Haworth.

Kelly, J. G., Azelton, L. S., Lardon, C., Mock, L. O., & Tandon, S. D. (in press). On community leadership: Stories about collaboration in action research. *American Journal of Community Psychology.*

Kelly, J. G., Mock, L. O., & Tandon, S. D. (2001). Collaborative inquiry with African American community leaders: Comments on a participatory action research process. In P. Reason & H. Bradbury (Eds.), *Handbook of action research* (pp. 348–355). London: Sage.

Kingry-Westergaard, C., & Kelly, J. G. (1990). A contextualist epistemology for ecological research. In P. Tolan, C. Keys, F. Chertok, & L. Jason (Eds.), *Researching community psychology: Issues of theory and methods* (pp. 23–31). Washington, DC: American Psychological Association.

Koch, S. (1992). Psychology's Bridgman vs. Bridgman's Bridgman. *Theory & Psychology, 2*(3), 261–290.

Oja, S. N., & Smulyan, L. (1989). *Collaborative action research: A developmental approach.* London: Falmer Press.

Park, P., Brydon-Miller, M., Hall, B., & Jackson, T. (Eds.). (1993). *Voices of change: Participatory research in the United States and Canada.* Westport, CT: Bergin & Garvey.

244

244   KELLY

Reason, P. (Ed.). (1994). *Participation in human inquiry: Research with people*. London: Sage.
Reason, P., & Bradbury, H. (Eds.). (2001). *Handbook of action research*. London: Sage.
Scheinfeld, S. (1992). *Documenting the community research panel*. Paper presented at the American Psychological Association Annual Convention. Washington, DC.
Shapin, S. (1994). *A social history of truth: Civility and science in seventeenth-century England*. Chicago: University of Chicago Press.
Tandon, S. D. (1995). *Sample responses from the DCP Interview*. Unpublished manuscript, University of Illinois at Chicago.
Tandon, S. D., Azelton, L. S., Kelly, J. G., & Strickland, D. (1998). Constructing a tree for community leaders: Contexts and processes in collaborative inquiry. *American Journal of Community Psychology, 26*, 669–696.
Tandon, S. D., Kelly, J. G., & Mock, L. O. (2000). Participatory research as a resource for developing African American community leadership. In D. L. Tolman & M. Brydon-Miller (Eds.), *From subjects to subjectivities*. New York: New York University Press.
Tolman, D. L., & Brydon-Miller, M. (Eds.). (2001). *From subjects to subjectivities*. New York: New York University Press.

III

The Consultation Process—Dialogues Across Settings and Disciplines to Activate Conceptual Change

The chapters in this section describe techniques and processes involved in consultee-centered consultation that promote engagement in the process and new conceptualizations in both the presentation and representation of the professional problem.

16

Complicating the Thinking
of the Consultee

Eva Marion Johannessen

INTRODUCTION

The object of consultation could be stated very simply; it is to complicate the thinking of the consultee (Caplan, 1977). These words from Caplan refer to consultation as a cognitive restructuring process, similar to what Sandoval (this volume) refers to as "conceptual change" and Hylander's (this volume) concept of "conceptual shift." The definition of *consultee-centered consultation* (Lambert, this volume) states that "one primary task of the consultant is to choose and translate knowledge about intrapersonal, interpersonal, and organizational effectiveness and well-being so that the work role of the consultee is enhanced" (Lambert, this volume). "Choosing and translating knowledge" means that if the consultant manages to transmit knowledge that is relevant to the consultee, a restructuring process will be initiated that results in the consultee developing more explanations to the problem presented and also more solutions. But this is a reciprocal, not one-way process, as the consultant also changes his or her perception of the case.

The consultant's transmission of knowledge differs from that of the traditional teacher. In the classroom, the teacher decides on the topic, whereas in consultation it is the consultee who raises the topics that the consultant has to pay attention to. By listening to how the consultee presents the problem, the consultant gradually gets cues as to which knowledge to transmit.

The examples are drawn from my own research on consultation (Johannessen, 1991) with staff in a day care center as well as from experience training future consultants.

THEORETICAL ASSUMPTIONS
IN CONSULTEE-CENTERED CONSULTATION

Consultee's Theoretical Perspectives About a Work Problem

The cognitive restructuring starts when the consultee describes the case, through which the consultant's questions gradually become more detailed. Together the consultant and the consultee reflect on the reasons behind the client's behavior, i.e. the causal explanations. In this process the consultees' theoretical assumptions are uncovered and expanded. It is rare to find a consultee who reflects on how her own beliefs and practices contribute to the problem she experiences with the client. Instead she tends to see the client (child) as "difficult" or to blame the parents for their inadequate upbringing of the child. Consultees who lean on such explanations may be experiencing a professional crisis that results in a projection of the consultees' problems to the client. Other reasons may be that the consultee does not have a wide repertoire of explanations due to a lack of theoretical knowledge, experience, and training (Caplan 1970).

Changing one's theoretical assumptions is not an easy process. But consultees are eager to know more about the reasons behind the client's behavior. They have some theoretical background, but not always a very deep knowledge. Fragments of theories have merged with common-sense knowledge and become part of a personal belief system. The consultant's task is to understand the ways that the consultee perceives the work problem and to assist the consultee to present his or her explanations or personal theories about the case.

Psychological theories are constructs that enable one to draw a map showing how to interpret human behavior. As the consultant begins to understand the important features of the client's problem from the perspective of the consultee, relevant theoretical explanations will be identified. Theories, however, are powerful and can do harm to the client. History has lots of examples on how theoretical explanations and research produced dogmas about mental illness and psychological disturbances that were not well founded. Consider, for instance, how autism was explained not many years ago. The consultant, therefore, has to be sensitive to which theoretical assumptions are introduced and have confidence in the scientific support for them.

Consultant's Theoretical Assumptions About a Work Problem

Since the 1980s to 1990s system theories (Bateson, 1979) have become part of the literature for training in various helping professions. This theoretical approach focuses more on the relationship between individuals, groups, and systems than on individuals. A case cannot be solved without focusing on the relationship between consultee and client, and between the consultant and the consultee. The consultant may contribute to the problems experienced with the consultees. The professional consultee will soon read the consultant's theoretical preferences and adjust his or her reflections accordingly although he or she does not subscribe to the consultant's theoretical position. One may avoid the consultant's questions resisting the theoretical playing with ideas and risk being characterized as "not accessible to change" by the consultant. If the consultant, for instance, adheres to psychoanalytic theory and the consultee believes in behavior therapy, the latter will rarely feel free to share his or her ideas, and instead comply with the consultant or saying what he or she thinks the consultant likes to hear. It is essential that the consultant create a climate that encourages the consultee to share his or her ideas. This calls for the consultant to inspect his or her theoretical preferences.

In order to complicate the thinking of the consultee, the consultant has to question and revise his or her own theoretical assumptions and how they affect the relationship with the consultee. The reason why the consultant does not succeed and the consultation process fails may not be due to unwilling and unresponsive consultees but the consultant's own lack of theoretical flexibility.

THE CONSULTATION PROCESS

Challenging the Consultee

Hylander (this volume) underlined the process from the perspective of the consultant as one where the consultant constantly oscillates between confirming and challenging the consultee's story.

Sometimes the consultee states his or her ways of reasoning very clearly; at other times the consultee's explanations are more difficult to uncover. The following example shows how the consultant may detect and explore the consultee's theoretical assumptions about a case.

Consultee: He [the child] makes a lot of noise and is always screaming when his mother comes to fetch him at the day care center.

She tries to calm him down, but never succeeds. She may threaten him, or try to convince him, but he always manages to manipulate her and get it his way. I think it is the mother who is the problem.

Consultant: Mm. Have you talked to the mother?

Consultee: Yes, but she is not easy to talk to. She keeps telling me about all the problems she has with his father who is away a lot. She is very evasive.

Consultant: Have you met the father?

Consultee: Yes, but only briefly. I have not talked to him about his son. It is always the mother who comes in the morning and in the afternoon. She is in a hurry and often comes very late.

"I think it is the mother who is the problem" is a significant statement and a cue the consultant should follow up. The consultee's theoretical assumption is that the mother causes the child's problems. When this statement comes so early in the conversation, it indicates that the consultee has something important he or she wants to share with the consultant. The consultee states that he or she wants to talk to the mother about her relationship with the child, whereas it appears as if the mother wants to talk more about her relationship with her husband.

By communicating more effectively, the consultant could have focused more specifically on the consultee's assumption. When the consultee says "I think it is the mother who is the problem" (which is a general statement), the consultant could have asked him or her to be more precise by asking "Can you say more about that?" or "What do you base your conclusion on?" Such questions would allow the consultee to come up with more details, and give the consultant a chance of questioning the basis on which he or she draws the conclusion that the mother is the problem. The consultant asks him or her to describe episodes he or she has noticed, or episodes the mother has said are taking place at home.

Consultee: I believe it is the mother who is the problem.

Consultant: What do you base that conclusion on?

Consultee: Well, I think she is not very firm and lets the child decide too much. If she had tried to stop him and be more consistent, he would have reacted differently.

This exchange confirms to the consultant that the consultee believes that it is the mother's relation with her son that is the problem. It tells us that he or she has an understanding of the importance of relationships. The fact that the consultee has a lot to say about the mother, and keeps coming back to how the mother is and what she does, shows the consultee's interest in the mother and may indicate that the consultee's relation with the mother is also part of the problem. The consultant may want to explore this further.[1]

To complicate the consultee's thinking in this case may be to challenge:

- The consultee's perception of the mother–child relationship. He or she has seen them at brief moments in the morning and the afternoon when the other members of the staff in the day care center are present. The relationship may be different at home and in other settings.
- The belief that the mother is the only person responsible for the son's problems. The father's role and the relationship between the parents, and the son's contribution play a part.
- The consultee's relationship with the mother and how that influences what he or she pays attention to and how he or she interprets the situations he or she observes.

The consultant's way of challenging the consultee's theoretical assumptions is by asking "what if" questions, thereby introducing new ideas. By explaining these ideas through examples he or she transmits new knowledge linking alternatives to the consultee's existing ideas.

Questioning the consultee's conceptions, not stating that they are wrong, helps the consultee to understand that there are various theoretical assumptions that may be valid, not only one. The consultant's task is to engage the consultee in a dialogue aimed at the expansion of possible explanations. This is done by questioning and wondering together with the consultee, not by lecturing.

Challenging the Consultant

This issue may be more difficult to deal with. If the consultant is firmly established in one tradition and does not use or is not familiar with other approaches, it may be difficult for the consultant to take a critical look at his or her favorites. Recognizing this pitfall, the consultant can speculate and come up with several hypotheses that need to be tested in order to find the most plausible. As the conversation moves on, the consultant has more opportunities to reevaluate his or her hypotheses.

Consultants expand their understanding of work problem and relevant theoretical explanations in the consultation process through training and practice. A thor-

---

[1]That is, the consultee may become too involved in the mother and less in the mother–child relationship. At the same time involvement is a positive sign that the consultant can use in the restructuring process.

ough training experience explores different theories. An important element of this training is to focus on differences and similarities between theoretical explanations and their relevance for various work problems. The training of the consultant provides them with the opportunity to understand the reciprocal cognitive restructuring that takes place between the consultee and the consultant. The objective is to motivate the consultation students to become interested in theory, and above all, to be familiar with an array of theories and how they can be combined. The result of this process is often that the students increase their sensitivity to relevant knowledge and take the first steps in developing their own personal approach.

From consultation practice, the trainee consultants expand their understanding of the consultee's professional work and the range of theories consultees use in explaining the clients' problems. Students are given cases or create their own cases based on their experience, which they role-play. This provides opportunities for the consultants-to-be to try out their theoretical approaches. At this stage they find out how applicable the theory is in practice. The result of the process is that the students become more aware of the relation between themselves and the consultees and how they communicate their ideas verbally and nonverbally.

It is my belief that the open-minded consultant with a broad knowledge base, which he or she is able to apply in various contexts, has a better chance of succeeding in a dialogue about theoretical assumptions. It may be argued that it is overwhelming for the consultee and the consultant to relate to many and various theories. However, consultant training should combine a high theoretical level with practical training. It is the trainer's job to single out the main features in the various theories focusing on how they are similar and different in their explanatory power for different work problems. The objective is not to present theories for the sake of storing knowledge in the students' heads, but to create positive confusion, thus complicating the thinking of the consultation student. It gives them a chance to find their own way in the jungle of theories.

Another and different skill consultants must acquire is to know how and when to communicate the theoretical explanations. This is acquired from the consultant's experience. As Hylander (this volume) points out in her chapter, the cognitive restructuring process in consultee-centered consultation does not only include the consultee but also the consultant. As the process unfolds, the consultant has to change his or her way of conceptualizing and interpreting the case presented. Thus the consultant's theoretical framework is modified. In a successful consultation process, the original case is gradually restructured on the part of both the consultant and consultee as they exchange ideas and are open to seeing the case from various angles.

SUMMARY

In this chapter I have focused on the consultant's pedagogical task of questioning the consultee's theoretical assumptions. It requires a varied theoretical knowledge base and pedagogical sensitivity to know how and when it is appropriate to complicate the thinking of the consultee. The consultant contributes to this process of complication, but it is the consultee who actually develops a more complicated perception of the client. By observing the changes in the consultees' ways of interpreting the case, the consultant may conclude that the consultation has been successful.

The consultee-centered consultation process includes two dimensions: to complicate how the consultee perceives the client and to analyze the consultant–consultee relationship and how it affects the consultee's willingness to share his or her ideas. Two strategies have been presented: asking more specific questions regarding the consultees' assumptions, and reflecting on how the consultant communicates his or her ideas with the consultee. The consultant must question theoretical preferences, be able to combine different approaches, and be willing to change hypotheses and theoretical constructs. We may conclude that the aim of consultation is to complicate the thinking of the consultees *and* the consultant.

More knowledge indeed complicates our lives. It opens up for new reflections, contradictory evidence, and solutions of which we were previously not aware. The aim is to move from certainty to uncertainty regarding the complex nature of human beings.

REFERENCES

Bateson, G. (1979). *Mind and nature.* London. Fontana paperbacks.

Caplan, G. (1970). *The theory and practice of mental health consultation.* New York: Basic Books.

Caplan, G. (1977). Mental health consultation: Retrospect and prospect. In S. Plog & P. Ahmed (Eds.), *Principles and techniques of mental health consultation.* New York: Plenum Medical Book Co.

Johannessen, E. (1991). *Group consultation in a day care center.* Oslo, Norway: Institute for Special Education. University of Oslo.

17

How to Respond to Teachers, Who Ask for Help but not for Consultation

Gunilla Guvå

Swedish psychologists have practiced psychological consultation as a method in child care, preschool, and school since the beginning of 1970. Our experiences of rapid turnings in consultation have inspired Hylander to study turning points (2000). She found that there are no distinct turning points but rather a turning processes, where the consultee's representation of the client is changed as result of an interactive process between the consultant and the consultee. In this process both the consultees' and the consultants' representations of the client are changed as a result of the consultant's alternation between confirming and challenging the presentation, that is, the story that is been told.

Since the 1970s, I have written articles and given workshops about a Swedish model of consultation, based on Caplan's definition of consultee centered consultation (Caplan, 1970, 1993; Guvå, 1989.) In this chapter, I describe this model in a somewhat new way, in the light of my latest research project (Guvå, 2001) and using some of the concepts emerging from Hylander's research.

Consultation is by definition a process of interaction (Caplan, 1970) in which the consultant has a special competence, which the consultee needs, in order to be able to solve a work problem. As a consultant, the psychologist must accept no direct responsibility for the client. The consultant has (one type of) competence, but no authority to handle the problem and help the client. The consultee has the responsibility, but not necessarily all the competence, knowledge, or confidence to help the client in a professional way. This juncture is often the beginning of an interaction process between a teacher, who wants a solution of the problem and the psychologist who wants to help the teacher to help the client (Guvå, 1999).

Teachers ask for help when they have come to a critical point in their professional work (Guvå, 2001). If they are in a professional crisis, they have lost their sense of competence and do not trust themselves to be able to handle the child in a successful way, even if they normally are quite capable. In this situation, they do not always ask for consultation when they ask for help. Sometimes they want to hand over a *question*, (i.e., they want an assessment that can prove that the child has to be placed in a special class or a special group), or they hand over a *task* (they want the psychologist to take over the problem), or they hand over the *feeling* that "something has to be done." Thus, the consultation must start from different points of departure, depending on what kind of help the teacher demands. The consultant must meet the consultee where he or she is in order to be able to build up a nonhierarchical side-by-side relationship and establish the agreements that are the prerequisites for starting a consultation process. That is, the consultee must be aware of and accept retention of his or her professional responsibility for helping the client and accept that the psychologist as a consultant is a specialist with competence but without responsibility for the client.

Hylander (2000) described a model for conceptual change resulting from an interaction process in which the consultant and the consultee are oscillating between their different representations of the client's problem by moving away and approaching through a free neutral position. The consultee's representation of the client must be made clear before the consultee can move away, leave it, and be open for a change in understanding. Whereas the consultant is approaching the consultee's representation, the consultant presents it in a more distinct way. When the representation is made clear to the consultee, the consultee feels that he or she is being confirmed and the consultant may start an oscillation between confirming and challenging this representation.

I earlier described the process of consultation as three different sessions (Guvå, 1995) that can be seen as successive steps. I have grown increasingly aware of the importance of the first session as a meeting where the special prerequisites for further consultation may be both examined and created.

In the first session, the consultant has to make the consultee's representation of the client clear. In a consultee-centered consultation, the consultant must keep in mind that the presentation of the client always reflects the consultee's representation of the client. It is more or less distorted, but it is always a subjective picture of the client and can also be seen as a conceptual construction (Sandoval, 1996). I previously labeled that client-in-mind the consultee's representation of the client the *subjective client* to make a difference from the *client in reality* (Guvå, 1989). By asking questions about this client-in-mind, the consultant gains insight into the consultee's representation. The consultant will also create a representation of his or her own. However, before the consultant can present his or her own representation he or she must have his or her construction of the consultee's representation confirmed.

By answering questions and listening to his or her own presentations through the ears of the consultant, the consultee will make his or her own representation more explicit and clearer to him or herself. It will move from being an inner representation to the outside—at a good-looking-distance, not too distanced, not to close—where it may be examined. If the consultee has been too far away from the client, he or she approaches and comes closer and if the consultee has been too close, he or she moves away to become more distanced in order to see the representation.

I use a special interview guide for this first session that makes it possible to oscillate between confirming—challenging and approaching—moving away. Through different kinds of questions, I can steer between approaching and moving away to a free neutral position in which I also can change from confirming to challenging.

Consultation is like putting together the pieces of a jigsaw puzzle. By asking questions, I try to find out the consultee's story of the client. Like all dramas, this narrative includes a past, a present, and a future. In contrast to a therapist, the consultant is an active and distinct person, who asks questions and interrupts the consultee's stories (Caplan & Caplan, 1993). The following interview guide is set up with different areas of questions that make it possible to alternate between not only approaching—moving away or confirming—and challenging, but also between the client-in-mind and the child-in-reality. With these alternating questions, an oscillation may start, which is of special importance in order to avoid being stuck in blind alleys. It is similar to getting a car out of the mud by creating a swinging movement back and forth. The following questions can be seen as "break" questions to be used when the intent is to move the consultation process from one area to another. Within these areas, it is possible to use a wide range of questions. Asking questions is neither an examination nor an inquiry, but a way of showing curiosity and knowledge. Asking good questions means putting different phenomena into words, which make the consultees feel that the consultant knows what they are talking about. Sometimes the consultant seems to know what the consultee wants to describe better than the consultee knows him or herself.

INTERVIEW GUIDE

The First Session

Focus on the Client and the Client's Problem.

You have a child you want to discuss?
You have a child you want me to see?
You have a child you want me to assess?

By starting in this way, the consultant confirms the consultee request from the very beginning, and shows that he or she has noticed what the consultee is asking for. Starting in this way does not necessarily mean that the consultant has to make an assessment or see the child. It merely means that the consultant respects the consultee's request.

What is the problem with the client? Can you tell me about him or her?

In this phase, the consultant should focus on the client's problem, not the consultee's problem with the client. The questions help the consultee to present his or her story.

Focus on the History of the Client and His or Her Problem.

For how long a time has it been like this?
What has happened since the first time you met the client?
Did you know something about the problem before you saw the client?
Are there any critical incidences of importance in the client's life-story?

Focus on Here and Now.

Can you tell me when during a school (pre-school) day the client is at his worst?
Can you describe some critical incidents and what is happening then?

Focus on the Consultees Thoughts of What is Causing the Problem.

Why is it like this?
Is it something that can help us to understand the client?

At this point in the process, the consultees often tell the consultant about the child's family. The consultees describe a situation outside school or pre-school, which helps them understand the problem of the client. However true these facts might be, they are also the story of the consultee and tell us through which glasses the consultee views the client's problem. In a similar way, as a child in play-therapy uses the toys to tell a story, the consultee will use family members to illustrate those conflicts in preschool, which are hard to talk about. In a consultee-centered consultation information about the child and his or her family is treated as facts reflecting the consultee's way of thinking that, in turn, influences the way the consultee relates to the client and interprets the child's behavior.

Focus on the Consultee's Picture of the Client.

What does he look like?

This question makes it possible for the consultee to meet the client-in-mind and in doing so, the client gets a face.

Does he say hello to you when you meet him?

Thinking of this question may make the consultee so curious that the next time he or she will meet the client in such a way that he or she says hello, which in itself could lead to a turning process. Brodin has elaborated the question "What does he or she look like?" in her chapter in this volume.

Focus on the Consultee's Fantasies of the Future.

What do you think will happen if nothing is done?

The purpose of this question is also to search for theme interference.

Focus on Other Imaginations of Importance (Ghosts).

Have you met similar problems before?

The purpose of this question is to find out about earlier experiences of similar problems. The question also may be a way of detecting theme interference.

With the questions just presented, the consultee not only gets an opportunity to discharge feelings and thoughts about the client but also a chance to reflect about the client and his or her problem. This process may make an uninvolved consultee more interested in and curious about the child and give an over identified consultee somewhat more distanced from the problem. For this reason it is necessary to have this reflecting dialogue before asking what kind of help the consultee is expecting from the consultant.

Focus on the Consultee's Expectations of the Consultant.

What did you expect me to do for you when you asked for my assistance?

Depending on the answer, the consultant can make a judgement of the feasibility of consultation. If the consultee asks for help to help the client, he or she will ask questions like: How can I help this child in school? Is what I do good enough or shall I relate to the client in another way? Those questions make it possible to be a consultant and together with the consultee find out the best way to work with or teach the client in school or preschool. The consultant can conclude the session with, "Let us meet again and continue our talk."

If the consultee, however, answers that he or she wants the consultant to talk with the child or the parents or make an assessment, the consultant must find out what the consultee is thinking by asking what the consultee wants the consultant to say to the parents and why. How does the consultee think that this would help the child in school or preschool? The responsibility for the client and his or her difficulties are usually not clearly negotiated between the parents and the teachers and this confusion has to be made obvious. Talking to parents is a task within the consultee's area of responsibility and the consultant only can help the consultee to prepare for such a session.

The consultee may say that the child must be tested or helped in some other way. This happens when the consultee has come to a critical point where he or she does not think he or she is able to help the child any longer. Everything is already done. The consultee states firmly that the child is in need for something more or something else and that it would be impossible to take the responsibility for the child any longer. In this case, the consultant must be able to contain the consultee's feelings of powerlessness and inadequacy, neither taking over the responsibility for solving the problem nor immediately returning it. Sometimes the consultant just has to share these feelings, without doing anything, until the next session by saying, "Let us meet again and continue to talk about this."

Many consultants are afraid of encountering the demands from the consultee, because they are afraid of being forced to do what the consultee asks. If, however, the consultant dares to discuss these wishes and demands, this discussion can constitute the starting point for a dialogue in which both parties work toward a cooperative alliance. Within this framework the other necessary prerequisites can be created (a work problem, noncoercive relation, responsibility remaining with the consultee). By asking questions the consultant might have convinced the consultee that he or she is a professional person to be trusted and someone the consultee wants to see again.

In my study (Guvå, 2001), I found that even psychologists come to critical points in their work, where they choose to take over a *question* by making a psychological assessment; to assume a *task*, by talking to the pupil or the parents, or by *handing over* of the question or the task to other specialists (child guidance clinics). The decision at this critical point is often based on the psychologist's opinion about the teacher's ability and motivation to help the client. If the teacher is seen as good enough, the psychologist will handle the problem as a consultant, but if the teacher is seen as a poor teacher, the psychologist tends to reformulate the problem as a question (task) for the psychologists or a specialist outside the school. In such cases the psychologist implies that the task is too difficult for the school or for the teacher.

When teachers are in crises, they regard themselves as unable to help the client and by projecting these feelings onto the psychologist, they may get the psychologist to believe that this is true. That is why it is important for the consultant to reflect and understand that such thoughts about teachers actually originate from the teachers themselves.

The Second Session

Some therapists describe the process of psychotherapy as a chess game, where the therapist can decide how to start and end a session. A consultation process varies in the same way between start and ending, depending on a great variety of circumstances. Anything may happen between the different sessions, and as a consultant, one may never know what one will meet and how to continue when one comes back for the next session. The interview guide for the second session is different and the questions have another focus as compared to the first session. In the first session, the questions focus on the client. In the second session, the focus is shifted to a client-consultee-interaction perspective. First, the consultant has to find out where to meet the consultee on this occasion. *What has happened since our last session?*

If the consultation is seen as a process, where the representation of the client's problem has to be changed, the consultant has to find out in what way the consultee is describing the client this time compared with his earlier descriptions. The consultant can open the session by *asking if something has happened since the last time*. Often, the consultee describes a quite different situation, where the client behaves in a new way. *Of course he or she still is his or her usual self but ….* Perhaps they say that they cannot understand why the client has changed, because they still interact with him or her in the same way as before. They have not changed. Sometimes they can describe how they have been more aware of how to meet the child in another way than earlier. By talking about the problem, it has been possible to see the client in a new way.

Another question to the consultee is *whether the first presentation of the client corresponds with the current picture of the client?* By asking this question the consultant can find out if the representation of the client is changed or not. If the consultee says that there is no difference between the earlier presentation and the current one, I ask, *if there is something that has surprised them since the last time*, to see if I can make them more curious about the child.

In any case, the process continues by focusing on the interaction between the consultee and the client, by asking questions about critical situations in which the client involves the consultee. *When and how is the client acting in a way that gets the consultee involved? In which way is the consultee reacting and what happens then?* By this analysis of interaction, the consultee will become more aware of the client as an actor, and see that his or her own reaction is a consequence not only of the child's behavior but also of his interpretation of that behavior. For example, if the consultee regards the child's behavior as hostile, he or she will meet the child differently than if he or she can see it as an expression of fear or shame. If the consultant can offer another interpretation of the client's behavior it may be possible for the consultee to see it in another way and meet it quite differently. The consultant makes it feasible for the consultee to reflect on his or her own behavior towards the client, without putting blame on him or herself. *"What will happen if you try this or that?"* By playing with many different thoughts about possible actions, a neutral zone, like the playground in therapy with children, (Winnicott, 1971) is created. Thereafter, the consultee may feel more free to try different kinds of behavior toward the child until the next consultation session.

The Third Session

This session is a very important meeting. Sometimes the problem is solved and the consultee describes it as a turning. The client is quite different and there is no problem anymore. The consultant can leave the consultee by saying that they can call him or her again if the situation changes or the problem comes back. Hopefully the consultee will be more competent in similar situations in the future. Sometimes, however, the situation is unchanged or perhaps worse than ever. The consultee is in a crisis and it is not sufficient to meet the consultee with empathy or questions, nor new discussions about how to interact with the child. Instead, it is necessary to contain those feelings of powerlessness, shame, helplessness, anger that the client evokes. (Perhaps the consultee's approaching to the client has made the situation more difficult than before and could be interpreted as a necessary but difficult step in the right direction toward solving the problem.) If this is the case, the consultant has to identify the psychological dilemma that the client has evoked in the consultee. The consultee may describe feelings of split and claim that the client forces them to handle things in such a nonprofessional way that they become afraid of their own feelings. First of all the consultant has to identify his or her own feelings of helplessness, anger, and powerlessness. The consultee is disappointed and behaves in a way that makes the consultant angry and sad. In the same way as the consultee has been unsuccessful in helping the client, the consultant feels that he or she has not been able to help the consultee. In this situation, the consultant tends to mistrust the consultation as a feasible method to help teachers to help the client. The consultant can share these feelings of failure and mistrust by saying something like: "You must be very angry because I have failed to help you .... You must think that it is a mission impossible to help this client and want him where the pepper grows." In this way the consultee's feelings of mistrust may be put in words. The consultant may also ask for critical incidents in which they have not been able to help the client. The consultant may meet these stories with humor, which will tell the consultee that he or she is not afraid to listen to the worst situations where the consultees behave in a way they cannot believe they allowed themselves. This is the time for the consultee to tell about the most forbidden things, their most unprofessional behavior and their most dangerous thoughts. The consultant makes it clear that thoughts are never forbidden and that behaviors are understandable although not desired or legitimate. The critical incidents may be analyzed. Why does it happen? Perhaps the client forces the consultee to handle matters in that way. What is the client telling the consultee by this scene? How is it possible to understand the client, who is the actor and setting the stage where the consultee is reacting? Is there a way to act professionally on this stage? How is it possible to meet a client who evokes ambiguous affects, for example anger and fear? By these questions and by talking about what happens and what kind of dilemma the client evokes within the consultee or between the consultees (in a group of consultees), it is possible to analyze the client. The dilemma gives information about an unstructured and chaotic client, who is in conflict with him or herself and therefore puts his or her conflict outside him or herself and thereby influences the consultee.

By making the forbidden acceptable, the consultee may become aware of his or her own conflicts in relation to the client and begin to use the conflicts professionally. These discussions may lead to a turning. When the consultant helps the consultee to recognize his or her own feelings and the dilemmas, he or she may encounter the client the way he or she is. The representation of the client is changed, but probably also the consultee's self-representation.

During the process of consultation, there are many representations. As Hylander described (2000), the consultant must identify the consultee's representation and her own representation. In the cases where their representations correspond too much, the consultant must challenge his or her own representation of the client by on-going questions. When the consultant believes that he or she has a clear representation of the client, warning bells should ring. By new questions this picture will be challenged and make it possible for the consultant to challenge the consultee's representation as well.

When the consultation is ended the consultant has challenged not only the consultee's representation, but also his or her own, and this has led to a change of the consultee's representation of the client. But when the consultant thinks in the same way as the consultee, when they are sharing the same representation of the client, the consultant must begin to challenge this picture—sometimes by asking for supervision him or herself.

REFERENCES

Caplan, G. (1970). The theory and practice of mental health consultation. New York: Basic Books.

Caplan, G., & Caplan R. B. (1993). Mental health consultation and collaboration. San Francisco: Jossey-Bass.

Guvå, G. (1989). Klientmysteriet. Ett fall för förskolepsykologen. Om personalinriktad fallkonsultation. (Sfph:s monografiserie nr 32).

Guvå, G. (1999). The first consultation session. How to meet a teacher who asks for help but not for consultation. In Explorations in process in practice (Seminar proceedings). Stockholm: 2nd International Seminar on Consultee-Centered Consultation.

Guvå, G. (2001). Skolpsykologers rolltagande: Överlämning och hantering av elevvårdsfrågor. (Dissertation). Linköping: Linköping University. Department of Behavioural Science.

Hylander, I. (2000). Turning processes. The change of representations in consultee-centered case consultation (Dissertation). Linköping: Linköping University. Department of Behavioural Science.

Sandoval, J. (1996). Constructivism, consultee-centered consultation, and conceptual change. Journal of Educational and Psychological Consultation, 7, 89–97.

Winnicott, D. (1971). Playing and reality. New York: Basic Books.

18

What Does He Look Like?
From the Inner World of the Consultee to the Inner World of the Client (With a Little Help From a Question)

Marianne Brodin

When teachers request psychological consultation, they are usually stuck in their professional relationship with a child. Their current understanding of the child and their own emotional involvement limit their ability to handle the situation in a fruitful way. In consultation, the consultee gets an opportunity to perceive the child in a new way. By expressing and reflecting on thoughts and feelings evoked by the child, and by gaining new knowledge and making new observations of the child, consultees may develop a new way of thinking about and a new feeling for the client. This process, in turn, gives the consultee new ideas about what to do, and how to interact with the child. The consultee has made a *conceptual change* (Sandoval, 2001). The problem is reframed and the consultee *presents a new representation—a turning* has taken place (Hylander, 2000).

In the consultation process the consultee's representation of the client changes from a distorted and confused image, often overloaded with affect, toward a more coherent and understandable image, with not so overwhelming emotion. Teachers in childcare often describe what has happened in consultation in words like: "I see him with different eyes today," "I have obtained a totally different picture of him," "I have obtained a new point of view" or "I can see the little child in him now." They talk in terms of *viewing, pictures, images, or perceptions.*

Consultation is a matter of changing the image of the child in the mind of the consultee. For me this "image" can be thought of as a symbol for a total experience of the child, with all its emotional, sensual, and cognitive aspects. My focus in this chapter is on the impact of the experiential and affective elements in this image, and their connection with verbal language and cognitive reflection.

Possibly the most important events in the consultation process are when the vague and unspeakable aspects of the image of the child connects with the logical, understandable ones, for which there are words. Following this connection a new image appears.

Winnicott's (1971) theory about the transitional space and Stern's (1985) discussion of the gap between global, amodal, sensual experiences and the verbal expression of these experiences give hints for understanding what happens. There are also parallels between consultation and expressive therapy techniques using nonverbal or verbal symbols as tools for expressing images and connecting them with verbal language and reflection (Robbins, 1980). Affective theories (Nathanson, 1992) are useful models since changes in the affective communication between the child and the teacher often is the key to progress. This chapter provides a very brief presentation of the theories just mentioned and applies them to the consultation process. I also apply them to some examples of consultation dialogues, starting with the question "What does he look like?" one of the questions in the structured set of questions used for consultation, developed by Guvå (1989). I have focused on this question because it is an actual request for a picture that often starts a dialogue between the inside and outside reality, and it gives the consultant information about the affective communication between the child and the caregiver.

LANGUAGE—A DOUBLE-EDGED SWORD

Stern's (1985) theory of self-development described the emergence of different, but parallel selves, and corresponding "worlds" or channels for experience and communication. Before the verbal self emerges the child experiences the world in an immediate, global way, with all senses involved. There seems to be a flow between the senses, called *amodal perception*. What the child sees with his or her eyes is immediately translated to sensations in the other senses too. When the verbal self emerges the child gets a new fantastic tool for sharing meaning with other people, but at the same time, something is lost. The amodal sensations are hard to translate into words. The words will never be enough to catch the total experience. The elements that are put into words will be prominent and distinct, whereas others fade and stay as diffuse memories in the mind. The language creates a split in the self between the amodal individual sensations and the experience as verbally formulated.

This unavoidable split, Stern (1985) says, is the reason why people always have a need for art experiences. The language of art is a dense symbolic language that can express what the common verbal language has no possibility of capturing. The symbol is like a bridge that connects the split parts in the self. The consultee's very personal, nonverbalized experience of meeting the child probably has a large impact on their relationship. A colorful, expressive language, using verbal pictures, symbols and metaphors in the consultation dialog opens possibilities for expression and examination of those experiences.

FROM PLAY TO REALITY

Winnicott has formulated a theory about the *intermediate area*—a position between the inside fantasies and creative capacity and the objective perception of the outside world. It is a safe area, where fantasy and reality can merge—one can play with reality. When you are in this area there are no demands for objective reality testing, nothing is right or wrong. It is an area for creative activity, for experience of art and religion, for play, jokes and humor.

Children playing together share each others' intermediate areas. In the same way, the consultant and the consultees can create a shared intermediate area in consultation. If the consultant can create a safe and allowing atmosphere and use his or her ability to play and symbolize this will stimulate the consultees to do the same thing. In the intermediate area, one can play with the language, using an expressive, colorful language with symbols and metaphors. One can play with thoughts, but also with pictures, images from the inner reality of the consultees as well as perceptions of the child seen from the outside. In this creative process the inside and outside world will meet and something new will be created. Different pictures from different persons may also meet, and new pictures emerge. It is a way of bringing order out of chaos. Being in the playground between the inner and outer world gives one an opportunity for distance and control. The creations that appear in this state of mind can be helpful for understanding the reality in a new way.

THE EXPRESSION OF IMAGES
AS TOOLS IN CONSULTATION

An *image* is a subjective response to an objective reality. It is a subjective personal creation, founded in the perception of internal and external stimuli (Robbins, 1980). Symbolic expression of images as a tool for change is used in expressive therapy. Parallel to that, in consultation, the consultee's expression of his or her images of the child, can be a tool for transforming the relationship between the consultee and the child.

A picture, whether it is painted on paper or painted in colorful expressive language, can capture the sensual and emotional experiences that are ambiguous, contradictory, illogical, and vague. When they have found a form for expression, they can then connect more easily with verbal reflection and understanding. This learning process is a process of reorganization, but it is not merely a cognitive change. It becomes a total experience in which perception, affect, and sensation join cognition at the same point in time and space.

Another parallel to art therapy is that consultants do not focus on the caregiver's own mental life but on a picture created by the consultee—the consultees presentation of the child. The important thing is that a third object is created. The consultant and the consultee may look at it together twisting and turning it around, to explore it, understand it, and discover new elements and meanings in it. The consultee controls the picture of the child and because the consultant has never met the child, there are no truths, no rights or wrongs. In this way the picture functions both as a defense and as a channel for expression of feelings and conflicts. The consultee may express something about his or her inner life in an indirect way, and at the same time be protected from confronting it too directly. The consultant catches the picture as described by the consultee, and mirrors it for critical examination. In this way the picture serves as a tool for reality testing, but is still controlled by the consultee.

The essential element in this is the movement back and forth between inner and outer reality and between creative playing and reality testing/reflection. In consultation we move back and forth between the expressive colorful presentations of the consultee's image of the child seen from the inside, and the consultant's questions, which force the consultee to look at the child from the outside. The consultee also shifts between a state of being totally absorbed in presenting an image and taking a step back, critically looking at this creation from a distance, reflecting over it, seeing new things in it.

WHAT DOES HE LOOK LIKE?

As change of images is so essential in consultation, the question "What does he look like?" (Guvå, 1989) has an important place. It is a powerful intervention, one that may change the consultee's image of the child. It stimulates the process of moving between inner and outer reality, and enhances reality testing and integration of contradicting images. In responding to this question, playing with metaphors and deep reflection about a child, often starts.

Listening to the consultee's presentations of the problem begins the discussion in the first consultation session. The emotional temperature is often high; and there is a flow of expressive "painting" from the consultees' inner realities. The question "What does he look like?" interrupts this flow. The consultant asks for a picture from the outside, at a time when the consultees are absorbed in their inner images. It is as if the consultees have to freeze their inner films, and confront the picture of the real child in their minds. This task can be difficult; the consultee may need time to shift perspective. Typically, there is a pause and quiet ensues. The images of the child from the inner world and from the outside will meet and the process of integration and bringing order out of chaos will start.

CONSULTEE ANSWERS TO THE QUESTION

Most consultees, after pausing to develop the picture of the child in their mind, give a description "from the outside" first. They describe haircolor, face and body characteristics, and some summarizing impression (e.g., "cute"). The description from the outside is, however, also an inner image, a subjective answer to an objective reality. What does the consultee see when looking at the child in his or her mind? What does he or she choose to describe?

When one paints a real picture, one can use form and color to express inner experiences, or one can place an object in front of one's self and try to picture it as detailed and realistic as possible. These two ways of painting can be seen as the extremes of a continuum between expressing inner reality and picturing the outside reality. Parallel to that, the consultees' answers to the question "What does he look like?" can belong to different positions in the continuum between inner and outside reality.

If the atmosphere in the consultation is allowing, safe and playful the consultees can activate their intermediate areas when answering the question. A movement back and forth in the continuum starts and new images, feelings and thoughts develop. I present some examples from my own consultations that I transcribed during the consultation sessions.

Toward Integration

To stop the film in the mind and really look at the face and body of the child often seems to remind the consultee of more positive aspects of the child. Until now, the negative sides have dominated the image. Suddenly the consultee can express that the child is, for example, charming, sweet, has a humorous twinkle in his or her eye, and is a happy guy *after all*. "I like him very much!" is not an unusual comment. It is as if this aspect of the child suddenly occurs to the consultee. A new image, integrated with positive elements, develops. The next three excerpts are all examples of how consultees arrive at more integrated pictures, when trying to see the child from the outside. The first example is illustrated graphically to show the shifting positions in the continuum between inside and outside pictures. All the following examples may be illustrated in the same way.

Consultees, in the example here, have a flow of negatively loaded images from within, (e.g., their representation of the child, of their relation to the child and of the problem the child evokes). Responding to the question "What does he look like?" they become quiet and then one of them says, "*Very cute, small, red curly hair, and big brown eyes.*" There is a little pause again and then the integrated picture comes: "*He is rather funny after all!*"

Another example concerns a little girl whom a consultee describes, saying, "*She has blond hair, blue eyes ....*" There is a long silence after the short description. I am waiting for her to say that she is sweet, but in vain. It seems like the caregiver tries to maintain her inner image, without succeeding. The inner and outer pictures meet, and give the consultant new information about her relation to the child. The caregiver says, "*We don't see that little pretty girl, she makes us so angry!*"

Sometimes, consultees are not able to look at the child from the outside at all. The inner image is so strong that it becomes dominating, like in the next example. The consultee's answer to the question comes immediately, without the usual pause, "*like a little devil!*" She says it with an angry voice, immediately followed by a laugh. When the consultee listens to her own words, the inner image conflicts with reality. The symbolic expression becomes a tool for reality testing. Her image of the child is expressed, and in that way it is possible to look at it. When she confronts her own image, she begins to laugh. It is so obviously far from reality. The laugh covers her shame over what has been revealed, and suggests that it was just a joke. When the image is presented in this way, it can also be changed. Images that do not find their expressions are not easily accessible for change.

FIG. 18.1.   The flow of pictures from inside and outside—an example of integration

Joking and Laughing

The use of humor, joking, and laughing are often effective in the consultation process and belong to the playful intermediate area. Here follows two examples, the first one illustrated graphically to show the movement between inside and outside reality once again.

The consultee in this example described the boy as *"big, rough, dark, and strong,"* then, with a certain resistance, she added *"cute,"* last in the description. To handle the contradiction she had to face, she said jokingly, *"He is very charming and that's his good fortune!"* The joke can help her to integrate the contradicting elements. In the joke, she can express both warm and aggressive feelings in the same phrase, and escape the shame of her negative feelings.

Another consultee describes a boy as being *big and sturdy*, then with a laugh she expresses her inner image: *I'm always thinking of the bear-team* (some of the figures in Donald Duck). Then she adds: *He is like a boxer type—he is always being so tense.* An interaction between the outer and the inner images starts. The atmosphere is playful and the consultee begins to laugh when talking about the bear-team, but becomes serious and reflective when she becomes aware of how tense the boy is. The image of the child develops through the shifting positions in the continuum between the inside and the outside.

A Hidden Story

The image of a child can be loaded with a "hidden story." One consultee answers the question with these words: *nice, proper, cute and well cared for.* Her voice sounds indifferent. She gives an outside picture however rather much seen from the inside This is also one way to describe the parent's relation to the child. That image, in turn, evokes another image from inside, which also

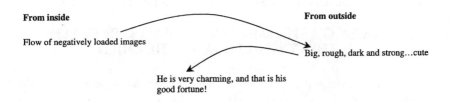

From inside   From outside

Flow of negatively loaded images

Big, rough, dark and strong...cute

He is very charming, and that is his good fortune!

FIG. 18.2. The flow of pictures from inside and outside—An example of joking

deals with the parents' relation to the child. The consultee says *But he has got a hole somewhere!* and now she is very upset. In the consultee's representation of the case the parents were the problem. Her image of the child is colored by her image of the parents.

Metaphors

To find a metaphor to express a mess of vague, diffuse sensual and emotional experiences can be a big step towards new reflections. A consultee describes a girl as being *tall, very tall.* The outside description evokes an inner image that is expressed in a metaphor. She says, *"She is like a foal, like a giraffe."* In the metaphor, the bodily felt sensations are caught. The consultee shows with her arms and hands as if she had the girl on her lap with her long arms and legs difficult to reach around. This metaphor accompanied by her body-expressions leads to a new reflection. It forces the consultee to realize something about her own relation to the child. *"You are not likely to take her on your lap!"* she says slowly and reflectively, as if she simultaneously realizes what she is saying as she is saying it.

After this session the consultee may have actually taken the child in her lap! What seems to happen in the consultation process is a new awareness that produces small changes in the behavior of the consultee. The consultees will not necessarily tell consultant about this awareness, still it may have such a powerful influence on the child that the consultation at times feels like magic.

A Neutral Description

The consultees answer may sometimes be just a neutral description causing no movement between inner and outer reality. The question seems uninteresting and irrelevant. Maybe it is a matter of timing. The consultant has to find the right moment for the question. A neutral description may also be a defense toward presenting unwanted feelings. For different reasons consultees are not always able to play. Maybe there is such a big distance and so little communication between the consultee and the child that there is no inner flow of images.

FOCUS ON THE EMOTIONAL DIALOG BETWEEN THE CONSULTEE AND THE CHILD

Because the emotional dialog is essential for the self-development of the child in childcare, this dialog or the lack of it, needs focusing in the consultation. The consultee has to shift perspective from his or her subjective, inner world to the outside reality to be able to take the child's perspective and gain a better understanding of the child's inner world. This focus in the consultation process deals more with observations of the reality, reflecting over these observations, making new interpretations and reflections over the consultee's own emotions. It is a more reflecting than expressing phase.

Affect Theories

Modern developmental psychology (Havnesköld & Mothander, 1995; Nathanson, 1992; Stern, 1985) stresses the importance of the primary affects and the communication of these affects. Tomkins (Nathansson, 1992) identified nine different affects: *interest* and *joy*, which are regarded as positive affects; *surprise*, which is a neutral affect; and *fear, distress, anger, disgust,* and *shame,* which are regarded as negative affects. Their biological aim is the survival of the human race. Each one of these inborn affects has its own specific expression in the human face. The affects give the infant information about how to behave in relation to the surrounding world. But they also give other people information about what is going on in the child's mind. Our inborn capacity to communicate affects, and be sensitive to others, is the basis for intersubjective communication and organization of the self.

The child learns about his or her own feelings, beliefs, desires, and intentions through sharing understanding of his or her own mental world with others. If the child's self-expression is repeatedly thwarted or misinterpreted, it becomes a threat to its psychological self, and the child will develop defense-strategies, in particular avoidance or aggression (Fonagy, Moran, & Target, 1993). The affective expression of a familiar adult guides the child as to what to feel and how to handle an ambiguous situation. Sharing, ignoring or misunderstanding affective expressions and guiding children through affective responses, are frequent ways of communication between teachers and children in preschool and child care. In fact, the verbal message from the teachers is probably often overwhelmed by the emotional message. The affective communication between children and teachers will have a large impact on the children in their formation of scripts for future relations and self development.

Focusing on diminishing a child's negative affects will not be enough. The positive affects constitute a system of their own and are not only emerging from the escape of unpleasant experiences (Emde, 1992). Interest and joy need outside stimulation and are the basis for growth and learning. Interest motivates the child to seek mastery. When the child succeeds, the feeling of competence evokes pride and joy, which, in turn, evokes more interest and more activity. It is basic in educational institutions like child care, preschool, and school to stimulate this cycle. Thus, keeping this circle in mind, becomes of prime importance, in consultation to these institutions.

The Affective Communication Between Child and Consultee

When teachers in child care call for psychological consultation, there is typically something problematic or lacking in the contact and communication with the child. The affective expressions of the child may seem inadequate or impossible to understand. As a consequence, the teachers probably will fail in giving an accurate reflection of what is going on in the child's mind. The teacher's own affective and verbal messages in communication with the child may be incongruent, and the response from the child may therefore seem confusing and inadequate.

Teachers' affective reactions may be so overwhelming that they obscure the awareness of what is going on in the child's mind. Teachers may have difficulty reflecting and handling their own reactions. The opposite may also be true, there may be too little affective communication between the teacher and the child. The problem with the child becomes an intellectual question about what is wrong with the child and what to do about it. What seems to be a distant approach to the child may, however, be a defense against the overwhelming feelings that the child evokes. Teachers have tried so hard and now they have given up.

A new awareness and a new interpretation of what is going on in the child's mind may change such problematic relations. Reflecting over what is in the child's mind, will probably result in new ideas about what to do, and maybe also a new awareness of the consultee's own affects. If the consultee in dialogue with the consultant reflects on his or her own affects that are evoked by the child, he or she will probably find new ways of communicating with the child. As a result of this changed communication, the child will most probably respond in a new way.

Affective Communication and the Question
"What Does He Look Like?"

To answer this question the consultee has to see the child in his or her mind. The affective expression in the child's face when it appears in the consultee's mind says something important about the contact and communication between the consultee and the child. The facial expression that first appears in the mind of the consultee is probably the one most frequent *in the dialogue* with that consultee. As described earlier, the consultee often presents a flow of images of the child's problematic behavior and the affective temperature is high and negative. When the consultant interrupts this flow with the question "What does he look like?" there is typically a positive presentation of a cute, good-looking child, with glittering eyes and a happy expression on his or her face. This is the image of the child, in a positive emotional communication with the caregiver. They have eye contact and they share the affect of joy. To verbalize and reflect over this image is often a step toward integration of the good and the bad image of the child, as described earlier in this chapter. The consultee is reminded of all the good moments together with the child. The reason for the consultation, however, is all the situations when *the dialogue is broken*. So, the next step is to find the facial expressions of the child in the problematic situations, when the communication mostly is thwarted or broken.

My experience is that it is difficult for the consultee, to try to "see" the child's face in those problematic situations. They have to stop their endless description of what the child does, focus on the child's facial expression in their minds, and finally try to interpret it. Not only have they to move from their own inner reality to the outside world, they also have to take the child's perspective and try to understand what is going on in his or her inside world. The process may then develop into focusing on the affective communication on the consultee's part, and what is going on *between* the consultee and the child.

The Provocative Smile

In the following example (from one of my own consultations) the consultees have described a boy who constantly gets into conflicts, who destroys the other children's games, who is unpredictably aggressive and just laughs when the teachers tell him not to do these things. Through the consultant's questions they start reflecting over what is going on in the child's mind, and what his facial expression actually stands for.

C-t: If you try to see him in your mind—what does he look like?

C-e: Sweet as candy, joyful, glittering eyes—it's very easy to like him! Other consultees now begin to give a lot of positive descriptions of the boy.

C-e: When we visited the bakery he was fascinated, he was exemplary and didn't touch a thing!

C-t: When he does all these other troublesome things you have told me about, what does he look like then?

C-e: He just smiles, in a provocative way.

C-t: Mostly when people smile they feel happy. You have described his joyful, glittering eyes when he is happy, but what do you think he is feeling when he smiles the way you think of now?

C-e: I think he is scared and uncertain.

C-e: Perhaps he doesn't understand **our** signals either.

C-t: So what do you think about your signals?

C-t: I think I look very tense .... I get so very angry when he does these
         things. At home I shout at my children when I'm angry, but as a
         teacher I hold it back. Maybe it would be better to show him that
         I'm angry?

What follows is a discussion of what happens if they show anger in relation to
the boy. One consultee thinks that when she does he listens to her. We also discuss how to understand his smile if he feels scared. Is it his way of trying to make
them smile at him again? And what about the smile if he feels uncertain? Perhaps he does not know what to feel and wants to read in their faces what they
feel? Can the smile serve as a protection from confusion, shame, and fear?

C-e: If you don't think of it as a provocation, I guess that you wouldn't
         get so angry ...

At the end of the session the consultant reminds the consultees of the expression of fascination the boy showed at the bakery, perhaps they can look for
more moments when he shows interest in something?

The Girl With the Wrinkled Face

In the following example the child and the consultee are emotionally far away
from each other, and perhaps there is a mutual misinterpretation in the communication. If the descriptions of the child until now have been neutral and
intellectual, the question "What does he look like?" can provide an opportunity for consultees to uncover more of their own affects. The image that occurs spontaneously in the minds of the consultees in this example is the one
that is loaded with negative affect. Beginning to reflect on what might be going on in the child's mind can reveal different interpretations and give new
hints about what to do.

The consultees have described a girl with a strong will, and a bad temper. She
is always trying to dominate the other children, and they are afraid of her. She
creates an unpleasant atmosphere in the group. The description is like a neutral
observation, the consultees don't give any expression to their own involvement.

C-t: What does she look like? Try to see her in front of you ....

C-e: Her face is always wrinkled together. She always has that wrinkle
         between her eyebrows ....

C-e: She reminds me of "Little My" (a very angry little girl in Tove Jansson's literature)

C-e: She always seems discontent.

C-e: As if she is thinking, "What can I figure out to do next …." (The consultee imitates the girl's hoarse and evil laughter.) She laughs like a witch.

C-e: (a bit startled) No, I don't think that's what she is thinking ….

C-e: She is nicest in the morning ….

C-e: When we rest she always wants to lay in my lap ….

C-e: But her voice … she sounds so unpleasant, she is really unpleasant.

C-t: What happens with you when she is so unpleasant?

C-e: I get angry!

C-t: You have told me about a girl who seems angry and unpleasant, always seeking new naughty things to do. But you also say that she looks discontent and unsatisfied. Why is she feeling that way, do you think?

C-e: Could it be that she needs more stimulation? If we find something that she likes to do, she is O.K.

C-e: Doesn't she feel loved?

The discussion turns to how difficult it is for the other children to understand her, they cannot predict her behavior, and she constantly misinterprets them. She is always expecting something negative, and the other children are always expecting something aggressive and evil from her.

In the next session the consultees tell the consultant that the girl has made progress.

C-e: She is easier to reach now.

C-e: We are close to her, and encourage her.

C-t: Do you remember how you described her face the last session? You told me that she always had that wrinkle …

C-e: (A bit astonished) It's gone!

C-t: So how would you describe her face now?

C-e: She looks … expectant! She is easy to stimulate. She wants to do things.

In this example the progress of the child is followed by another description of the child's facial expression. The problem with the girl was not solved that easily, but the consultees had found a good strategy to relate to the girl and to get on with the work with her.

My experience is that the face that occurs *spontaneously* in the consultees' minds never has the expression of interest, curiosity, fascination, surprise, and expectation. If that were the case, there would probably be no need for consultation. However, the task for a teacher is to look for, or elicit that expression, which is the basis for learning, and to share the joy of competence with the child. If the consultant is able to transmit his or her own curiosity and interest for the case to the consultees and share these feelings with them, this will create a basis for learning and change in the consultees. Then, they can experience the pride over their feeling of competence, having solved their problem with the child.

My intent in this chapter has been to focus on the importance of catching and expressing the affective and sensual aspects of the image of the child in the mind of the consultee to open it for reflection and change. The next step is reflection on what's going on inside the child to change the affective communication between client and consultee. The question "What does he look like?" opens many possibilities for working with these areas.

REFERENCES

Emde, R. N. (1992). Positive emotions for psychoanalytic theory; surprises from infancy research and new directions. In I. T. Shapiro & R. N. Emde (Eds.), *Affect: Psychoanalytic perspectives*. Madison: International University Press.

Fonagy, P., Moran, G., & Target, M. (1993). Aggression and the psychological self. *International Journal of Psycho-Analysis, 74*, 471–485.

Guvå, G. (1989). Klientmysteriet. *Sfph:s monografiserie nr 32.*

Havnesköld, L., & Risholm Motander, P. (1995). *Utvecklingspsykologi. Psykodynamisk teori i nya perspektiv*. Stockholm: Liber Utbildning.

Hylander, I. (2000). Turning processes. The change of representations in consultee-centered case consultation. *Linköping Studies in Education and Psychology No. 74*. Linköping: Linköping University, Department of Behavioural Sciences.

Nathanson, D. L. (1992). *Shame and pride. Affect, sex and the birth of the self*. New York: Norton.

Robbins, A. (1980). *Expressive therapy*. New York: Human Sciences Press.

Sandoval, J. (2001, August). *Conceptual change in consultee-centered consultation*. Paper for the Third Seminar on CCCC, San Francisco.

Stern, D. (1985). *The interpersonal world of the infant*. New York: Basic Books.

Winnicott, D. W. (1971). *Playing and reality*. New York: Basic Books.

19

Allowing Ambiguity
and Listening
to the Contradictions

Solweig Thörn

In consultee-centered consultation the consultant and consultee embark together on a journey—one of mutual exploration. The starting point is the
consultees' presentation of their work problem. The consultant's first task is to
ask questions and listen in order to understand and confirm the consultee's presentation of the problem. At the same time the consultant listens in order to understand the representation behind the presentation and what the underlying
dynamics might be. The consultant can later use this information when challenging the consultee's presentation. Such challenges are intended to introduce
new thoughts and to facilitate new discoveries. A goal of the consultation process should be deep and complex thinking (Sandoval, 1995).

This approach corresponds to my experience as consultant in Swedish preschool and day care. The way the consultee describes and views the child and
the situation becomes more complex as the consultations move forward. The
change in the consultation progresses from a one-sided, sometimes stereotypical description of the child and the relationship, to a more complex image where
contradictory aspects and emotions can be experienced simultaneously and be
integrated to a more composed and complete image.

During this process it is particularly important for the consultant to listen to
contradictions and ambiguity in different ways, and to explore them together
with the consultee. In this chapter, I discuss ways to support the examination of
ambiguity and to broach the subject of contradictions noted. In the following

279

examples the *consultee* is a teacher in the Swedish preschool, the *client* is a pre-school child and the *consultant* is a psychologist using *consultee-centered consultation*. As consultants we do not work with the client directly. The focus is on the consultee's perspective of the client, that is, on the consultees' presentation and representation of the client and their relationship.

LISTENING FOR WHAT HAS NOT BEEN EXPLICITLY EXPRESSED: THE BOY WHO WAS BOTH BIG AND SMALL

Setting

The consultees are three teachers and the client is a 5-year-old boy. The work problem presented is that the boy is provocative and bossy. The teachers notice how he deliberately ruins the activities. "We have to stop this, but how?"

Consultation Process

The teachers are very annoyed with the boy; he is provocative, always needs to be the center of attention, screams and has continuous conflicts with both children and adults. "He always wants to decide everything. He shows no respect, he teases us by loitering and dithering in all situations." At the same time the consultant detects an ambiguity in their description. On one occasion the boy is described as clever and calculating, but on another occasion as a small child who is not capable of dressing himself—he expresses himself in an advanced way and later on he "whines like a one year-old child." These contrasts become apparent to the consultant who keeps this to herself and only comments that "the situation appears to be all over the place."

At the beginning of the second session the teachers are really tense, but toward the end they feel more playful and relaxed and think of how they can handle the boy. During the session it becomes more and more apparent that the teachers shift between describing the boy as actively manipulating and bossy, and describing him as passive and not wanting to take part in activities. But the teachers' attention is focused on the provocative behavior. The turning point in the consultation occurs when they describe the boy's behavior when all the children have to go and put their coats on. In this narrative they graphically describe how he runs back and forth and does lots of different things and ends up hanging from the clothes rack. The consultant gets the impression that the boy is not able to handle the situation, but loses control. "Is he at loose ends?", the consultant asks. The group of teachers stop, turn quiet, and then start reflecting on how the boy might not be able to deal with the situation, and is at a "loose end" and unable to get connected.

The teachers associate this incident with other situations where they previously thought that he had been consciously provocative, but now they start to wonder whether the boy might not be able to handle the situation. Next they start to think about how they can handle the boy in various situations. One teacher expresses the psychological dilemma that they find themselves in with the question: "I wonder if that is why you get furious with him but at the same time you want to comfort him?"

The consultation comes to an end with the third session. The teachers now know how to handle the boy with confidence, they can tell when he needs support and he no longer acts in a provocative way. Conflicts still arise, but now the teachers feel that they can handle them more effectively.

Reflections on Development in the Consultation

At first the teachers describe one aspect of the situation, that is, the boy is provocative and bossy. At the same time their description of the boy and their interaction with him also conveys another aspect (i.e., how the boy is passive and unable to do things himself). First the consultant has to consider this ambiguity and listen to more accounts of the boy's behavior. This is where the consultant realizes that the teachers cannot as yet see that they portray different sides of the child. The consultant picks the metaphor of the boys being at a "loose end" because of the teacher's graphic description. The consultees probably reacted so positively to this because they were close to discovering the boy's difficulties themselves.

Sandoval (1995) pointed out that in the conceptual change process, metaphors will often be used to introduce the new ideas and conceptualization. Metaphors serve to enable the consultee to gain a different view of the client's problem, to take a look at the issue from a related yet different perspective (Mang, 1995). The Danish science journalist Nörretranders (1991) compared figures of speech to the Trojan Horse. Symbolic language allows us to smuggle new thoughts into our consciousness just like the Greeks smuggled their warriors into the besieged Troy in a giant wooden horse. On the one hand, the symbol is familiar and can easily be taken to heart, but on the other hand it contains ammunition for new associations.

As consultants, we challenge the consultee's perception of the situation, and we base this challenge on the consultee's own accounts of the situation. After a successful intervention, the consultees can reflect on the situation in a new way.

Once the teachers discover that the boy is both actively bossy and confusingly passive they become more flexible in their interaction with the boy. They can act more freely based on their professional knowledge.

LETTING AMBIGUITY EMERGE: THE GIRL WHO MADE THE TEACHERS FURIOUS

Setting

The consultees are two teachers and the client is a 6-year old girl. The work problem presented is that there are many conflicts with both children and adults. The teachers are confused and want to know how to handle the girl. "We can't reach her."

Consultation Process

The teachers describe a hyperactive girl who is constantly having conflicts with other children. When they intervene and stop her, she jeers at them and slips away. The teachers describe various provoking situations, but at the same time they say that "if there is a grown-up next to her, she can handle relations and interplay in a better way." But the teachers cannot approach the girl.

The development between the sessions is adverse. The next time things have become more "messy than usual." The consultant continues to ask about difficult situations that they have experienced with the girl. The teachers then describe an incident when all the other girls were going to do some acting and she was not allowed to participate. She then had to stand and watch, and they "almost felt sorry for her." But later they describe how the girl tries to manipulate, threaten, and provoke the others to let her join them. "When she behaves like that we get so angry with her. It is her own fault and it is hopeless trying to help her."

Is it because of these mixed emotions that the teachers find it difficult to approach the girl?

The fact that she gets left out and they feel "sorry" for her makes them feel uncomfortable when they get angry with her. The teachers are torn between emotions and find it difficult to approach the girl.

During the session the ambivalence becomes more apparent. The ambiguity is obvious to the consultant and this gradually becomes obvious to the consultees as well. When the consultant describes the mixed emotions she has heard and verbalizes what is happening, both of the teachers remark: "That is exactly how it is, we often experience that with her." They start to talk about the difficulty in experiencing "feeling sorry for her " and "it serves her right" at the same time, as well as discussing what situations they find difficult to approach her in and what happens when they do. They also discover that the girl approaches them and turns them away at the same time. The psychological dilemma that the teachers find themselves in is the girls own problem as well. The teachers reactions are a parallel to the girl's difficulties.

Reflections on Development in the Consultation

At the beginning the teachers see these two reactions as separate experiences. They *either* feel sorry for her *or* feel that it serves her right. They feel uneasy, uncomfortable and irritated, which stops them from getting closer in the relation. Mixed emotions that are not made conscious and understood will inhibit the relationship from developing any further. First of all the consultant has to listen and accept the teacher's description of the girl who is impossible to get close to. The intervention of the ambivalence with both the teacher and the girl will have to wait. Later the consultant verbalizes both sides. This is a child that makes the teachers approach her *and* "feel sorry for" her, as well as reject her *and* "become furious with" her. We are talking about same child and same adults in both situations. The mixed emotions that they have about the girl can now exist simultaneously. She is "both ... and" and not "either ... or."

Conflicting reactions can be integrated into a more complex image of both the child and the interaction. Based on this, the teachers can adopt a different attitude toward the girl. Now they can have their own approach to the work, which means that they do not have to give in to the child's temper tantrums.

NOTICING AND ACTING ON WHAT IS OMITTED: THE BOY WHO WAS BOTH TOUGH AND SCARED

In some cases the ambiguity and ambivalence is not as clearly expressed in the consultation conversation. Instead the message is communicated to the consultant through what is omitted, what is being left out. For this situation the consultant can use his or her own reactions and feelings to understand the dynamics behind the teacher's descriptions and later also use this in the consultation. For instance in this case:

Setting

The consultees are two teachers and the client is a 5-year-old boy. The work problem presented is that the teachers are tired and are not sure whether they can cope with the boy who is very demanding. "Maybe he needs something else."

Consultation Process

The teachers tell a story of a boy who is constantly in conflict with adults and children alike. He swears, kicks, spits, and does not obey. They portray a hopeless, demanding boy, who rejects adults, is tough and quarrelsome. The consultant listens, asks questions, and confirms their story. At the same time they tell the consultant of the boy's private life that contains painful experiences of separations and parents who cannot understand the boy's needs. The teachers speak of the situation in a matter-of-fact manner and do not convey an understanding for the boy's situation. The consultant, however, imagines feelings of loneliness, helplessness, being lost, and scared. But the teachers only describe the boy as tough, rejecting, and demanding. Initially the consultant becomes angry: "Can't they see ... can't they understand .... " And she is tempted to explain, to make them understand the boy. But as a consultant she has to contain these feelings and keep them as information about the boy and the teachers' difficulty with him. She has to continue to listen to the teachers in order to better understand their difficulty with the boy's problems. Therefore, the consultant keeps confirming the teacher's presentation and keeps asking questions about how the boy reacts in certain situations, and for details about the confrontations she also expresses empathy for their difficulties with this "bad boy." The consultant realizes that the teacher's strong reactions toward the intolerable boy are working as a defense because they find it painful to consider his troubled life situation. The consultant decides to wait before approaching this aspect of the work problem. Then, together with the teachers, the consultant begins to approach "the lonely, sad boy" through questions. "I wonder what happened to cause him to cry that much?" "What do you think he thought when his mother and younger sister left?" "What was the look on his face when you gave him ... ?"

The next step in the consultation is concerned with keeping both aspects of the case alive. This is a boy, who is both scared and lonely as well as tough and rejecting. Through the consultation process the teachers gradually begin to approach the two aspects of the boy, the tough and rejecting side as well as the weak and needy side. The teachers regain their empathy for the boy without pitying him. Now they can also set adequate limits in their work with him and give him support and comfort when he needs it.

Reflections on Development in the Consultation

The consultant has to oscillate between listening, confirming and later on also challenging and confronting the consultees if new perspectives are to emerge and carry the process forward. However the consultees must first be convinced that the consultant understands their situation before they can proceed. Forward movement is difficult when the consultant feels that he or she has a more valid understanding of the child's problems and wants to impart this to the consultees rapidly, maybe even lecturing them. The consultant's task is to engage the consultee in a dialogue of which the aim is to expand the consultee's knowledge base. This is done by questioning and wondering together with the consultee, not by lecturing (Johannesen, 1999). When this temptation to lecture arises the consultant must stop and think. The teacher's strong reactions and their lack of empathy can be a result of becoming far too engaged and affected by the child's problems. The ambiguity and ambivalence is communicated to the consultant through what is being left out. The consultant has to be able to stop, keep information for later interventions and focus on what the teachers are describing, try to get closer to and confirm their side of the story. This has to be done in order to ask the teachers the right questions that will, step by step, approach the omitted aspect of the case and help the teachers meet the child in a new way.

DEALING WITH CONTRADICTORY REPRESENTATIONS BETWEEN CONSULTEES: WHAT A DIFFERENCE THREE WORDS MAKE

Setting

The consultees are two teachers and the client is a 4-year-old boy. The work problem presented is that the teachers are worried about the boy's development and behavior.

"Something is not right." He changes his mood too rapidly.

Consultation Process

The boy has been taking part in preschool activities for 6 months and his difficulty in taking part in group activities and daily routines has increased. The teachers tell a story of a boy who has trouble concentrating, cannot handle routine situations and shouts and screams and shouts or hides. As soon as they try to engage all the children in playing games or singing songs he slips away, hides, keeps doing what he was doing, or hits a child who happens to be nearby. The teachers describe very difficult situations in their work with the boy, yet have the intention to get to know him better. The consultant has previously worked with these teachers and perceives them as very competent in their work. The first conversation ends with a joint description of the problems. "This seems to be a boy who hasn't found his place in the group—he has difficulties with all routines and activities with the other children." During the day the teachers are allowed to make observations on different situations and in detail account for what happens in order to understand what makes it so difficult for the boy.

The consultation continues with discussions between the teachers and the consultant on what measures the teachers can use in order to try to help the boy. The conversations roughly follow the same pattern. They start with the teachers describing how difficult it is with the child, and the consultant listens and confirms their story. After that they focus on observations and how you can try different ways of working. The teachers go back to work and try the measures that have been decided. However there is no progress in the consultation process. The consultant is starting to doubt her ability to help the teachers and thinks that this boy is probably too difficult to work with.

After four sessions, the consultant analyses her work and realizes that there is a lot of information about the boy and what he does but very little information about the teachers' reactions, how they perceive and feel about his actions. The consultation has been too focused on coming up with measures. At the next session it becomes clear that the consultant is stuck in a blind alley. Again the teachers describe the same situations and same reactions with the child. "What are we going to do?" they ask. The consultant avoids answering this question and tries to understand how the teachers perceive the boy in these situations, how they perceive the look on his face, how they feel about him and what he does. One of the teachers uses words such as demanding, controlling, manipulating as well as not willing to adapt to routines. The other teacher describes the situation in another way—the boy cannot find his place in the group, he watches inquisitively, runs around and swings his arms about. The teachers have two different interpretations of the boy in these situations: one where he has a conscious, active role and one where he seems to be lost. The consultant asks: "Is it the case that the boy becomes angry and wants to make his own decisions but at the same time is taken by surprise?" A discussion about the words "taken by surprise" follows. The teachers look thoughtful.

During the next session the teachers bring this up again. They say that "it became obvious when we spoke about being taken by surprise the last time." Once they came to that realization it became easier to work with the boy and understand his strong reactions. The consultation is then focused on these two aspects. If you perceive the boy as "always bossy and wanting to make his own decisions" confrontations arise and the grown-up takes up the conflict. If you perceive him as "taken by surprise" and as having no strategy you try to calm him down instead and make him see the situation differently and give him other alternatives to his actions. The attitudes become different. After this realization the consultation became more vivid and the participants could concentrate on the opposite perceptions "bossy" and "taken by surprise." The consultant could use the ambiguity when trying to understand the boy. Furthermore, the teachers now had concrete concepts that helped them to work with the child.

Reflections on Development in the Consultation

The fact that the consultant knew the teachers previously and was aware of their competence contributed to a consultation that rapidly focused on how to approach the problems through the teacher's presentation. At the same time, however, it prevented the consultant in noticing the teachers' different perceptions of the child's reactions. Therefore, the teachers' presentation of the problem will increasingly differ from how they perceive and feel about the boy's reactions. This disjunction also affects how the teachers will be able to carry out the measures that are being discussed. The consultant defined the problem from her own perception that she thought the teachers also shared. The consultant did not find out what theories the teachers had about why the boy reacted the way he did, but assumed that they had the same perceptions as her. The feeling of not being able to act is passed on to the consultant who also doubts her own ability. The consultant is stuck in a blind alley. During the consultation the consultant must constantly change her own perception in order to find out how the teachers perceive the problem, what their explanation and theory of the child is. The consultant is stuck in a blind alley when she does not challenge her own representations enough (Hylander, 2000).

The change will come when the consultant can listen to the differences in the teacher's accounts and perceptions of the child, their representations. This also enables the teachers to handle their own different perceptions and gain more freedom in their work. The dynamics in the contradiction between "bossy" and "taken by surprise" fueled the consultation. Choosing right words is a powerful intervention. Words that both mirror the consultee's feelings and contain a challenge, a difference that will give new perspectives of the problem. "Taken by surprise" made a difference in this case.

Listen to the contradictions in the consultation. These can mirror the child's own problems and better describe what he is going through. Diversity of opinion can prove to be fruitful and has to be verbalized and perceived as something interesting, for instance in the case of a question like "how can we use this in our efforts to understand the child."

LISTEN TO THE CONTRADICTORY
AND EMPHASIZE THE AMBIGUOUS

In the cases described, I show how the consultant, in different ways, can listen to and emphasize ambivalence and contradictions and use it in the consultation in order to promote conceptual change. Teachers seek consultation when they cannot handle contradictions or ambiguity in their perception and experience of the child, the relationship, or the work situation. They cannot bring forth both sides simultaneously, yet instead, try to create a comprehensive picture out of a limited perception. When only one of the sides is represented the scope and control of the situation is limited. At the same time, there is a desire to change something when teachers seek consultation. Descriptions that consultees give often convey a feeling of "being stuck; something is not right; we don't understand the child."

Consultation Process

During the consultation we start a dialogue where the consultant and the consultee can discover things together. The consultant's consenting attitude paves way for more difficult and more conflicting descriptions. The consultee's account, in other words, what they convey during the consultation, contains the material we need to understand and make things intelligible. The consultant's task is to stimulate the consultee to reflect and to listen to contradictions and ambiguity in order to discover the consultee's dilemma, thereby facilitating new discoveries and promote change.

Ambivalence and Ambiguity—A Stage in the Change

Barth and Näsholm (1997) pointed out that a strategy to create movement and to facilitate change can be to carefully create an ambivalence or to make clear and emphasize one that already exists relating to an issue, relation, or situation. They also stress that when one examines and explores ambivalence, one can understand behavior that seems irrational. The ego can control the complex situation and contradictory emotions and thoughts can be coordinated. It is possible to understand and make changes. But to dare bring forth and explore contradictory emotions and thoughts can be both a sensitive and delicate matter. An atmosphere and a relationship characterized by empathy and concern is needed. We create a consenting, yet limiting atmosphere in the consultation, which gives the consultee the opportunity to explore. The consultee is encouraged to widen his or her own frame of reference and cognitive focus because the consultant supports him or her in feeling safe while dealing with emotionally sensitive issues (Caplan & Caplan, 1993).

In order for development and change to take place, the consultant must bring forth the ambiguity and contradictions and explore them together with the consultee. The consultant should challenge the consultee's accounts, feelings, and thoughts in order to make a change, and the consultant bases this challenge on material taken from the consultee's own presentation of the client and their interaction. The change is both emotional and cognitive and will help the consultee to develop the interaction with the client.

REFERENCES

Barth, T., & Näsholm, C. (1997). Vankelmodets dynamik. *Psykolog Tidningen*, 16, 4–7.

Caplan, G., & Caplan, R. (1993). *The theory and practice of mental health consultation* (2nd ed.). San Francisco: Jossey-Bass.

Hylander, I. (2000). *Turning processes. The change of representations in consultee-centered case consultation*. (Dissertation). Linköping: Linköping University. Department of Behavioural Science.

Johannesen, E. (1999). How to complicate the thinking of the consultee. In *Explorations in process in practice*. (Seminar proceeding). Stockholm: 2nd International Seminar on Consultee-centered Consultation.

Mang, M. (1995). *Use of metaphors in consultee-centered consultation. School-based applications*. Stockholm: 1st International Seminar on Consultee-centered Consultation.

Nörretranders, T. (1991). *Märk världen. En bok om vetenskap och intuition*. Stockholm: Bonnier Alba.

Sandoval, J. (1995). Constructivism, consultee-centered consultation and conceptual change. *Journal of Educational and Psychological Consultation*, 7(1), 89–97.

20

Anger and Gender in Consultation

Elin Michélsen

Swedish day care and preschool are places where almost only women are employed. The consultants too are almost all women. The most frequent problem when preschool teachers and nurses ask for psychological consultation concerns boys—particularly angry and aggressive behavior among boys. The consultee is worried about the angry emotions and actions of the child and wants to understand both the boy's and his or her own reactions in order to help the boy to cope with his anger in a more varied and flexible way. It is often hard for the consultee to communicate with angry boys, as it evokes affective expressions and fear of losing their professional composure. Nevertheless, helping to understand children and coping with their negative affects is one of the most important and challenging tasks both for primary and secondary caregivers. As a consultant, my task is to help the consultee understand and find strategies to handle these work problems in a successful way.

GENDER DIFFERENCES IN ANGER

This frequently presented question about male anger—raised and handled by female consultees and consultants—made me curious about anger from a gender perspective. The following describes my thoughts in planning a study aimed at widening the frames of reference in consultation about anger in girls and boys.

Different Expectations and Affective Responses to Girls and Boys

Sheridan and Henning-Stout (1994) explored the implication of gender in school and preschool consultation. They pointed at research showing that teachers do respond differently to girls and boys. For example, there is research showing that teachers interact with girls and handicapped children in ways that encourage passive learning, docile conduct, and lack of initiative and perseverance. Other studies show that teachers encouraged imitation, rule learning, help seeking, and nurturing in girls games. Boys, on the other hand, were encouraged in exploration, problem solving, creativity, and independence.

We also know from experiments that if individuals expect that a child is a girl, they will respond to her in a different way than if they expect that the same child is a boy. For example, teachers and nurses are likely to interpret the same behavior as anger or rage if it is a boy and as sadness if it is a girl. We also communicate differently with girls and boys about anger and this influences and restricts the development of the scripts for interactions and the development of the reflective self of the child (Fonagy, Moran, & Target, 1993).

The Difference Between Aggression and Anger

Aggression

In everyday language, the concept of anger and aggression is often confused. Psychoanalytic thinking on aggression focuses either on aggression as an innate instinct for destruction or as a reaction to a frustrating phenomenon (Fonagy et al., 1993). It is generally recognized that aggression may be part of a healthy mental state influencing professional rivalry, humor, sports, and so on. Senseless and cruel destructiveness is seen as pathological manifestation of aggression. Fonagy (1993) described the development of a psychological self and argued that if the caregiver is unpredictable aggression will be invoked frequently as a defense against the threats to the psychological self. It may become an organizing influence in the construction of the self. Pathological destructiveness then takes place. Aggressive behavior involves the intent to harm in reality or fantasy.

Anger

Tomkins (cited in Demos, 1995) developed an affect theory and postulated nine primary innate affects; anger, fear, distress, startle, joy, interest, contempt, disgust, and shame. He described anger as an affect activated by a very high density level of stimulation—higher than distress. Anger can be caused by pain, distress, or frustration when stimulation is sufficiently dense to activate the affect system of anger. Nathanson (1995 also emphasizes the wide range of expressions of anger) consistent with Tomkins' affect theory.

> Some people explode like a thunderstorm .... Some yell or hit, others clam up and withdraw ... each of these people is experiencing the same affect assembled in ways developed over lifetime magnified and dampened by virtue of their having grown up in a particular family, neighborhood and era. (p. 103)

As a psychiatrist, Tompkins was especially interested in his patients manifesting and coping with their anger. He also pointed out that anger calls attention to the need to change something. He further discussed the sources for anger and emphasized that in normal interpersonal life the most prominent stimulus to anger is humiliation. He considered that the slings and arrows of everyday life that create that perceived outrageous fortune to be some as-yet-unexplained link between shame and anger.

According to Fredelius et al. (1994)

> anger is an affect that can be expressed verbally or non verbally, giving us immediate information of discomfort and motivating us to change (p. 127)

She also highlighted the paradox of living in a culture so much dominated by anger, hatred, and violence and in the same time suffering from prohibitions of expressing anger.

To summarize, anger can be seen as a forceful affect often expressed in different ways when ordinary self-expression is stopped or inhibited (Fonagy et al., 1993). It is the intention to harm that makes the difference between aggressive and angry behavior. Angry behavior does not necessarily involve the intent to harm, but aggressive behavior does.

CONSULTEE-CENTERED CONSULTATION

In helping the teacher to solve his or her work problem with the child, I practice the Swedish elaboration of the early Caplan (1970) model of mental health consultation, namely, consultee-centered consultation. This involves posing a number of questions in a special sequence to the consultee about the client (Guvå, 1989, this volume). The aim is to solve the consultee's work problem by increasing the reflective and affective thinking about the problem making emotional and cognitive change possible (Sandoval, 1996). In this volume Sandoval describes consultation as a conceptual change process. The consultant asks questions to elicit both descriptions of the child's behavior as well as what is going on in the minds of the consultees as a consequence of the child's behavior.

Using Hylander's concepts, also presented in this volume, the consultant is interested in the consultee's presentations and representations of his or her work problem. The attitudes and affects—the representations—of the consultee are of great importance and are dealt with by the consultant sometimes as parallel processes, which means that the affects of the consultee are seen as unconsciously communicated affects of the child.

According to Hylander (2000) the starting point for subsequent conceptual shifts is the ability of the consultant to change his or her own representation of the problem to start with *to the point where he or she totally accepts and understands the teacher's representation of the case.*

ANGER IN THE CONSULTEE

Women and Anger

Anger is seldom openly discussed among the consultees. Bernadez-Bonesatti (1978) and Lerner (1977) assumed that anger is a difficult affect, one which is taboo to express and, for women, even to feel in our society. Theories of the psychology of women (Baker Miller, 1976) claim that women develop their identity based on similarity with their mother and her way of functioning in a network of relations. As a consequence a woman's identity is dependent on the mutual recognition and confirmation by other women. She described women's fears of hurting or losing a relationship as they move toward greater authenticity and personal growth. According to these theories most women have difficulties in recognizing their anger and in expressing anger because of their fear of being excluded from the sisterhood.

Boalt-Boëthius (1983) studied staff group processes in day care centers. The research focus was on individual autonomy and was defined as:

> The degree to which an individual (a) has access to his intellectual capacity and prior experience (capacity), (b) has a perspective of the situation and a certain degree of access to in regard to his own behavior alternatives, and (c) is able to listen and understand what other persons in the group say and do (empathy). (p. 35)

In her observations of the teachers' interactions, working with authentic planning tasks, she found their main strategies were to avoid confrontation, criticism, taking initiatives and responsibility. Obviously, they seemed to avoid expressing anger toward each other.

Fredelius (1994) also writes that female anger is taboo. Openly expressed anger is not allowed. Women have been told and taught that it is improper to express anger. Relatively weak emotional expressions of anger evoke strong reactions of contempt. What does this mean to the consultees/teachers? Does this difficulty make it more troublesome for the consultee not only to recognize her own anger but also to recognize or identify anger in girls rather than boys? Or is it rather the opposite?

Daily Experiences Working With Children

Working with children in preschool, day care centers, and school often arouses all sorts of emotions in the teacher, including anger. If anger is taboo to express (or even to feel it in the moment) when surrounded by female colleagues, helping children with their affective expressions of anger would be an extra demanding task. Afterwards in consultation—a situation where one is allowed and free to express one's anger—the consultees/teachers do express anger. This is illustrated in the following statements made during consultation; statements rarely made in other conversations at the preschool (Michélsen, 1995).

> He is making me mad.
> I get furious.
> I would like to scream to him that I won´t tolerate him talking to me like this.
> I want to take him and shake him.

Still the consultees' questions and problems in consultation are mostly about angry boys.

Why are angry girls such an unusual problem in consultation? There must be angry girls in day nurseries and preschools. The question is how the girls express their anger and whether their angry expressions are recognized, tolerated, encouraged or not. If the angry expressions of the girls are invisible or not tolerated by the teachers there is a gender problem.

Gender Attitudes and Affects

Sheridan and Henning-Stout (1994) recognized the gender attitudes and affects as potential barriers to effective practice. They argue *"these attitudes and personal issues can take the form of gender stereotypical beliefs about differential abilities or of appropriateness of behavior of boys and girls"* (p. 93). They also pointed out the importance of consultation efforts directed at changing the subjective judgements, stereotypical attitudes, and other personal factors of the consultee in order to provide a more gender-fair learning environment. They proposed confrontation and reframing as a way this can be accomplished.

I have found the following confrontational technique to be a useful as well an unexpected query.

Introducing a Surprising Question

The use of a particular question can be illustrated in the following case. Recently in consultations about angry children, I have been confronting the consultee with the gender comparative question *if he had been a girl?* or *if she had been a boy?* The question is posed late in the first session or during the second session, when the consultees have already described the behavior of the child and their own responses, thoughts, feelings, and beliefs about the child in question. It is not meant to interfere with the ordinary process in the beginning of the consultation when the consultant mostly listens to and confirms the consultee's presentations. Hylander (2000) described the consultation process as oscillating between the consultant confirming and challenging the consultee's presentations and representations as well as his or her own presentations and representations of the problem. My question to the consultees is intended to be challenging. The aim is to widen the frames of reference and to increase further reflections, consciousness, and emotional and cognitive understanding of anger in girls and boys and the consultee's interactions with angry children. When I have posed this question it has been successful in arousing interest and reflections. The consultees, women only, look at the consultant somewhat surprised and confused, then say that it is a difficult question but after a while they answer.

Responses to "If He Had Been a Girl?"

It seldom happens that a girl is angry in that manner.

I don't know why .... Perhaps younger girls when they are two or three years old. Yes I remember one girl she hit me ...

The consultee reflects about differences in boys and girls expressing their anger presuming their modes of expressions to be acquired.

Then I would not have been afraid and uncertain. I know what to do if it is a girl.

I think I understand her better. .... Perhaps I intervene earlier if it is a girl.

I think I have a better relation with the girls so it is easier for me to understand and help them.

The consultees tell us that they are more familiar with and knows better how to handle the angry problem when it is a girl, which typically means to intervene earlier. This is contradictory to the hypothesis of the invisible female anger.

> I think the girls don't express anger in the same way so it is more difficult to see if they are angry.
>
> You don't expect girls to hit each other like this when they get angry.

On the other hand these reflections and presentations of their expectations seem to confirm theories and research in woman psychology about the invisible female anger.

Response to "If She Had Been a Boy?"

> Do I tolerate more if it is a boy? I hope I react in the same way, but probably not ... We have the same rules for girls and boys.
>
> I prefer noisy and troublesome boys. I don´t know why but it has always been like this ... Girls are so complicated ....

There is no right or wrong answer and it is interesting to notice that these examples both seem to verify and falsify the theories of the psychology of women.

This question has been successful in starting the reflective process. Now I am curious to learn how this question influences the consultation process. How does it influence the consultee's affects and behavior toward the child? Does it help the consultee to look at her work problem with new eyes and thus lead to successful turnings? Is it easier to consider anger in a boy or in a girl by this reversed gender question?

ANGER IN CLIENTS

Helping the Child to Cope With Anger

Children's anger can be expressed without observed direction; toward objects, other children, other adults, and the consultee. One can distinguish different roles for the consultee in helping the child to cope with his or her anger.

In Direct Angry Interactions With the Child

This happens when the consultee and the child are involved in a conflict and both are angry. This is a difficult role and calls for a professional attitude including empathy and self reflection. Yet, if these interactions are successful it is probably one of the most powerful ways for a child to learn how to cope with anger.

As a Model Interacting With Other Teachers or Nurses

Children also learn from observing the grown-ups. When teachers are angry at each other and express this in the presence of the children, they serve as models to learn from. However, this does not happen very often and according to the theories of psychology of women previously mentioned, one would expect children to find it troublesome to learn from because of the ambivalent and ambiguous expressions of female anger.

As a Model Interacting With Another Child

When another child and the teacher are angry at each other, the other children often show great interest and pay attention to the teacher's behavior and expressions. This will be a good learning opportunity for those children who are observing this interaction.

As a Helping Preschool Teacher not Personally Involved

In these cases the consultee helps the angry child to handle the situation that makes the child angry, but not the consultee. In my experience as a consultant, this role of the consultee is often an empathetic one and is very successful in helping the child.

In all these roles, it is of great importance for the consultee to be aware of her gender-specific expectations and responses.

Fonagy et al. (1993) discussed the importance of an accurate mirroring by the caregiver in early interactions as being very important in the development of a psychological (reflective) self of the child. Thus children's anger in preschool can be seen as an affect often expressed when ordinary self-expression is stopped or inhibited.

DEVELOPING AN OPEN MIND ABOUT ANGER AND GENDER

As a professional teacher, the consultee has to develop more or less conscious strategies to cope with her own anger and to handle angry expressions by the children. Perhaps daily experience and helping young children cope with their anger stimulates the consultees/teachers and nurses to develop more adaptive and conscious strategies concerning their own anger and ways of handling angry expressions by the children.

Thus, compared with other women, one would expect female teachers and nurses be more reflective, relaxed, and open minded about their own anger and anger expressed both by girls and boys.

It is my impression that Swedish teachers and nurses are more interested, observant, and reflective about gender aspects among the children than the average woman. Whether this helps them to recognize girls' anger or not is still an open question. This will be of great importance in fulfilling their main task of encouraging children in their all-inclusive development, which includes helping both girls and boys to cope with and understand their anger.

REFERENCES

Baker Miller, J. (1976). *Toward a new psychology of women*. Boston: Beacon Press.

Bernandez-Bonesatti, T. (1978). Conflicts with aggression in contemporary women. *Journal of the American Medical Women's Association, 33*, 215–219.

Boalt-Boëthius, S. (1983). *Autonomy coping and defence in small work groups*. University of Stockholm: Department of Psychology.

Caplan, G. (1970). *The theory and practice of mental health consultation*. New York: Basic Books.

Demos, E. V. (Ed.). (1995). *Exploring affect. The selected writings of Silvan S. Tomkins*. Cambridge, MA: Cambridge University Press.

Fonagy, P., Moran, G., & Target, M. (1993). Aggression and the psychological self. *Journal of Psycho-Analysis, 74*, 471–485.

Fredelius, G. (Ed.). (1994). Kvinnoidentitet. *Natur och Kultur*. Stockholm: Om Personalinriktad Fallkonsultation.

Guvå, G. (1989). *Klientmysteriet*. Sfph:s monografiserie nr 32. Stockholm: Norstedts.

Hylander, H. (2000). *Turning processes. The change of representations in consultee-centered case consultation*. Linköping University: Department of Behavioural Sciences.

Lerner, H. (1977). Taboos against female anger. *Meninger Perspective, 8*, 4–11.

Michélsen, E. (1995). *Hur uttrycks ilska i konsultation. En fråga för handledaren*. Stockholm: Uppsats i Ericastiftelsens handledarutbildning.

Nathanson, D. (1992). *Shame and pride: Affect, sex, and the birth of the self*. New York: Norton.

Sandoval, J. (1996). Constructivism, consultee-centered consultation, and conceptual change. *Journal of Educational and Psychological Consultation, 7*, 89–97.

Sheridan, S. M., & Henning-Stout, M. (1994). Consulting with teachers about girls and boys. *Journal of Educational and Psychological Consultation, 5*(2), 93–113.

21

Use of Metaphors, Parables, and Anecdotes in Consultee-Centered Consultation: School-Based Applications

Michelle Mang

There are many examples of the use of metaphors in the consultation literature (Berlin, 1967, 1977; Caplan, 1970). In fact, several articles have used
various metaphors to describe and better understand the consultation process as a whole (Kitchner & Greenstein, 1983; Smith, 1984; Trickett, 1987).
However, very little attention has been given as to how—through the consultant's conscious and deliberate use of metaphors—the consultation process itself can be enhanced. Furthermore, outside of the linguistic literature,
the underlying structure of metaphors has seldom been addressed. Consequently, the issue of how metaphors can be constructed in an active manner,
using a specific set of principles, and then applied to the consultation situation at hand has yet to be examined. The goal of this chapter is to explore the
effective use of metaphors during the consultation session as a way of challenging the consultee and introducing the consultant's representations. The
use of metaphors is thereby expected to increase the consultee's repertoire of
choices in working with the client that will, in turn, help the consultee overcome the difficulties with the client.

METAPHOR, PARABLE, AND ANECDOTE

What exactly does it mean to use metaphors, parables, analogies, or anecdotes effectively during consultation? For that matter, how does one differentiate between a useful metaphor and one that simply wastes the consultation time, or worse, does damage to the relationship? How are metaphors constructed? How do school-based consultants learn to use metaphors within their training programs? It could be that just as it is important for the consultant to understand the manifest and latent content of the consultation session, so it is important for the consultant to have a similar understanding of the structure and latent meaning of the metaphors used during the consultation process. Metaphors serve to enable the consultee to gain a different view of the client's problem, a way to step back verbally and take a look at the issue from a related, yet different, perspective. In this manner, new insights into the client's behavior and issues can be gained and taken into consideration by the consultee during further interactions with the client.

Before going further into an analysis of metaphor use, it is important to distinguish between the terms *metaphor, analogy, parable*, and *anecdote* as they relate to the consultation process. Although there are similarities and overlap between these terms, for the sake of clarity they are defined as they will be viewed within the consultation framework.

Webster's dictionary defines a *metaphor* as a figure of speech in which a term is transferred from the object it ordinarily designates to an object it may designate only by implicit comparison or analogy; or the application of a word or phrase to an object or concept it does not literally denote in order to suggest comparison with another object or concept. A *parable* is a short allegorical story designed to convey a truth or moral lesson; a statement or comment that conveys meaning indirectly by the use of comparison, analogy or the like. An *analogy* is a correspondence in some respects between otherwise dissimilar things; a form of logical inference, based on the assumption that if two things are known to be alike in some respects, then they must be alike in other respects. An *anecdote* is a short narrative concerning an interesting or amusing incident or event: a short, often oral, account of a real or fictitious occurrence.

As a general statement, an anecdote, parable, analogy, or metaphor can all serve as interventions within the context of the consultation setting. Stories, anecdotes, and parables all have the potential to convey a message or new learning about a particular area of difficulty. Essentially, in these forms a person encounters a type of challenge that is somehow mastered. The process by which this challenge is resolved may offer a possible solution for others in a similar situation.

Thus, if the conflict that is occurring in the story is similar to the one the listener also happens to be facing, the story increases in significance (Gordon, 1978). Most people have had the experience of listening to a parable, or anecdote and identifying various characters that are similar to people actually known to them. Usually, when this occurs, the story's resolution becomes increasingly important as the listener begins to wonder how the story characters handled the situation. Other examples of sources for such stories include novels, fairy tales, songs, epic poems, movies, even gossip (Gordon, 1978; Mills & Crowley, 1986).

According to Gordon (1978), when any of these narrative sources are presented with the goal of instructing or advising the listener, even if the listener imports for him or herself such a relationship, then that story becomes a metaphor for that person. A metaphor is a novel representation of the consultee's world. During consultation a metaphor is being used each time an image or association is transposed from one arena to another in order to exhibit similarities, differences, or ambiguities. In fact, the two most important characteristics that define a metaphor are in terms of movement; movement from one situation to another, and a transformation (Ricoeur, 1986). This can result in new awareness and the construction of new meaning by connecting the two ideas, events, or experiences.

For example, a teacher was having difficulty with a child who was an excellent student but had begun to fall drastically behind in completing assignments and had difficulty finishing even the easiest tasks presented to her; she was also a perfectionist. Although this child had started to stay in at recess and after school to catch up on her work, she continued to fall further behind and became even more concerned about making mistakes or doing poorly. The consultant told the teacher a story about a track student on his wife's team who was an excellent runner but whose times began to deteriorate drastically shortly before a very important race. His wife found out that the student, concerned about getting an athletic scholarship to college, had begun to train even harder, often doing double the workout that was given. This had resulted in an increase in stress and a decrease in performance because of overtraining. When the student was forced to slow down and stick to a reasonable amount of training, his performance slowly improved and his race times ultimately became faster. Later, the teacher reported that he had set limits as to how much time the student was to spend working on assignments and made her spend recess on the playground with the other kids. He also spoke with her parents and had them set the same limits at home. By the end of the year, the student was completing all of her assignments in a timely manner although she still remained overly concerned about making mistakes.

ISSUES IN USING METAPHORS IN CONSULTATION

There are several components to the metaphors used by the consultant that seem to promote the most effective reception by the consultee. First, there must be what Rossi (1985) called a "shared phenomenological reality" which includes a sense of identification with the story. In other words, the consultee should be able to identify with the character in the narrative being presented. The story should provide a subtle parallel to real events. This parallelism ensures that the consultee's sense of isolation can be replaced with a sense of shared experience. Also, there must be a metaphorical conflict that is analogous to the issue, producing concern, anxiety, or other unpleasant emotions for the teacher. Along with this conflict, there is a crisis where the protagonist is faced with a major threat. The hero utilizes resources and resolves the problem, whereby the consultee identifies with the victorious role model (Mills & Crowley, 1986).

The primary feature of a metaphor is that the characters and events that occur in the story are isomorphic or equivalent with those people and events that characterize the teacher's problem. In this manner, all of the important people in the teacher's area of concern are represented in the metaphor's cast of characters (Gordon, 1978). Although these representations are not always equal per se, the relationships are the same in the metaphor as those presented in the actual problem situation. In addition to maintaining the relationships, it is important to preserve the sequencing of the story to insure that the teacher will accept it as a significant representation of his or her situation. However, the teacher may or may not be consciously aware of this representation. Conscious awareness is not necessary for the metaphor to be effective although most consultee's will have this awareness to some degree.

Because the isomorphic transformations are concerned only with relationships, the consultant is given quite a deal of flexibility regarding content (Mills & Crowley, 1986). This allows the consultant to draw on his or her wide range of experience and creative flexibility to fashion a metaphor designed especially for the situation, or in perhaps the best approach, a combination of experience and creativity.

As the metaphor is being told, it is important for the consultant to insure that it is being well received and that rapport is still being maintained. This can be accomplished through careful observation of the teacher's nonverbal communication. Perhaps the most important component of a successful metaphor is the desired outcome, the resolution of the conflict, which is presented via a connecting strategy (Gordon, 1978). The resolution and strategy that will have the greatest chance for success is the one that originates with the consultee. This information will be indicated either directly or indirectly during the initial phases of the consultation session. Being mindful of these components enables the consultant to use metaphors successfully during the consultation process. When the consultant is using the same kind of language as the consultee—repeating some of the words and phrases as the consultee is using—it is easier to come up with metaphors that fit the consultee work problem.

An experienced consultant asks consultees specific questions about how they have tried to resolve the problem in the past (Caplan, 1970). From the information presented in the details of past failures, there will also be an implicit description about how the issue can be resolved. In this manner, the consultees provide information about how they got stuck in resolving the problem and the areas where their conceptual frameworks are limited. Given this information the metaphor can be constructed. In summary, the process of formulating a basic metaphor using the following steps.outlined by Gordon (1978).

Gathering Information

The consultant looks for the answers to the following questions: Who are the significant persons involved and what are their interpersonal relationships? What are the events that are characteristic of the problem situation? How does the problem progress? What changes does the consultee desire to make? Are they well formed? What has been tried unsuccessfully in the past to deal with the problem?

Building the Metaphor

This involves selecting a context. Then the consultant needs to construct and structure the metaphor so that its form is isomorphic with the information gathered in step one. Finally, the consultant must determine a resolution that includes a strategy, the desired outcome, and a reframing of the original problem situation for the metaphor.

Tell the Metaphor

The consultant should insure that rapport is maintained. Also, whenever possible the consultant should use unspecified verbs and nominalizations such as know, understand, and wonder, to assist in the likelihood of the metaphor being assimilated by the consultee into his or her unique conceptual framework (Gordon, 1978; Haley, 1973; Mills & Crowley, 1986).

METAPHORS IN CONSULTEE-
CENTERED CONSULTATION

In consultee-centered consultation the consultant works with the consultee to indirectly impact on the client (Berlin, 1977; Caplan, 1963). Generally, in the school system, the teacher is the consultee whereas the student is the client. During the consultation conversation the consultant may use analogies, anecdotes, or parables as a way of helping the teacher master the situation. These may be applied to address any of the four categories of difficulty outlined by Caplan (1970) that the teacher is experiencing. It is important to remember, however, that metaphors may have varied levels of applicability that depend both on the individual situation as well as the specific difficulty which the teacher is experiencing.

Using Anecdotes to Increase the Teacher's
Psychological Understanding

During consultation, the consultant may discover that the teacher has a lack of understanding of the psychological factors underlying the student's difficulties. Using an anecdotal method as a vehicle to provide the information that the teacher may need to understand the student better has several potential benefits.

First and foremost, it allows for the teacher and consultant to maintain the equal, coordinate nature of their relationship and thus avoids the potential pitfall of the teacher placing the consultant into an "expert other" role during the consultation process. Second, it provides the consultant an opportunity to share and reflect the affect that the teacher is experiencing as a result of lack of knowledge. Finally, it provides a more indirect approach of providing information and lessens the chance of the consultation session becoming one where the consultant solves the problem for the teacher. This also guards against the consultant using extensive psychological language that may not be appropriate for the teacher's conceptual framework. As a result, the use of metaphoric language to assist the teacher in seeing the connections in the psychosocial patterns can be useful.

For example, during consultation, a consultee was expressing concern about one of her students who was having social difficulties due to his intrusive behavior and rudeness toward other children. He would frequently interrupt other children in the classroom and on the playground in unsuccessful attempts to join the group activity. According to her description, he was simply unaware of the disruptiveness of his actions and the teacher was at a loss to understand why he could not simply "play nicely" with the other children. This child came from a very chaotic home environment.

The consultant mentioned that the situation reminded him of a story told to him by another psychologist about a porcupine who kept having difficulty interacting with the other forest animals because he was unaware of the impact of his quills. However, the consultant continued, it was necessary for the porcupine to keep his quills as they served to protect him in certain situations. Fortunately, the porcupine encountered a wise old owl who helped him understand that there were times when his quills were helpful and necessary, and other times when they hindered him in his interactions with other animals. The consultee laughed at this and remarked "That's funny, I'm sure that he has to be very intrusive at home to get any attention at all, it sure doesn't work on the playground though. I'll bet I could teach him a different way here at school."

Use of Metaphor or Analogy to Address a Consultee's Lack of Skill

A second difficulty frequently encountered during the consultation process is often termed *lack of skill*. Lack of skill differs from lack of understanding in several important ways. When the teacher is experiencing this difficulty, he or she usually has an understanding of the student's problems but is unaware of how to access the resources necessary to help the student. These resources might be internal, residing within the teacher, or external such as availability of school or community assistance. Use of a metaphor to address an issue that derives from lack of skill can indirectly suggest plans of action to the teacher that have not been previously considered. In this manner, the teacher's professional integrity is preserved and the consultant does not fall into the role of technical supervisor that may be perceived as an authority role and would alter the consultation relationship.

Use of a metaphor in this case can also help with what Hollister and Miller (1977) described as using trait-cause analysis to deal with lack of skill or knowledge. In this manner, a metaphor can allude to possible causes for the trait that is resulting in the teacher's difficulty. Then, once the focus is shifted through the use of metaphor from the trait to the cause the teacher may be able to generate interventions based on eliminating the causes rather than focusing on the symptoms. Possible interventions may be suggested indirectly through the resolution portion of the metaphor.

An illustration of this involved an older teacher new to a community with a high percentage of ethnic minorities. She felt that one of her students was experiencing difficulties because of the absence of a father in the home environment. There were very limited opportunities for male role models within the school system and she was at a loss to help the student. An analogy was drawn between her predicament and that of the consultant who, during her first year in graduate school, had not made the best choices for academic courses because she had studiously avoided her academic counselor, assuming that she was too old for such advice and should have learned it on her own. However, on inquiry, she found that the advisor not only expected such questions, but that he also provided some information that helped the consultant solve a current academic dilemma. The next week the teacher mentioned that she had spoken with the principal about the child in question and that he had provided her with a point of contact for a local agency who could offer male volunteers interested in working with students such as hers who did not have any such role models in the household.

Metaphor Use to Promote Consultee Confidence

A third area where the teacher may experience difficulty stems from a lack of confidence or self esteem. Frequently, this occurs as a result of inexperience, illness, or fatigue. Providing nonspecific ego support through the use of a metaphor assists the teacher without calling undue attention to the difficulties that have led to the lack of confidence and/or self esteem. Additionally, a metaphor may also allow the teacher to gain perspective through a realization that "this too shall pass." The teacher may then become more hopeful about the successful resolution of the student's difficulty along with his or her ability to deal with the problem.

This process may be demonstrated best by exploring an interaction that took place between a student teacher and a consultant. The student teacher came into the consultation very dismayed and feeling hopeless about her ability to teach. She repeatedly mentioned that she did not feel that she had learned enough in school and was in over her head. She was also concerned about the other student teachers who were older than she and presumably had more experience.

In reality, the evidence was that this teacher was very well trained and competent. She simply suffered from a lack of self confidence in her abilities. The consultant shared with her a story about his prior military experience where he had been a platoon leader right out of officer basic training and was interacting with people who were older, more experienced, and who had gone to West Point, a very prestigious military school. However, as time went on, he found that although he was young and inexperienced, he had some specialized training that the other older folks had not received because it was very new information that had not been taught when the others had attended their training. As he continued, he found that he was able to take this knowledge and apply it to situations that continued to surprise and delight him during that difficult first year.

Theme Interference Reduction With Metaphors and Parables

The final, and perhaps most important area where the use of metaphor could be effective, is when dealing with the issue Caplan (1970) called lack of objectivity, also termed *theme interference*. This occurs when consultees are unable to utilize their skills and knowledge with a client because of some distortion of the situation based on an intruding problem theme on the part of the consultee. As a result of this, the consultee becomes immersed in the client's situation and is unable to see the situation clearly. According to Caplan (1963) this theme interference is a "symbolic inhibition of free perception and communication between consultee and a concomitant disorder of objectivity." Generally, this is marked by a degree of emotional upset in the consultee that can vary considerably from person to person. At times it may even approach the crisis stage. During this difficult period, consultees often attribute their discomfort to the problem they are having with the client. It is important to understand that the feelings that the consultees attribute to the client's situation may primarily originate in their personal lives or in an aspect of the work situation unrelated to the client.

Most of the references in the consultation literature that use metaphors in their examples focus on the issue of how to deal with theme interference. This is not surprising when one stops to consider the potential applications of metaphors in such a situation. Initially, using a metaphor helps to diffuse the issues surrounding the work problem and get the teacher thinking about the "other" possibilities that the consultant is describing. Caplan (1970) cited the use of a parable as a technique for dealing with these particularly sensitive themes. According to Caplan, by using a parable, the consultant diverts discussion away from the student onto a case that appears completely different but resolves essential theme elements. This is where the process of building the metaphor gains in importance. The manifest content of the metaphor should be different but the latent content retains the common threads that make it isomorphic.

Caplan (1970) emphasized that during the consultation process the consultant does not confront the consultee's defensive displacement. However, the consultant also recognizes the importance and value of helping the consultee resolve the personal problem in a vicarious manner through the client's problem thereby improving the consultee's work functioning. Using metaphors during this process can help keep the problem "out there" especially when focusing on the client is too intense for the consultee. Working through problems presented by the consultee that involve affect indirectly by inference is key to theme interference reduction (Altrocchi, 1972). Because the consultee is not cognizant of the link between his or her client's difficulties and his or her own emotional issues, a metaphor can be used to help resolve the difficulty. This method will help keep the displacement from weakening. Moreover, a metaphor does not require conscious intent for it to be effective (Haley, 1973).

An example of using a metaphor to address an issue of theme interference occurred during consultation with a first grade teacher. This particular teacher was experiencing difficulties with a student who, in her words, "kept defying her," was stubborn, and refused to do what she told him. As the consultation continued, the consultee made frequent references to the student not responding to her directions or respecting her authority in the classroom. The consultant told the teacher a story about his niece who continuously refused to get into her pajamas when it was bedtime. His sister was exasperated, angry, and at her wits end when the child's new babysitter provided the solution to the problem. It seems that his sister had arrived home early from a night out to find her child happily dressed in her pajamas and being read a bedtime story.

Later, she asked the babysitter how she had managed to get the child into her pajamas without a fuss. "Oh, I simply told her that she could wear either her blue pajamas or her red ones and then told her it was her choice which ones to wear" replied the babysitter. "A few minutes later, she was downstairs in her blue pj's asking to be read a bedtime story," she continued. "That's an old trick my mom taught me when I first started babysitting, give the child some kind of freedom and choice, while still getting the job done," she finished. The consultant told the consultee that that story often helped him when he was working with kids. Later that week, the teacher reported that the student was responding more positively to her directions in the classroom especially with completing his work assignments, generally choosing to finish them before recess and/or quiet time rather than after.

Perhaps the most important reason for using a metaphor to reduce theme interference is in order to avoid falling into the pitfall of providing psychotherapy to the teacher. Although this is an issue that may occur anytime during the consultation relationship, the danger is often increased because of the unique nature of theme interference (Caplan, 1970). In this case, to separate the teacher's personal issues from the student's problem and return the teacher to a normal level of effectiveness and functioning, it is useful to devise a metaphor that will help accomplish this task. Because theme interference generally involves preconscious syllogistic propositions about the world, the use of metaphoric language should be designed not to unlink all the syllogistic statements but instead, to invalidate the fixed expectation that accompanies such statements. Furthermore, this principle is very important to understand when using metaphors so as to avoid unlinking the teacher from the specific situation at hand without any resolution of the theme interference. When this occurs, the original situation may be successfully resolved but the theme will persist and the teacher will probably find a different student or situation in the future on which to displace this personal issue (Caplan, 1963). With an accurate understanding of the preconscious syllogisms and the stereotypical expectations that usually follow them, a metaphor can be devised to correct the irrational elements contained in the teacher's expectations. In essence the "initial category" Altrocchi (1972) outlined, is maintained through careful construction of the metaphor, and what is changed is the "inevitable outcome" or expectation, usually through the metaphor's resolution. Therefore, the metaphor can be a very elegant indirect way of dealing with theme interference.

Berlin (1967) discovered that if the consultant discusses problems similar to the one that the teacher is currently experiencing, the teacher's anxiety is reduced. Also, the teacher feels that the consultant understands his or her feelings and difficulties. Berlin (1977) believed that all feelings aroused in the teacher by a pupil can be talked about. Using case examples to support this statement, he utilized successfully several principles of metaphor-building in his "related" story told to the teacher designed to help her deal with a student's problem that was also arousing intense feelings on her part. In both of his examples, Berlin (1977) provided a successful resolution to the difficulty in his metaphor that was internalized and generalized by the teacher and used as a way of dealing with the teacher's similar problems with the students.

It is important to note that often metaphors used by consultants do not include all of the components previously outlined. Frequently, they are designed to show the teacher that the consultant empathizes with the situation and can understand the difficulty that the teacher is experiencing. However, with a little creative application, a resolution can easily be incorporated into the sharing experience and may provide the teacher with an avenue to generate alternate forms of behavior.

Metaphors are a way of talking about a person's experience. Many people who are involved in the helping profession, such as counselors, psychologists, psychiatrists, and other mental health professionals, often have an intuitive sense of the value of parables, analogies, and anecdotes to facilitate communication. The same is true for the consultation process. Several well-known practitioners in the field cite examples of the use of such stories in their articles on consultation techniques (Berlin, 1967, 1977; Caplan, 1977; Davis & Sandoval, 1978). However, very little research has been devoted to making metaphor use more explicit and understandable to the novice or student learning consultation skills.

This chapter has outlined four areas of difficulty that can occur during consultation and how the consultant's use of metaphor can be useful in overcoming these difficulties. Learning how to formulate such metaphors can greatly facilitate the consultation process. Consultants in training would be well advised to studying the underlying techniques of metaphor creation.

REFERENCES

Altrocchi, J. (1972). Mental health consultation. In S. E. Golann & C. Eisdorfer (Eds.), Handbook of community mental health (pp. 477–507). New York: Appleton-Century Crofts.

Berlin, I. N. (1967). Preventive aspects of mental health consultation to schools. Mental Hygiene, 51(1), 34–40.

Berlin, I. (1977). Lessons learned in 25 years of mental health consultation to schools. In S. C. Plog & P. I. Almed (Eds.), Principles and techniques of mental health consultation (pp. 23–48). New York: Plenum Medical Books.

Caplan, G. (1963). Types of mental health consultation. American Journal of Orthopsychiatry, 3, 470–481.

Caplan, G. (1970). Building the relationship with the consultee. In The theory and practice of mental health consultation (pp. 48–78). New York: Basic Books.

Davis, J., & Sandoval, J. (1978). Metaphor in group mental health consultation. Journal of Community Psychology, 6, 374–382.

Gordon, D. (1978). Therapeutic metaphors. Cupertino, CA: META.

Haley, J. (1973). Uncommon therapy. New York: W. W. Norton.

Hollister, W. G., & Miller, F. T. (1977). Problem-solving strategies in consultation. American Journal of Orthopsychiatry, 47, 445–450.

Kitchner, I., & Greenstein, R. A. (1983). A model for psychiatric consultation in the general hospital. Psychiatric Quarterly, 55(1), 42–46.

Mills, J., & Crowley, R. (1986). Therapeutic metaphors for children and the child within. New York: Bruner/Mazel.

Ricoeur, P. (1986). The rule of metaphor. London: Routledge & Kegan Paul.

Rossi, E. (1985). Dreams and the growth of personality. New York: Brunner/Mazel.

Smith, K. (1984). Toward a conception of organizational currents. Group and Organizational Studies, 9(2), 285–312.

Trickett, E. J. (1987). Consultation as a preventive intervention: Comments on ecologically based studies. In The ecology of prevention (pp. 187–204): Haworth Press.

22

Promoting Student Learning by Consultee-Centered Consultation With a Vygotskian Framework

Petri Partanen

Carl Wistrom

INTRODUCTION

In consultee-centered consultation the consultant applies a theoretical perspective that is appropriate for the work problem the consultee brings to the discussion. In this chapter, we hope to show that a Vygotskian framework is appropriate for school staff working with students with learning difficulties. This theoretical perspective could be applied in understanding interactions in consultation process between the three parties; the consultant, the consultee, and the client. However, we will center our attention on its value in illuminating the problems of the student with learning difficulties. The concepts of the Russian psychologist, Lev Vygotsky, are a good fit with the theme of this book—consultation as a conceptual change process derived from a reciprocal exchange of presentations and representations of the consultee's work problem and the consultants responses to them.

Since the mid-1980s, psychologists in Sweden have been using an originally psychodynamically influenced method of consultee-centered mental health consultation in their work with preschool teachers. An evaluation of consultee-centered mental health consultation in a preschool and senior school settings in the municipality of Ostersund in 1995 showed that the majority of consultation cases were in the 3- to 8-year-old age group. Consultee-centered consultation involving students between the ages of 9 and 15 was less frequent. In the 9 to 15 age range students with learning difficulties are a major problem for school staff. Traditionally, teachers have sought help for student learning problems by requesting help from school psychologists, usually in the form of psychological assessment.

Both approaches, assessment and the psychodynamically oriented consultee-centered mental health consultation, have their limitations with regard to students with learning difficulties. Assessment does not always lead to identifying the necessary learning processes needed in the environment of the student to solve the teacher's work problem. Our experience showed that multiple theoretical frameworks, rather than the single psychodynamic framework was needed to respond to teachers' requests for help with student learning problems at ages 9 to 15. In this chapter, we describe how we used Vygotsky's theories to discuss issues regarding learning and development as they relate to student learning problems.

THEORETICAL BACKGROUND

Our choice of Vygotskian theory may need some explanation. Wistrom (1995) described a transition between preschool and school in terms of organizational factors and how these factors relate to consultation. One can see a clear shift in the aims of the senior schools compared with those of the preschool. The primary aim of preschool can be described as care and social training. In school, there is an emphasis on education and learning that becomes more emphasized as students become older. This transition also takes place at an individual level, when the child develops into a student when he or she leaves the preschool.

In Sweden, the preschool has a team-oriented work organization. As the child progresses through the school system, the school organization tends to be more and more hierarchical. Responsibility moves from the shared responsibility of the preschool teacher-team to the individual responsibility of the senior school teacher, where the teacher is primary professional responsible for his or her student's academic development. The preschool teacher-team has a general responsibility for the child's development and coping whereas the senior school teacher is less-focused on the well being of a student and more on the child's success in learning. There is a parallel between work organization and organizational culture. Preschools represent a caring female culture, whereas schools represent a traditional rigid male culture.

The consultee-centered mental health consultation method, which was developed in a preschool setting in Sweden in the late 1970s, was heavily inspired by Caplan's psychodynamic approach (Guvå, 1989). The theoretical underpinnings of the psychodynamic approach were well suited to explain the work problems of the teacher consultees within the aims, system of responsibility, work organization, and organizational culture of the preschool.

We decided to apply a theoretical framework in our consultations with teachers that would enable us to be responsive to the learning and educational problems teachers presented us, and one that took the crucial social aspects of the school context into consideration. The classical learning theories in western Europe and in the United States focused on aspects of student learning and did not take the social contextual elements of learning and development sufficiently into account. The theories of Russian psychologist Lev Vygotsky offered a richer understanding.

CENTRAL CONCEPTS IN VYGOTSKIAN THEORY

The central concepts in Vygotskian theory that we found interesting in our approach to consultee-centered consultation were concerned with student learning and the social context in which it occurred. These concepts are the zone of proximal development, activity, and tools.

The best known concept in Vygotskian theory is "the zone of proximal development." Vygotsky (1978; Moll, 1990) defined the zone as the *difference* between the actual level of independent problem solving and the level of potential development that can be achieved under adult guidance or in collaboration with more capable peers. One main idea is that if development is to occur in the individual, it needs to be mediated through social interaction, in an appropriate manner taking into account the level of difficulty of the problem to be solved.

The concept of activity is the main way to describe and analyze events occurring and actions taken by students. All human activity is to be understood as mediated and goal oriented. The mediating factor is the tool. Tools can be external and internal. External tools can be textbooks and teaching materials. Internal tools can be the specific thinking and the concepts used by the student in solving the problem. Language or inner speech is definitely seen as internal tools. Social speech can be understood as an external tool, mediating the communicative activity between the teacher and student or between a student and student.

The interplay between thought and language, manifested in inner speech and external social speech, is one of the key elements in development and change. This reciprocal process of change can also be described in terms of a change in the presentations and representations of the individual, and in terms of conceptual change, which is the overall theme of this book.

According to Hedegaard (1990), one key element in the process of change and the development of knowledge is exploratory activity. Knowledge evolves out of the contradictions between what is explored or observed and what is understood at a given point in time as described by Sandoval. Vygotsky stressed that learning and development occur as a result of the student's exploration of real-life phenomena, rather than from using second-hand information handed out by the teacher or from textbooks. Vygotsky focused on the teachers' responsibility for the process of learning, rather than the content of knowledge.

VYGOTSKIAN THEORY IN CONSULTEE-CENTERED CONSULTATION

These concepts from Vygotskian theory can be used to understand activities in the consultation between consultant and consultee, and in the educational context between the consultee and the student. The objective of the consultation is to exchange ideas with the teacher so that the teacher can solve or handle a work problem that he or she is experiencing with a student who has learning difficulties. We define learning difficulties as problems regarding academic and social skills, and we see them intertwined, as would Vygotskian theory.

The concept of the "zone of proximal development" can explain the interaction between consultant and consultee as well as the interaction between the teacher and student in a learning task. In consultation, the consultant observes the zone of proximal development between the teacher's current presentation and representation of the problem, and the revisions of those concepts as the consultation proceeds and the teacher adopts a new way or a revision of the learning task and context in which it is presented. As this zone of proximal development is created in the consultation process—the teacher's presentation of the problem and the range of solutions to the problem adopted from the consultation process—it is expected that this conceptual change in the teacher will go hand in hand with the creation of a zone of proximal development for the student in the learning task facilitated by the social context in which the learning takes place. The consultant's mission is to guide this process appropriately. The consultant's responsibility is to support the process of developing more ways of thinking about the problem, but the consultant is not responsible for teacher's conceptualizations that evolve. This is accomplished by the consultant's efforts to establish a nonhierarchical relationship with the consultee where the consultant and the consultee have a reciprocal exchange about the nature of the student's problem and ways of resolving it.

Consultation is an active and directed process. From an activity perspective, the consultant uses language, and more precisely, questions, as tools for the exploratory activity about the student and the student's learning activities. This encourages the teacher-consultee to explore different aspects of the student's learning problem and context of the educational setting in which it occurs. The consultee is requested to take notes, both in the session and between the sessions. According to Vygotsky (1928), the process of writing stimulates thinking, similarly as speech does. These notes are a tool for the consultee's further exploratory work. The exploratory activity and material generated by the consultee between the first and the subsequent sessions are used in consultation to formulate hypotheses about the student, the classroom activities and the setting. These hypotheses are evaluated in subsequent sessions, eventually leading to change and development, both in the teacher-consultee and the student.

MANUAL FOR THE INITIAL CONSULTATION SESSIONS

The questions in the consultation session emphasize the exploration of different aspects of the student's learning and behavior and the classroom context. The consultant often asks the teacher about the reasons for identifying the student as one with a learning problem. Then, as appropriate, the consultation process includes the following interactions.

Exploring Activities

"What is the problem? In which activities? When is the problem more or less evident?"
It is important to distinguish behavior from activity. The teacher's perception of the manifest behavior or problem may not be the same as what is manifest in the learning activities taking place. The manifest behavior of the student is determined by a number of factors. Some relevant factors or questions that the consultant has to bear in mind when analyzing the interaction are: What kind of educational activities does the teacher think he or she is setting up for the student? What student behavior actually results from these ideas and plans? What activities does the student think he or she is doing? What does the student actually do? How do the teacher and the student communicate these thoughts and actions about the learning plans?

"What kind of activities does the student choose optionally?"
This question refers to the notion that human activities have a meaning to the individual. The meaning of language and activities are an important aspect of Vygotskian thinking. Therefore, the question of what the student chooses intentionally and optionally can carry information about what the student values compared with what is going on in the student's educational setting.

Exploring the History of the Problem

"When did the problem occur first? How has the problem changed over time?"
The consultant explores the history and possible changes over time in the learning and difficulties the student encounters, as they are perceived by the teacher.

Exploring the Base of the Zone of Proximal Development

The individual skills of the student constitute the prerequisite for the student's ability to solve problems independently, that is, the base of the zone of proximal development (Fig. 22.1). The consultant thoroughly explores the teacher's per-

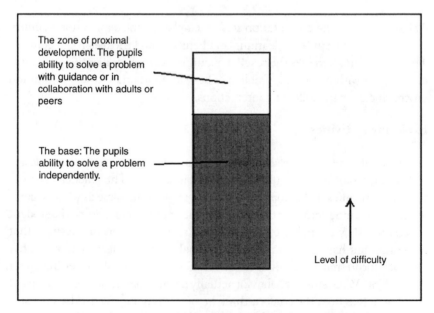

The zone of proximal development. The pupils ability to solve a problem with guidance or in collaboration with adults or peers

The base: The pupils ability to solve a problem independently.

Level of difficulty

FIG. 22.1.   The zone of proximal development. Development occurs when the guidance is at appropriate level (i.e., in the white square above the base).

ception of the student's use of psychological tools relevant for the school situation, that is, the student's skills in reading, writing, arithmetic, memory, perception, language, speech, and so on. For example: *"How are the arithmetic skills of the student?"* Still, the questions have to focus as well on the activity-perspective of these skills and abilities: *"In what kind of activities do you see this?"* And next the consultant discussion explores the student's independent problem-solving ability with questions such as: *"How does the student work independently with a given task? Does this vary over time? Why?"*

Exploring Aspects of the Student's Zones of Proximal Development in Relation to the Teacher

The consultant then focuses on mapping the teacher's conception of the student's zone of proximal development.

"Does the student ask questions? About what? In what manner?"

"Is the student letting himself be instructed? In classroom situations, group situations? When alone with the teacher?"

The next set of questions focus on the student's ability to work with tasks, in relation to the guidance provided by the teacher, in different settings.

"When the student is guided by you, does he handle the task?"

"How much assistance does he need before he handles a given task?"

These questions focus on the level and type of assistance needed. If there is a need for frequent assistance, it raises questions about the level of difficulty in the task. Sometimes this can be formulated as a specific question in the consultation:

"Is the task too difficult for the student?"

"Can you discuss the school situation with him?"

Questions that follow can focus on the student's perception of the school situation and the quality of communication between the teacher and the student.

"Do you have a schedule or a plan for the student? How does it look?"

These questions reveal the structure of the learning activities, as they are set up by the teacher. The questions lead to a discussion of the structure, what activities it involves, and in which ways it is communicated between teacher and student.

Exploring Aspects of the Student's Zone of Proximal Development in Relation to Peers

"How does the student co-operate with a peer?", "Does the student ask peers for help? If you ask him to do so, will he?", "Are there peers he or she can work with?", "How does the student work in a group?"

These questions focus on the student's ability to work with tasks, in relation to peers and peer collaboration, working in pairs as well as in a group.

Exploring Development

"Have you observed development in the student's learning? Is there progress? How?"
This question maps the teacher's perception of the student's development.

Exploring the Role of the Parents

"What do the parents think about the student's school situation?", "Have they told you what have they seen at home?"
These questions focus on the student's school situation in relation to the parents. They map the communicative activities between teacher and parents and between parents and student.

Summarizing Questions to Explore Further

At the end of the initial consultation sessions, the consultant summarizes the case and tries to formulate questions in need of further exploration. These questions constitute the base for the teacher's exploration between sessions.

In short, these questions are expected to help the consultant and teacher formulate jointly a set of hypotheses about the student and the activities undertaken by him or her, eventually leading to a creation of constructive learning activities in the student's educational environment.

The structure of the subsequent sessions is based on the previous sessions and the process of further exploration and generation of hypotheses. The consultation is ended when the teacher can handle the work problem and identify progress in the work with the student. It is the responsibility of the consultant to evaluate the consultation and initiate the termination.

DISCUSSION

It is clear to us that the work problems presented in consultee-centered consultation can be explored from a Vygotskian perspective. This framework provides tools that can suitably be used to understand and promote the process in consultation. In the school organization, with its objectives of learning and development, a theoretical framework concerned with human development in classroom learning can promote understanding and new instructional activities and contexts. Concepts from Vygotskian theory, namely the zone of proximal development and the activity-perspective, offer a base for the interpretation of the phenomena presented in the consultation sessions, in the teacher-consultee-student relationship, and in the everyday activities of the student.

In the context of school psychology, a Vygotskian framework in consultation can complement the psychodynamic perspective as well as other theoretical perspectives to promote conceptual change in consultee-centered consultation. The theoretical perspective selected depends of the nature of the work problem the consultee presents in the initial consultation sessions. These first interactions help the consultant to map the type of work problem the consultee faces and to choose relevant points for discussion in the consultation. In cases where the consultee formulates a problem primarily regarding student learning activities, the consultant needs to use a theoretical framework that fits this work problem and choose a consultation strategy that focuses on how the consultee can structure relevant learning activities that promote development. In cases where the consultee's main concern is with the client's emotional and social functioning, the consultant may need to stress the psychodynamic aspects of the work problems in the consultee-centered consultation in order to promote development in that area. We have also found that focusing on these different theoretical perspectives may be relevant in one and same consultation case, according to how the formulation of the work problem proceeds and changes in the consultation process over time.

Different theoretical perspectives in consultee-centered consultation, including a Vygotskian perspective can be understood as part of the consultant's set of tools. An important aspect of the consultant's professional development is to broaden the set of consultation tools, in order to meet a variety of types of work problems, and a variety of emphases in the consultation processes.

REFERENCES

Caplan, G. (1970). *The theory and practice of mental health consultation.* New York: Basic Books.

Caplan, G., & Caplan, R. B. (1993). *Mental health consultation and collaboration.* San Francisco: Jossey-Bass.

Guvå, G. (1989). *Klientmysteriet.* Sfph:s monografiserie nr 32. Stockholm: Norstedts.

Hedegaard, M. (1990). The zone of proximal development as basis for instruction. In L. C. Moll (Ed.), *Vygotsky and education: Instructional implications and applications of sociohistorical psychology.* New York: Cambridge University Press.

Moll, L. C. (1990). Introduction. In L. C. Moll (Ed.), *Vygotsky and education: Instructional implications and applications of sociohistorical psychology.* New York: Cambridge University Press.

Vygotsky, L. S. (1978). *Mind in society. The development of higher psychological processes.* Cambridge: Harvard University Press.

Wistrom, C., & Qvarustrom (1995). *Psychological consultation in educational settings. Analysis and evaluation.* Ostersund, Sweden: Pedagogica.

Wistrom, C. (1995). *The relationships between the organisation, the child and consultee-centered consultation in different settings in the Swedish educational system.* Paper at international seminar on consultee-centered consultation in Stockholm, Sweden, May 4–7.

SUGGESTED READING

Alvesson, M., & Skoldberg, K.(1994). *Tolkning och reflektion. Vetenskapsfilosofi och kvalitativ metod.* Lund: Studentlitteratur.

Campione, J. C., Brown, A. L., Ferrara, R. A., & Bryant, N. R. (1984). The zone of proximal development: Implications for individual differences and learning. In B. Rogoff & J. V. Wertsch (Eds.), *Children's learning in the "zone of proximal development".* San Francisco: Jossey-Bass.

Griffin, P., & Cole, M. (1984). Current activity for the future: the zoped. In B. Rogoff & J. V. Wertsch (Eds.), *Children's learning in the "zone of proximal development".* San Francisco: Jossey-Bass.

Leont'ev, A. N. (1981). The problem of activity in psychology. In J. V. Wertsch (Ed.), *The concept of activity in Soviet psychology.* New York: Sharpe.

Pryzwansky, W. B., & Noblit, G. W. (1990). Understanding and improving consultation practice: The qualitative case study approach. *Journal of Educational and Psychological Consultation, 1*(4), 293–307. Mahwah, NJ: Lawrence Erlbaum Associates.

Vygotsky, L. S. (1986). *Thought and language.* Cambridge: MIT Press.

Wertsch, J. V. (Ed.). (1985). *Culture, communication and cognition. Vygotskian perspectives.* Cambridge, UK: Cambridge University Press.

Wertsch, J. V. (1984). The zone of proximal development: Some conceptual issues. In B. Rogoff & J. V. Wertsch (Eds.), *Children's learning in the "zone of proximal development".* San Francisco, CA: Jossey-Bass.

Winnicott, D. W. (1981). *Lek och verklighet (play and reality).* Stockholm: Natur och Kultur.

Zinchenko, V. P., & Gordon, V. M. (1981). Methodological problems in the psychological analysis of activity. In J. V. Wertsch (Ed.), *The concept of activity in Soviet psychology.* New York: M. E. Scharpe.

23

To "Create
a Conversation That
Is a Little Bit Different"

Anders Wachter

When we meet consultees for the first time we have been invited to engage with them in problem solving. They think that we, as mental health experts, can help them to solve a work-related problem. The way the session starts is most important because it will affect the development of the session and our chance to explore and create new meaning and understandings. The following sessions were all taped for a project, exploring the ideas of social constructionism in consultation to day-care centers. In these sessions my intention as consultant is to create a dialogical space, a conversation, with the consultees that proceeds differently from a usual conversation responding to their concerns.

THE INVITATION TO EXPLORATION

I (K) serve as a consultant to a child-care center. The center staff wants me to help them with a 4-year-old girl, Johanna. The day-care staff are consultees: Irene (I), Maria (M), and Vera (V). I report the conversation as it occurred along with my thoughts about how I made the conversation "a little bit different" from others the staff might have, a difference that makes this discourse consultee-centered consultation.

Opening Up the Discourse

K: How do you want to use this conversation?

I: We feel that this girl needs a lot of support and help and she has clearly got problems. To have some … well have the opportunity to talk to someone that can ask adequate questions.

K: Yes.

I: To be sure of how we wish to proceed … or?

K: Do you all think about the girl in the same way?

M: Well, it's difficult … for me to communicate with her.

K: With the girl?

M: Yes with the girl, I've almost no contact at all …. When I came back in June last year she had entered a few months earlier. She began here in March and I can't communicate with her. It's only on rare occasions, when she needs help with something like getting dressed, that she allows me to do something with her. She stands and waits and looks, and if I don't say something to her, she doesn't react.

K: Do you think she is more difficult to communicate with than other children?

M: Yes … in the beginning if I came near her she started to ….

V: She is very rejecting against male staff. She is afraid of them.

K: Oh, so it's a difference between male and female staff?

V and M: Yes.

I: No, she accepted John our student.

V: Mmm, so she did.

I: But that is the only one since I started as I ….

K: Do you have any thoughts about why she is so afraid of male staff?

I: No, she has a father and a mother … I mean it's not that there is only a mother.

K: No, have you met the father?

I, M, and V: Yes.

K: Do you think he is different from other fathers you met?

I: No.

K: No, how old is the girl?

M: She will be 4 years in April … I think.

K: How would you like to use this conversation (to V who hasn't responded)?

V: To me it's also that I think it is difficult to get in touch with the parents …. To talk to them about things we think is important to talk about. Anyway, they are positive about the center and like it here but still … "this we know and this is ours" and still I think we have been very … yes, we have not been hard on them nor have we had demands … we have talked a lot about how she is doing here and we have been honest that we think that she has certain problems … with peers and, well, with all relations.

This session starts in a different way from a usual conversation. I ask how they (the consultees) would like to use the session, what they want to talk about. By asking that question, I am indicating that it is the consultees who are the experts in their own situation. They know best themselves what they need to talk about. When I ask this question it appears that they want to talk about different things. Irene wants some adequate advice about how to handle the girl. Mario does not know how he should communicate with the girl and Vera wants some help in reaching the parents. These differences are the start of three separate narratives that might be openings to different thoughts and theories about the girl existing among the three consultees. This is the beginning of the creation of a conversation.

When we tell a story about a child, we can do it in many ways depending on which distinctions we make and what situations we choose. The interactions between my questions and their answers are what create the narratives about the child. By asking somewhat different questions than they asked themselves, and by trying to listen for each individual narrative about the child, we together create a conversation that is a "little bit different." This is a prerequisite for new meaning and understanding of the child to develop. The differences between the narratives and conflicts among them give rise to new narratives that create a space for reflection and new possibilities.

This process can be compared to a kaleidoscope. When one looks in, one can see a completed pattern. If one twists it slightly, the pattern dissolves and for a moment all the pieces are in chaos before they fall into a new pattern. In the same way, you can keep twisting and create new patterns. When the staff calls me and asks for help they already see a pattern as I do when I look in the kaleidoscope for the first time. There is not anything wrong with the pattern that the staff has constructed. The problem is that it does not help them in their work with the children and that they do not see any alternative pattern. They are caught in their own explanations. In that situation, I imagine that my questions can be seen as a twist of the kaleidoscope that contributes to the creation of a new pattern.

The Impatient Girl—The Second Meeting

K: Is there anything, thoughts or ideas that you been thinking about since the last session?

I: Yes, we talked yesterday about how we thought it had ....

M: Yes, we have worked on as usual, and thought a little extra instead ....

I: Well, this with the attention ...

K: What did you talk about?

I: At first we did not see anything that had changed, but then I remembered when I took her to Akalla (small town) by, to this ... what is its name again.

M: Helreklam (a firm)

I: That's right, we were there all together and played, and then I took her to Helreklam to buy some pearls. She chose which pearls we bought. It was really positive and she only talked about those pearls ... it was like she grows ...

V: She really liked it.

I: Yes.

K: That you chose to take her, was that because you have been thinking a little extra about her or would you have done it anyway?

I: Yes, it was because of that, otherwise we would have taken someone else. You know we have 13 children.

M: Mmm, it was also to test ...

K: Was that something new that you chose to take her with you?

I: No, she has been with us many times, but we actually have 13 children and if you choose someone ... it is not so often you take only one child.

M: Yes, so you may feel chosen.

Every session is like a first session in that one can never know what has happened between sessions. One can never anticipate what in the conversation the consultees were affected by or attended to. Therefore, I begin every session by asking whether the consultees have been thinking about something new since last time. The first session ended with my proposal that they should consider how they wanted to proceed. I suggested two ways; either talk about the child or about the mother, because it seemed to me they were very angry with her. It seems that the consultees did not take any notice of the invitation to discuss the mother. Instead they chose to go on with the girl. They decided to try different ways of giving her more attention. If I were to remind them about the question we ended with, it is unlikely they would remember the question or recognize that they made a choice. Instead it seems as if an idea or representation had come up, an idea that I did not think about which they call *"need for attention."* This idea has influenced them to go with her alone to a store. Something they can do once in a while despite having 13 more children in their care. This time it seems like they did it deliberately to see if it had any effect.

Where did that idea come from? Did it come from our conversation? Or would they have tried this anyway? "To have a conversation that is a little different" means in this case, that when the consultees talk about the child with me, whom they have not been talking about before, an opportunity arises to have a conversation that is a little bit different than the conversation they already have had with each other. I ask them questions that sometimes are different from those they already have asked themselves. In the conversation, if we succeed in creating a dialogical space, a space for multiple views at the same time, it will produce new information and points of view. The consultee's picture of the child builds on the distinctions they have made out of what they have thought about the situation so far. When I participate in the consultation, my questions shift the attention to other distinctions equally valid as the ones they made so far. It creates new representations, which, in turn, contribute to the possibilities of change. Another outcome of a conversation is that the child is not the same child after having talked about her. When one expresses some of the impressions one has of a child—impressions mostly felt or have been taken as given—it will be different when one sees the child next time. One could say that the child no longer is the same child.

In this case, the consultees have been thinking a bit extra about Johanna and also decided to test different ideas, including something we did not talk about during our first session.

The Session Continues

Let's return to the idea about having a conversation that is a little bit different and see if the continuing of this session can illustrate the point.

I: Like when we were at Skansen (an amusement park) last Friday ... and we were having a good time and with only a few children. And then she is nagging all the time about her stockings.

M: Did they go down in her boots?

I: She was wearing stockings that were hopeless ... with no elastic and that gets loose in your toes.

K: Mmm.

I: And it does not feel good to walk in, I know that too. It was snow out and you do not pull off your boots in the snow. I tried to explain to her, can't you wait until we get to the toilets were there are warm. Where we can ... and then she started to stamp and want to take off her boots. The others in the group went on and they seemed to have a nice time and there I was with her in the snow and mud and I felt ... oh good I can't take any more of this ....

M: It is like yesterday in the wood when she was going to take off her overall. The boots, the hat everything off and then she was trying to take off the overall too.

K: Mm, What was it you felt that you couldn't stand anymore?

I: It is that she .... Always, always will ... when we go somewhere ... not destroy, what, what shall I say ... it is so difficult ... be in the center ... makes a scene.

M: Yes, it was not so big, it did not need to be like this.

I: No, it was not, I told her we were on the way to the toilet, you can see it over there. We only need to go this way to get there. I can hold your hand. I know it feels nasty to have the stockings like that, but it is not dangerous. I really tried but she only threw herself on the ground and screamed and kicked and .... I stood there yelling; I don't want to hear one more word about your stockings, not a word (with loud voice). It was like I was yelling at my own kids, I felt, oh good (laughs), I am a professional, this is awkward (laughing). Well then finally, she just came because I went. I just felt that I can't go on like this.

K: No, so when you think about it afterwards, what do you think you should have done?

I: Be as patients as M (laughs).

K: What would you have done if you had M's patience?

I: She would have been joking about it, and then she .... Well, whatever you would have done, but you would ...

K: How come, do you think, that she can't wait a couple of minutes. Though you have told her that you will walk with her to the toilet?

I: Well, that's what I don't know. That is what I think is strange. I tried to explain to her, I mean she is 4 years old, she ought to be able to understand and say; "Okay let's go then, we are on our way to the toilet and everything is all right. I want to die because the boots are so uncomfortable." It was so close, we saw the toilets, and still it turned out this way.

K: Is it possible to understand her lack of patience in any way?

I: They are probably yelling at each other like that at home, two strong wills standing there yelling and stamping on the floor.

K: Is it so that you think that if you had more patience then it would be easier? If you had M's patience?

V: Yes, but at the same time it feels like the kids are starting to think; why does she get all the attention and we not.

I first try to understand how the consultees feel and think about the girl. They seem to recall the situations that Johanna wants attention. They believe that to be able to give it to her, one must have patience. This presentation is possible to explore and work with to see if there are any other possible ways to understand Johanna's behavior. By examining their thoughts more closely, this idea is challenged—an idea that is so self-evident to them that they do not even see it anymore. In this way, the conversation becomes a little bit different than the conversation they usually have. In the usual conversation among colleagues, they probably confirm each other's conceptions by supplying with new stories that confirm the picture they have already formed. Colleagues do not normally challenge each other.

K: What would it mean to have more patience?

I: I should maybe ... not get so mad at her. Be like you (M), make a joke of it, in spite of the fact that she gets mad. You always find something, she can still look sour, but somehow you see that she thinks it is really funny ... but I am not like that [sigh] we are so different in that way. I can also joke with her but not when she is like that.

K: What demands does she make on you—if one would could put it in words—that are hard to meet.

V: It is that you should be with her all the time. She expects attention every minute. As soon as she needs something one ought to be there instantly.

K: You are saying that one must be with her all the time. If we go
          back to this situation when you offered to go with her to the toi-
          let, but still .... How come that is not enough for her?

V: One has to do exactly as she says. She does not want to wait. She
          is the one that makes the decisions; "Now we are going to the toi-
          let or now we are going to change clothes out in the snow because
          I want to do it."

K: Is it more important for her to decide than for someone to take
          her to the toilet?

V: I think she is testing us. She needs a clear boundary because
          she knows ... Then she understands that it is not acceptable
          that she yells.

K: Whom do you think she is testing?

V: Well, if she is going to change her mind, okay we skip the toilet,
          we do the changing out in the snow instead.

K: Do you also think she is testing you?

M: Well ... I think it is strange ... it is so weird that one should ....

I: You test your parents at home, I mean day-care staff do you need
          to test them? I think that is strange behaviour.

K: If it would be so that she is testing you, let's try that idea, what is
          she testing if you look at this situation?

V: She is testing how far she can go?

I: She wants a reaction.

K: What kind of answer would she like? Does she want you to say no
          or does she want you to do as she wants?

I: As she wants.

K: Would she be satisfied then? Would she stop testing if she could
          have everything as she wants?

M: No, I don't think so. Then after a few meters she probably finds
          something else to be bothered about, like the hair getting in her
          face, there is always something, even if you do as she wants,
          something else turns up.

As I see it, the consultees are struggling with two ideas, one that Johanna
wants *attention*, wants to be seen. The other is that she is testing their limits.
None of the ideas are really satisfactory, however. We try to twist and bend
them, but there is always something that doesn't fit. I try to stay as close as possi-

ble to their stories and together with them explore the stories to try and find ideas for some new way to apprehend the client's behavior.

At this time, I have no opinion of my own about their thoughts. I'm just trying to follow them from a *"not knowing"* position. I try to keep a position of genuine curiosity where I try to understand how each of the consultees thinks and what they mean when they make a statement. This curiosity challenges their own thoughts when they have to express their ideas and explain how they think. Andersen (1980) observed that, *We don't know what we think before we have expressed ourselves. When we express ourselves we also learn, what we think.* I think that is exactly what is happening here. When the consultees express themselves, they also discover what they think, how they contradict themselves, and what they do not know. Possible differences among them about how they perceive Johanna gives them an opportunity for reflection and consideration.

Questions asked from a position of curiosity usually create a space for dialogue—a play area—where the curiosity of the consultant is spread to the consultees and makes them curious about different ways of understanding and thinking about the child.

K: What is most important for her, to be with her or to let her decide?

V: Be with her.

K: Be with her. How do you mean? How come you think that is the most important?

V: It is more important to be with her and show that one cares, than she has her own way.

K: Yes, that's what you think is most important. But if we imagine, what is most important for Johanna? To have her own way or that you are with her?

V: I think, that I'm with her, at least I hope so anyway.

K: What is it that makes her satisfied when you make a joke with her?

V: I think she likes it that one doesn't react as her mother does. I don't think it is just the joke. It is this ....

M: I think she needs the kindly glance in the eyes and that one likes her though she does what she does.

I: Yeah, maybe that's what she needs.

V: As much as the joke.

M: Yes, because the joke is with quotation marks.

K: Well, is it the joke, or is it something else you do, that she appreci-
        ates.

V: It is that one likes her that one cares, one doesn't get angry.

M: One shows that one still likes her.

K: Could that be a difference between you? Could it be that you like
        her better than S and L do and that makes it easier for you to han-
        dle her?

V: I think it is easier for her to understand Johanna, in some way ... I
        don't know how you were when you were a child, if you were shy
        and so ... but maybe you see ... Johanna in yourself.

K: If you would tell us what she sees, what do you think she sees?

V: I think she sees a girl that is neglected.

M: I can recognise my own childhood a little ....

V: And you feel that you have to give a little extra.

K: And that makes it easier?

V: I think so.

K: And what do you see when you look at her?

V: One has learned to like her actually. Okay she is like that but you
        interact all day long, one has learned as to speak.

M: I feel sorrow for her ... one can't know how it is ... she really wants
        to have ... she comes first in the mornings and is the last to leave ....

In this part, the session changes. M's engagement and understanding of
Johanna add something to the conversation that has not been there before and
it seems like they all look at Johanna in a new way—as a neglected child who has
had a hard time. The conversation is not about attention or having patience any
more. Something new is emerging instead.

When we, for a moment, change perspective and try to understand what it
would be like to be Johanna, the consultees come up with a new idea. Maybe
she wants us to like her as she is, M says. This is an opening for new thoughts
and possibilities. Thoughts that have been in the group but maybe most in M,
ideas that have not had any space to come through before. M's patience and
humor are reframed. She sees something else in Johanna than a girl only trying to get attention. This becomes a sort of "a-ha" experience for the group and
they look at her with new eyes. They understand her in a new way that makes
it possible to relate to her a little bit different and maybe be a little more patience with her as they wished.

Where did this new and a "little bit different" view come from? It was there
all the time within them. But it had no space to emerge because they were

locked up in certain beliefs. The result was that they could not see anything beyond their own explanations. When we began to talk about what they already knew, they discovered what they did not know. They learned that there was more to discover. One could say that they had not realized all of what they had understood.

How is it that these experiences are not expressed? What is it that oppresses our "tacit knowledge" so that it never becomes expressed?

Dominating Discourses

Kathy Weingarten (1991) defined the concept *discourse* by five criteria that provide a framework for "having a conversation that is a little bit different." These criteria describe what you do and what is going on in a normal conversation.

1. A Discourse Consists of Ideas and Practices That Share a Common Value

Any conversation is always in a context of expressed and unexpressed conceptions and rules that together, create a shared culture of values (i.e., that this is a problem and shall be regarded in this way and how you can talk about it).

2. Any Discourse Reflects and Constructs a Specific World View

Any conversation is based on a map—the way the participants in the conversation conceive of the world. This map is the foundation for how the subject talked about is understood and explained. If we regard a child as acting-out, we will talk about and construct a narrative and an explanation that fit, this denotation.

3. There are Dominant and Subjugated Discourses. Dominant Discourses Contain and Constrain What We Can Feel, Think and Do

Of all conversations that one can have about a child, there are some that dominate. The dominant discourses are consonant with the dominant conceptions and values, and control what we can think and feel in relation to a child. If the dominant discourse is about an acting-out child, testing boundaries and hard to control, it will be difficult to talk about other perceptions, ideas, and feelings at the same time. Perhaps the child, due to his or her behavior, is also very lonely, outside the group, deserted by children and staff. A discourse that reflects this perception will be hard to hold at the same time because it will differ and conflict with the dominant discourse.

4. That Which Is Not Part of the Discourse Shapes Our Experience as Critically as the Discourse Itself

All experience, feelings, and so forth that are not part of the discourse, not talked about, and that do not fit in the dominant discourse—all the conversations one could have had—shapes us as much as the ones we have.

5. Changes of Discourse Occur When the Collective Conversations People Have About Their Lives Transform Culturally Available Dominant Narratives About People's Lives

When the collective conceptions we have change, our conversation also changes, such as the collective conception that children who watch television too much become overactive and violent. This idea creates conversation about overactive children being so because they watch video too much. In the 1950s, this conception was connected to comic books, which were considered stupefying and could lead to violent behavior. In the 1960s, it was western movies. Today, we talk about video games and role play games as causing the violence among youngsters. When these conceptions change, the conversations about the children's behavior also change.

These criteria give us a tool to catch sight of which discourses dominate; which narratives are told and the explanation to these; and finally, which narratives are not told, spoken about, and remain silent.

In the previously mentioned session, the dominant discourse, at first, is a narrative about Johanna, as an "impossible" girl who always wants to decide and oppose without any real reason and who has a minimum of patience. To this narrative also belongs a narrative about a self-centered mother, with a minimum of time for Johanna and not very empathic or sensitive to her child. Indeed, she has been known to slap Johanna.

In the day-care center, the manager has the opinion that one should handle parents with care and try to do as much as possible at the center. This idea has forced the group in to a deadlock because they think that Johanna's behavior is a result of her mother's treatment. Because there is something one cannot talk about, one has to pretend that it does not exist instead. The consultees dominant conception is that Johanna's behavior is caused by the mother and that it is necessary that she change her ways with Johanna. This idea is in conflict with the manager's decree. The manager does not offer any alternative way out of the situation. On the contrary, she prevents the group from seeking help when they cannot control the girl.

It is into this context I have been invited. Something I, of course, do not know anything about when I arrive. At first the consultees stay in the dominant

discourse and only talk about the girl. In that conversation, ideas and conceptions are missing about why the girl does what she does. When we, due to my
questions, come closer to this forbidden subject the conversation changes and
narratives about the mother start to dominate. Narratives develop about how
dreadful she is and about her aggression against Johanna, which they are not allowed to do anything about because of the mangers prohibition.

Viewed in this way, one can say that they surrender to the dominant discourse of what one can or may talk about. They probably felt that it was impossible to do anything else, because they did not want to talk about this with their
manager. To do something with the mother would have meant that they went
behind the manager's back and violated her explicit instructions. Instead, they
discovered another way to talk about the girl—as a matter of attention. An idea
that still was within the dominant discourse because its origin was that the
mother had to little time and was not enough sensitive to her. It is also these
permanent demands for attention that make them lose their patience and think
that if they only had more patience then ....

As long as the conversation is within the dominant discourse, the consultees
describe the girl from a distance, from the outside. Although they tell how irritated and mad they are, they are not *in* their narrative, they are relating it from a
position of standing outside, following the explanations they have. It is only
when we look at the girl from another perspective—an *inside* perspective—that
changes in their conceptions take place. When they for a moment change perspective and try to feel what it is Johanna wants—"*that someone is with her, gives
her that friendly look in the eyes, that one likes her, though she behaves as she does.*"
When they let go of the idea they have had so far and view the girl from a personal perspective, a new conversation arises.

Suddenly, it becomes clear that they view Johanna a little bit different. M's
"patience" is due to a different idea about the girl. So far, it has seemed as they all
agreed on Johanna's behavior. The only visible difference between them has been
M's patience. When we look closer for that difference, it appears that the others
have ideas about why M has more patience. S thinks it is because M identifies herself with Johanna—that she views her as a neglected child. The fact that S expresses this idea permits M to give her view that has had no space cut out in the
dominant discourse so far; that she can identify with her a little and that she can
give Johanna "a little extra." This thought opens the conversation and gives an
opportunity to let out experiences and feelings that had no space so far.

In the dominant discourse there is no room for personal, individual, or
unique ideas, feelings, and experiences. There can be room only for the
consultees' total generalized experiences and conceptions that together shape

the dominant discourse. It will, in its turn, determine and prescribe how it is and how one can feel. To break through to the subjugated discourses one has to be close to the personnel. One must re-establish multiplicity, which they have had to keep back. That, in a way, forces them to express experiences and feelings that did not fit with the dominant discourse.

If one views it in this way, we can see the depth to the notion to "create a conversation that is a little bit different." We as consultants, have to listen for what is not said or talked about, and try to create a context where it is possible to talk even about these experiences.

REFERENCES

Andersen, J. (1991, 1994). *Reflekterande processer: Samtal och samtal om samtalen.* Stockholm: Mareld.
Weingarten, K. (1991). The discourses of intimacy: Adding a social constructionist and feminist view. *Family Process, 30*(3).

24

Consultation as Dialogue: The Right Words at the Right Time

Sylvia Rosenfield

Many of us grew up with the saying, "Sticks and stones will break your bones, but names will never hurt you." In the world we all live in, however, words have tremendous impact, as recently documented in the book, *The Right Words at the Right Time* (Thomas, 2002), which tells the stories of remarkable men and women across multiple professions and walks of life for whom words spoken in conversations at the right time changed their lives. Similarly, Acosta and Prager (2002) described how "Verbal First Aid" (p. xix)—that is, the right words at the right time by doctors and emergency personnel in traumatic situations—can alter the outcomes through physiological and emotional changes in patients and victims.

Words play a critical role as well in consultee-centered consultation, whose form is essentially a conversation between consultee and consultant. Through the words spoken between the participants, the consultee's initial story about a situation is impacted, leading to the resolution of a work-related problem if the process is successful. One perspective on consultation is that it is a constructive activity, fostered through dialogue, in which the consultee's understanding of a work-related problem is jointly reconceptualized.

If consultee-centered consultation, as an activity, is mediated largely through language, it is essential to understand the nature of the verbal interactions that define consultation and to study language strategies that would facilitate high quality consultation interactions, thus harnessing this powerful tool. The purpose of this chapter, then, is to describe how the basic assumptions of a

337

language-based framework for understanding the process of consultation can be applied to consultation, as it has to other change processes in the helping professions; to explore some examples of the communication strategies that arise from a narrative perspective; and, third, to suggest some techniques designed to facilitate skill in using these language tools.

LANGUAGE AS A TOOL FOR CHANGE

The power of language can be understood from several perspectives as one of the essential tools in consultation. One source of theory for attending more fully to language arises from Social Constructivist Theory (e.g., Vygotsky, 1978). Vygotsky's theory has been applied to consultee centered-consultation by Knotek, Gravois, Babinski and Rosenfield (in press), who specify three aspects of the theory that are relevant:

1. Higher order learning is fundamentally a social process in which intrapersonal growth occurs as a result of exposure to cultural tools such as problem solving skills and the consultation process itself.
2. Development is mediated through language as individuals are exposed to new ideas.
3. Supportive facilitators, such as consultants help individuals to reach higher levels of functioning.

Other discussions of language as applied to the helping professions are also found in the literature. The power of language in clinical interactions has been explored in therapeutic work in the psychotherapy (e.g., Malcus & Kline, 2001; Wachtel, 1993; Watzlawick, 1978), counseling (e.g., Monk, Winslade, Crocket, & Epston, 1997), and family therapy literature (e.g., Anderson & Goolishian, 1988; Friedman, 1993). Watzlawick (1978), writing on the language of psychotherapy, traced reluctance to consider communication "as a phenomenon *in its own right*" (p. 6) from an historic context stemming back to the study of ancient rhetoric, particularly the fear that manipulation is involved in how language can be used to make others change. He acknowledged that it is difficult to accept that "language does not so much reflect reality as create it" (p. 16). He suggested multiple strategies for therapeutic interactions focused on language, including reframing, paying attention to the language used by clients for the therapist's own verbalizations, and preempting resistance by anticipating it in how suggestions are given.

Wachtel (1993) contributed to an understanding of the importance of what therapists actually *say*, moving "from understanding the patient to putting that understanding into words" (p. vii). He gave multiple illustrations of how the actual words therapists use might be the source of resistance, noting the ease with which therapists describe the resistance of the client rather than examine the impact of their own language on the client's behavior. He then focused on what the therapist can say that will contribute to the process of change, on the "nuances of phrasing and meaning ... that can make a crucial difference between comments that are genuinely therapeutic and comments that unwittingly perpetuate the very problems the patient brings for treatment" (p. vii). His focus on language is framed within theoretical and contextual factors that support these verbal tools.

Significant exploration of language strategies has been undertaken in the family therapy field, where the "language systems approach" has been developed. The "language-systems approach" (Anderson & Goolishian, 1988) assumes that we generate meaning in interactions with one another through language. This approach, derived in part from the social constructivist movement, treats meaning as "a negotiated reality that does not occur outside of the context of human interaction" (Loos & Epstein, 1989, p. 152). It also draws on cybernetics, in that the helper is inextricably a part of the linguistic system under observation and by participation, changes what occurs (Loos & Epstein, 1989). Friedman (1993) also focuses on language as the crucial medium for change in working with families, and demonstrates how options and possibilities emerge as meaning takes shape within the conversation. The work of the family therapist includes, in his view, knowledge of how to provide a context that enables those one is trying to help "to see a world of expanding options rather than a world of limitations and constraints" (p. xiv).

CONSULTATION COMMUNICATION

The concepts described earlier can appropriately be applied to consultee-centered consultation, which is, at its core, a linguistic event, a setting where new meanings are constructed through dialogue (White, Summerlin, Loos, & Epstein, 1992). If consultation is a conversation, the role of the consultant is that of architect of the dialogue, creating space for and facilitating the consultation conversation (White et al., 1992). White et al. (1992) applied the language systems approach, drawn from the family therapy literature (Anderson & Goolishian, 1988; Goolishian & Anderson, 1987), to school consultation, seeing the concepts as a rich source of theory and practice enhancing the consultation process. The approach introduces a new perspective to understand how the consultant defines or diagnoses the problem(s) and how language is used to develop and enhance the relationship between the consultation participants.

Problem Definition as A Constructive Activity

Perhaps nowhere in the consultation process is communication more powerful than in the critical stage of problem identification. If humans create realities through communication, then it is through the consultation conversation that the problem is both constructed and critical steps taken to resolve it. It is within the boundaries of the conversation that the reality of the problem is created, rather than found. According to Loos and Epstein (1989), the consultant "must be fully responsible for his or her active participation in the creation of the problem definition" (p. 16).

Within the consultation literature, the study by Tombari and Bergan (1978) provided a classic example of this process in action. They reported the impact of the specific words used by the consultant in introducing the problem-solving process on the eventual outcome. Depending on how the consultant framed the initial opening interaction designed to elicit the problem statement, that is, whether the statements by the *consultant* reflected a "medical" model ("Tell me something—anything you would like to talk about ....") or a behavioral orientation ("Tell me about ___'s behavior in your class") (p. 214), future verbalization, judgments, and teacher expectations about their capacity to resolve the problem were affected.

Research on the problem identification stage in instructional consultation (Rosenfield, 1987) also has examined the co-construction through language of the consultee's initial problem. In a simulation study, Jones (1999) found the same initial teacher concerns were constructed differently as a result of the consultant's verbal interactions with the teacher role player. The teacher role was scripted to provide cues that could lead to different problems being identified (family problems, emotional problems, behavior problems, or academic problems), and the consultant participants engaged the teacher role player in a consultation session at the problem identification stage. The different consultant participants focused on the child's behavior, the family problem, or the adequacy of the classroom instruction, depending upon what aspects of the teacher's concerns they thought most relevant. The consultant and teacher then developed the assessment process to gain further information about that "problem." For example, although there was a high likelihood that the "student" in the simulation might have a reading problem, it was ignored by consultant participants who were focused on the behavior or the family. The study corroborated the Tombari and Bergan (1978) conclusion that how the consultant uses questions and verbal prompts to understand the problem might also inadvertently create the problem from the consultant's perspective. Practitioners can be lulled into "limited, stereotypical, and unreflective understandings" (Malcus & Kline, 2001, p. 189) unless they are aware of the influence that the words they use play on problem definition.

Using Communication to Build the Consultation Relationship

Individuals see the world differently, and our language, to some extent, structures that view. Practitioners from different professions have different worldviews and different language systems.

Reflecting the impact of differences in perspective and language, the consultation literature has focused on communication with respect to relationship building skills in order to develop trust, rapport, and empathy (e.g., Kurpius & Rozecki, 1993). Generic interpersonal communication skills, such as listening, effective questioning, and conflict management have been viewed as critical. Consultant and consultee communicative behaviors on variables such as questioning, dominance, and message elicitors have been studied from both an independent and relational perspective using coding systems (e.g., Benn & Rosenfield, 2002; Bergan, 1977; Erchul & Chewning, 1990; Gutkin, 1996; Witt, 1990). Gender differences in communication and in ways of knowing (e.g., Henning-Stout, 1994) have also been examined. But the actual dialogue used in consultation sessions has rarely been the focus of this type of investigation.

In a recent study, Benn and Rosenfield (2002) examined questions and alternatives to questions, based on a coding system, in problem identification interviews. Using videotapes of consultants interacting with a teacher role player in a simulation case, each consultant was evaluated as a competent, partial mastery, or novice instructional consultant. With the exception of clarifying questions used more frequently by competent consultants, questioning strategies were relatively uniform across the different competency levels. However, a qualitative analysis of the verbal interactions was more productive in differentiating competent from less competent consultants. For example, the consultants judged as more competent framed more collaborative questions ("Does this work for you?") rather than just information oriented questions ("When is he out of his seat?") that helped them to build a working relationship with their consultee. Some of the novice consultants' statements and questions lacked focus or were inappropriately timed, such as moving into a discussion of assessment prior to having a problem clearly identified. Thus the codes may have looked similar, but closer analysis reflected language that disrupted the smooth flow of the process.

White and Loos (1996) suggested that sophisticated interpersonal communication strategies developed in the family therapy field have potential application to consultation. The questioning and reflection techniques that they described change the nature of the relationship between consultant and consultee; the role of the consultant becomes less the one who is charged with deciding what the problem is and more a participant in helping the consultee to reflect on the situation under examination and consider alternatives. In the language-systems approach, questions have purposes such as uncovering patterns and relationships that help to frame a new perspective on a problem. These include "if" and future oriented questions under the premise that "future questions suggest that change is possible" (White & Loos, 1996, p. 301) and help the consultee to picture a new reality. When the focus of the consultation is on the current state of the problem, the fixed nature of the situation may be reinforced.

Such strategies would be innovative in consultation, where typically questions have served the function of gathering information by the consultant on the consultee's or client's problem (e.g., Anderson, Kratochwill, & Bergan, 1986). In building consultation relationships, it has been suggested that relying on alternatives to questions, such as clarification statements, might be more effective (e.g., Benn & Rosenfield, 2002). However, in both instances, the point of the verbal exchange is typically on gaining information to develop an accurate picture of the problem from the perspective of the consultant, whereas the language-systems approach focuses more on reframing the problem from the perspective of the consultee.

Social psychology also provides research that is useful for considering how communication affects consultation relationships. Higgins (1999) described several empirically supported concepts that impact verbal interactions in consultation. He discussed the concept of "audience tuning" (p. 33) in which speakers spontaneously tailor their messages to their listener to suit what they perceive as the immediate informational needs of their listener. In addition, Higgins (1999) found that communicators "tune their message about a target person to suit the attitude of their audience toward that person" (p. 35). For example, teachers frame their concerns about students in terms of disabilities when speaking with school psychologists, rather than in terms of the classroom behaviors they might discuss in conversations with another teacher. But even more important, the speaker "can develop a position on an issue for the first time during the communication itself" and "can change … judgments and knowledge as well … as memory for the original information that was the basis for the message" (p. 34). These "saying-is-believing effects" (p. 36) persist over time, and may even increase weeks after the interchange. In other words, it fits Goolishian's comment to family therapists that "you never know what you think until you say it" (Goolishian, cited in Loos & Epstein, 1989).

The strength of saying the words is enhanced when they are listened to by others, creating a "shared reality." Higgins' (1999) research has demonstrated that "our individual experiences are established as valid and reliable to the extent that they are shared with others" (p. 42). It is through interpersonal communication that a shared reality is developed:

> communicators consider their audience-tuned messages to be about the topic of the message rather than about the audience. They also consider their audience-tuned message to provide objective, accurate information on the message topic because it was shared with the audience ... communicators treat their audience-tuned message as if they were simple statements of fact. (Higgins, 1999, p. 45)

The verbal interchanges between consultant and consultee have a significant effect on how problems are identified and resolved, and it is critical that consultants become more aware of the power of words and the communication experience in consultation.

DEVELOPING LINGUISTICALLY COMPETENT CONSULTANTS

Effective use of linguistic strategies in consultation requires considerable skill (Rosenfield & Gravois, 1993). McKenzie and Monk (1997) found that narrative approaches seem obvious when described, but are complex to integrate into clinical practice effectively. The final section of the chapter presents some reflective teaching techniques, in which consultants are assisted in becoming aware of the assumptions that govern their conversations and develop effective communication techniques to facilitate the consultation dialogue.

The education and supervision of consultants, in general, have been neglected topics within the consultation literature (Cramer & Rosenfield, in press; Rosenfield, 2002), and there has been even less attention to providing feedback on the verbal strategies used by novice consultants (Anton-Lahart & Rosenfield, in press). Yet it is critical to listen to consultants' verbal behaviors in their interactions with consultees in order to provide feedback on their communication. Consultants are often surprised at what they actually have said during a consultation session, sometimes even denying that they have made a particular type of comment. Extensive use of audio and video-taping provides the opportunity for consultants-in-training to hear themselves at work, and to understand more clearly their impact on consultee responsiveness. Growth emerges from the experience of replaying tapes of consultant–consultee interactions and generating appropriate verbal strategies for use in the future.

Two techniques, drawn from Senge and his colleagues' (Senge, 1990; Senge, Kleiner, Roberts, Ross, & Smith, 1994) work on mental models, have been used to help consultants examine their verbal behavior and the underlying thought processes. First is the "left-hand column" (Argyris & Schon, 1974), a technique in which students draw a line down the middle of a page. Student consultants select a problematic consultation interaction from a tape of their consultation session, and transcribe on the right hand side of the page what they actually said. On the left-hand column, they indicate what they were thinking and feeling, but did not say. Or, they can indicate what message they intended to convey. Supervision then focuses on finding the best way to understand the discrepancy between what was said and what was intended, followed by developing language to present the content more effectively. Questions for reflection include:

1. How did what I said contribute to the difficulty of the situation?
2. Why was I unable to say what was in the left-hand column?
3. How can I improve the communication based on this reflection?

Many consultants believe that developing a collaborative working relationship precludes a discussion where differences are aired. Too often, their attempts to engage the consultee in reframing a situation are ineffective at best. Supervision that includes both the actual language and a systematic structure to work on more effective verbal strategies enables consultants at any stage to improve their skills.

A second technique is orientation to the "ladder of inference" (Argyris, 1990), which provides a visual heuristic to assist consultants in unpacking the inferential language used in discussing problems. Consultants are taught how to understand links in their own and their consultees' reasoning from fact or observation to conclusion, and the importance of moving inference statements (the child has an attention deficit disorder) made by consultees down the ladder to statements of observable behaviors (the child does not complete his or her work in reading). Ladder of inference techniques enable reflection on one's own thinking and reasoning, as well as inquiring into the thinking and reasoning of others (Senge et al., 1994). It involves asking questions that reflect issues such as: "what is the observable data behind that statement?" or "How did we get from that data to these abstract assumptions?" (p. 245). Moving to the observable behavior allows alternative explanations to be considered.

A third example is a technique supportive of meta-reflection on the consultation process between consultee and consultant. In family therapy, Andersen (1987) described the process by which a neutral party or team listens to the dialogue and comments on what they hear, omitting normative judgments. In applying this technique to consultation, the consultee and consultant discuss their work together in front of a team when progress is slow or not evident, and the team helps the dyad to reflect on their work together. In instructional consultation teams, the process of "temperature taking" (Rosenfield & Gravois, 1996), in which teams regularly schedule time to evaluate their work together, also develops a language for meta-reflection by team members on their process.

SUMMARY

In this chapter, the language of the consultation process has been moved from background to foreground, from relationship variables and coding systems, to the actual words people say. Theoretical underpinnings taken from the language systems approach, developed originally by family therapists, social constructivist theory, and social psychology research, have been applied to consultation communication. Finally, a few techniques useful in assisting consultants in developing language skills have been presented. But only the surface of the relevance and power of language has been touched upon here, and the research base in this area is limited to non-existent. Further study of the language of consultation is needed if consultee-centered consultation is to reach its maximum potential.

REFERENCES

Acosta, J., & Prager, J. S. (2002). *The worst is over: What to say when every moment counts.* San Diego, CA: Jodere Group.

Andersen, T. (1987). The reflecting team: Dialogue and meta-dialogue in clinical work. *Family Process, 26,* 415–428.

Anderson, H., & Goolishian, H. A. (1988). Human systems as linguistic systems: Preliminary and evolving ideas about the implications for clinical theory. *Family Process, 27,* 371–393.

Anderson, T. K., Kratochwill, T. R., & Bergan, J. R. (1986). Training teachers in behavioral consultation and therapy: An analysis of verbal behaviors. *Journal of School Psychology, 24,* 229–241.

Anton-Lahart, J. M., & Rosenfield, S. (in press). *A survey of preservice consultation training and supervision.* Journal of Educational and Psychological Consultation.

Argyris, C. (1990). *Overcoming organizational defenses.* Needham, MA: Allyn & Bacon.

Argyris, C., & Schon, D. (1974). *Theory in practice.* San Francisco: Jossey-Bass.

Benn, A. E., & Rosenfield, S. (2002, July). *Comparison of consultants' competence levels and communication skills during problem identification.* Poster presented at the International School Psychology Colloquium, Denmark.

Bergan, J. R. (1977). *Behavioral consultation.* Columbus, OH: Merrill.

Cramer, K., & Rosenfield, S. (in press). Clinical supervision of consultation. *Clinical Supervisor.*

Erchul, W. P., & Chewning, T. G. (1990). Behavioral consultation from a request-centered relational communication perspective. *School Psychology Quarterly, 5,* 1–20.

Friedman, S. (Ed.). (1993). *The new language of change: Constructive collaboration in psycho-therapy.* NY: Guilford Press.

Goolishian, H., & Anderson, H. (1987). Language-systems and therapy: An evolving idea. *Journal of Psychotherapy, 24,* 529–538.

Gutkin, T. B. (1996). Patterns of consultant and consultee verbalizations: Examining communication leadership during initial consultation interviews. *Journal of School Psychology, 34,* 199–219.

Henning-Stout, M. (1994). Consultation and connected knowing: What we know is determined by the questions we ask. *Journal of Educational and Psychological Consultation, 5,* 5–21.

Higgins, E. T. (1999). "Saying is believing" effects: When sharing reality about something biases knowledge and evaluations. In L. L. Thompson, J. M. Levine, & D. M. Messick (Eds.), *Shared cognition in organizations: The management of knowledge* (pp. 33–48). Mahwah, NJ: Lawrence Erlbaum Associates.

Loos, V. E., & Epstein, E. S. (1989). Conversational construction of meaning in family therapy: Some evolving thoughts on Kelly's sociality corollary. *International Journal of Personal Construct Psychology, 2,* 149–167.

Jones, G. (1999). *Validation of a simulation to evaluate instructional consultation problem identification skill competence.* Dissertation Abstracts International, 60(12A), 4317.

Knotek, S., Rosenfield, S., Babinski, L., & Gravois, T. A. (in press). The process of orderly reflection and conceptual change during instructional consultation. *Journal of Educational and Psychological Consultation.*

Kurpius, D. J., & Rozecki, T. G. (1993). Strategies for improving interpersonal communication. In J. E. Zins, T. R. Kratochwill, & S. N. Elliott (Eds.), *Handbook of consultation services for children* (pp. 137–158). San Francisco: Jossey-Bass.

Malcus, L., & Kline, J. (2001). Language as a saboteur: The case of "case management." *Professional Psychology: Research and Practice, 32,* 188–193.

McKenzie, W., & Monk, G. (1997). Learning and teaching narrative ideas. In G. Monk, J. Winslade, K. Crocket, & D. Epston (Eds.), *Narrative therapy in practice: The archaeology of hope* (pp. 82–117). San Francisco: Jossey-Bass.

Monk, G., Winslade, J., Crocket, K., & Epston, D. (Eds.). (1997). *Narrative therapy in practice: The archaeology of hope.* San Francisco: Jossey-Bass.

Rosenfield, S. (2002). Developing instructional consultants: From novice to competent to expert. *Journal of Educational and Psychological Consultation, 13,* 97–111.

Rosenfield, S. (1987). *Instructional consultation.* Hillsdale, NJ: Lawrence Erlbaum Associates.

Rosenfield, S., & Gravois, T. A. (1993). Educating consultants for applied clinical and educational settings. In J. E. Zins, T. R. Kratochwill, & S. N. Elliott (Eds.), *Handbook of consultation services for children* (pp. 373–393). San Francisco: Jossey-Bass.

Rosenfield, S., & Gravois, T. A. (1996). *Instructional consultation teams: Collaborating for change.* New York: Guilford Press.

Senge, P. M. (1990). *The fifth discipline: The art and practice of the learning organization.* NY: Doubleday.

Senge, P. M., Kleiner, A., Roberts, C., Ross, R. B., & Smith, B. J. (1994). *The fifth discipline fieldbook: Strategies and tools for building a learning organization.* New York: Doubleday.

Thomas, M. (2002). *The right words at the right time.* New York: ATRIA Books.

Tombari, M. L., & Bergan, J. R. (1978). Consultant cues and teacher verbalizations, judgments, and expectancies concerning children's adjustment problems. *Journal of School Psychology, 16,* 212–219.

Vygotsky, L. V. (1978). *Mind in society: The development of higher psychological processes.* Cambridge, MA: Harvard University Press.

Wachtel, P. L. (1993). *Therapeutic communication: Knowing what to say when.* New York: Guilford Press.

Watzlawick, P. (1978). *The language of change: Elements of therapeutic communication.* New York: Basic Books.

White, L. J., & Loos, V. E. (1996). The hidden client in school consultation: Working from a narrative perspective. *Journal of Educational and Psychological Consultation, 7,* 161–177.

White, L., Summerlin, M. L., Loos, V., & Epstein, E. (1992). School and family consultation: A language-systems approach. In M. Fine & C. Carlson (Eds.), *Handbook of family-school interventions: A systems perspective* (pp. 347–362). Boston: Allyn & Bacon.

Witt, J. C. (1990). Face-to-face verbal interaction in school-based consultation: A review of the literature. *School Psychology Quarterly, 5,* 199–210.

25

Developing Through Discourse: Speech Genres as Pathways to Conceptual Change

Steve Knotek
University of North Carolina, Chapel Hill

There is little doubt as to the centrality of speech in the interpersonal process of consultee-centered consultation (CCC), for it is through the interpersonal communication between the consultant and the consultee(s) that work problems are described, multiple perspectives explored, and solutions generated (Hylander, in press; Rosenfield, 1991). Eventually, facilitated by the consultative process, participants can even develop new understandings and create new conceptions of work related problems (Caplan & Caplan, 1995; Sandoval, 1996). It is therefore useful, and perhaps even crucial, for the consultant to pay attention to the forms of speech that occur during consultation sessions.

This chapter uses the example of CCC applied to student study teams (SSTs) to discuss how consultants can identify and use forms of social speech (Bahktin, 1986; Wertsch, 1991) to both monitor the progress of consultation and also as a means to promote conceptual growth.

STUDENT STUDY TEAMS

Student study teams are school-based, problem-solving teams that are widely used as a means to meet students' educational needs in the regular education classroom (Chalfant, Pysh, & Moultrie, 1979; Pugach & Johnson, 1989;

349

Ysseldyke & Algozzine, 1983). Although their makeup can vary, SST's typically consist of several members; such as a teacher, an administrator, a school psychologist, and a counselor, who each individually represent a particular education profession and who each possess a unique professional knowledge. During the course of an SST meeting, the members each present their profession's views about a student's problems and also suggest their remedy to the problem based on their disciplinary knowledge. Ultimately, the team should process their disparate understandings of a student's functioning collaboratively and form a synthesized, integrated action plan (Fuchs, 1991). Student study teams have become popular because research has shown that early intervention can decrease the number of students who need special education (Ross, 1995; Zins, Curtis, Graden, & Ponti, 1989).

One barrier to effective SST's is that each member's allegiance to his or her personal and professional knowledge can limit true collaboration and inhibit problem-solving within the SST process. Unfortunately, teams often do not have a formal mechanism to support participants' construction of new understandings and approaches to problems. Accordingly, there is a danger that, as the members of these disparate groups individually present their own understandings, information will merely be exclaimed and not synthesized and mutually negotiated by the team. The potential of the SST to effect change in the participants' work problems may not be realized if its members are not interacting, negotiating, and problem solving. Inclusion of a consultant into this problem-solving process can support interactions that lead members to mutually construct understandings of the issues and collectively solve work problems (Knotek, 2003a,b).

Providing consultation in the complex, interpersonal environment of the SST presents many challenges, and the consultant will need some means or strategy to assess and gauge the progression of the consultation. With so many personal and professional perspectives to consider, the consultant may become overwhelmed with the multiple threads, themes, and issues that are presented across the span of even a single meeting. One approach to scrutinize this bewildering process is for the consultant to monitor the evolution of the forms of social language used by the members over the course of the consultation.

LANGUAGE AND CONCEPTUAL DEVELOPMENT

Language plays a key role in the interpersonal process of both the SST and consultation in that in both instances individuals rely heavily on speech to communicate their knowledge, values, ideas, and opinions. The talk used in these settings is not random, and often reflects personal and professional forms of discourse. Language is the functional key to both the SST and consultative processes, for it is through interpersonal conversation that the participants arrive at alternative solutions and perhaps change their conceptions of the problem. Therefore, when consultation enhances problem solving and conceptual change in an SST's participants, consultees' development in these areas will be reflected in the team members' speech.

Speech Genres

The concept of speech genres provides a useful construct with which consultants can describe and assess the team members' perceptions, as well as illuminate pathways to promote consultees' conceptual development. Speech genres are defined as a common language used between members of the same social group (professional, social, and cultural) to discuss and understand common experiences and salient issues (Bahktin, 1986; Wertsch, 1991). Genres consist of ways of speaking and expressing meaning that includes a specialized vocabulary that has semantic congruence. For example, when a teacher tells a parent, "John exhibits lots of gross motor movement and he consistently disrupts my class. Boy, about all I can say is that he is a handful." she really means she can think of nothing positive to say about the disruptive boy.

Groups that use speech genres include both professional groups (i.e., administrators, teachers, psychologists), in which the speech is initially acquired in a formal setting, and personal groups (i.e., teen cliques, teachers' lunch group), in which speech may be acquired more informally. Speech genres can be thought of as semi-privileged speech that only people with the right training and/or experience can fully understand or use. Communication in SSTs is saturated with both professionally and culturally acquired speech genres.

SPEECH GENRES IN SSTS

Communication in SST's occurs within four predominant speech genres: personal, professional, folk, and negotiated (Knotek, 1997, 2001). Each of these genres has particular characteristics that work to either serve or inhibit the process of collaborative problem solving.

Personal Speech Genre

Personal discourse describes members' working relationships and experiences with the students. It consists of the words and phrases that members use to describe their own (i.e., others not privy to) experiences with and impressions of a student. The language is ubiquitous in the sense that it is nonprofessional and is typical of everyday speech. For example, if a teacher were to say "I've had it with Patsy, she's always interrupting and slowing down the other kids. Patsy is in my doghouse!", she would be using her own colloquial speech to describe her unique experience with a student. Within the SST process, personal speech is especially prevalent in the beginnings of the meetings when staff individually describes their prior experience with the student in question.

Professional Speech Genre

Professional speech is characterized by references to professional knowledge and infused with terminology containing terms associated with particular disciplines. Because SSTs are designed to be a collaborative process, each member is responsible at times for providing "expert" knowledge about specific content domains, and the team's members variously use their professional language to accomplish this task. For example, when a student's "presenting problem" is first discussed in an SST, each of the members, using the language and concepts appropriate to their discipline, provide their "professional opinion" about a child, and the members then alternately engage in the "expert speak" of their professional genre. Teachers may talk about current achievement levels, counselors talk about the child's family situation, and principals may talk about administrative concerns.

Folk Speech Genre

Folk speech is characterized by a team's common vocabulary about a student and represents the team's manner of adopting the same problem descriptors and semantic understandings of a student's situation to fashion a working description of the students' functioning. For example, it is likely that not every member of a team would know the technical, DSM-IV definition of *Attention Deficit Disorder with Hyperactivity*; however, the team may commonly adopt the quasi-professional usage of the term *ADD* to use to refer to all students who have difficulty staying on task and who have difficulty sitting still.

This speech has a least-common-denominator quality to it, in that, the speech is ubiquitous enough that everybody knows what it means when it is used and it tends to be colorful and appeal to individuals' evaluative common sense. It is constructed and adopted by the team as members arrive at a shared "meeting of the minds" about the children.

Negotiated

The negotiated genre, like the folk genre, consists of a common vocabulary that is worked out and adopted by group members: However, unlike folk speech, negotiated speech contains problem descriptors and explanatory mechanisms that consist of an integration of the team's various professional perspectives. For example, a folk term such as *hyper* could be subsumed into negotiated speech as the term *hyperactive* if a team were to overtly discuss and then adopt the clinical usage of the word.

In summary, four basic forms of speech genres are found in SSTs: two are profoundly personal genres, personal and professional; and two, folk and negotiated, represent mutually constructed, shared perspectives. Although each of these four forms of speech no doubt serves a social or cognitive function, they are not all equal hallmarks of professional, collaborative, systematic problem solving. Additionally, they do not all equally foster consultees' professional, conceptual development.

CONSULTEE CENTERED CONSULTATION
AND CONCEPTUAL CHANGE IN SSTS

SSTs do not routinely have a trained person assigned to facilitate and support interpersonal communication, negotiation, and problem solving. Because teams do not have a dedicated facilitator to support the interpersonal, problem-solving *process* of the SST, they are often immersed in personal, professional, and folk speech, which leads to the creation of disjointed, superficial problem descriptions and interventions (Knotek, 2003b). Meaningful conceptual negotiation is not a given outcome of this interpersonal process. However, the addition of consultee-centered consultation to the SST process is an excellent means to support bona fide collaborative problem solving and reconceptualization of the work problem.

In order to facilitate the teaming process and support collaboration, the SST consultant should be aware of two embedded stumbling blocks that exist within the process: conceptual chaos in the individual genres, and conceptual congruence within the folk genre.

Conceptual Chaos

At the beginning of the SST process, when team members primarily use personal and professional speech in their interactions, the discussions suffer from a form of conceptual chaos, in that there are low levels of congruence between the members' descriptions and explanations of student's functioning. This occurs especially during the problem identification phase when the interpersonal space in the SST is filled with the team members' competing descriptions of the students. Within these genres, there is little to no conceptual negotiation. For example, when a team first discusses a student whose main referral complaint is "finishes comprehension questions on the assigned readings less than 90% of the time," the team's professionals may cite very different concerns about the child's functioning, including: a processing problem, poor self-esteem, a lack of motivation, and being from a problem family. Although it is good procedure to construct a multilayered portrait of a student, the portrait should be coherent and congruent, and not consist of individuals' disconnected observations. However, as the typical meeting progresses, and after members have first referenced their personal and professional genres to contribute "their piece," the discourse normally shifts, and then, folk speech, a form of mutually negotiated and shared speech begins to dominate.

Conceptual Congruence

As SSTs unfold, they may move from the conceptual chaos inherent in the individual, privileged speech genres to a form of *conceptual congruence* associated with the folk genre. At the folk level, the team members tend to mutually conceptualize a student's issues at surface levels of common sense; that is, the team members mutually adopt common terms in place of professional terminology. Typically these folk conceptualizations began to appear as the team reaches a point in the SST process that requires a summary statement of the child's functioning.

Although the folk genre differs from the two individual genres in some important ways, it is similar in that it often leads to a relatively unsatisfactory problem description and a diffuse sense of the team members' problem ownership. Students are often described in delusory terms and their complex issues reduced to some surface generalizations, (said of a third grader who was achieving 2 years below grade level) "Joel has no motivation and he's completely illiterate."

The discourse in these three genres is either parsed and individualistic or surface and diffuse. Group problem solving is supposed to be the hallmark of the SST process, yet in the speech in these three genres there is little to no integration of ideas or truly collaborative interactions—each person gives their personal and professional piece and the team then mutually engages in a forum at the level of least common denominator. Accordingly, the collaborative potential of the SST is not fully realized. In all three of these speech genres, the problem-solving process is clouded by a lack of appropriate conceptual coherence combined with a lack of interpersonal negotiation and as a result the teams' goals suffer.

CONSULTEE CENTERED CONSULTATION
AND CONCEPTUAL NEGOTIATION

Consultants' can use the teams' social language as a guide to facilitate the consultee(s): conceptual integration, problem reframing, and integrated generation of hypotheses.

Conceptual Integration

When team members engage each other in the personal, professional, and folk speech genres, the problem-solving process is clouded by a lack of appropriate conceptual coherence. Because the team members do not sufficiently negotiate a deep, multidimensional conceptualization of their students' issues, the teams' goals can suffer—students may be unnecessarily referred for assessment and not adequately supported in their regular education settings. Consultee centered consultation can be used to: facilitate the teams' awareness of conceptual chaos, help unpack the various assumptions inherent in the differing perspectives, and to maximize the power of multiple perspectives to construct a robust representation of the students' functioning (Caplan & Caplan, 1993; Lambert & Hylander, 2001; Knotek & Sandoval, in press).

The consultation goal is to foster a noncoersive, supportive environment so that team members can experience their own perplexity and be trusting enough to reflect on discrepancies of opinion, and understanding of fact as a group move toward a negotiated conceptualization of a student's functioning (Knotek, Babinski, & Rogers, 2002; Rogers & Babinski, 2002; Webster, Knotek, Babinski, & Rogers, in press).

Reframing the Problem

A key issue in the problem-solving process is the group members' lack of objectivity with relation to troublesome students—usually those children who are furthest below grade level or behaviorally the most challenging (Knotek, 2003b). Lack of objectivity often becomes evident in the discourse during the problem-identification phase of the SST, when the students' actual abilities are underestimated and their actual problems were overestimated; for example, as a third grade girl (who was later found to be only one year below grade level) was described by her teacher "Shareena is completely illiterate, she can't do anything with letters or books!" Consultation can be used to help the team reframe pejorative descriptions by facilitating the consultees to shift their problem descriptors and explanatory attributions of the students.

Integrated Hypotheses

Nowhere will the lack of group problem solving and conceptual cohesion be more evident than during hypothesis generation. Sometimes teams may generate hypotheses throughout the meetings without following an explicit problem-solving format, and thereby couch hypotheses in personal and folk terminology. Such hypotheses suffer from: multiple linearity and disjointedness in the case of personal speech, or reduction and oversimplification of a child's issues in the case of folk speech. The goal of consultation in these instances is to support team members' active questioning of each other's implicit assumptions, and to facilitate their explicit negotiation of the descriptors and attributions ascribed to the work problem.

SUMMARY

The members of SSTs are given the daunting task of collaboratively piecing together valid, multifaceted, mutually resonant descriptions of students who are at educational risk in the regular classroom. Collaboration in these settings can be very ephemeral, and it is difficult to achieve the process goal of genuine, multidisciplinary collaboration. There is the risk that when members adopt certain genres of speech, they may not reach the collaborative potential inherent in the assembled individuals, and correspondingly, unwittingly distort the images of the children they have been discussing.

Being mindful of the forms of speech used in these high stakes assessments offers a road to better examine one's assumptions about students and a means to deepen interdisciplinary collaboration and better serve the needs of diverse students.

Consultee centered consultation may be used to support the use of "negotiated speech" to enhance the qualities of collaboration and negotiation within an SST. When a consultant facilitates a team's use of negotiated speech, he or she is promoting: mutual negotiation of "professional" descriptions and explanations; a deeper, more interactive communication process on the interpersonal level of the SSTs; and a broader sense of problems faced by the students and the corresponding interventions necessary to ameliorate their obstacles. By being aware of the forms social speech used during an SST, a consultant has access to pathways with which to provide the basic conditions necessary for promoting change in consultees' conceptual understanding of their work problems.

REFERENCES

Bakhtin, M. (1986). *Speech genres and other late essays*. Austin: University of Texas Press.

Caplan, G., & Caplan, R. (1993). *Mental health consultation and collaboration*. San Francisco: Jossey-Bass.

Caplan, G., & Caplan, R. (1995). The need for quality control in primary prevention. *Journal of Primary Prevention, 15*(1), 15–29.

Chalfant, J. C., Pysh, M., & Moultrie, R. (1979). Teacher assistance teams: A model for within-building problem solving. *Learning Disabilities Quarterly, 2*, 85–96.

Fuchs, D. (1991). Mainstream assistance teams: A prereferral intervention system for difficult to teach student. In G. Stoner, M. R. Shinn, & H. M. Walker (Eds.), *Interventions for achievement and behavior problems* (pp. 241–267). National Association of School Psychologists.

Hylander, I. (in press). A grounded theory of the conceptual change process in consultee-centered consultation: Successful turnings in representation and blind alleys. *Journal of Educational and Psychological Consultation*.

Knotek, S. E. (2003b). Bias in problem solving and the social process of student study teams: A qualitative investigation of two SSTs. *Journal of Special Education, 37*,1, 2–14.

Knotek, S. E. (1997). *Student study teams and discourse across disciplines*. Poster presented at APA annual convention. Chicago.

Knotek, S. E. (1999). *Development through discourse: Speech genres as pathways to conceptual change in consultee-centered consultation*. Invited paper presented at 3rd International Seminar on Consultee-Centered Consultation: Explorations in Process in Practice. San Francisco, CA.

Knotek, S. E. (2003). *Making sense of jargon during consultation: Understanding consultees' social language to effect change in student study teams*. Journal or Educational and Psychological Consultation, 14(2), 181–207.

Knotek, S. E., Babinski. L. M., & Rogers, D. (2002). Consultation in new teacher groups: School psychologists providing collaboration and support for teachers. *California School Psychologist, 7*, 39–50.

Knotek, S. E., & Sandoval, J. (in press). *Introduction to special issue: Consultee centered consultation as a constructive process*. Journal of Educational and Psychological Consultation.

Lambert, N. M., & Hylander, I. (2001, August). Principles underlying consultation methods in general and consultee-centered consultation in particular. In N. Lambert, *Promoting conceptual change*. Symposium conducted at meeting of the Third International Seminar on Consultee-Centered Consultation, San Francisco, CA.

Pugach, M. C., & Johnson, L. J. (1989). Prereferral interventions: Progress, problems, and challenges. *Exceptional Children, 56*, 232–235.

Rogers, D., & Babinski, L. M. (2002). *From isolation to conversation : Supporting new teachers' development*. Albany: State University of New York Press.

Rosenfield, S. (1991). The relationship variable in behavioral consultation. *Journal of Behavioral Education, 1*, 329–336.

Ross, R. P. (1995). Implementing intervention assistance programs. In A. Thomas & J. Grimes (Eds.), *Best practices in school psychology, III* (pp. 227–238). Washington, DC: NASP.

Sandoval, J. (1996). Constructivism, consultee-centered consultation and conceptual change. *Journal of Educational and Psychological Consultation, 7*, 89–97.

Webster, L., Knotek, S. E., Babinski, L., & Rogers, D. (in press). *Mediation of consultee's conceptual development in new teacher groups: Using questions to improve coherency*. Journal of Educational and Psychological Consultation.

Wertsch, J. V. (1991). *Voices of the mind: A sociocultural approach to mediated action.* Cambridge, MA: Harvard University Press.

Ysseldyke, J. E., & Algozzine, B. (1983). On making psychoeducational decisions. *Journal of Psychoeducational Assessment, 1*(2), 187–195.

Zins, J. E., Curtis, M. J., Graden, J. L., & Ponti, C. R. (1989). *Helping students succeed in the regular education classroom: A guide for developing intervention assistance programs.* San Francisco: Jossey-Bass.

26

Reflectivity
in Consultation

Margaret Garcia

The practice of consultee-centered consultation is based on several principles that are not only most *effectively* achieved in a reflective practice, but are almost marked for failure without a reflective approach. These principles include:

1. An understanding of the interactions between sociocultural and psychosocial forces.
2. The need for an explicit agreement between the parties involved.
3. A noncoercive relationship between the consultant and the consultee.
4. Objective focus on the case rather than on the interpersonal conflicts of the consultee.
5. An objective to widen the consultee's frame of reference.
6. The necessity for consultant training.

The role of reflective thinking in the consultation process is particularly relevant to examination of the consultant's espoused theories versus theories-in-action. Both espoused theories and theories-in-action are similar to Hylander's (2000) concept of representation or internal conceptualizations. When theories-in-action contradict espoused theories, the consultant's presentation (verbal statements and nonverbal behavior) may be more consistent with the automatic responses of theories-in-action than with the planned behavior of one's espoused theories. This examination entails an analysis of the factors that lead to incongruency in the consultant's explicit goals of consultation (representation) and his or her actual behavior toward the consultee (presentation). A consultant may adopt the just-named principles, but fall short of executing them due to automatic responses and a lack of reflective thinking that leads to a cycle of failure. Automatic responses may be triggered by fear, such as fear of appearing incompetent to the consultee. Responses by the consultant that are automatic rather than reflective will evoke reciprocal ways of thinking by the consultee. The consultant, serving as a model for thinking about a case, may inadvertently lead the consultee to be less reflective and more reactive. The role of the consultee-centered consultant is to help the consultee resolve a work problem more effectively by reducing obstacles such as lack of knowledge, lack of skill, lack of self-confidence, or lack of objectivity. The consultant, however, is not immune to these same obstacles that limit thinking about any given case. The characteristics inherent in a reflective thinking process are discussed as tools for practicing effective consultee-centered consultation.

REFLECTIVITY IN CONSULTATION

Teachers face many challenges as they strive to carry out their roles in today's schools. These challenges may be due to sources within their control, outside of their control, or the interactive effects of internal and external causes. If this results in less effective teaching performance, the challenges have become obstacles. Caplan (1970) described four obstacles against working effectively: lack of knowledge, lack of skill, lack of self-confidence, and lack of objectivity. Overcoming these obstacles through consultee-centered consultation can often be a challenge in itself, particularly if the consultants are experiencing similar types of obstacles in knowledge, skill, self-confidence, and objectivity. For example, school psychologists may engage in consultee-centered consultation with teachers while lacking sufficient knowledge in psychology or skills in rapport building. Or due to a lack of self-confidence, a school psychologist may fail to use one-downsmanship and instead attempt to elicit favorable remarks from a teacher. Consultants must consider obstacles impeding their own effectiveness in the consultation process.

This chapter examines six of the principles Caplan and Caplan (1993) regard as crucial to the success of consultee-centered consultation along with the difficulties of following each principle in practice. Elements of reflective thinking that can help the consultant work more effectively are discussed with a focus on school teachers as consultees and school psychologists as consultee-centered consultants. The primary purpose is to raise awareness among consultants that reflective thinking in consultation is essential for their own professional success and the success of their consultees.

HISTORICAL PRECURSORS TO CONSULTEE-CENTERED CONSULTATION

The early principles of consultee-centered mental health consultation are the foundation on which consultee-centered consultation evolved and is reflected in the sections in this volume.

Understanding Sociocultural and Psychosocial Forces

An understanding of the ecological forces of a workplace is a prerequisite for mental health consultation (Berlin, 1967; Caplan & Caplan, 1993). Consultants should be familiar with the various aspects of an organization including the community, the groups and individuals within the organization, and the clients served by the system. If the consultant enters the system temporarily and knows very little about it, then time must be invested into becoming more informed. The information is not to be used to form prejudices, but to develop clear understandings of the consultee's framework. The danger here is that a consultant may become informed with the good intention of understanding the consultee's frame of reference but fail to recognize the factors most relevant to a consultee's problem. A school psychologist who works 2 days a week in a particular school will undoubtedly know a good deal about that school. But what is known is known from the school psychologist's perspective, not from the teacher's perspective. In the interest of time, the school psychologist may simply use what he or she already knows as a basis for understanding the consultee's problem and fail to seek clarification from the teacher consultee's perspective.

An Explicit Agreement Between the Consultant and the Consultee

Caplan and Caplan (1993) make clear the necessity for a formal contract to be established between the consultant and the consultee. What are not as clear are the techniques in changing from the agreement established at the initial contact to an agreement derived after further analysis of the problem. The reflective consultant may decide that consultee-centered consultation is the best approach to the problem because it involves the analysis of the consultee's work problem from an array of theoretical perspectives. Although a teacher may have initially sought consultation from a single pedagogical viewpoint, a broader perspective may develop through the consultation process. Some school psychologists gain a great deal of training in behavior analysis and behavioral consultation. They are trained to focus on the behavior of clients and may find it difficult to switch their consultation to a consultee-centered approach—one that is more conducive to inward reflectivity (Korthhagen & Wubbels, 2001). This may be due to the prescriptive nature of special education laws surrounding behavior problems or limited training in consultee-centered consultation. In either case, the model of consultation must be made clear (Reschly, 1976) and that carries significance in forming the consultation agreement. If lacking an explicit theoretical structure for consultation various barriers are likely to be encountered (Brack & Brack, 1996).

The Noncoercive Agreement Between Consultant and Consultee

It is very difficult to train school psychologists to build coordinate, non-hierarchical relationships with their consultees. School psychologists in training are eager to appear competent and will inadvertently "one-up" a teacher to do so. Training school psychologists to be effective consultee-centered consultants involves helping them strike a balance between establishing their own expertise in psychology and recognizing the teacher's expertise in pedagogy and the classroom. Consultants may fortuitously present their knowledge about a case with the expectation that the teacher either accept it as relevant and true or run the risk of being viewed as resistant. The consultant must deliberately and actively work toward equilibrium in the relationship as it will naturally go in and out of balance throughout the consultation process. A noncoercive agreement is not simply established at the onset of consultation nor is it a matter of attitude. It requires a constant monitoring of one's own behaviors in consultation, the consultee's responses, and one's responses to the consultee.

Objective Focus on the Case

To focus on the case rather than on the interpersonal conflicts of the consultee requires a keen sense of consultation versus psychotherapy. This is not as difficult when the consultation model is behavioral than when it is consultee-centered. In consultee-centered consultation, the school psychologist attempts to improve a teacher's objectivity and presentation of the case without working out the teacher's personal problems. This is understandable as a concept but difficult as a practice. A consultant may covertly recognize subtle characterological disorders or personal distractions in the consultee and consider whether such factors are affecting the consultee's work. If so, the consultant must maintain focus on the case and invite the teacher consultee representation of the case to reduce his or her own subjective views about the consultee. By doing so, the consultant encourages a nonhierarchical relationship with the teacher consultee because both perspectives are needed to shed light on the child's difficulties.

Widen the Consultee's Frame of Reference

According to Covey (1989), Albert Einstein observed, "The significant problems we face cannot be solved at the same level of thinking we were at when we created them" (p. 42). The consultant serves to help the consultee arrive at a level of thinking that includes more alternatives for problem solving. The consultant must work toward widening the consultee's frame of reference but may serve to limit it in some ways. For instance, some consultants work from a deficit model of consultation in response to crisis situations, which limits the possibilities for primary prevention (Dougherty, 1990; Parsons & Myers, 1984). I once asked a class of graduate students in a teacher education program to give me examples of problems they experience in the classroom. In response, they said things such as lack of materials, not enough support from administration, low parent involvement, among other things. As I looked at all that had been written on the board, I shared with the class my observation that not one of them identified a problem but instead they all had given me solutions they felt they were not receiving. They took another glance at the list and then engaged in a discussion of the problems and subsequently allowed for a wider discussion of the ways to address those problems. Consultants often have this experience with their consultees who state the "problem" in narrow terms of pre-identified alternatives that they have determined do not work. It serves the process well to widen the consultee's perspective by clearly identifying the problem. Frame analysis is an important skill in this process and is discussed in more detail in this chapter.

The Need for Training Consultants

Caplan and Caplan (1993) exhort that consultee-centered consultation requires systematic training and does not simply come naturally to mental health workers. Although training is undoubtedly important for the consultant, it is similarly important for the consultee and the consultee organization (Brown, Pryzwansky, & Schulte, 1991). Knoff and Batsche (1993) engage their entire staff at Project ACHIEVE in consultation training. The staff includes teachers, administrators, office and cafeteria staff, bus drivers, counselors, and school psychologists. The process uses problem-solving referral question consultation based on Caplan's model and serves as much as a collaborative process as it does a consultation process. However, the training in consultation provided to the staff could not be, nor should it be, as intense as the training given to the school psychologist interns.

I have taken six basic principles of consultee-centered consultation and addressed some of the problems consultants face in turning these principles into practice. In the next section, I discuss the concepts of reflective thinking that are critical for the best practice of consultee-centered case consultation.

THE CONSULTANT AS A REFLECTIVE PRACTITIONER

Definition of Reflective Thinking

Reflective thinking is a popular term that generally refers to thinking about one's thinking and behavior. Specifically, reflective thinking cannot be defined as much as described because it entails an entire thinking process ranging from problem identification through frame analysis. Reflective thinking is an essential process for consultee-centered consultants. Without the readiness to reflect-in-practice, school psychologists will not be effective in consultee-centered consultation.

Problem Identification

By identifying the problem in consultation, the school psychologist has chosen what will be noticed. The direction for action is set by the selective attention and the organization of ideas (Schon, 1987). This is important for the consultant to be able to test hypotheses about the case. But the consultant must use selective attention not to limit thinking but to give it direction. If the consultant does not engage in active inquiry before, during, and after problem identification, then the consultant has simply restricted the possibilities of the case. A school psychologist who decides from the outset that the consultee's problem with a case stems from poor classroom management skills will focus on the teacher's lack of skill. If, in reality, the teacher's problem stems from theme interference, the school psychologist will not recognize it and will not employ theme interference reduction. The trouble is not in original misdiagnosis of the problem, but in failure to engage in active inquiry.

Frame Analysis

Dewey (1964) warned of the hazards of reflective thinking that is limited in scope, "It is a matter of common notice that men who are expert thinkers in their own special fields adopt views on other matters without doing the inquiring that they know to be necessary" (p. 223). School psychologists have different frames of reference than classroom teachers. Elementary school teachers have different frames of reference than secondary school teachers. School psychologists as consultee-centered consultants will be unable to help teachers widen their frames of reference if they are unaware of their own frames of thinking. Consultants cannot form the right questions to ask about a consultee's situation, community, organization, or clients if they are unable to recognize the subtleties in their own field of practice. For instance, some people may have a limited appreciation for cultural diversity because they do not have a strong sense of their own cultures. They may focus on a universal way of thinking about themselves and others and feel safe in assuming that others should do the same. Taking a monocultural approach may feel inclusive but the over-simplicity of it actually excludes many ideas, values, and behaviors. Likewise, the consultant might narrow the scope of thinking about a case to his or her own, possibly less relevant framework if he or she loses insight into the diversity of existing perspectives.

Frame analysis is important in order for professionals from different fields to be able to reach a common ground. The consultation relationship will engage all parties involved into thinking about how one frames the problem. It is particularly important for the consultant to be able to help a consultee view a problem from a professional frame of reference rather than from a personal frame of reference. Lack of objectivity can be viewed as the latter. If frame analysis results in the consultee's observation of the problem from a professional frame of reference, then the problem in turn will be re-evaluated to focus on more relevant matters.

Reflection-in-Action Versus Reflection-on-Action

Reflective thinking is the process of active inquiry about the problem, the frame of reference, and the behaviors that follow. In a consultation relationship the parties engage in reflection-on-action. They discuss behaviors that have been acted or will be acted. The school psychologist inquires about what the teacher has done or will do to solve a problem. Reflection-in-action is the process of inquiry while doing. Teachers may ask themselves whether a particular lesson is successful while actually teaching the lesson. They may choose to make changes on the lesson plan during the instruction. Likewise, consultants reflect-in-action when they think about the questions they are asking consultees. A school psychologist may decide to change the focus of questioning in the middle of a consultation session based on the reflection-in-action.

Espoused Theories Versus Theories-in-Action

Espoused theories are the explicit theories used to explain behavior that is sometimes distinct from theories-in-action (Argyris & Schon, 1974, 1996; Schon, 1987). *Theories-in-action* are the implicit theories of our spontaneous behavior that may contradict our espoused theories, especially during stressful or difficult situations (Schon, 1987). Without a reflective practice, one is at risk for engaging in spontaneous behavior that is inconsistent with what one believes to be true about a case. Through reflectivity, one's espoused theories are guiding one's actions. If the consultee-centered consultant experiences anxiety during consultation, he or she may use theories-in-action that are contrary to the basic principles of consultee-centered consultation. The consultant, for instance, may adhere to the principle of establishing noncoercive relationships with consultees. But when encountering an abrasive and overbearing consultee, the consultant may spontaneously respond by using one-upmanship to be perceived as competent to the consultee. The theory-in-action during this feeling of threat to the consultant's competence might be "I must convince this teacher that I have more expertise than she does so that she will take me seriously. I need more power in this dyad." Such a theory-in-action may backfire by making the consultee more reactive and a vicious cycle has begun. The consultant "choked" by not reflecting on the consultee's behaviors and guiding his or her own behaviors by espoused theories. Theories-in-action are often the automatic responses that can lead to a cycle of failure.

Herbert and Tankersley (1993) observed that "With guidance, teachers can be helped to explicate their thoughts about teaching, to reconcile them with in-class behaviors, and to examine critically the fit between the two" (p. 35). Consultee-centered consultants can serve in that guiding role. But in order to do so they themselves must be reflective. In this next section I briefly discuss some methods for promoting reflection in consultation.

Promoting Reflective Thinking in Consultee-Centered Consultants

There are two very basic methods for promoting reflective thinking in consultee-centered consultation. The first method is to engage in active inquiry about one's thinking with others. Consultants in training have many discussions about their consultation relationships with their supervisors. These discussions should focus on helping the consultant to engage in problem and frame analysis through active inquiry. The supervisor serves as a coach and models the reflective consultation practice. This can be very difficult because consultants are not always motivated to engage in reflective-thinking processes. They can learn and believe the espoused theories but often follow theories-in-action. The coach can involve them in consultation that helps them to reframe the problems.

The second method to promote reflective thinking in consultants is to require consultation logs and analyses of them. Although this writing can be quite a chore, it does help the consultant to reflect-on-action. Without the task of writing, the consultant does not develop the skills of looking back on a consultation session and analyzing the course of action taken. This is important not only to recognize error in consultation, but to recognize successes as well. Reflection-on-action allows the practitioner to notice which actions resulted in which outcomes. In their review of models to promote reflectivity in professional development, Platzer and Snelling (1996) suggested that journal writing may only be effective to promote initial stages of reflection and that other methods may be needed to promote more advanced levels of reflection in professionals.

For consultants who have long since left their training programs, I strongly encourage them to meet with their colleagues regularly to discuss their consultation sessions. In these discussions, consultants can promote reflectivity in one another.

CONCLUSION

Consultee-centered consultation requires the consultant to be a reflective practitioner. The principles of consultee-centered consultation promote more than one espoused theory that will guide consultation practice in ideal situations. But when encountering some challenges in meeting with consultees, the consultant is in danger of behavior based on theories-in-action, rather than reflection-in-action. School psychologists are faced with conflicts of interest, resistance, strong emotional reactions from teachers, and their own personal biases. All of these serve to impede effective consultation. Through a reflective process, consultants can become aware of and address obstacles that keep them from doing their jobs effectively. In turn, consultees will more clearly view the obstacles to their own performance. Ultimately, the clients will be better served when consultee-centered consultants engage in reflectivity.

I am confident that promoting reflective thinking in school psychologists will help them become competent consultee-centered consultants. They can also use their reflective thinking as they provide other school psychological services. Reflective practitioners will bring school psychology to a new level of influence in the field of education.

REFERENCES

Anserello, C. & Sweet, T. (1990). Integrating consultation into school psychological services. In E. Cole & J. A. Siegel (Eds.), *Effective consultation in school psychology* (pp. 173–200). Toronto, Canada: Hogrefe & Huber.

Argyris, C., & Schon, D. A. (1974). *Theory in practice: Increasing professional effectiveness.* San Francisco: Jossey-Bass.

Argyris, C., & Schon, D. A. (1996). *Organizational learning II: Theory, method, and practice.* Reading, MA: Addison-Wesley.

Berlin, I. N. (1967). Preventive aspects of mental health consultation to schools. *Mental Hygiene, 51*(1), 34–40.

Brack, C. J., & Brack, G. (1996). Mental health consultation: In defense of merging theory and practice. *Journal of Mental Health Counseling, 18*(4), 347–357.

Brown, D., Pryzwansky, W. B., & Schulte, A. C. (1991). *Psychological consultation.* Boston: Allyn & Bacon.

Caplan, G. (1970). *Theory and practice of mental health consultation.* New York: Basic Books.

Caplan, G., & Caplan, R. B. (1993). *Mental health consultation and collaboration.* San Francisco: Jossey-Bass.

Conoley, J. C., & Conoley, C. W. (1992). *School consultation* (2nd ed.). Boston, MA: Allyn & Bacon.

Conoley, J. C., & Wright, C. (1993). Caplan's ideas and the future of psychology in the schools. In W. P. Erchul (Ed.), *Consultation in community, school, and organizational practice: Gerald Caplan's contributions to professional psychology* (pp. 177–192). Washington DC: Taylor & Francis.

Covey, S. R. (1989). *The seven habits of highly effective people.* New York: Basic Books.

Dewey, J. (1964). Why reflective thinking must be an educational aim. In R. D. Archumbault (Ed.), *John Dewey on education.* Chicago: University of Chicago Press. (Original work published in 1933)

Dougherty, A. M. (1990). *Consultation: Practice and perspectives.* Pacific Grove, CA: Brooks-Cole.

Herbert, J. M., & Tankersley, M. (1993). More and less effective ways to intervene with classroom teachers. *Journal of Curriculum and Supervision, 9*(1), 24–40.

Hylander, I. (2000). *Turning processes: The change of representations in consultee-centered consultation.* Linköping, Sweden: Linköping Studies in Education and Psychology, No. 74.

Knoff, H. M., & Batsche, G. M. (1993). A school reform process for at-risk students: Applying Caplan's organizational consultation principles to guide prevention, intervention, and home-school collaboration. In W. P. Erchul (Ed.), *Consultation in community, school and organizational practice: Gerald Caplan's contributions to professional psychology* (pp. 123–147). Washington DC: Taylor & Francis.

Knoff, H. M., Sullivan, P., & Liu, D. (1995). Teachers' ratings of effective school psychology consultants: An exploratory factor analysis study. *Journal of School Psychology, 33*(1), 39–57.

Korthagen, F., & Wubbels, T. (2001). Evaluative research on the realistic approach and on the promotion of reflection. In F. Korthagen (Ed.), *Linking practice and theory: The pedagogy of realistic teacher education* (pp. 88–107). Mahwah, NJ: Lawrence Erlbaum Associates.

Parsons, R. D., & Myers, J. (1984). *Developing consultation skills.* San Francisco: Jossey-Bass.

Platzer, H., & Snelling, J. (1996). Promoting reflective practitioners in nursing: A review of theoretical models and research into the use of diaries and journals to facilitate reflection. *Teaching in Higher Education, 2*(2), 103–122.

Reschly, D. J. (1976). School psychology consultation: "Frenzied, faddish or fundamental?" *Journal of School Psychology, 14*(2), 105–113.

Schon, D. A. (1983). *The reflective practitioner.* New York: Basic Books.

Schon, D. A. (1987). *Educating the reflective practitioner.* San Francisco: Jossey-Bass.

Shulman, L. S. (1988). The dangers of dichotomous thinking in education. In P. P. Grimmett & G. L. Erickson (Eds.), *Reflection in teacher education* (pp. 31–38). New York: Teachers College Press.

IV

Evidence of the Impact of Consultee-Centered Consultation

Models for evaluating change in the consultation process focus on the interplay between the consultant's and consultees' presentations of the problems and representations of its underlying dynamics. Documenting the impact of consultation involves assessing the conceptual development that occurs for the two or more participants in the process and the effects of this change on the clients.

27

Identifying Change in Consultee-Centered consultation

Ingrid Hylander
University of Linköping, Sweden

How do we know that what we do in consultation is good practice and beneficial for clients, consultees, and consultee organizations. To approach an answer to this question, this chapter reviews research and evaluation methodology, and discusses problems inherent in consultation research and evaluation design. One goal is to achieve congruence between consultation theory and evaluation methodology that requires a consideration of different types of research and evaluation strategies within the main methodological paradigms. A wide variety of evaluation methods and perspectives may be required if we want to understand, explain, and develop successful consultation approaches that can guide practice and advance the art of consultation.

A first question to ask in planning research is what kind of change do we want to explore? Is it a change in attitude, motivation, conceptual development, or a change of behavior? Do we foresee a conceptual change in the client or the consultee, a change that perhaps also will guide the consultee's further practice? Do we believe that a conceptual change in the consultant is a successful and necessary outcome of a consultation process or do we regard it as irrelevant in the research design? Do we expect an organizational change as result of consultation interventions, and in such case what kind of an organizational change do we believe that is possible to identify? Are we interested in exploring the *interaction* between the parties or the interaction between the consultation process and the contextual environment, or would we like to study the *features* of the client, the consultee or the consultant? The next question is how do we explore change? Do we want to use interviews or inventories to document feelings and conceptions or do we want to make observations to produce objective data about behaviors or do we want to use official reports for descriptive statistics? Are we interested in what is going on in professional practice or do we want to manipulate the environment and interventions to document change based on experimental studies?

The last question is why do we want to evaluate or explore consultation? Is it because we want to describe and understand what is going on in a consultation process, or is it because we want to explain how different kinds of interventions relate to different kinds of problems, different kinds of settings, different kinds of processes? Or, do we want to verify that one method is superior to another?

No single study can address all these questions, but different studies may highlight specific aspects of consultation. The kind of question asked determines the feasibility of the evaluation method or research methodology. It may seem rather obvious that different research problems require different research methods (Allwood, 1997; Guba & Lincoln, 1994; Starrin, Larsson, Dahlgren, & Styvborn, 1991). Arguments around which is the best research or evaluation method frequently focus on the polarity between quantitative and qualitative methods, although many researchers today claim, that the important issue is what kinds of philosophical underpinnings guide the method (Allwood, 1997; Guba & Lincoln, 1994). Both quantitative and qualitative methods can be used reflecting very different belief systems. The question of method is secondary to the question of paradigm. Three main research perspectives give three different types of information: hypothetico-deductive methodology, giving information about the probability of occurrence of certain hypothesis; interpretative methodology, giving descriptions and deeper understanding of a phenomenon; and theory generating methodology, giving probable explanations for complex interactions and social processes. Many researchers propose triangulation, that is, the use of different research approaches, different types of data, and different types of settings, in order to secure both objectivity and an understanding of the diversity of human processes.

During the mid-1980s there was a common agreement that earlier research on consultation had been lacking in rigor, had failed to answer vital questions, or did not even state the questions in a meaningful way (Hughes, 1994; Meade, Hamilton, & Yuen, 1982; Pryzwansky, 1986; Wiström, 1990). Meade et al. (1982) stated that the empirical literature on consultation was in about the same state as empirical literature in counseling and psychotherapy 20 to 30 years back. Few results rendered theories that could explain what is happening in the consultation process, that is, showing how the consultant's intervention relates to the consultee's interaction with the client and to the problem that originated the consultation. During that time new perspectives were aimed at finding a common model for identifying and defining what should be investigated in consultation. For examples, Meade, Hamilton, and Ka-Wa Yen (1982) constructed a research matrix, delineating different research methodologies, variables under study and consultation approaches. Pryzwansky (1986) proposed a set of variables to cover a basic minimum of information in each study. Gallessich (1985) outlined a metatheory of consultation, giving examples of broad questions that theory should address and postulates that might be advanced. Authors of scientific articles on consultation in the 1980s were optimistic about the future of research (Bardon, 1985; Meade et al., 1982). Enthusiasm was short-lived, however, and since the middle of the 1980s, there has been a decline in general consultation studies. There have been theoretical discussions about the power base in consultation (Erchul, 1987; Erchul & Chewning, 1990), which is an attempt to find theoretical links between consultation interventions and outcome, but these discussions apply only to prescriptive models of consultation.

During the 1990s, research on consultation has developed mainly within the traditional hypothetico-deductive research paradigm. Experimental designs for consultation research have become more rigorous and solid but focus almost exclusively on behavioral consultation (Bramlett & Murphy, 1998). On the other hand, there are authors who believe that meaningfulness has been lost on behalf of rigor. Hughes (1994) uncovered no consultation studies that were methodologically rigorous reporting clinically or socially meaningful outcomes for students, that the best outcome studies predated the 1980s, and that the prevalent behavioral consultation model had restricted outcome assessment.

One reason for this outcome may be that consultee-centered consultation has not been very prevalent in the United States. Research has been carried out, in countries where consultee-centered consultation is a well-known and widely used practice. There are but a few studies from other countries than the United States: Israel (Caplan & Caplan, 1995; Bar-El, Mester, & Klein, 1982), Norway (Johannesen, 1991), Sweden (Brodin & Hylander, 1995; Guvå, 1995, 2001; Hylander, 2000; Wiström, Hanson, Qvarnström, & Westerlund, 1995), Russia (Pakhal'ian, 1990), and Greece (Hatzichristou, 1999).

CONSULTATION RESEARCH PARADIGMS

Perhaps the most salient limitation with many of the experimental studies is the fact that young students with no professional experience and limited training in consultation are used as consultants. Few experienced professionals would regard results from such studies as meaningful and leading to the promotion of further development in the field. Evaluation studies of professional practice, on the other hand, often share a common weakness, the consultant and the evaluator or researcher is often the same person and thereby interested in giving a "good" answer to the evaluation question. All kinds of consultation studies, with a few exceptions, lack follow-up data. In earlier studies, different approaches of consultation are not well defined in terms of their concepts and processes (Hughes 1994; Meade et al., 1982; Pryzwansky, 1986). In later studies, this has been improved but on the other hand only behavioral consultation is studied.

The Hypothetico-Deductive Perspective

Researchers certainly recognize the immense difficulties in conducting rigorous experimental research on consultation. Many researchers have addressed the lack of methodological rigor that characterizes most consultation studies (Hughes, 1994; Meade, Hamilton, & Yuen, 1982; Pryzwansky, 1986; Wiström, 1990). Outcome studies generally demonstrate a positive change of some kind, but these changes are difficult to interpret, as the methodology is unsophisticated (Medway & Updike, 1985).

Those few studies that have used control group designs use a prescriptive consultation method. One good example is the well-controlled and sound study by Dunson, Hughes, and Jackson (1993). They studied consultation with ten teachers who had students with ADHD, using ten teachers with the same type of students as a control group. In order to have a common set of problems that were disturbing in a classroom, children with ADHD problems were selected. Behavioral consultation was selected as the consultation method because it is well-defined with precise behavioral goals. (Bergan, 1977; Kratochvilll & Bergan, 1990). Target behavior was specified clearly in behavioral terms, prior to consultation. The child's behavior was assessed by a variety of measures of ADHD. Three consultation sessions, equal for all, were completed during a period of 6 weeks. The evaluation design required the consultant to ask the teachers what they had implemented, and the teachers' answers were compared to the consultant's plan of implementation. Observations before and after showed that the intervention group of children improved in classroom behavior, whereas the control group did not. A strong positive relation was found between teacher's evaluation of the consultant and their ratings of the behavior improvement of the child. There was, however, a negative relationship between teachers' reports of self-efficacy and their evaluation of consultation.

This experimental design, although appropriate for the behavioral consultation method would not have been appropriate for a consultee-centered model of consultation for several reasons. It left very little space for a joint problem identification interaction between the consultant and the consultee because the client problem was identified prior to consultation. The consultation ended after three sessions, not when the problem was solved. Also, change was expected after a very short period of 6 weeks. There was a consultant's plan to be implemented and an assessment of how well the teachers followed the consultant's plan. Although such a research method fits a prescriptive consultation model very well, it would not fit a nonprescriptive consultee-centered model.

Measurement of consultee-compliance, in particular, becomes specifically linked to prescriptive models of consultation and is impossible to use with nonprescriptive consultation methods. Treatment acceptability, the extent to which the consultee is accepting the consultant's plan and integrity of interventions, the measurement of how well the consultant's plan is implemented by the consultee, is model specific for prescriptive consultation (Bramlett & Murphy, 1998; Erchul & Martens, 1997; Greshham & Kendell, 1987). In consultee-centered consultation if the consultee accepts the proposal or advice of the consultant without being given the opportunity to reject it, the consultation would not be judged to be successful. In such a case, the necessary co-ordinate relation between the consultant and the consultee would not have been established.

One can argue that experimental methods are easier to apply to prescriptive methods of consultation than to nonprescriptive models. Does this mean that it is impossible to use hypothetico-deductive strategies for consultee-centered consultation? Probably not. But measures have to be adjusted to fit the expected outcome of nonprescriptive models of consultation. For example, if one expected outcome is the reframing of goals, goal attainment is not a suitable outcome criterion.

What can be measured? The expected outcome of consultee-centered consultation is the conceptual change of the consultee, and consequently, an expected change in the interaction between the consultee and the client. This is what should be assessed. The consultees' conceptual change, their attitudes, and their relation to the client may be assessed by different types of inventories, before and after consultation. The client's conception of the interaction with the consultee may also be assessed before and after consultation. There are, however, significant difficulties in linking measured change in the client to a specific consultation intervention. On the other hand, there is a great amount of literature showing that good quality interaction between adults and children is the single most important aspect for a positive development for children (Hundeide, 2001; Werner, 1979, 1990). Thus, it might be possible to deduce positive indicators from earlier research on teacher–student interactions and general adult child interactions that could be used as criteria for measuring change. Furthermore, the change resulting from con-sultee-centered consultation is supposed to have long lasting effects for cli-ents. But these kinds of long lasting effects can only be expected in contexts where there is a long tradition of consultee-centered consultation, with expe-rienced consultants and consultees who know that they always may be able to turn to a consultant when stuck in relation to a client.

Simple consumer satisfaction measurements are the most common out-come studies. Although such studies may not provide precise measures of out-come, they may give indications of effect. However, when comparisons between consultation models are made, it is important that they reflect au-thentic professional practice. In a Swedish study (Brodin & Hylander, 1995), 119 consultees answered an inventory after consultee-centered consultation. The return rate was 98%. Among all consultees 86.5 % thought that the prob-lem had either been completely solved or partly solved—but could be han-dled. There were no effects of teachers' training or experience on their ratings of consultee-centered consultation outcome, or their willingness to consult again if a new problem would appear. The most common answers to the ques-tion about what consultants had contributed were "someone coming from the outside," "giving new perspectives," "a neutral person"—such as issues focus-ing on overcoming subjectivity. In contrast, Gutkin (1981) reported that lack of objectivity was an infrequent focus in school-based consultation, as com-pared to lack of knowledge. The difference in these results may reflect the fact that teacher consultees as well as consultants refer to the kind of consultation approach they are used to, a fact that has to be considered, when assessing and comparing the outcome of different models. Consultees used to a consultee-centered approach express their need for a consultant who can help them to see more clearly and more objectively in order to handle the problem. Consultees used to a behavioral approach rather express a wish to get clear ad-vice or a program on how to handle the problem.

The Interpretative Perspective

When one explores complex processes characterized by ambiguity where simple relationships of cause and effect through the manipulation of a single variable are not likely to be found, there is a need for research methods other than those that reduce life phenomena to objective measurable entities. If the experimen-tal designs become so rigorous that real meaning is lost, there is a call for other types of research methods. Rosenfield, (1991) suggested that consultation prac-tice, not scientific experiments should be the primary source of research questions. Such an approach may lead to a greater understanding and knowledge of what is really going on in a consultation process in practice, where models of practice seldom are as clear and well defined as in experimental settings. Case studies and other qualitative methods to explore consultation have been advocated during the 1990s by a wide variety of researchers. (Henning-Stout, 1994; Meade et al., 1982; Meyers, 1995; Pryzwansky, 1996; Pryzwansky & Noblit, 1990; Rosenfield, 1991; Sandoval, 1999).

The interpretative perspective primarily involves methods that rely on phenomenological and hermeneutic philosophies. The aim is to give a deeper understanding of a phenomenon by "thick descriptions" or interpretations giving rise to new social meanings. This perspective is used when the researcher is interested in the life-world of the individual or how people perceive phenomena. Qualitative descriptions, narratives, and concepts are used instead of statistical treatment. During the last few decades qualitative research-methods, have gained influence in social and human science, but have been much more predominant in sociology and education, than in psychology.

Case Studies

Case studies may be used for a variety of reasons, to understand both unusual and typical cases (Patton, 1987). Pryzwansky and Noblit, (1990) have shown how case studies may be used to evaluate consultation programs. In Norway, Johannesen (1991) explored the process of group consultation to child day care. It is one of the few studies focusing on interactions between the consultee and the consultant as seen in praxis. She addressed the content of the consultation, as well as the process of consultation using a qualitative approach inspired by Bateson (1979). She found a great gap between how consultation is described in theory and what it is like in actual practice.

Falck-Järnberg, Janson, Olsson, and Orrenius-Andersson (1980) studied different stages of the consultation process. In a study of ten consultation cases in Swedish child day care, they delineated three stages of the consultation process: problem identification, working through, and closure. They reported that the identification of the problem was crucial to goal achievement. They also found that consultants who identified the problem also used a directive style, (asking more questions, structuring the sessions and taking responsibility for the dialogue) as compared to those consultants who used a nondirective listening style.

Carlberg, Guvå, and Teurnell (1977) assessed the effects of psychological consultation/collaboration (methods were not so well-defined at that time) in

Swedish child care by focusing on 14 cases during a 2-year period, analyzing data from diary notes and interviews. They found that when the teachers thought that they had benefited from the dialog with the psychologist, the children had also improved (as assessed by the teachers, the psychologist, and the researcher). When teachers, on the other hand were negative or disappointed with the psychologist's intervention, no improvements were seen in the children. Their conclusion was that the best way to help children in child care was to work through the teachers.

Many of the contributions in this book reflect an interpretative perspective. Although not normally considered a research approach, they are qualitative evaluations of professional practice, and provide a broad understanding of the process of consultation that can guide further development of the method. Professional practitioners who evaluate their practice and develop their professional methods, provide the bases for sound research that is both meaningful and evidenced-based.

Theory Generating Perspectives

Theory may be generated either by inductive analyses or abductive analyses, which are the bases for grounded theory (Glaser, 1978; Glaser & Strauss, 1967; Strauss & Corbin, 1990). Abductive analysis means an empirical discovery that is astonishing and gives an idea about a theory, which if it was true, could explain the surprising discovery. In grounded theory such theoretical derivatives are checked against new data . Studies using grounded theory methods show how consultation theory can be generated by studying professional practice. The theory from such a study is presented in part I of this book.

Theories of consultation have to be made explicit before we know what to assess. We can not know what to assess before we know where we are heading and we do not know where we are heading before we know how the consultation process can be described and understood. My point of departure when exploring the consultee-centered consultation tradition in Sweden was the belief that consultants were not always doing what they said that they were doing and they were also doing things that they were not so aware of.

The grounded theory approach to developing consultation theory is a theory generating methodology particularly suitable when a researcher wants to explore a new field or give a new perspective on an old field. It does not test a given theory to verify it, but explores raw data, to discover new patterns permitting the generation of a substantive theory. As such, this theory consists of hypotheses that are grounded in data. Testing these hypotheses is a different matter and becomes a task for later. The criteria for a grounded theory are that the theory fits data, that it works, that it is usable, and that it is easy to modify (Glaser, 1978).

An Application of Grounded Theory in Consultee-Centered Consultation

The question I started out to explore was what has happened *when a teacher (consultee) tells the consultant (psychologist) that the child she worried so much about, now is doing much better and that now she apprehends the problem in a different way than previously.* What has changed? The child, the mind of the teacher, or the mind of the psychological consultant? What can be studied? The answer to these questions, as I realized it, was that the aspects that could be investigated were the *changes of the presentation of the problem* and the change of the *inner representation of the problem* i.e. the conception of the interaction to the client.

Participants and Data Sources

The data for this study were drawn from 23 experienced Swedish consultants trained in consultee-centered consultation. Theoretical sampling (Glaser, 1978; Strauss & Corbin, 1990) was used to generate the data. In this approach, the sample is taken from individuals who are in situations where the phenomenon under study is likely to exist. In later stages, participants from other situations challenging the generalizability of the phenomena are selected.

The theory developed from the study was based on data from audio-taped consultation sessions, interviews and responses to questionnaires with consultants and consultees in schools and preschool and child day care. The samples consisted of the following data sources:

- Six focus groups (three groups meeting twice) with 17 consultants.
- Six audio taped consultation cases (altogether 19 sessions) from six consultants.
- Twelve interviews with consultants and consultees from the taped cases.
- Open-ended responses to questionnaires from 119 consultees having completed consultation (with a 98% return rate).

Generating the Theory

Transcripts were prepared of all of the audio-taped data and the responses to interview questions and responses to open-ended questions. The data were repeatedly coded and sorted by computer. Every indicator, category, and subcategory was given letters and numbers. Every new code was compared to all other codes and categories of codes by constant comparison (Glaser, 1978). The emerging concepts, patterns, and theory were elaborated in memos that were also sorted at the end of the process. The study consisted of three different substudies, each with a separate and slightly different core process. The analysis was performed in four steps or substudies, which is an elaboration (Guvå & Hylander, 1998) of the more common three-step model (Hallberg, 1992, 1994; Strauss & Corbin, 1990):

1. From data to labeled indicators.
2. From labeled indicators to concepts.
3. From concepts to search for patterns.
4. Arriving at a theory.

The four steps and how they were used in this study are illustrated in Table 27.1. Steps 1 to 3 illustrate the general process in all three substudies while the fourth step has examples only from the fourth substudy.

Grounded theory is described as a procedure of four steps, but this is not a linear process. The research process may simultaneously include all the different steps of analysis in relation to different parts of data and different concepts, until the final integration of the model.

The result of the study is a theory about change in the consultation process, explaining: how consultee presentations and representations of the problem in interaction to a client, turns; the process in the interaction between the consultant and the consultee that precedes these turnings; and finally, the interaction between the consultant's presentation and representation and the consultee's presentation and representation when the consultation process is stuck.

A grounded theory is never a completed theory. It is always open for change. Not until the concepts and relations have been tried out in many different settings may it develop into a formal theory. But even if a grounded theory consists of hypotheses, those hypotheses should be well grounded in data. Thus, a grounded theory can be validated like any other scientific study. In the grounded theory approach, validation is built into the research process (Kvale, 1989), through the constant comparison between emerging theoretical concepts and new data. Verification is part of theory development and not some final product control.

Credibility is equivalent to empirical grounding or fit as Glaser (1978) stated it. The two first parts of the study are well grounded. Concepts have been derived from open coding and fit new data. Those concepts appearing late in the research process, such as blind alleys, have partly appeared from the emerging theory and are mainly grounded through selective coding. This means that they

TABLE 27.1
Procedure in grounded theory as applied in Turning processes.
The change of representations in consultee-centered case consultation.

Objective	Sample	Coding	Comparative Analysis
Step 1			
Labeled indicators	Open theoretical sample	Open coding	Sorting
	Three focus groups with consultants	Coding indicators resulted in a list of codes, 150 codes in 9 categories.	Constant comparison between indicators and codes.
Step 2			
Grounded concept	Strategic sample	Conceptual coding	Conceptual analysis
	Second set of focus group interviews	A coding list with categories and subcategories on five levels. Turnings, tuning points, and shifts appear as main categories. Different kinds of turnings appear as grounded concepts.	The variances within the concepts are analyzed.
Step 3			
Pattern	Variational/relational Sample.	Theoretical coding	Pattern analysis
	Inventories with consultees, reported cases, taped consultation sessions, interviews	Representations, presentations, movement, being stuck, closeness, distance appear as theoretical codes relating concepts to each other. A pattern of approaching, a free neutral position and moving away is discerned in the interaction between the consultee and the client as well as between the consultee and the consultant.	Relating concepts and their sub-categories by diagrams. Figures "Cross tabulation" Conceptual Case-stories. Interaction of theoretical codes (Consultant and consultee representations and presentations, related to being stuck give rise to the concept of blind alley)

(continued on next page)

TABLE 27.1 (continued)

Objective	Sample	Coding	Comparative Analysis
Step 4			
Theoretical model	Selective sampling	Selective coding	Integration
	Excerpts from the taped cases and descriptions from the interviews indicating that the process is stuck and starts to move.	The core process is identified: The sudden shift from being stuck in a blind alley to moving freely as an interaction between the consultee's and the consultant's representations and presentations	The blind alleys are linked to the emerging theory. Bind is the blind alley of approach, boredom is the blind alley of the free neutral position and break is the blind alley of moving away.

have strong theoretical bases, are well integrated into the model, but would gain credibility while grounded in new and different settings.

Applicability

The theory has several times been presented to audiences of psychological consultants and teachers. Concepts and hypothesis have also been discussed with psychological consultants in small groups and have been met by recognition and regarded as useful. In 1998, after a lecture to 95 psychological consultants an assessment showed that four out of five consultants found the model useable and comprehensible; the rest were unsure, none was negative (Hylander, 2000, p. 272).

Consistency

Concepts are generated and systematically related to each other. There are several conceptual relations and the categories are well developed. There is a great variability and a core process in the study. The following variety is addressed:

1. Different kinds of problems ascribed to the client.
2. Different kinds of relations between the consultee and the client as described by the consultee.
3. Different kinds of turnings in the process of consultation.

4. Variations in the interaction between the consultant and the consultee throughout the consultation process.
5. Different kinds of problems that consultants encounter in the consultation process.

Objectivity is seldom applicable in a qualitative study. Instead discourse criteria or communicative validity is used (Kvale, 1989), for example, how well the results are explained in comparison with other possible alternative explanations. A grounded theory study, however, never claims to be the best explanation, but should relate to and, if relevant, include parts of other possible theories. When similarities with other theories are found one could conclude that there are general and common phenomena that have been discovered and analyzed. The present grounded theory fits well within a constructivistic paradigm, whereas many of the grounded concepts have similarities with concepts within a wide variety of theoretical paradigms (e.g., the concepts of blind alleys have similarities to Bion's [Granström, 1986] concept of basic assumption groups. Argyris and Schon's [1974, 1978] way of differentiating between theory in use—what guides the action—and espoused theory—what people say they are doing—although not the same have apparent similarities with representations and presentations).

Most important, perhaps is that a grounded theory presents a *new perspective*, that will add to the theoretical field. Focusing on the change of the consultant has not yet been studied in consultation research. Thus, for the consultee-centered consultation method to progress, the difficulty that the consultant encounters in challenging his or her own representation when feeling stuck in blind alleys should be further investigated. Focus group interviews and taped consultation sessions with consultants from many different settings, would give data that may deepen the understanding and give a more varied picture. Stimulated recall with consultees and consultants after one consultation session would give information about the mutuality or lack of mutuality in interpreting what is going on in the process when the consultant feels stuck and identifies it as a blind alley.

In order for the theory to develop to a formal theory, much more work has to be done. The theory has to be tried out, adjusted and changed in accordance with other nonprescriptive consultation traditions.

A Constructivist Framework for Evaluating Consultee-Centered Consultation

The research method used and the consultation process that has been studied share common features, each of which fits into a *constructivist* framework. The links between symbolic interactionism—the roots of grounded theory and constructivism, have lately been emphasized (Annells, 1996; Guvå & Hylander, 1998; Pidgeon & Henwood, 1997; Starrin et al., 1991). Symbolic interactionism focuses the meaning of events and the symbols that convey this meaning. Phenomena are studied from the perspective of the actors in the environment where they act. The concepts are created in an interaction between the researcher and the empirical data. They reflect the social acts, but are constructions, getting their symbols and meanings from the interaction between researcher and participants (Blumer, 1969; Mead, 1934). This approach is in line with constructivist theory (Andersen, 1994; Anderson & Golishian, 1998), which underscores that there is no true social reality only constructions of reality that are kept by individuals and groups. Collecting information about actions, thoughts and behaviors, becomes in this view an interactive process between the researcher and those studied. This interaction is particularly true, in the present study, as focus group interviews (Hylander, 1998; Morgan, 1997; Morgan & Kreuger, 1993) have been used where new information is constructed during the interview. The final aim of constructivistic research is according to Guba and Lincoln (1994) "to distil a consensus construction, that is more informed and sophisticated than either of its predecessor constructions." This outcome could also be a description of the goal of nonprescriptive consultation.

Thus, a theory generating perspective in research seems to fit a nonprescriptive model of consultation. Could a theory generating method then be used to study behavioral consultation? Certainly! It can be used to study all practice. But the researcher has to be open for surprises and prepared that all results may not fit so well with the theory that is said to guide practice. Just as is the case in psychotherapy research, when trying to find out what the most powerful interventions are, one seldom finds great differences between models but instead differences between individual therapist-patient pairs. Establishing a relationship and making agreements are the common factors that predict therapeutic change. Likewise in consultation research one might find that the main concern as the actors see it may not be model specific (like the implementation of reinforcement schedules) but rather factors having to do with establishing a relationship between consultant and consultee. Thus, there is a need for research generating new theories about what is actually going on and what is vital in the consultation process, and research using theory as a point of departure for revisions, refinements and further development of concepts and postulated relations.

REFERENCES

Allwood, M. (1997). Välj metod efter forskningsuppgift. *Psykologtidningen, 4*, 4–7.

Annells, M. (1996). Grounded theory method: Philosophical perspectives, paradigm of inquiry and postmodernism. *Qualitative Health Research, 6*, 379–393.

Argyris, C., & Schön, D. (1974). *Theory in practice*. San Fransisco: Jossey Bass.

Argyris, C., & Schön, D. (1978). *Organisational learning*. Reading, MA: Addison-Wesley.

Andersen, T. (1994). *Reflekterande processer. Samtal om samtalen*. Stockholm: Mareld.

Anderson, H., & Goolishian, H. (1998). Human systems as linguistic systems: Preliminary and evoking ideas about the implication for clinical theory. *Family Process, 27*, 371–394.

Bardon, J. (1985). On the verge of a breakthrough. *The counseling psychologist, 13*, 355–361.

Bar-El, I., Mester, R., & Klein, H. (1982). Experience in community mental health consultation. *Israel Journal of Psychiatry and Related Sciences, 19*, 173–180.

Bergan, J. R. (1977). *Behavioral consultation*. Columbus, OH: Merrill.

Bramlett, K., & Murphy, J. (1998). School psychology perspectives on consultation: Key contributions to the field. *Journal of Educational and Psychological Consultation, 9*, 29–55.

Bateson, G. (1979). *Mind and nature. A necessary unity*. Toronto: Bantam Books.

Blumer, H. (1969). *Symbolic interactionism: Perspective and method*. Englewood Cliffs, NJ: Prentice Hall.

Brodin, M., & Hylander, I. (1997). *Att bli sig själv. Daniel Sterns teori i förskolans vardag*. Stockholm: Liber.

Caplan, G., & Caplan, R. (1995). *Recent advances in mental health consultation and collaboration*. Paper presented at The International Seminar on Consultee-Centered Case Consultation, May 5–7. Stockholm: Hasselbacken.

Carlberg, M., Guvå, G., & Teurnell, L. (1977). *Konsultation i förskolan*. (Rapport från förskoleteamet.) Stockholm: Stockholms läns landsting, Sociala nämnden.

Dunson, R., Hughes, J., & Jackson, T. (1994). Effect of behavioral consultation on student and teacher behavior. *Journal of School Psychology, 32*, 247–266.

Erchul, W. (1987). A relational communication analysis of control in school consultation. *Professional School Psychology, 2*, 113–124.

Erchul, W. P., & Martens, B. K. (1997). *School consultation. Conceptual and empirical bases of practice*. New York: Plenum Press.

Erchul, W. P., & Chewning, T. G. (1990). Behavioral consultation from a request-centered relational communication perspective. *School Psychology Quarterly, 5*, 1–20.

Falck-Järnberg, B., Janson, U., Olsson, S., & Orrenius-Andersson, A. M. (1980). *Konsultationsprocessen*. (Rapport 2 från förskoleteamet). Stockholm: Stockholm läns landsting, Sociala nämnden.

Gallessich, J. (1985). Towards a meta-theory of consultation. *The Counseling Psychologist, 13*, 363–354.

Glaser, B., & Strauss, A. (1967). *The discovery of grounded theory*. Chicago: Aldine.

Glaser, B. (1978). *Theoretical sensitivity. Advances in the methodology of grounded theory*. San Francisco: The Sociology Press.

Granström, K. (1986). *Dynamics in meetings. On leadership and followership in ordinary meetings in different organisations*. Linköping: Linköping Studies in Art and Science.

Gresham, F., & Kendell, G. (1987). School consultation research: Methodological critique and future research directions. *School Psychology Review, 16*, 306–316.

Guba, E. G., & Lincoln, Y. S. (1994). Competing paradigms in qualitative research. In N. K. Denzin & Y. S. Lincoln (Eds.), *Handbook of Qualitative Research* (pp. 105–117). Thousand Oaks, CA: Sage.

Gutkin, T. (1981). Relative frequency of consultee lack of knowledge, skills, confidence and objectivity in school settings. *The Journal of School Psychology, 19,* 57–61.

Guvå, G. (1995). *Professionsutveckling hos konsulter. Om konsultativ handledning och självutveckling.* (FOG-Rapport No. 25). Linköpings universitet, Institutionen för Pedagogik och Psykologi.

Guvå, G. (2001). *Skolpsykologers rolltagande. Överlämning och hantering av elevvårdsfrågor.* (Doktorsavhandling.) Linköping: Linköpings Universitet. Institutionen för beteendevetenskap.

Guvå, G., & Hylander, I. (1998). *Att tillägna sig grounded theory.* (FOG-rapport nr 43). Linköping: Linköpings universitet. Institutionen för pedagogik och psykologi.

Hallberg, L. (1992). *Hearing impairment, coping and perceived handicap, in middle-aged individuals with acquired hearing loss: An interactional perspective. (Doktorsavhandling).* Göteborg: Göteborgs universitet, Psykologiska institutionen.

Hallberg, L. (1994). *En kvalitativ metod influerad av grounded theory-traditionen.* Göteborg: Göteborgs universitet. Psykologiska institutionen.

Hatzichristou, C. (1999). Alternative school psychological services: Development of a model linking theory, research and service delivery. In *Explorations in process in practice.* (Seminar proceedings.) Stockholm: 2nd International Seminar on Consultee-Centered Consultation.

Henning-Stout, M. (1994). Consultation and connected knowing: What we know is determined by the question we ask. *Journal of Educational and Psychological Consultation, 5,* 5–22.

Hughes, J. N. (1994). Back to basics. Does consultation work? *Journal of Educational and Psychological Consultation, 1,* 77–84.

Hundeide, K. (2001). *Vägledande samspel.* Stockholm: Rädda Barnen.

Hylander, I. (1998). *Fokusgrupper som kvalitativ datainsamlingsmetod. Focus groups as a research method for collecting qualitative data. (Fog-rapport nr 42).* Linköping: Linköping University. Department of Behavioural Science.

Hylander, I. (2000). *Turning processes. The change of representations in consultee-centered case consultation.* (Dissertation). Linköping: Linköping University. Department of Behavioural Science.

Johannesen, E. (1991) *Group consultation in a day care center.* Oslo, Norway: Institute for Special Education. University of Oslo.

Kratochwill, T. R., & Bergan, J. R. (1990). *Behavioral consultation in applied settings.* New York: Plenum.

Kvale, S. (1989). To validate is to question. In S. Kvale (Ed.), *Issues of validity in qualitative research.* Lund: Studentlitteratur.

Mead, M. (1934). The use of primitive material in the study of personality. *Character and Personality: A Quarterly for Psychodiagnostic and Allied Studies, 3,* 1–16.

Meade, C. J., Hamilton, M. K., & Yen, R. KW. (1982). Consultation research: the time has come the walruss said. *The Counseling Psychologist, 10,* 39–51.

Medway, F. J., & Updike, J. F. (1985). Meta-analysis of consultation outcome studies. *American Journal of Community Psychology, 13,* 489–495.

Meyers, J. (1995). A consultation model for school psychological services: 20 years later. *Journal of Educational and Psychological Consultation, 6*(1), 73–81.

Morgan, D. (1997). *Focus groups as qualitative research.* Qualitative Research Methods Series, 16. 2. ed. Thousands Oaks, CA: Sage.

Morgan, D., & Kreuger, R. (1993). When to use focus groups and why. In D. Morgan (Ed.), *Successful focusgroups. Advancing the state of the art* (pp. 3–19). Newbury Park, CA: Sage.

Pakhalian, V. (1990). The work of the psychologist in preparing and conducting a pedagogical consultation. *Voprosy Psikhologii, 2*, 86–90.

Pidgeon, N., & Henwood, K. (1997). Using grounded theory in psychological research. In N. Hayes (Ed.), *Doing qualitative analysis in psychology* (pp. 245-272). London: Taylor & Francis.

Pryzwansky, W. B. (1986). Indirect Service Delivery: Considerations for future research in consultation. *School Psychology Review, 15*, 479–488.

Pryzwansky, W. B. (1996). Professionals peer-mediated learning experiences: Another idea whose time has come. *Journal of Educational and Psychological Consultation, 7*, 71–78.

Pryzwansky, W. B. & Noblit, G. W. (1990). Understanding and improving consultation practice: The qualitative case study approach. *Journal of Educational and Psychological Consultation, 1* (4), 293–307.

Rosenfield, S. (1991). The relationship variable in behavioral consultation. *Journal of Behavioral Education, 1*, 329–336.

Sandoval, J. (1999). Evaluation issues and strategies in consultee-centered consultation. In *Explorations in process in practice. (Seminar proceedings)*. Stockholm: 2nd International Seminar on Consultee-centered consultation.

Starrin, B., Larsson, G., Dahlgren, L., & Styrborn, S. (1991). *Från upptäckt till presentation. Om kvalitativ metod och teorigenerering på empirisk grund.* Lund: Studentlitteratur.

Strauss, A., & Corbin, J. (1990). *Basics of qualitative research. Grounded Theory procedures and techniques.* Newbury Park, CA: Sage.

Werner, E. (1979). *Cross-cultural child development: A view from the planet Earth.* Monterey, CA: Brooks/Cole.

Werner, E. (1990). Protective factors and individual resilience. In S. Meisel, och J. Shonkoff (Eds.), *Handbook of early intervention.* Cambridge, MA: Cambridge University Press.

Wiström, C. (1990). Konsultation i skolan. Teori och metodik under 2 decennier. *Psykologtidningen, 20*.

Wiström, C., Hanson, M., Qvarnström, G., & Westerlund, S. (1995). *Psykologisk konsultation i pedagogisk verksamhet. Analys och utvärdering av konsultationsarbete i banomsorg och skola.* Östersund: Östersunds kommun, Konsult & Service, Pedagogica.

Hylander, I. (1995a). Konsultation och handledning. En jämförelse mellan två professionella, psykologiska processer. Consultation and supervision, a comparison between two professional psychological processes. (FOG-rapport 23.) Linköping: Linköping University. Department of Behavioural Science.

Hylander, I. (1995b). Evolvement of Consultee-Centered Case Consultation in Sweden. Paper presented at The International seminar on Consultee-Centered Case Consultation May 5–7. Stockholm: Hasselbacken.

Hylander, I. (1999). Identifying change in the consultation process. Turnings and turning points. In Explorations in process in practice. (Seminar proceedings). Stockholm: 2nd International Seminar on Consultee-Centered Consultation.

Meyers, B., Valentino, C. T., Meyers, J. Boreti, M., & Brent, D. (1996). Implementing prereferral intervention teams as an approach to school-based consultation in an urban school system. Journal of Educational and Psychological Consultation, 7, 119–149.

Sandoval, J. (1996). Constructivism, consultee-centered consultation, and conceptual change. Journal of Educational and Psychological Consultation, 7, 89–97.

28

Evaluation Issues and Strategies in Consultee-Centered Consultation

Jonathan H. Sandoval
University of California at Davis

Consultation, as an activity, is not exempt from accountability. We owe it to our employers, to our consultees, and most of all, to the clients to demonstrate that our consultation work has been helpful. This chapter reviews traditional strategies for evaluating individual consultations rather than consultation as a program of services. Hylander addressed the evaluation of consultation as a process in a companion chapter. My choice to center on individual consultation is not to avoid or neglect much needed program evaluation, but to acknowledge that individual consultations must be evaluated and made to be effective before a program of consultation can be shown to be effective.

Information from evaluation is important to identify professional strengths and weaknesses on the part of the consultant and to learn whether the process is at an end and has achieved its goal. The goal is, of course, improving the job performance of the consultee with regard to the client and future clients. Responsible consultants continue to engage in reflective practice (Garcia, this volume, Rosenfield, this volume) aimed at improving their personal development as consultants and take time to collect information and review their professional practices. Simple reflection, with or without the aid of a peer, can be thought of as part of the consultation evaluation process. But reflection alone is not sufficient. There is a danger that reflection in the absence of data from other sources can become self-serving and self-deluding, and subject to a number of cognitive biases (Sandoval, 1998). Reflection combined with multi-source data can lead to improved service, however.

Two general types of evaluation data can be considered: changes in the client and changes in the consultee. Many scholars believe that the first, changes in the client, is the most important of the two types, and ignore or minimize changes in the consultee. Purists from the behavioral tradition, for example, would even limit evaluation to an examination of changes in the client's observable behavior around the identified problem. Changes in target behaviors, determined in the early stages of consultation, are the primary, or the only, types of evaluation data deemed useful.

Although changes in client behavior are important and informative, I argue that changes in conceptualizations, which are not directly observable, are also critical criteria to use in determining consultation effectiveness. By conceptualizations, I mean our broad understandings of phenomena and the network of associations we have to them (some of which may be affectively loaded). Changes may occur in the consultee's understanding of the problem, or of the client, or of her or himself. Changes may occur in his or her thoughts about an issue, problem, or client, or changes may occur in the understanding of the process of consultation. Changes in consultee conceptualizations are certainly more accessible than changes in client conceptualizations. Moreover, changes in consultee conceptualizations are of most interest to consultee-centered consultants. I return to this point later. Finally, in consultee-centered consultation it is also important to examine changes in affect in the consultee as additional sources of information or indicators about the course of the consultation process.

It also may be important to examine changes in the behavior, conceptualizations, and affect in the *consultant*. The consultant finding it easy to cancel consultations, or arriving late, the consultant forming negative attitudes about consultees or clients, and the consultant anxious or bored during consultation has data at hand that things are not going well. Hylander (this volume) points out that reflection is an important tool used to recognize blind alleys in consultation. Reflection and peer review should look at what is occurring in the consultant's behavior and thoughts as well as changes in the consultee and client. In addition to self-examination on the part of the consultant, several measures of consultee satisfaction with consultation have been developed (e.g., Brown, Pryzwansky, & Schulte, 1987; Conoley & Conoley, 1982; Gallesich, 1982; Parsons & Myers, 1984). These measures include reports of consultant behavior that provide important feedback.

Evaluation efforts may be focused on the whole of the consultation process or on the parts. For example, one might evaluate success with a consultee following a course of consultation; or one might evaluate the success of a particular strategy or technique in the consultation process, such as reframing or the process of theme interference reduction. If the focus is on the entire consultation, there may be an interest in learning if one has reached an end point, or if one must alter his or her approach. If the focus is on a specific technique, the intent may be to improve the consultant's use of that technique with all consultees or to determine if the technique works with this particular consultee. In any case, the same evaluation considerations may be kept in mind.

Increasingly psychologists are concerned with identifying and promoting the use of empirically validated interventions in changing behavior. The focus has been on interventions with clients, rather than on interventions with consultees. Because consultation is a *vehicle for delivering interventions to clients* rather than an intervention itself, consultants will be interested in introducing validated interventions into consultation. Consultee-centered consultation is not an intervention for clients. However, as a vehicle, it may be that consultee-centered consultation does have virtue in increasing the level of "buy-in" or treatment acceptability among consultees and subsequent implementation of interventions.

As an intervention with *consultees*, however, consultee-centered consultation may be subject to validation. Studies are beginning to emerge that document changes in consultees as a result of consultee-centered consultation (Knotek & Sandoval, in press). At this stage of development, both qualitative and quantitative methods of validation are in use.

CHANGES I N CLIENT BEHAVIOR

Although changes in the client have been considered by many as the goal of evaluation in most forms of consultation, under consultee-centered consultation it is also important to examine the effect of the consultation process on a whole range of clients who are the responsibility of the consultee, as well as the identified client. One central premise is that consultation will result in improved performance of the consultee with other clients. This improvement occurs because effective consultation interventions work to bring about changes in consultee perceptions and attitudes and then, in turn, changes in consultee-client behavior and, finally, changes in client behavior and performance. One hopes for what Gagne (1977) called horizontal transfer of learning. He noted, however, that this form of transfer is often difficult to bring about.

Traditional evaluation focuses on identifying behaviors in the client that are causing difficulty for the consultee and then documenting changes in these client behaviors following interventions generated during consultation. This strategy makes sense to the extent that the behaviors are real and are the central issues in the consultation predicament. Consultation may be effective, particularly in reducing the consultee's lack of confidence, when it changes the way the behavior is framed by the consultee. Consequently, consultation may be effective even when observable behavior does not change or changes subtly. Nevertheless, change in client behavior remains an important outcome to evaluate and is a key to accountability.

Unless the consultant is part of the system serving the client, there is little chance to observe first-hand changes in the client or other similar clients. These changes can be observed by supervisors or may be reflected in data routinely collected by the institution such as attendance data, achievement data, and disciplinary or other referrals. The consultee will also be able to report changes in the client, but the consultee must be considered a biased source of information. There are observational technologies available to record the frequency and intensity of target behaviors that can be applied and that will increase the objectivity of the consultee. These should be used when possible. Others in the consultee's system, such as peers or assistants, can also be given the task to look for and record client behavior in a systematic manner. However, information about changes in the client must be cross-validated using more than one source.

The consultant can examine shifts in the sort of referrals or types of problems brought to consultation by the consultee. If the same predicaments or types of clients continue to show up in consultation, it may be a sign that positive transfer is not occurring. One may be misled, moreover, if there is a reduction in the number of clients brought to consultation over time. This reduction may represent transfer, but may also represent increased *comfort* with clients with a particular behavior, but not necessarily increased *competence* in meeting the needs of these clients. Additionally, a reduction in the number of problems presented may also indicate that the consultant is not perceived to be of help with this sort of case. Nevertheless, coupled with other evidence, a reduction in the number and type of referrals generally would be a sign that consultation is working.

Because the goal is change in behavior with respect to new clients with similar profiles, a comprehensive evaluation needs to extend over some time in order to determine if the desired outcomes occur with new clients. As a result, it is useful to build in long-term follow-ups, either by questionnaire or interview, to get an accurate picture of success.

CHANGES IN CONSULTEE BEHAVIOR

Changes in consultee behavior and performance can be noted by the consultee, the consultant, the consultee's supervisors and peers, and by clients. Each of these sources can contribute useful information, but each has its drawbacks.

The consultant can usually only judge changes in behavior indirectly. Changes in behavior that are reported by the consultee are difficult to evaluate because they may be influenced by conscious or unconscious motivation. Caplan points out some of the problems of consultee self report, "Moreover, a consultee's report to his consultant about changes in his behavior with a client must be accepted with some caution, since it will often be colored by the consultee's awareness of what he thinks the consultant would like to hear and by the complexities of the consultee-consultant relationship. A consultee may reward or punish his consultant by such a report" (1970, p. 296). Nevertheless, self-reports are one source of information.

In addition to self-reports on the part of consultees, the consultant can observe the consultation process. To permit the observation of change, the consultant must keep a careful record of the consultation conversation. Using notes collected during or after each session, the consultant keeps track of the problem or predicament discussed, the thread of the discussion focusing on presentations and representations, the consultation strategies or approaches used, the consultee's emotional responses, and the consultant's thoughts and feelings. Additionally, after the session, the consultant should record the result of reflections on the session. These notes can be used as one source of evaluative information, about the consultant as well as the consultee.

The consultee's supervisors and colleagues may also provide information about behavior change and increased competency if asked. As Caplan (1970) pointed out, these reports may also be biased. Indirect evidence, such as increased requests from administrators for consultation services, may support observations of improvement in the job performance of consultees. The consultant, because of different professional training, may or may not be able to tell if changes in performance are for the better or worse, but peers and supervisors from the peers' profession can note changes and evaluate them. Changes in behavior may be noted on routine performance evaluations collected by the consultee's organization. Alternatively, the consultant and consultee may design questions and probes designed to identify changes in behavior.

Clients, too, can be brought into the evaluation process, although often this will be awkward. In some situations, such as high school and college teaching, there are attempts to get information from clients about professionals. These evaluations may be examined to detect changes in performance following consultation.

One observable change that may occur in teacher consultees is a shift to becoming more learner-centered (Lambert & McCombs, 1998) in their approach to teaching. As they come to see their clients as more complex through the process of consultation, they may be inclined to shift their teaching practices in the direction of being more responsive to the classroom as a whole, focusing on learners rather than curriculum. Measures of learner-centered orientations have been devised, including questionnaires for use with children (McCombs, Lauer, Bishop, & Peralez, 1997).These may provide useful sources of evaluation data. Perry (1999) and Donohue (2001) have reported that teachers of kindergarten and first grade children who are perceived by their students to more learner-centered have higher levels of achievement and lower rates of peer rejection.

CHANGES IN CONSULTEE ATTITUDE AND AFFECT

The consultant also can observe changes in consultee attitude. Attitude change is often revealed in both verbal and nonverbal behaviors. Traditional signs of reduced anxiety that can be observed are relaxed body language and appearance, improved sense of humor, and a reduction in the level of confusion and distractibility. Additionally, the consultant can note the gradual shift in anxiety across clients with similar features, as the consultee's capacity to cope improves.

The consultee, too, can be a source of information. The consultant can ask about changes in attitude and affect, but, as with other self reports, the responses will need cross-validation. Talking about problems with a skilled and empathic listener typically brings about a reduction in tension. If consultation is effective, however, this relief will not be temporary, but lasting. The consultant should expect a gradual increase in signs of coping on the part of the consultee. If the consultee returns week after week at the same level of agitation, there is evidence that new strategies must be employed.

Consultee self reports and consultee satisfaction or the reduction in anxiety about the consultation issue are legitimate factors to evaluate and document. In developing a protocol for evaluating consultee satisfaction it is important to consider all possibilities: lack of knowledge, lack of skill, lack of self confidence, and lack of objectivity. Items must be developed to tap each of these domains. The literature contains many examples.

Clients might also be a source of information about changes in consultee attitudes and understandings. To the extent that clients react to the climate established by the consultee, they may also reflect the disposition of the consultee. They may be observed to be more relaxed and comfortable with the consultee, quite apart from changing their behavior, as a result of a successful consultation. In general, the consultee needs to be the major source of information about changes in conceptualization.

Current theory in evaluation stresses the need to involve the recipient of the program in the process of evaluation. New directions in evaluating consultee-centered consultation would suggest an early partnership between the consultee and the consultant in planning and executing the evaluation process. Questions might be posed to the consultee such as "how will we know when this process has been helpful?" Follow-up questions (which the consultant would also try to answer in the spirit of brain-storming) would include "How would you feel different if we were successful?" "How would your understanding of the problem and possible interventions change?"

CHANGES IN CONSULTEE CONCEPTUALIZTIONS

I conclude with a description of a new strategy for consultation evaluation focused on examining changes in a consultee's conceptualizations and understandings. This method of looking at consultee cognitive change I call *consultee mapping*. Examining changes in the consultee's understanding is only an intermediate step in evaluation, but a step in right direction, if one assumes that changes in behavior flow from changes in understanding. But it must be acknowledged that consultee professional performance does not necessarily change as a result of changed conceptions and improved coping.

I have been experimenting with an approach that can directly examine a consultee's conceptualization of a problem, a client or a situation. In this approach, consultees and consultants construct diagrams of the identified problem both before and after consultation has taken place. A relatively short period of training is necessary to learn to construct these maps, which consist of concepts placed in circles and labeled arrows connecting them. The labels on the arrows indicate the nature of the relationship (see Sandoval, 1995).

Training in the use of maps can be integrated into consultation as part of the problem exploration process where the initial problem and all of the factors impinging on it can be graphically represented. In this context, it can be a tool to aid understanding of the issues as well as serve as a benchmark against which to guage changes. At the end of consultation about a particular predicament it can again be used as a way of summing up what has been learned. Not everyone is comfortable with graphic representations, but we have found them to be possible to score for their complexity and relatively reliable. It is well known that the maps constructed by experts in a field are much more complex than those produced by novices and vary in a way that can only be described as more elegant

and efficient. We will be interested to learn if consultee's maps of the consultation process will shift in parallel ways.

Another virtue of maps is that they easily reveal misconceptions in understanding. I believe these misconceptions should be the focus of consultation
and be replaced with more complex understandings that the consultee views as
fruitful in solving the consultation predicament. Quite apart from the use of
these maps as tools for evaluation one can consider their utility in facilitating
the consultation process.

Figures 28.1 and 28.2 are some illustrative maps produced by a consultee
dealing with a client with attention deficit hyperactivity disorder. The first is a
map produced at the beginning of discussions about the problem. The second
map was produced after a long period of group consultation and discussion. Is
the consultee more effective in working with children with this condition?
Other evidence from supervisors and self-reports suggest it is the case.

Unfortunately, I can only show a few examples of this technique, as I have not
been able to implement it widely in consultation, although we have validated it
for use in changes in pediatrician understanding (West, Park, Pomeroy, &
Sandoval, 2002). I offer it as an example of one possibility in a quest for new ways
to document consultation effectiveness. No one method or source of information

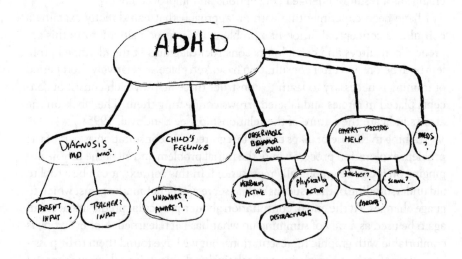

FIG. 28.1.   Map drawn by consultee near the beginning of consultation.

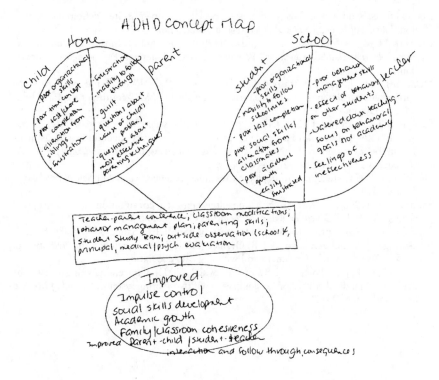

FIG. 28.2. Map drawn by consultee at the end of consultation.

should be used exclusively in evaluation. We need to continue to develop additional assessment devices. We must be systematic, honest and thoughtful—and rely on evidence of many kinds—if we are to grow as consultants.

REFERENCES

Brown, D., Pryzwansky, W. B., & Schulte, A. C. (1987). *Psychological consultation.* Newton, MA: Allyn & Bacon.

Conoley, J. C., & Conoley, C. W. (1982). *School consultation.* New York: Pergamon Press.

Caplan, G. (1970). *The theory and practice of mental health consultation.* New York: Basic Books.

Donohue, K. M. (2001). Classroom instructional pratices and children's rejection by their peers. *Dissertation Abstracts: Section B. The Sciences and Engineering, Feb. v. 61.*

Gagne, R. M. (1977). *The conditions of learning* (3rd. ed.). New York: Holt Rinehart & Winston.

Gallesich, J. (1982). *The profession and practice of consultation.* San Francisco: Jossey-Bass.

Knotek, S., & Sandoval, J. (Eds.). (in press). Special issue on consultee-centered consultation. *Journal of Educational and Psychological Consultation*.

Lambert, N. M., & McCombs, B. L. (Eds.). (1998). *How students learn: Reforming schools through learner-centered education*. Washington, DC: American Psychological Association.

McCombs, B. L., Lauer, P. A., Bishop, J., & Peralez, A. (1997). *Researcher test manual for the learner-centered battery (grades 6–12 version)*. Aurora, CO: Mid-continent Regional Educational Laboratory.

Parsons, R. D., & Meyers, J. (1984). *Developing consultation skills*. San Francisco: Jossey-Bass.

Perry, K. E. (1999). The role of learner-centered teaching practices in children's adjustment during the transition to elementary school. *Dissertation Abstracts International Section A: Humanities and Social Sciences*, December v. 6.

Sandoval, J. (1995). Teaching in subject matter areas: Science. *Annual Review of Psychology, 45*, 355–374.

Sandoval, J. (1996). Constructivism, consultee-centered consultation, and conceptual change. *Journal of Educational and Psychological Consultation, 7*, 89–97.

Sandoval, J. (1998). Critical thinking in test interpretation. In J. Sandoval, C. L. Frisby, K. F. Geisinger, J. D. Schueneman, & J. R. Grenier (Eds.), *Test interpretation and diversity* (pp. 31–50). Washington, DC: American Psychological Association.

West, D. C., Park, J. K., Pomeroy, J. R., & Sandoval, J. (2002). Concept mapping assessment in graduate medical education: A comparison of two scoring systems. *Journal of Medical Education, 36*, 820–826.

Index

A

accessible reasoning, 161
activity, 315
administrative setting, 28, 29
advocacy for children, 164, 168
affect theories, 266, 273
affective communication, 274
agreement for consultation, 30
aggression, 292
amodal sensations, 266
ambiguity, 279, 289
analogy, 302
anecdote, 302, 306
anger, 276, 291, 299
applicability, 384
approach, 50, 51
approaching, 51
art therapy, 268, 296, 299
assessment, 314, 355
audience tuning, 342
attention, 51

B

behavioral consultation, 10, 46, 375, 376
bind, 52
blind alley, 52, 206, 210, 286, 287
boredom, 55
break, 56
break questions, 257, 291

C

California State Department of Education, 6
Canada, 151
Caplanian consultation, 23, 25, 32
case studies, 379
causal attributions, 123
challenging the consultant, 251
challenging the consultee, 249, 279, 289, 296,
change in attitude, 396
change in conceptualization, 392, 397
changes in affect, 392, 396
changes in client, 392, 393
changes in consultee, 392, 393
child care workers, 150
client, 13
client-centered consultation, 4, 5, 12, 13
coding system, 341
cognitive mapping, 95
cognitive restructuring, 248
collaboration, 350, 354
collaboration defined, 80, 83, 189, 207
collaborative problem solving, 81, 354
collaborative research, 233
collective conceptions, 134
communication, 341
competence, 256
complicate thinking, 248, 253, 279
conceptual change in consultation, 17, 46
conceptual change, 33, 39, 42, 44, 45, 83, 107, 142, 265, 281, 293, 313, 377